YALE STUDIES IN ECONOMICS, 17

COLLECTIVE BARGAINING

IN THE AUTOMOBILE INDUSTRY

A Study of Wage Structure and Competitive Relations

by ROBERT M. MACDONALD

New Haven and London, Yale University Press, 1963

Preface

This book is the result of an inquiry into the economic consequences of collective bargaining in the automobile industry,
conducted under a grant of funds from the John Randolph
Haynes and Dora Haynes Foundation. The Foundation's gen-
erous financial assistance and the support and encouragement
received from Gordon S. Watkins, chairman of the Foundation's committee on research and grants, are gratefully
acknowledged.

As in many undertakings of this sort, where the objective
is to examine critically a sensitive area of business practice, a
major source of frustration was the difficulty encountered in
gaining access to the kinds of data and other records essential
to an informed appraisal and evaluation. It is only proper to
note that this difficulty has helped to determine the orientation
of the study; for while I have sought to explore the full range
of issues connected with the behavior of the industry's wage
structure and pattern of labor costs, and have not hesitated to
speculate beyond the evidence where necessary, the treatment
of topics was inevitably influenced by the amount and quality
of the information available. However, to those union and
management officials who contributed their time and knowledge
to the study, I express my gratitude and appreciation. Without
their cooperation, no useful analysis of collective bargaining

practice in the industry would have been possible. In particular, I wish to thank Nat Weinberg of the United Automobile, Aircraft and Agricultural Implement Workers of America for permission to use the extensive library facilities maintained by the union at its Detroit headquarters and Edward L. Cushman of the American Motors Corporation for a stimulating discussion of the manuscript.

In the course of the study I incurred additional obligations which I am happy to acknowledge. My wife, Mado R. Macdonald, assisted in most of the field research, served throughout as a thoughtful and sympathetic critic, and assumed major responsibility for typing the manuscript. Anita R. Summers was my research assistant for two years and prepared much of the background material essential to the analysis. The contributions of these talented assistants are not easily overstated.

I have also profited from the comments of a number of scholars. The entire manuscript was read and criticized by Lloyd G. Reynolds and Neil W. Chamberlain of Yale University and by Robert H. Guest of the Amos Tuck School of Business Administration at Dartmouth. Earlier drafts of chapters 6 and 7 were reviewed by Charles A. Myers of the Massachusetts Institute of Technology, Mark W. Leiserson of Yale University, and by my colleagues at the Amos Tuck School— Karl A. Hill, Kenneth R. Davis, and John W. Hennessey. I am indebted to these commentators for their many helpful suggestions, though it should be understood that they are in no way responsible for the orientation or conclusions of the book.

R.M.M.

Hanover, New Hampshire
December 21, 1962

Contents

TABLES

COLLECTIVE BARGAINING IN THE AUTOMOBILE INDUSTRY

A Study of Wage Structure and Competitive Relations

CHAPTER 1

Wage Structure Analysis:
Some Methodological Issues

This study is concerned with the influence of collective bargaining upon the structure of wages and interfirm labor costs in the automobile industry. Since wage structure, or the complex of wage relationships among occupations, firms, industries, and geographic areas, is a key concept of contemporary wage theory, its study requires no special justification here.[1] There are, however, a number of specific reasons for undertaking this particular project which may appropriately be stated at this point since they serve to indicate the scope, direction, and general objectives of the analysis.

1) Wage-structure analysis often proceeds on the basis of wage-rate or earnings data of fairly broad coverage. This procedure raises two kinds of dangers—first, that the statistical averages employed may so conceal or distort the true pattern

1. For discussions of the theoretical and practical importance of wage-structure analysis, see Lloyd G. Reynolds and Cynthia H. Taft, *The Evolution of Wage Structure* (New Haven, Yale, 1956), pp. 1–13; John T. Dunlop, "The Task of Contemporary Wage Theory," in John T. Dunlop, ed., *The*

of wage differentials as to lead to quite erroneous conclusions; and second, that the measure of wages adopted, since it encompasses only a part of the "wage bargain" or agreement, may yield an incomplete and hence misleading picture of wage and cost relationships. By limiting the scope of the study to only one segment of industry—passenger-car producers—these dangers are minimized; for it is then possible to conduct the analysis on the basis of actual job-rate data (or at least on the basis of known rate distributions) and to consider the consequences of broadening the wage concept to include nonrate elements such as fringe benefits. The latter are an integral part of worker compensation and should therefore be included in the analysis of wage structure. This need for a broader concept of wages is especially acute when interest is focused on the behavior and determinants of interfirm labor-cost differentials. To view the wage bargain in these circumstances as little more than a wage-rate agreement is quite unsatisfactory, since labor costs are affected by all the terms of the agreement, including the manner in which these terms are administered. Except under unusual circumstances, therefore, hourly wage-rate or earnings data are an inadequate guide to interfirm costs. By confining the analysis to the five automobile manufacturers, it is possible to explore the pattern of labor-cost differentials in terms of the total union–management relationship.

2) An important objective of wage-structure analysis has been the determination of union influence—the issue of whether unionism has "warped" the pattern of wage relationships, interfering thereby with the allocative function of the competitive market mechanism. Though extreme views exist, the present consensus is that unionism has had a mixed effect, distorting

Theory of Wage Determination (London, Macmillan, 1957), pp. 3–30; Frank C. Pierson, "An Evaluation of Contemporary Wage Theory," in George W. Taylor and Frank C. Pierson, eds., *New Concepts in Wage Determination* (New York, McGraw-Hill, 1957), pp. 3–31; D. J. Robertson, *Factory Wage Structures and National Agreements* (London, Cambridge, 1960), pp. 192–220.

the wage structure in some respects but improving it in others.[2] Since the method of measuring union impact involves, however, certain assumptions that are of questionable validity, there is reason to doubt, or at least to entertain serious reservations about, the significance of much of the contemporary analysis. A second purpose of the study, therefore, is to examine this methodological issue and to point up possible weaknesses in our present approach to the measurement of union influence.

3) A final reason for undertaking the study was the desire to explore wage relationships and the wage system in this key manufacturing industry and to clarify the nature and basis of union and management wage-structure policies.[3] The United Automobile Workers, under the leadership of Walter P. Reuther, is generally regarded as one of the most progressive unions in the country. Along with auto managements, it has evolved a system of labor relations which has profoundly influenced the course of collective bargaining in American industry. This fact alone justifies intensive study of the union's objectives and effects. Beyond that, however, interest is sharpened by the remarkable changes in structure and policy which the organization has recently undergone in response to a series of internal and external pressures. It is yet too early to judge the full implications of these changes, but it is clear at least that industrial unionism has entered a period of crisis and is in the process of being transformed into a new and different kind of organization. A final objective of the study is to appraise these changes in terms of their consequences for wage (and cost) relationships.

2. For a summary and appraisal of the literature in this area, see George H. Hildebrand, "The Economic Effects of Unionism," in Neil W. Chamberlain et al., eds., *A Decade of Industrial Relations Research,* 1946–1956 (New York, Harper, 1958), pp. 115–27.

3. Despite the importance of the automobile industry in the American economy and the pace-setting character of its labor relations, there has been no systematic investigation of collective bargaining in this industry since the early studies by William H. McPherson: *Labor Relations in the Automobile Industry* (Washington, Brookings Inst., 1940); "Automobiles," in *How Collective Bargaining Works* (New York, Twentieth Century Fund, 1942).

The Structure of Bargaining Relations

The automobile industry is the classic example in the American economy of large-scale mass production. Since the mergers of the 1950s, the production of automobiles has been concentrated in only five firms—the General Motors Corporation, the Ford Motor Company, the Chrysler Corporation, the American Motors Corporation, and the Studebaker-Packard Corporation.[4] In 1960 these five companies, employing close to 600,000 hourly rated workers, produced and sold 6.7 million passenger cars with a total wholesale value in excess of $12 billion. The companies vary widely from the standpoint of size, range of products manufactured, and degree of vertical integration. Nevertheless, their relative importance as automobile producers can be judged from the statistics in Table 1.

TABLE 1.   Passenger-car Output, 1959–1960

Company	Share of Passenger-car output	
	1959	*1960*
General Motors	45.6%	47.7%
Ford	31.2	28.2
Chrysler	13.2	15.2
American Motors	7.2	7.3
Studebaker	2.8	1.6

Source. *Automobile Facts and Figures,* Automobile Manufacturers Assn., 1961 ed.

Over 90 per cent of the hourly rated workers employed in the auto industry are members of the United Automobile, Aircraft and Agricultural Implement Workers of America. Although this union represents workers in several industries, its strength lies primarily in the automobile and parts industries, and indeed in the five auto companies listed above which together account

4. The reduction in the number of automobile companies from nine to five (through merger, acquisition, and retirement from passenger-car production) during the period 1953–55 is discussed in chap. 6.

for about one half of the union's total membership. In mid-1961, the number of UAW members employed by these companies was approximately 550,000, distributed as follows: General Motors, 310,000; Ford, 122,000; Chrysler, 90,000[5]; American Motors, 23,000; and Studebaker, 6,000.[6] It is these five firms and their bargaining relationship with the UAW that provide the framework for this study.

Collective bargaining in the automobile industry is conducted on a single-company basis. This does not mean, of course, that the negotiations are unrelated. On the contrary, there is a well-defined system of pattern bargaining whereby the key settlement reached with one company establishes the standard for agreement with other companies. Through strong, centralized direction of negotiations, the international union has been able to pursue a tightly coordinated strategy that takes full advantage of the intense sales rivalry between firms. Auto managements, recognizing their vulnerability, have long deplored this system of bargaining and have called repeatedly for legislation to reduce or eliminate the power of the international union. More recently, however, the Big Three producers, aware that nothing was to be accomplished through legislation, have sought to protect themselves against the union's whipsaw tactics by presenting a united front based on joint acceptance of common goals and a common strategy. In the 1958 negotiations, this cooperation took the form of "parallel bargaining."[7] It was judged sufficiently successful to cause one knowledgeable ob-

5. Slightly more than 10 per cent of the members in Chrysler are salaried office, clerical, and engineering workers.

6. UAW press release, June 6, 1961; *New York Times,* July 29, 1961.

7. According to William H. McPherson, in "Cooperation Among Auto Managements in Collective Bargaining," *Labor Law Journal* (July 1960), p. 607, parallel bargaining "involves the establishing and maintaining of a united front by the companies. It means that the bargaining goals and limits of acceptability are the object . . . of joint determination. Under these circumstances the separate negotiations of the companies will develop along similar lines with the companies making identical, or at least comparable, proposals and concessions."

server to "safely forecast that the auto companies will not enter their next negotiations without some definite plans for strike assistance."[8] Whatever the over-all strategy of the Big Three in 1961, however, the union's countermoves in that year cut short its effectiveness. Confronted, as in 1958, with more or less identical (and not unattractive) offers presented simultaneously by the three larger firms, the union induced American Motors to set a substantially higher pattern in return for improvements in its competitive position through concessions in the work-rules area.[9] This maneuver, which defeated the united front by outflanking it, adds an interesting new dimension to the union's bargaining strategy and a new complication to employer cooperation; for if the pattern can be set outside the Big Three and if the union is willing to offer concessions to the pattern setter, effective cooperation must embrace a wider range of firms and include an agreement to resist union enticements offered to individual firms for the purpose of disrupting the united front. At this point, the status and future of employer cooperation must therefore be regarded as uncertain.

Despite the high level of coordination on the union side and efforts toward effective cooperation on the management side, the basic bargaining unit in the industry remains the single firm. The organization of this unit for bargaining purposes is illustrated in the case of General Motors. This corporation has bargaining relations with more than 20 international unions. Our concern, however, is in its relationship with the UAW, which represents about 90 per cent of the company's unionized workers.[10]

In June 1961, there were 310,000 GM workers covered by UAW agreement in 131 local bargaining units located in 66 different cities in 18 different states.[11] For bargaining purposes,

8. Ibid., p. 614.

9. These negotiations are discussed in some detail in chap. 5.

10. Other unions include the Electrical Workers, the Machinists, the Rubber Workers, the Teamsters, the Die Sinkers, and the Pattern Makers' League.

11. UAW press release, June 6, 1961.

these local unions are grouped together in the UAW National General Motors Council—an intracorporation council whose function is to coordinate local demands and formulate policies for dealing with the common employer. Each local union is entitled to at least two council delegates who are automatically the president and the chairman of the plant shop committee. Larger locals are entitled to one additional delegate for the first 3,000 members above 5,000 and one more for each 2,000 members above 8,000. The voting strength of each local in the council is proportional to its membership, and all matters coming before the council are decided by majority vote. This national council has one regular meeting each year, but special meetings may be called at any time by the director of the National General Motors Department (see below) or upon the written request of a majority of the General Motors National Negotiating Committee after consultation with the Department director.

Affiliated with the National GM Council are eleven GM subcouncils, organized along functional lines as follows: Chevrolet Assembly; Fisher Body Assembly; Fisher Stamping; Accessories and Parts; Foundry and Forge; Heavy Equipment; Buick-Oldsmobile-Pontiac; Design-Engineering-Model Maker-Pattern Shops; Tool-Die and Maintenance; Assembly Manufacturing and Motor; and Bearings, Transmission and Axle.[12] The purpose of these subcouncils is to permit discussion of common problems and the formulation of appropriate solutions for consideration in the national council's bargaining program. Each subcouncil has a regular annual meeting and may, at its own discretion, schedule two additional regular meetings each year. An important function of the eleven subcouncils is the election of one member each to the National GM Negotiating Committee. This committee, in turn, elects the officers to preside over

12. Prior to 1957, subcouncils were organized on a regional basis. The change to functional groupings was part of the union's reorganization of its bargaining structure undertaken to accord greater representational rights to the rebellious skilled trades (see chap. 4).

all national council meetings and participates with members of the international union in negotiations with the corporation.

The international union guides and coordinates the work of the various intracorporation councils through a system of parallel international departments. The director of each department is appointed by the UAW president subject to the approval of the International Executive Board. The General Motors Department, which is under the direction of UAW Vice-President Leonard Woodcock, calls all meetings of the GM Council and subcouncils, assists in formulating bargaining demands, participates actively in national negotiations with the corporation, advises in local bargaining and grievance handling, and is responsible for the processing of unadjusted grievances appealed to the umpire. In the absence of the international president, the department director is the union's chief spokesman at the bargaining table. The former participates frequently, however, and is always present in the final stages of negotiations. It appears that the international officers and staff handle the major economic issues while members of the national negotiating committee (elected by the subcouncils) tend to concentrate their efforts on modifications of the working agreement.

Although the National GM Council, working with the National GM Department, is responsible for formulating the bargaining demands to be served on the corporation, the basic economic program is established by the International Executive Board, subject to ratification by a special collective bargaining conference of the UAW convened a few months before the opening of negotiations. The function of the council, therefore, is to develop a set of proposals which incorporates these basic economic demands and the contract proposals originating in the GM locals. In the bargaining itself, any agreement reached must be approved by a majority of the negotiating committee and of the national council before it is presented to the local membership for ratification. Consistency with international policy is assured by the participation of international officers and staff in the negotiations and by the requirement that all agreements be approved by the international union before they become operative.[13]

On the management side, major policy decisions at General Motors are handled by two principal committees of the Board of Directors, one of which—the Operations Policy Committee —is responsible for the operating affairs of the business, including labor relations.[14] This committee is made up of members of the board who are also executives of the corporation. Functioning under the jurisdiction of the Operations Policy Committee is the Administration Committee whose membership consists of the members of the parent committee and the general managers of representative divisions of the corporation. The Administration Committee is responsible for recommending policies and methods of administration to the Operations Policy Committee on all matters referred to it by the latter or by the Board of Directors. Assisting the Administration Committee are a number of functional policy groups headed by staff vice-presidents and group executives. One of these policy groups, headed by the vice-president in charge of personnel, handles matters relating to labor relations. Its membership includes top executives, divisional managers, and specialists

13. The balance between local autonomy and international authority is maintained through Article 19, Section 3, of the UAW Constitution: "No Local Union Officer, International Officer or International Representative shall have the authority to negotiate the terms of a contract or any supplement thereof with any employer without first obtaining the approval of the Local Union. After negotiations have been concluded with the employer, the proposed contract or supplement shall be submitted to the vote of the local union membership . . . at a meeting called especially for such purpose; should the proposed contract or supplement be approved by a majority vote of the Local Union . . . , it shall be referred to the Regional Director for his recommendation to the International Executive Board for its approval or rejection. In case the regional Board Member recommends approval, the contract becomes operative until the final action is taken by the International Executive Board."

14. The Operations Policy Committee was renamed the Executive Committee in 1959.

from the labor relations staff. This group is the instrumentality whereby suggestions and recommendations originating in line and staff organizations are passed along, if acceptable, to the Administration Committee and Operations Policy Committee. All individuals affected by proposed policies are given an opportunity to express their views before the policy group.

Once major policy lines are established, it is the function of the labor relations staff of the vice-president in charge of personnel to administer these policies throughout the corporation. This staff is responsible for negotiating and administering the national agreement and for handling all grievances appealed to the corporation and the umpire. During actual negotiations with the union, the labor relations staff is supported, where necessary, by specialists from other areas. It also has ready access to members of the top policy committees who are kept informed of all progress made in the bargaining sessions. Consequently, there is little delay in seeking and being granted the authority to make proposals and decisions at the bargaining table. But while the whole management group is thus mobilized to help out at the time of negotiations, the actual bargaining is conducted by members of the labor relations staff.

Each division and plant of the corporation has its own labor relations personnel who work closely with, and receive instructions from, the central labor relations staff. These plant and divisional staffs handle day-to-day relations and see to it that corporation policies are adhered to by all levels of supervision. They also negotiate local agreements covering such matters as wage rates, seniority, and shift preference, though all such agreements are subject to approval by the central staff before becoming operative.

This brief description of the formal structure of the bargaining unit at General Motors does not, of course, do justice to the complexity of modern-day collective bargaining or to the efforts and talents involved on both sides in negotiating and administering agreements in the large, multiplant corporation.

Nevertheless, it is sufficient to indicate the general framework within which bargaining is conducted between the UAW and the Big Three. Before we leave the subject of bargaining structure, however, a few points are in order concerning the bargaining relationship with smaller companies such as Studebaker and American Motors.

Up to the mid-1950s, the international union was not an active participant in negotiations with these two companies. This can be attributed mainly to the fact that local unions had been organized in the plants of these companies and had already established bargaining relations and agreements with management prior to the chartering of the UAW. They were therefore accustomed to handling their own affairs and prized highly their autonomy. As Dubin notes in the case of Studebaker:

> The "grass roots" aspect of this local union has perhaps been most evident in its relations with the International Union. It has been the general practice within the International to have central administration officials, regional directors and their staffs, participate in contract negotiations and the settlement of grievances at the higher levels of the grievance procedure. No International representative has ever been called in to assist the Studebaker local in dealing with management. Local 5 has been in no sense a "hot house" growth which needs constant ministrations from the parent organization.[15]

The crisis of the mid-1950s, when intensified competition threatened to engulf the smaller firms, brought the international union more actively into negotiations—partly to relieve the pressure on local union officials who, in the face of considerable rank-and-file opposition, were forced to recognize the need for granting some concessions to management. Since then, the international union has played a more prominent part in

15. Frederick H. Harbison and Robert Dubin, *Patterns of Union-Management Relations* (Chicago, Science Research Associates, 1947), p. 124.

bargaining with the Independents, though still not quite the commanding role assumed in the Big Three, especially in the handling of local issues. At least this is the impression given at American Motors where close to fifty representatives from the five local unions in the company's plants attend bargaining sessions with management. As Edward L. Cushman, American Motors' vice-president, explained the union situation in 1960: "In Kenosha and Milwaukee [the principal production centers] the International Union is present only when invited by the locals. The international representative speaks only when called upon, and the local people are not loath to express to Mr. Reuther and his associates their very strong convictions on matters they feel fall solely within their jurisdiction. The locals may request technical assistance from the international, but little beyond this as far as daily operations are concerned."[16]

This measure of local autonomy on the union side is fully endorsed by American Motors. The management structure is highly decentralized and there is virtually no central labor relations staff. Periodic contract negotiations dealing with "economic" issues such as wage and benefit levels are handled by top executives of the corporation, but local managements enjoy some discretion in the settlement of other contract matters. This arrangement has resulted in variations among local agreements, which in turn have given rise to pressures among local unions for extension of the most liberal contract provisions to all plants. Management frankly acknowledges these pressures but is convinced that they are a price worth paying for local determination of labor relations issues. As Edward Cushman notes, "We have no arbitration in any of our agreements. The local unions and plant managers are opposed to arbitration and see no need to develop any such terminal settlement procedures in their agreements. We have a long tradition of letting the people work out their problems together. Frankly on some

16. Edward L. Cushman in Arnold Weber, ed., *The Structure of Collective Bargaining* (Graduate School of Business, Univ. of Chicago, 1961), p. 73.

occasions we aren't too happy with the solutions, but we are willing to go along with the local decisions."[17]

American Motors' approach to labor relations issues at the local level affords an interesting contrast, incidentally, to the more centralized labor policy developed and pursued at General Motors. The rationale for the latter's approach to labor relations has been explained as follows:

> Through experience the corporation learned that the union would use concessions secured in one plant as a means of pressing its demands in others. Central control has existed as a guard against the "inchworm tactics" of the union. The entire strategy of "containing the union" could be wrecked by union encroachments at the weak points in management's organization. . . .
>
> Decisions which might ultimately affect the whole corporation could not be left to the judgment of hundreds of divisional managers and personnel directors. Those down the line might not be well informed on the details of what was transpiring throughout the corporation and in some cases might not have mastered the fine points of even ordinary management-union strategy. It has been logical, under such conditions, that the area of local managerial discretion in labor relations matters should be narrowly circumscribed. The very size of the corporation and the fact that it has been a major target of UAW pressure has made such a policy plausible in the light of the issues involved.[18]

The relative merits of these two approaches have been debated at length in the literature on collective bargaining. At this point, however, our purpose is simply to note any major differences that exist in bargaining arrangements between the union

17. Ibid., p. 74.
18. Harbison and Dubin, *Patterns of Union-Management Relations,* pp. 61–62.

and firms in the industry. The issue of how effectively the individual companies have handled the labor relations function is of course a central concern of the study, but it can only be judged after a careful appraisal of actual operating policies and results.

The Measurement of Wages

Empirical studies of wage behavior are hampered by certain conceptual and statistical problems for which no satisfactory solutions have yet been found. Nevertheless, since the definition and measurement of wages are of critical importance in interpreting the results, these problems must be met and resolved where possible—and any limitations of the data used duly noted. This is the purpose of the present section.

The term "wages" itself is deceptively simple: it may refer to wage rates or to gross or straight-time earnings calculated on an hourly, weekly, annual, or lifetime basis; it may or may not include fringe benefits and other supplements; it may relate to income currently received or to costs currently paid out—measures which differ because of withholding taxes, pension programs, and other deferred benefits; and so on. Clearly, a variety of statistical measures is available, and the selection of the appropriate measure must therefore rest on the concept of wages judged most significant for the problem at hand.

In theories of wage determination, wages are normally defined in terms of the "net attractiveness" of the job rather than of the wage rate per se. This all-inclusive term embraces the entire range of factors that influence the worker's job choice and constitute the employer's job offer. Thus it includes, along with the wage rate, all supplementary wage payments and nonwage terms of employment. The "wage" equalities and inequalities with which our theories deal are consequently not the narrow concepts for which we have rough statistical equivalents (in the form of wage-rate or earnings data) but are instead comparisons between composites of a number of factors that enter into the worker's preference system. This complicates the task of wage-structure analysis considerably, for it follows that the wage rate provides an unambiguous measure of the price of labor (and hence an appropriate basis for wage comparisons) only under the most restrictive conditions—e.g. that workers in the same occupational category are of equal efficiency and have identical preference systems, that they are paid by the hour and are offered the same number of hours of work, and that fringe benefits and working conditions are either uniform or uniquely correlated with the wage rate.[19] But such conditions, often assumed in theoretical discussions, are seldom met in actual situations. Workers do differ from the standpoint of efficiency; methods of wage payment and hours of work often vary from one job or establishment to another; and while wage supplements and working conditions are important aspects of job attractiveness, little is known about how they enter into workers' preference systems or how they are correlated with wage-rate levels.[20] It is dangerous, therefore, to rely on wage rates alone as the appropriate data in wage-structure analysis.

In analyzing the behavior of the wage structure in the automobile industry, we are interested in "wages" both as employee income and as employer costs. In the first instance, our concern is with the behavior of relative income flows to groups of workers in different occupations, plants, firms, and geographic areas;

19. For a discussion of these conditions, see Reynolds and Taft, *Evolution of Wage Structure*, p. 7.

20. With reference to the role of supplementary wage payments (or fringe benefits), Clark Kerr has this to say: "What has happened to 'compensation' differentials (wages and 'fringe benefits' taken together) is a different and more complex question; and an increasingly important one with the growth of 'fringe benefits.' The compensation structure is a more meaningful, if less tractable, concept than the 'wage structure.' On the currently available evidence it is almost foolhardy to estimate whether occupational 'compensation' differentials are or are not behaving similarly to occupational wage differentials": Clark Kerr, "Wage Relationships—The Comparative Impact of Market and Power Forces," in John T. Dunlop, ed., *The Theory of Wage Determination* (London, Macmillan, 1957), p. 178 n.

in the second, it is with the behavior of labor costs in different firms. In both cases, a major purpose is to establish the extent to which unionism may be viewed as an independent influence —affecting, on the one hand, income relationships among the various categories of workers and, on the other, competitive relations among the various firms.

It may be argued that the concept of wages employed in these two instances is essentially the same—i.e. that any labor cost incurred by the employer on behalf of his employees yields satisfactions which have a money equivalent and should therefore be considered a part of worker income. This view is persuasive, but not altogether satisfactory. If one is to define income in terms of worker satisfaction, then all significant job elements, whether they involve actual cost outlays or not, should be included. This would accord with the definition of wages or income encountered in theoretical reasoning; but it also introduces a major difficulty already alluded to—namely, the difficulty of converting "satisfactions" to their money equivalents. It is reasonable to assume, of course, that the major variables entering into the worker's preference system are in some degree substitutable, but we know little about the actual rates of substitution. We may suspect that there are certain vague socially or culturally determined minimum requirements with respect to at least some of the key variables (i.e. certain minimum levels for wage rates, fringe benefits, and working conditions) below which reasonable substitution possibilities do not exist (i.e. the marginal rates of substitution are extremely high). Again, we know little about the nature and location of these minimums. Finally, there is considerable evidence that preference functions differ significantly between individuals and for the same individual at different times. Other things equal, older workers place a higher value on pensions and an easy work pace, female workers on sick leave, lower seniority workers on layoff benefits, workers with heavy family responsibilities on life insurance and perhaps overtime opportunities, and so on. We know little, however, about how the valuations placed on these various items by any individual worker relate to their cents-per-hour cost.

Unfortunately, there is at present no satisfactory way of solving these problems—at least as far as quantifying the several "income" variables is concerned.[21] Many economists would argue, of course, that wage-earner income (or compensation) ought to be more narrowly defined, including at most, along with actual money wages, the value of so-called fringe benefits. But while this narrower definition may simplify the problem, it does not remove it—for fringe benefits cover a wide variety of practices ranging from those that are fairly described as wage supplements (e.g. paid vacations and pension plans) to those that are more in the nature of working conditions (e.g. subsidized cafeterias and recreational facilities). Although there are numerous ways of classifying fringe benefits, there is no firm basis in principle for distinguishing those items that constitute a part of worker compensation. As Neil Chamberlain concludes in his discussion of the issue: "It is not easy to know where to draw the line. Perhaps one definition of wages or earnings might be that they include any cash payment made to, or on behalf of, an individual worker (in distinction to payments made, or labor costs incurred, on behalf of the work force as a whole)."[22] The tentative manner in which this definition is presented indicates that the issue is by no means resolved at the

---

21. Occasionally it is possible to circumvent some of these difficulties in wage-structure analysis. In certain situations it may reasonably be assumed that the satisfactions derived from one or more job elements are roughly the same for two groups of workers so that for comparative purposes their influence may be disregarded. Similarly, in studying relative wage behavior over time, we may justifiably ignore the influence of those job elements which have not changed significantly, even though they may affect the groups in question differently. Such procedures rest on personal judgments and have limited applicability, but their use, wherever the circumstances warrant, permits us to approach the issues of wage structure with somewhat greater assurance.

22. Neil W. Chamberlain, *Labor* (New York, McGraw-Hill, 1958), p. 359.

conceptual level. The definition does, however, represent a reasonable balance between conflicting viewpoints as to what should be included.[23] Major fringe benefits are realistically a part of labor's compensation and, at least as a first approximation, may be incorporated at cost. It is always possible in the analysis to make allowance for such evidence as may suggest an alternative treatment and even to indicate, where necessary, the effect on conclusions of broadening or narrowing the wage concept—all subject of course to the availability of the relevant data. This is essentially the procedure adopted here, though the main emphasis of the analysis is on wage rates modified to take account of the estimated value of major fringe benefits.

In viewing wages as costs we encounter fewer conceptual difficulties since the definition of labor costs per hour or per unit of output is relatively unambiguous. It includes all payments made to, or costs incurred on behalf of, a firm's workers, whether as individuals or as a group. It follows, therefore, that the question of how unionism affects relative costs or competitive relations among firms must be approached in terms of the entire range of union-management activities. We cannot afford to focus simply on the behavior and determinants of relative wage rates and major fringe benefits, but must also

23. At the statistical level, the recent estimates of wage-earner compensation (per hour at work) compiled by Albert Rees are based on a concept of compensation that closely parallels Chamberlain's definition. Thus, Rees includes in earnings such items as paid vacations, holidays, and sick leave and excludes other items such as lunch periods, washup time, and call-in pay only because of the absence of reliable data. His estimates of wage supplements (which are added to earnings) include employer contributions to public and private pension and insurance systems, but do not include Christmas bonuses, cafeteria subsidies, and employee discounts on company products. The basis for distinguishing the items to be included in wage supplements is not stated explicitly. It may be that some items were excluded because they are not easily interpreted as a part of compensation. It is also possible that they were omitted simply because their costs were either unknown or insignificant. [Albert Rees, "Pattern of Wages, Prices and Productivity," in Charles A. Myers, ed., *Wages, Prices and Productivity* (American Assembly, Columbia Univ., June 1959), pp. 12–13.]

take account of any differential influence of unionism on work standards, idle-time allowances, grievance procedures, seniority practices, and so on. (We may not know how these variables enter into workers' preference functions and hence how to incorporate them into income, but no similar difficulties arise in their measurement as costs.) Given the necessary statistical information, we could readily estimate the influence of these variables on producers' costs and hence on competitive relations. This would provide the logical starting point for our analysis of determinants. Unfortunately, however, there are few, if any, cost data available and we are compelled, therefore, to approach the issue of cost differences on a piecemeal basis, utilizing whatever evidence exists (whether direct or indirect, quantitative or qualitative) that is relevant to the labor-cost situation of the firms in question. The shortcomings of such a procedure are obvious; gaps in the analysis are unavoidable and the role of personal judgment is considerably enlarged. As a result, any conclusions must remain tentative and subject to possible revision either as new evidence emerges or as superior judgment is applied to the available facts.

The Measurement of Union Impact

Attempts to measure the independent influence of unionism upon wage structure and competitive relations—or, for that matter, upon the wage level, productivity, or any other economic variable—raise a complex methodological problem. One aspect of this problem is the analytical difficulty of separating the effects of any one of a number of causal factors when many, if not most, of these factors are not susceptible to quantitative measurement. This difficulty and what it implies for wage-structure analysis have been noted by Reynolds and Taft:

> These factors [i.e. changes in demand and supply conditions, inflation, union and employer bargaining policies, and government relations] do not operate independently

but interact on each other in complicated ways. Several of them will frequently be found to have operated in the same direction, so that a particular change in differentials may be over-explained. . . . The problem of several independent variables impinging on a dependent variable is common enough in economics, and statistical techniques are available to deal with it. In this case, however, most of the independent variables either cannot be, or at any rate have not been, subjected to quantitative measurement. . . . We are forced back, therefore, onto qualitative appraisal of the forces at work and an intuitive "feel" of how the economy operates.[24]

This difficulty, which is a familiar one to students of labor economics, requires no special emphasis. There is, however, another aspect of the problem which has been seriously slighted in much of the contemporary analysis—the question of what is really being measured in studies of union impact. Economists, it is true, have displayed considerable ingenuity in their approach: at best, though, their conclusions have rested more on personal judgment, on a blending of insight and intuition, than on any rigorous analysis of *feasible* alternative systems of economic relations; at worst, they have been little more than a description of events and developments that have taken place in a unionized economy. This aspect of the problem, because of its importance, warrants further comment.

The customary assumption underlying conclusions about union impact is that economic trends and developments, in the absence of collusive or cooperative action, would reflect primarily the outcome of "individual responses" on the part of workers and employers to a more or less competitive market environment. The distinction between the two processes is neatly expressed by Kerr in his study dealing with the comparative impact of market and power forces on wage relationships.

24. Reynolds and Taft, *Evolution of Wage Structure,* p. 13.

The customary dichotomy of "market" and "power" forces lacks full precision. . . . It might be more useful to speak of "individual responses" on the one hand and "institutional behavior" on the other.

"Individual responses" are the expressed preferences of individual workers and unorganized employers in response to the environmental context in which they find themselves. While in totality their actions affect the result, their individual actions taken separately do not succeed in manipulating their environment. "Institutional behavior" is comprised of the policies and practices of groups of individuals in the dominant corporation, the employers' association, the trade union or government.

When a market responds largely to the first type of action, it might be designated as a "natural" market, however imperfect it may be aside from collusive action itself; and when to the latter, an "institutional" market. Most actual markets will, of course, have characteristics of both of these types; and then some evaluation is in order of the comparative influence of these two types of forces. Our question is then, to rephrase it, to what extent have wage differentials been affected by the entry of "institutional behavior," in addition to "individual responses," into the supply side of the labor market.[25]

It is well to note that this "natural" market admits of imperfections other than collusive action. It is therefore not the perfectly competitive labor market but rather the imperfectly competitive nonunion labor market. This distinction, implied in Kerr's statement, receives forceful expression in the study of wage

25. Kerr, "Wage Relationships," p. 174. For a similar distinction between "individual responses" and "organizational behavior," see *Evolution of Wage Structure*, pp. 4–5. These writers, also concerned with the impact of collective bargaining on relative wage levels, see as their problem the determination of "how far, in a particular economy, the results of individual responses in the labor market have been modified by group behavior."

structure by Reynolds and Taft: "There is a growing body of evidence that the labor market is by nature an imperfect instrument and that all kinds of wage distortions exist even under nonunion conditions. To compare the wage structure that develops under collective bargaining with a hypothetical wage structure which might exist under perfect competition is an arbitrary and unreal procedure. The significant comparison is between the bargained wage structure and that which actually exists in imperfect nonunion labor markets."[26]

Recognition of the imperfections which distinguish the actual nonunion labor market from the model of the perfectly competitive labor market is, of course, desirable and necessary in the study of wage structure and competitive relations. The critical question in measuring union impact, however, is whether the "natural" market governed by "individual responses"—even when allowance is made for imperfections in the form of immobilities, incomplete knowledge, and apparently "irrational" job-choice behavior—constitutes in fact a realistic and practical alternative to the "institutional" market governed by "organizational behavior." In our view, it can be argued that just as the concept of the perfectly competitive market has value mainly as a norm in measuring the performance of the institutional market, so too in its way the concept of the imperfectly competitive nonunion market, though yielding a more "realistic" model, represents more a standard against which to measure the results of organizational behavior than a reasonable alternative to such behavior. If unionism performs a vital function, assuming away the institution does not remove the needs and pressures that unionism was specifically designed to meet and resolve. If workers had been deprived of this mechanism of protest and reform, can we easily predict what course society and the economy would have taken? Can we assume that all else, including the institutions of management and government, would have developed along precisely the same lines,

26. *Evolution of Wage Structure*, p. 168.

achieving precisely the same status? In short, is unionism to be regarded as an appendage to the system which might easily be dispensed with or as a vital institution, an integral part of the industrial system, that has affected the functioning and direction of other institutions and left its mark indelibly impressed on that system as we know it?

We do not presume to know the full answers to these questions; we raise them mainly to dramatize the nature and complexity of the issue involved. It may be that an alternative to unionism was (and is) possible which would serve the same needs and yet prove compatible with the functioning of free, unorganized markets. It is significant, however, that democratic societies have so far failed to discover such an alternative; and, indeed, the weight of historical evidence is against such a discovery. As one of our most perceptive labor scholars has written: "The union did not create the community of interest among workers; the factory system did that. The union did not originate industrial unrest but merely sharpened and took advantage of it. . . . Discontent is the prime mover of economic and social change. Ever since the emergence of a numerous wage-earning class, groups and movements of quite diverse tendencies have claimed the right to exploit this discontent and convert it into a vehicle for change. . . . It can be turned in more than one direction and used for more than one purpose. . . . Clearly it makes a great deal of difference which kind of organization has had the best luck."[27]

Given this historical perspective from which few, if any, serious scholars would dissent, an organized response to the industrial situation was inevitable and predictable except with respect to its specific form. In the nineteenth century, the three main channels of group protest against the industrial system were trade unionism, political action, and the cooperative

27. Arthur M. Ross, "The Natural History of the Strike," in Kornhauser, Dubin, and Ross, eds., *Industrial Conflict* (New York, McGraw-Hill, 1954), p. 23.

movement. Whether these instruments of change and reform were in fact effective substitutes is a moot point. We know only that all three converged under trade unionism (in the twentieth century) as the principal institutional device for serving the continuing needs of workers in a capitalistic industrial society. As William Leiserson has pointed out, one effect of the rise of industrial unionism in the early 1930s "has been to unite under the aegis of organized labor the three lines of activity which formerly were considered substitutes for one another and tended to develop separate labor movements. . . . The tendency today is to make organized labor synonymous with the labor movement, whereas in the last century the political and cooperative movements were usually separate from the union movements and were generally inspired and led by intellectuals, social theorists, and reformers, rather than by union leaders."[28] Historical evidence suggests, therefore, that workable alternatives to the institutional market which preserve the character and structure of a democratic capitalist society (in its familiar form) are not so easily formulated. This view is reinforced, moreover, by the widely held conviction that "business unionism"—the characteristic form of American trade unionism—is a conservative force, a shield against revolution, not only compatible with the free enterprise economy but probably essential to its survival.[29] Curiously enough, this conviction is apparently dismissed, its implications all too frequently forgotten, in evaluating the economic impact of unionism. Yet if unionism is indeed a conservative force, a bulwark of the free enterprise system, then surely its removal (or failure to materialize) would have repercussions beyond those normally envisaged in contemporary studies.[30]

28. William M. Leiserson, *American Trade Union Democracy* (New York, Columbia, 1959), p. 36.

29. See, e.g., E. Wight Bakke and Clark Kerr, *Unions, Management and the Public* (New York, Harcourt, Brace, 1949), pp. 5–6; Frederick H. Harbison, "Collective Bargaining and American Capitalism," in Kornhauser, et al., eds., *Industrial Conflict*, pp. 270, 276.

30. An interesting illustration of the possible shortcomings of our present

It goes without saying that the preceding comments are directed toward those studies whose purpose it is to discover the separate or unique influence of unionism. If, instead, the purpose is merely to demonstrate how the results of the present "bargaining" system differ from those of some other (arbitrarily chosen) system which abstracts from the problems of industrial unrest and discontent (i.e. from labor's response to the industrial system) then there is, of course, no reason to question the procedure but only the meaning and significance of the findings.

We have already noted that the influence of unionism is typically evaluated in terms of hypothetical models of the perfectly competitive system and the imperfectly competitive nonunion system. The latter model affords certainly a more appropriate basis of comparison—especially if it admits the fact of social and group behavior at the work place even in the absence of formal organization.[31] Nevertheless, the limitations of this model, and hence of analyses based on the model, should be acknowledged.

---

approach is provided in Shister's analysis of the impact of unionism on economic growth. Shister observes: "Conclusive evidence (one way or the other) would consist of this: A comparison of the patterns of economic growth in two nations that are identical in every conceivable way except that one has a powerful union movement and the other no unionism at all. But no such animal exists; nor should one realistically expect it to exist if for no other reason than the fact that if two nations are identical in every way they will not breed radically different patterns of union growth." Shister then goes on to offer "suggestive evidence" of union impact. Nevertheless, the nagging questions remain: Is not much of our analysis based on the assumption that this "animal" does in fact exist? What pattern of institutions, if any, is consistent with the absence of unionism? The latter may well differ radically from what we have known and experienced under unionism. [Joseph Shister, "Trade-Unionism, Collective Bargaining, and Economic Growth," *American Economic Review, 44* (May 1954), 224–25.]

31. For an excellent brief discussion of the nature and implications of informal organization among workers, see Leiserson, *American Trade Union Democracy,* chap. 2. The first and last paragraphs of this chapter are especially pertinent to the present discussion (pp. 17, 30–31):

Like other polities, union governments grow out of common needs, experiences, traditions, and aspirations of groups of people. Unionism is rooted in the customary practices and social habits of wage earners at

Our understanding of how nonunion markets operate derives largely from a sketchy knowledge of events and developments of the preunion era, from study of the operation of wholly or partially nonunion markets in a unionized environment, and from our notions of how individual managements and workers would behave in the absence of collective bargaining. Our knowledge of preunion markets may have greater relevance, however, as an explanation for the rise of unionism than as a guide to the sort of market model that provides an alternative to the institutional market. Similarly, studies analyzing the behavior of nonunion firms and local markets, while useful in many respects, are probably of limited value from the standpoint of constructing a realistic nonunion market model for industrial centers such as Detroit. Either the situations are too dissimilar, or the behavior of the participants in the nonunion situation is too strongly affected by the existence of unionism elsewhere. Finally, to repeat an earlier point, most of us would probably hesitate to predict the course of events over the last few decades (especially the role of government) had unionism for some reason or other failed to materialize.

---

their work long before formal organizations appear among them. To protect their customary ways of living and working, cliques and other informal groups of workers habitually adjust employers' shop regulations to bring them into line with their own traditional codes of behavior. Union rules and collective bargaining agreements, as we know them, are in effect legislative enactments, bearing the same relationship to the unwritten customs and codes of working people that statutes do to common law. . . .

In some quarters debates are still going on as to whether labor unions are desirable or not, as if this were a question that could be determined by argumentation. If, however, union organizations and their policies are expressions and formulations of the collective beliefs and sentiments which give rise to spontaneous, informal organizations in shops and factories, then of course logical disputation as to the merits of unionism are as irrelevant as they are futile. Attempts to evaluate their customs, practices, and rules in terms of technical efficiency, productivity, or economic effects, without reference to the traditions of the workers' own organizations for social control, are of little more worth.

In summary, unless one is willing to assume that the nonunion market provides a feasible alternative to the institutional market, conclusions based on a comparison of "individual responses" on the one hand, and "organizational behavior" on the other, must remain primarily normative judgments. They answer the question: What difference would it have made to the development of wage structure and competitive relations if "individual responses" had ruled in place of "institutional behavior"? Whether they answer, however, the more fundamental question concerning the *actual* influence of unionism depends on one's willingness to accept the proposition that the nonunion "natural" market—rejected in the rise of unionism—was and is a practical alternative to the organized "institutional" market.

Our own conclusions concerning union impact should be read with the above reservations in mind; for, while we have sought to judge the union's influence in terms of feasible alternatives (and in some cases in terms of a range of feasible solutions under collective bargaining), the basic model adopted for comparative purposes assumes a free enterprise economy in which the wage system is governed by the behavior of individual managements and workers responding to an environment not unlike the environment actually developed under unionism. We have tried, however, to retain awareness of the true dimensions of the "labor problem" in an industrial society, to make explicit the assumptions underlying the analysis, to recognize possible developments in other institutions, and to point out the limitations inherent in the method. To avoid excessive repetition, these matters are more emphasized in Chapter 2 (in the section entitled "Collective Bargaining and Employee Benefits") than in later chapters, but it is clear that similar considerations apply to the later analyses and conclusions.

The study consists essentially of two parts, the first dealing with wage structure and the second with competitive relations. These are, of course, related topics; but for our purpose it is desirable and even necessary to treat them separately. In Chapter 2 we examine the nature and growth of fringe benefits in the industry and their role in the wage (or compensation) structure. This sets the stage for Chapters 3 to 5 which are devoted in turn to a detailed exploration of wage relationships from the standpoint of personal, occupational and interplant differentials—the key dimensions of the industry's wage structure. The analysis in these chapters is conducted on the basis of wage-rate data modified, where appropriate, by our findings regarding the role of fringe benefits. Since Chapter 5 deals with wage relationships among the industry's firms, it represents the logical first step in our analysis of interfirm costs or competitive relations—the subject matter of Chapters 6 and 7. The principal findings are brought together in the final chapter of the study and are interpreted in the light of current ideas and views concerning the meaning and significance of collective bargaining in the economy.

CHAPTER 2

Fringe Benefits and the Wage Structure

It is an obvious, though still frequently neglected, fact that "fringe" benefits or wage supplements are a major component of employee compensation and hence an important variable in wage analysis. In this chapter, we trace briefly the evolution and current status of the principal wage supplements in the industry, analyze the role of such supplements in the compensation structure, and consider the part played by collective bargaining in their development.

The Development and Cost of Fringe Benefits

Wage supplements encompass a wide variety of programs and practices which may be classified according to the following categories: pay for time not worked; premium pay for time worked; pensions and welfare plans; and legally required benefit programs. Although some of these benefits have a long tradition in industrial relations,[1] evolution has been especially

1. The Studebaker Corporation, for example, had a variety of "cooperative plans" in operation during the 1920s. According to management, these plans were not compensation in lieu of wages (since the company had an established

rapid during the last two decades, with respect to both the proliferation of existing benefits and the initiation of new ones. This increase in the scope and complexity, as well as in the significance, of supplementary benefits is indicated below.

In the late 1930s, the principal benefit supplements to the wage rate were those embodied in the Federal Social Security and Federal-State Unemployment Compensation systems. The cost of these programs to automobile manufacturers in the early years of their enactment was probably in the neighborhood of 3 to 4 cents per hour per employee. At Nash-Kelvinator, for example, the combined hourly cost was 3.5 cents in 1937, 3.6 cents in 1938, and 3.7 cents in 1939—or 4 per cent of the company's average hourly wage rate in each year.[2] There were, it is true, some private benefit plans in existence; but whatever their actual value to employees, their cost impact on the companies was certainly modest. The GM programs are a case in point. In 1939, employees at GM could participate in a program of life, sickness, accident, hospitalization, and surgical insurance, but the major part of the costs was borne by the participants

---

policy of paying wage rates at least as high as the prevailing levels in relevant labor market areas), but represented a sharing of profits with employees who, by virtue of continuous employment and cooperative effort, had aided the company's progress. In 1919, this program included an Anniversary Check Plan whereby employees received checks of 5 per cent of earnings on the first four anniversaries and 10 per cent thereafter; a Co-partnership Plan permitting employees with 3 or more months' service to purchase company stock (up to 20 per cent of earnings) at half price; a Vacation Plan under which employees with 2 years' continuous service and a satisfactory attendance record were entitled to 1 week's vacation with pay; and a Pension and Life Insurance Plan whose principal provision, applicable to employees with 20 years' service, was a retirement benefit of 25 per cent of average annual earnings in the previous 5 years (with a minimum of $30 a month). In addition, the company operated an emergency hospital and recreational facilities for its employees. The cost of these plans in each of the years 1926 and 1929 was reported to exceed $2 million. As with most company programs, however, these plans at Studebaker did not survive the depression. (Information supplied by Studebaker Corp.)

2. Nash-Kelvinator Corp., *Annual Report, 1952.*

themselves. In addition, employees with the necessary "service" qualifications were eligible for interest-free loans under the company's income security plan which sought to meet the problem of gross fluctuations in weekly earnings by providing for limited borrowing against future earnings.[3] The level of participation in these programs gives adequate testimony that they were of some value to the majority of employees. Nevertheless, they were certainly not a substantial cost burden on the company.[4]

Apart from these benefit programs, the only other wage practices significantly affecting employee compensation in the early years related to premium (or penalty) payments. In 1939, Chrysler paid a premium of 5 per cent to workers on second and third shifts, and both Chrysler and GM paid time and one half for work in excess of 40 hours per week (double time if said work occurred on a Sunday), double time for work on six specified holidays, and a minimum of two hours' pay to employees called to work or not properly notified of lack of work. There are no estimates of the cents-per-hour cost of these practices in the late 1930s, but crude calculations place the cost in the neighborhood of 1.5 cents.[5]

3. Workers under 64 years of age and credited with at least 5 years of service could, in the event of reduced employment, secure advances against future earnings which would raise their earnings to 60 per cent of their standard weekly wage. The total advance was limited to 360 hours' pay, and repayment was by automatic deduction of one half of weekly earnings in excess of 24 hours' pay. For employees with 2 to 5 years' service, terms were less liberal: borrowing was limited to 40 per cent of standard weekly earnings and the total credit allowance was 72 hours. ["General Motors Corporation," Wage Chronology No. 9, *Monthly Labor Review* (Sept. 1949), 263.]

4. Even in 1947, GM's insurance plan cost the company only 0.6 cent per hour per employee (see Table 3, p. 40).

5. In 1939, average gross hourly earnings in the automobile industry (including parts producers) were 91.5 cents and the average workweek 35.9 hours. If we apply to these data the adjustment factor developed by the Bureau of Labor Statistics for converting gross earnings to straight-time, our estimate of overtime costs is 0.9 cent per hour. [See *Monthly Labor Review* (Nov. 1942), pp. 1053–54.] Since this adjustment factor is based on the as-

On the basis of these estimates, it is safe to conclude that the cost of wage supplements in 1939 was little more than 5 cents per hour, or about 6 per cent of the average hourly wage rate.[6] From these modest beginnings, however, the trend in benefit costs has been sharply upward, far outdistancing the rise in wage rates.

The year 1940 is credited with the introduction of shift premiums and vacation allowances into the automobile industry. In June of that year, General Motors granted a shift premium of 5 per cent to second- and third-shift workers, liberalized overtime practices by providing time and a half for work in

sumption that overtime is paid at time and a half and only on hours worked in excess of 40 per week, it fails to correct for Sunday and holiday work at double time and for shift premium payments. The omission of a correction for double time, however, appears to be of little consequence, partly because companies could be expected to hold payments at these high penalty rates to a minimum in 1939 and partly because the adjustment factor used above is for a 36-hour workweek and therefore tends to overstate the amount and cost of overtime. As for shift premiums, it is unlikely that these added significantly to costs for only a small minority of companies in the industry followed this practice in 1939. A study of over 500 UAW-CIO contracts as of May 1938 reveals that only 15 per cent contained any bonus provision for night work. Similar data were not compiled for 1939, but by June 1940 the proportion of contracts making such provision had risen to 53 per cent. There is a strong presumption that the bulk of this increase occurred in 1940 rather than in 1939, since the union lists the former year as marking the introduction of shift premiums into auto manufacturing plants. [R. J. Thomas, president, UAW-CIO: "Automobile Unionism, 1940–41," report submitted to the 1941 Convention of the UAW-CIO (Aug. 4, 1941), p. 57. "We Dared to Make Our Dreams Come True" (UAW-CIO Education Dept., Sept. 1955).] On the (liberal) assumption, however, that 10 per cent of the work force received a 5 per cent shift premium throughout the year, the cost amounts to less than 0.5 cent per hour.

6. The only reference to the cost of employee benefits in an automobile company in prewar years is a statement, dated July 1949, by Ernest R. Breech, then executive vice-president of the Ford Motor Company, to the effect that hourly rated employees at Ford received an average of 90 cents per hour plus 4 cents in "direct and indirect benefits, such as insurance" in 1939. ["Why No Postwar $1,000 Car?"] This somewhat lower figure for Ford is not inconsistent with the above estimate and may be attributable to Ford's nonunion status in 1939.

excess of eight hours per day, and agreed to pay employees with one year's seniority 40 hours' pay (at straight-time rates) in lieu of vacation.[7] Two years later, by directive order of the National War Labor Board, this vacation allowance was liberalized to provide 80 hours' pay in lieu of vacation to employees with five or more years' seniority. Apart from this improvement, however, the only other changes of note during the war period were in the area of premium and penalty payments. In late 1942, workers were granted time and a half for work on the sixth day of the calendar week and double time for work on the seventh day. (At the same time, overtime pay for work on Saturdays, Sundays, and holidays as such was abandoned for the duration of the war.) Call-in pay was also increased—to three hours at GM in September 1942, and to four hours at Ford in the following month. Finally, in mid-1945, premiums for third-shift workers at GM were raised, by order of the NWLB, to 7.5 per cent. This last provision was made retroactive to October 1943.

In the immediate postwar years, after the return to free collective bargaining, the focus of "fringe" negotiations was on improved vacation payments and holidays with pay. In March 1946, GM's vacation plan was revised and extended: employees with one to three years' seniority were granted 2 per cent of gross annual earnings in lieu of vacation; those with three to five years' seniority 3 per cent, and those with five or more years' seniority 4.5 per cent. This revision of the formula proved temporary; in the settlement of April 1947 the earlier formula was restored by reverting to 40, 60, and 80 hours' pay, respectively, for the three seniority groups. The principal "fringe" gain in 1947, however, was the negotiation of six paid

7. Actually, the vacation allowance was the only novel provision, for the same overtime and shift premiums were already in existence at Chrysler (as of Nov. 1939); and, indeed, the Studebaker-UAW contract of 1937 granted a 10 per cent premium to workers on all regular shifts ending between 10:30 P.M. and 8:15 A.M.

holidays for all hourly rated employees with seniority status—a gain estimated to be equivalent to 3.5 cents per hour.

The effect of these developments up to 1947 was an approximate trebling of the hourly cost of wage supplements. At GM, the total cost of benefits in this year was $96.5 million, or 18 cents per hour per employee. Since the company's average hourly wage rate was then $1.37, wage supplements added 13 per cent to hourly labor costs. How these supplementary costs were distributed among major programs is shown in Table 3, p. 40. These estimates, which are based on the only complete data issued to date, may be considered representative of the general magnitude of industry costs. The actual cost in individual companies will vary, of course, according to whatever differences exist between firms in programs, wage levels, seniority distributions, and employment experience.

In 1948 the union launched its drive to establish private security programs in the auto industry. Group insurance programs already in existence in such firms as Ford and GM were brought under union agreement and their terms revised and liberalized. The Ford plan, for example, provided the following benefits (geared to wage levels): $2,000 to $4,000 life insurance, $1,000 to $2,000 accidental death and dismemberment, and $18 to $30 weekly accident and sickness disability. Employee contributions to the cost of the plan ranged from $1.72 a month for employees earning less than $1.10 an hour to $3.44 for employees earning $1.90 and over. In addition, hospitalization and surgical insurance (Blue Cross and Blue Shield) was made available to workers at their own expense. In its September 1949 agreement, Ford improved its insurance package by adding in-hospital medical benefits (with a maximum of $4 per day up to 70 days). A more striking feature of this agreement, however, was the establishment of the industry's first pension plan for hourly rated workers. The main provision of this noncontributory retirement program was the guarantee of a $100-a-month pension benefit (including the primary federal benefit) to employees at age 65 or over with 30 years of credited service.[8] In the spring of 1950 (after a long and bitter strike over the issue of funding), Chrysler granted the Ford pension plan and agreed to pay one half the cost of hospital and surgical insurance for its employees. A few months later, in its celebrated five-year agreement, GM extended the latter provision to cover workers' dependents as well and introduced a number of significant improvements in major benefit programs. Group insurance benefits were raised; pay in lieu of vacation in the amount of 120 hours at straight-time rates was granted to employees with 15 or more years' seniority; and the earlier (Ford) pension formula was revised to yield to employees retiring at age 65 or over with at least ten years' service a monthly retirement benefit of $1.50 for each year of service up to 30 years.[9]

In the five years following the 1950 settlements, the only improvement in supplementary wage benefits occurred in 1953 when the UAW invoked the "living document" principle. At this time the pension formula was raised from $1.50 to $1.75 per month and a maximum benefit amount (inclusive of federal social security) established at $137.50.[10] The new agreements of 1955, however, contained a number of important advances. The Ford settlement—the first to be reached that year—granted a 2.5-weeks vacation with 100 hours' pay for employees with 10 to 15 years' seniority,[11] added two paid half holidays, and

8. Benefits were reduced proportionately for workers with less than 30 years' service, and provision was made for both early retirement and disability retirement.

9. The minimum retirement benefit (inclusive of the federal benefit) was set at $4 a month for each year of service up to 25 years. Reduced annuities were provided for retirement between the ages of 60 and 65; and employees totally disabled at age 50 or over with 15 or more years' service were granted a benefit of $3 a month per year of credited service up to 30 years.

10. Retired workers were also permitted to subscribe to Blue Cross–Blue Shield as part of the group plan covering employed workers.

11. Unlike the GM and Chrysler agreements which provide pay in lieu of vacation, the Ford and Studebaker agreements make provision for vacations with pay.

liberalized group insurance and Blue Cross–Blue Shield. On the pension front, it raised the benefit formula from $1.75 to $2.25 per month, eliminated the benefit maximum and the 30-year limit on credited service, and established vesting rights for employees separated from the company at age 40 or over with 10 years of credited service.

The most dramatic innovation in 1955, however, was the Ford-UAW Supplemental Unemployment Benefit (SUB) Plan. This plan, in brief, established a trust fund, maintained by company contributions of 5 cents per man-hour, to be used for the purpose of supplementing unemployment benefits received by laid-off Ford employees from the state unemployment compensation systems.[12] The company's liability was limited by a so-called maximum funding of the Fund for each month. This maximum was determined by multiplying $55 million (the maximum funding established for June 1955) by the ratio of the number of workers employed and laid off with credit units during the month in question to the number of workers employed prior to June 1, 1955. The market value of the Fund's assets divided by the maximum funding determined the Trust Fund position; and the company's obligation to contribute in any month was limited to the attainment of a 100 per cent Trust Fund position for that month.

Benefits under the 1955 plan were payable after June 1, 1956. To be eligible for benefits, a laid-off worker had to meet the benefit requirements of the state unemployment compensation system and have to his credit at least one quarter credit unit under the plan.[13] The basic benefit amount (including state unemployment benefits) was set at 65 per cent of weekly after-tax straight-time earnings for the first four weeks of layoff and 60 per cent thereafter—subject to a maximum weekly supple-

12. Actually, two separate funds—a General Fund and a Defense Fund— were established; for convenience, this distinction is disregarded.

13. Eligibility terms also required that the worker had not refused an offer of work by the company in the same labor market area.

mental benefit of $25 and a Trust Fund position of 13 per cent or above.[14] The duration of benefits for any laid-off employee depended on the number of credit units he had accrued, his seniority, and the Trust Fund position. Credit units were accumulated only by employees with at least one year's seniority up to a limit of 26 credit units at any one time. The rate of accrual was one half unit for each full workweek, except that during the first two years of the plan's operation workers with less than ten years' seniority were credited with only one quarter unit per workweek. The duration of benefits depended on the number of credit units canceled for each weekly benefit payment, and this in turn was a function of the worker's seniority and the applicable Trust Fund position. Table 2, from the

TABLE 2.   Schedule of Credit Units Canceled for Weekly Benefit Payments under the SUB Plan

If the Trust Fund position applicable to the week for which such benefit is paid is	If the seniority of the person to whom such benefit is paid is					
	1-5 years	5-10 years	10-15 years	15-20 years	20-25 years	25 years and over
	The credit units canceled for such benefit shall be					
85% or over	1.00	1.00	1.00	1.00	1.00	1.00
76–84.99%	1.11	1.00	1.00	1.00	1.00	1.00
67–75.99	1.25	1.11	1.00	1.00	1.00	1.00
58–66.99	1.43	1.25	1.11	1.00	1.00	1.00
49–57.99	1.67	1.43	1.25	1.11	1.00	1.00
40–48.99	2.00	1.67	1.43	1.25	1.11	1.00
31–39.99	2.50	2.00	1.67	1.43	1.25	1.11
22–30.99	3.33	2.50	2.00	1.67	1.43	1.25
13–21.99	5.00	3.33	2.50	2.00	1.67	1.43
4–12.99	10.00	5.00	3.33	2.50	2.00	1.67
Under 4%	No benefit payable					

14. If the Trust Fund position fell below 13 per cent in any week, benefits payable out of the Fund were reduced by 20 per cent (but not below $5). If it fell below 4 per cent, benefit payments were suspended.

Ford agreement, shows the precise nature of this relationship.

In the 1958 negotiations, concluded first at Ford, no new programs were initiated but many of the existing programs were extended. In the area of premium payments, time and a half was provided for work on Saturdays as such, and the differential for third-shift workers was increased from 7.5 to 10 per cent. Group insurance benefits were raised for workers in the higher wage brackets, and hospital and surgical benefits were improved by the inclusion of a provision for full payment of surgical services for employees with an annual income not in excess of $7,500, the cost to be shared equally by the company and the employee. On the pension front, the most significant change was the distinction drawn between present employees and retirees. In the past, improvements in the retirement program had been applied equally to both of these groups, but in 1958 management was successful in breaking this pattern. For present retirees, the benefit formula was raised from $2.25 to $2.35 a month for each year of credited service. For employees retiring on or after September 1, 1958, however, the formula was raised to $2.40 a month for each year of service prior to September 1, 1958, and $2.50 a month for each subsequent year. Early retirement benefits, deferred vested pension benefits, and disability retirement benefits taking effect on or after September 1, 1958, were similarly upgraded. Finally, the SUB plan, which had been conservatively financed in the first instance, was revised in a number of respects. Eligibility requirements were liberalized; the maximum supplemental benefit was raised from $25 to $30; and the reduction in the benefit base from 65 to 60 per cent of straight-time take-home pay after the first four weeks of layoff was eliminated. In addition, two new benefits were added. The first of these was a short-workweek benefit designed to raise income to 65 per cent of straight-time take-home pay in any week in which the employee's earnings disqualified him from state unemployment benefits. The second was a lump-sum separation payment made available to any permanently laid-off worker with at least two years' seniority. This payment was determined by multiplying the worker's hourly wage rate (including cost-of-living allowance) by the number of hours' pay to which his seniority entitled him (ranging progressively from 40 hours' pay for 2 years' seniority to 1,200 hours' pay for 30 or more years' seniority) and by the Trust Fund position.[15] These new and higher benefits were to be financed, however, within the existing framework of company contributions (i.e. 5 cents per man-hour).

The cost of these benefit improvements since 1947 has been substantial. In the second full year of operation under the 1958 agreement, General Motors estimated that its benefit costs amounted to 72 cents an hour—a fourfold increase over the 1947 level. This compares with an approximate doubling of the company's average hourly wage rate over the same period—from $1.37 in 1947 to $2.76 in early 1961.[16] In other words, despite a rapid increase in wage levels since 1939, the cost of employee benefits, relative to the average wage rate, had risen from approximately 6 per cent in 1939 to 26 per cent in 1960. The distribution of benefit costs in 1960 is shown in Table 3 along with the data for 1947. These estimates and the nature of the programs in force in the auto companies up to 1961 provide a basis for judging the role of employee benefits in the "compensation structure."

The Role of Fringe Benefits in the Compensation Structure

In analyzing the manner in which fringe benefits modify the wage structure, it is naturally desirable to consider the relationship of such benefits to each of the major types of wage

15. This payment was reduced by the amount of any supplemental benefits received during the period of layoff.

16. General Motors Corporation, "Free Collective Bargaining Works!" (1961), p. 9. To our knowledge, these figures have not been disputed by the union.

TABLE 3.   Costs to General Motors of Supplementary Wage
Payments, 1947 and 1960

	Cost of company contribution			
	1947		1960	
Type of benefit	Per man-year (dollars)	Per man-hour (cents)	Per man-year (dollars)	Per man-hour (cents)
a) *Private benefit plans*				
Pensions			135	6.5
Group insurance	13	0.6	97	4.7
Blue Cross–Blue Shield			87	4.2
SUB			102	5.0
b) *Public benefit programs*				
Federal social security	28	1.4	154	7.5
Unemployment compensation	48	2.4	125	6.1
c) *Other programs*				
Vacation pay	83	4.2	257	12.5
Holiday pay	57	2.8	151	7.3
Overtime and shift premiums	131	6.6	387	18.2
Total benefits	360	18.0	1,495	72.0

Source. "Free Collective Bargaining Works!", General Motors Corporation (1961). Only the cost of total benefits (per man and per hour) appears
in the publication. Other statistics are computed from information on the
total cost of individual items and average hourly-rate employment in the
two years.

differential—i.e. personal, occupational, and interfirm. In the
following discussion, we have chosen to comment rather briefly
on personal and interfirm differentials and to emphasize the
role of benefits in the occupational structure. This does not
imply that issues connected with the first two kinds of differential are unimportant, but simply that the nature of the information currently available precludes an exhaustive treatment

of these issues at this point. Moreover, insofar as labor-cost differences between firms are concerned, these are the main topic of subsequent chapters which deal with the influence of collective bargaining on competitive relations. At this juncture, it is sufficient to note simply the main findings of this analysis as they bear on the matter at hand.

In the absence of reasonably detailed comparative data covering the cost of major benefit programs in the various companies, it is impossible to estimate with any degree of precision how the inclusion of such benefits affects the interfirm structure of compensation. From the study of negotiations, contract provisions, and program administration, it would appear that the benefits (and costs) of major fringe items are more or less equal in the Big Three and American Motors and somewhat higher in Studebaker-Packard. If the definition of "fringes" is broadened, however, to take account of certain work practices, such as relief, rest, and washup periods, then benefit levels and costs have certainly been related inversely to the size of firms, though the differentials are smaller now than in the immediate postwar decade.[17]

In the search for more precise measures of interfirm fringe differentials, it is tempting to make use of the few scattered cost statistics that are available on an individual company basis. It is our judgment, however, that the quality of these data does not warrant their use as meaningful measures of compensation differentials. This judgment rests in part on the uneven and frequently unspecified coverage of the statistics. It is also based, however, on the questionable significance of those cost differentials which are admittedly valid. Our concern here, it will be

17. The issue of cost differentials between firms is dealt with at length in chap. 6 and 7 where an attempt is made to take account of a broader range of practices than is here considered. The improvements in work practices which have led to substantial reductions in the cost disadvantages suffered by smaller firms are thoroughly documented in these chapters. The 1961 negotiations reveal, however, that the process of adjustment toward a more uniform structure of labor costs is not yet complete.

recalled, is with the income rather than cost effects of benefit arrangements, although the cost of programs is accepted as an approximation of their value to employees except where other evidence indicates that cost and value clearly diverge. Consequently, if the cost differential associated with a particular program is traceable to some cause other than a difference in benefit arrangements, it is not an acceptable measure of the program's impact on the compensation structure. If insurance costs, for example, differ between two companies because of differences in the efficiency of program administration (including the ability of one company to drive a harder bargain or secure a more favorable contract with the insurance carrier), we should properly disregard this difference in the analysis of compensation flows, though it remains relevant in the study of cost flows. Similarly, if a pension (or vacation) plan imposes higher costs on one firm than another because of differences in the seniority distributions of the respective work forces, the differential in question is not properly a part of the interfirm compensation structure though clearly an important element of the cost structure.[18] It is not always possible of course to pinpoint the source(s) of fringe cost differences among firms in the industry; nevertheless, there is sufficient evidence in the comparison of benefit provisions and in the comments and complaints of individual managements to support the conclusion that interfirm cost differences (at least for the major ben-

18. Whether cost differences of this sort are relevant from the standpoint of the interfirm compensation structure depends on the measure selected as appropriate to interfirm comparisons. If our concern is simply with the average return to workers in the same occupation in each firm, then the negotiation of, say, a pension plan that provides a uniform benefit and full funding of past service obviously confers a higher income on that group with the higher seniority distribution. If, on the other hand, the (interfirm) comparison is made between workers in the same occupation group with identical service records, then no income differential is created. In our view, this latter measure is the appropriate one since the cost differences in question have no effect on the relative attractiveness of jobs in the different firms, either for an employee with given seniority or for a new entrant into the industry.

efit programs) derive primarily from nonbenefit sources of the type illustrated above.

While interfirm cost differences attributable to differences in seniority distributions do not enter into the analysis of interfirm compensation differentials, there is another way in which benefit programs tied to seniority affect the structure of compensation. The pension and vacation plans negotiated in the auto industry are, at least in their initial stages, a combination of a deferred wage payment and a transfer of income from low-seniority to high-seniority workers.[19] This transfer effect,

19. In 1948, the union argued that only contributory pension programs were discriminatory in this sense. In a pamphlet entitled "Facts about a Pension Program," issued to delegates at the UAW National Chrysler Conference, it was contended that contributory pension plans tended to create disunity and were often voted down by the membership because they resulted in younger workers paying much of the cost of benefits for older workers. By contrast, it was claimed that the UAW plan, because it was paid for by employers and the government, favored no one group at the expense of others. This distinction, intended no doubt to sell a plan which otherwise might appear unpalatable to younger members, is clearly without substance. A more acceptable statement, giving due recognition to the wide range of "transfer" possibilities, was made by Leonard Lesser of the UAW Social Security Department in 1953:

The issues (in pension negotiations) have . . . centered around the determination of basic questions of a choice as to who gets what, when and how much. These basic determinations have raised issues such as whether to allocate the bulk of the limited funds to assure maximum retirement security to older workers at the cost of generally foregoing, for the present, such desirable features as vesting of benefits, transfer of rights, and other provisions directed to the special needs of younger workers; whether to tie benefits to earnings and thus divert more of the available funds to higher paid workers, thus leaving less available for the pensions of lower paid workers, or whether, by gearing benefits to service only, to permit the payment of a more adequate benefit to all workers regardless of earnings; whether to provide a benefit for the permanently and totally disabled individual at the expense of a lower benefit for those who retire because of age; whether to give credit for past service and whether such past service should be credited on an equal basis with future service; what conditions of eligibility to require . . .

The principles which were established by the UAW-CIO in the area of benefits can be stated briefly: To provide within the limits of available

deriving from the crediting of past service, has its major impact during the early years of the plan when much of the company's contribution goes to the funding of past service credits. This effect diminishes over time, though it does not disappear entirely as long as benefit improvements are applied to past service and are made available to those already in retirement. In consequence, workers with high seniority at the time of the plan's introduction gain at the expense of workers with low seniority; and retired workers on pension, as a result of benefit improvements, gain at the expense of employed workers. Beyond these effects, however, the main impact of the pension program is to alter the time-shape of the worker's earnings' stream by the deferral of certain income payments to later years. The latter transfers, unlike those associated with the funding of past service, are not discriminatory in that they are transfers of income between periods rather than between persons.[20] The same transfer effects naturally apply in the case of other employee benefit programs, such as vacation pay and holiday pay, where receipt of benefits depends on seniority or on the attainment of some minimum service status. The only difference in these programs

funds maximum retirement security for the greatest number of older workers who will be eligible for retirement within the period for which the plan was originally negotiated; and to provide some measure of security for workers under the age of 65 who are forced to retire because of permanent and total disability and for whom no benefits are provided under the Social Security Act. ["Problems in Pension Contributions and Benefits," *Proceedings of the Industrial Relations Research Assn.* (1953), pp. 89–90.]

The fact that contributions to the plan were made directly by employers does not render these issues of choice any less important. Indeed, only by adopting the highly improbable assumption that employer contributions would otherwise have been distributed (say, in the form of a wage increase) among the various categories of workers according to the pattern of benefits established under the plan can we justify the nonexistence of transfer effects.

20. We abstract here from problems associated with differences in time preference, which cause individuals to place different valuations on such programs, and from the element of discrimination in any program which does not make provision for full vesting or transfer rights.

is that benefits are paid, with only minor exceptions, to workers currently employed and receiving wages.

If employee benefit programs which award benefits on the basis of seniority are incorporated into the compensation (or income) structure, one primary influence is then the effect on personal differentials. In the early period following their installation these programs represent a form of rate discrimination equivalent in principle to the negotiation of a wage increase based on length of service; in later stages, they are equally a part of the compensation structure, but discrimination is absent in that benefits are in the nature of a deferred income payment, earned in earlier years. Whether this (temporary) disruption of the pattern of personal differentials is attributable to collective bargaining depends of course on the role one ascribes to unionism in the development of such programs.

The role of fringe benefits in the occupational structure can be estimated with somewhat greater assurance and precision. From our earlier review of the development of these programs, it is clear that some tend to maintain the pattern of relative differentials (as revealed in wage-rate statistics) while others tend to narrow it. In the former category are group insurance, premium payments, and paid holidays and vacations. Under each of these programs, the benefits or payments involved are geared directly to wage levels. Consequently, the integration of these programs into the occupational compensation structure does not alter the pattern of relative (wage) differentials significantly.[21] In the category of employee benefits that do affect the occupational structure are pensions, hospitalization and surgical insurance, SUB, and the federal-state programs. The benefits accruing to workers under each of these programs

21. To avoid encumbering the text with excessive detail, we report here only our conclusions regarding the impact of the various programs on the occupational structure. The reader interested in the recent status of these programs or in the assumptions underlying their treatment in the compensation structure will find additional information in the appendix to this chapter.

tend mainly to preserve the pattern of absolute differentials and hence to compress the structure of relative differentials. This is readily apparent in the case of private pensions and hospitalization insurance where benefit amounts are the same for all participants regardless of wage or earnings level. It is less evident in the case of SUB and the public retirement and unemployment compensation systems which gear benefits partially to earnings. However, these wage-connected benefit differences are offset to some extent under SUB (and presumably under state unemployment compensation) by the lower incidence of layoffs among the more skilled and highly paid workers and are rather severely restricted under the public programs because of the relatively high earnings levels in the auto industry, which qualify the majority of workers for close to the maximum benefits. While the assumption of a level-benefit effect is not strictly accurate in the case of SUB and the federal retirement program, it involves, in our judgment, only a very modest overstatement of the degree of wage compression implicit in these programs.

Thus, the inclusion of major employee benefits in the compensation structure clearly reduces the range of occupational differentials (as measured by wage rates alone). If our conclusions with respect to the significance of each program are accepted as approximately valid, then we may estimate the value of benefits (assessed at cost) to different occupational groups from the data contained in Table 3. This is done in Table 4 for three principal categories of workers—janitors, assemblers, and tool makers. Given the wage rates for these occupations and the average wage rate for all workers in all occupations, the value of benefit programs geared to wage levels (i.e. that are equivalent to a percentage wage increase) is computed by multiplying the occupational rate by the ratio of the average cost of the program to the average wage rate. Programs that are the rough equivalent of a flat rate increase have of course the same dollar value to all occupations regard-

TABLE 4. Value of Major Employee Benefits to Specified
Occupational Groups in the Automobile Industry,
Early 1961

	Occupations			
Type of benefit	All	Janitor	Assem-bler	Tool-maker
a) *Private benefit plans*				
Pensions	$0.065	$0.065	$0.065	$0.065
Group insurance	.047	.041	.044	.060
Blue Cross–Blue Shield	.042	.042	.042	.042
SUB	.050	.050	.050	.050
b) *Public benefit programs*				
Federal social security	.075	.075	.075	.075
Unemployment compensation	.061	.061	.061	.061
c) *Other programs*				
Vacation pay	.125	.109	.118	.159
Holiday pay	.073	.063	.069	.092
Overtime and shift premiums	.182	.158	.172	.231
d) TOTAL	$0.720	$0.664	$0.696	$0.835
e) Wage rate (incl. cost of living)	2.760	2.400	2.600	3.500
f) Compensation rate (d + e)	$3.480	$3.064	$3.296	$4.335
g) Relative wage rate (assembler = 100)		92	100	135
h) Relative compensation rate (assembler = 100)		93	100	132

Source. The cost data and average straight-time hourly wage rate for all occupations are derived from "Free Collective Bargaining Works!"; wage rates for individual occupations are projections of late 1958 rate data and are representative of the Detroit area.

less of wage level. As the data in Table 4 indicate, the effect of including major employee benefits is to reduce the current assembler-tool maker differential from 35 to 32 per cent and the janitor-tool maker differential (roughly equal to the range of occupational earnings) from 46 to 42 per cent.

In summary, the incorporation of employee benefit programs into employee pay scales affects the industry's structure of compensation in a variety of ways. If we envisage the wage structure in terms of wage-rate differentials, as it is conventionally portrayed, the principal effects of adding to wage rates the cents-per-hour equivalents of fringe benefits are the following. First, there is possibly some tendency to raise the relative level of compensation for workers in the plants of the Independents. This effect is not significant if attention is confined to the programs discussed above. If the definition of employee benefits or wage supplements is extended, however, to embrace plant practices of the pay-for-time-not-worked variety, the effect is more marked. Second, employee benefit programs geared to seniority affect personal differentials, particularly in the years immediately following their introduction. Pension and vacation plans that credit past service constitute in effect a transfer of income from low- to high-seniority workers and therefore introduce a significant differential in earnings between workers in the same occupation but with different records of attachment to the firm. Third, benefit programs in the industry have the effect of slightly reducing relative wage differentials between occupations. This influence stems from the nature of private and public benefit programs which, with the exception of group insurance, either do not relate benefits to wage levels or employ formulas that in a high-wage industry provide essentially the same benefit for all. The effect of adding the value of fringe benefits to wage rates in 1960 reduces the range of the occupational structure by 9 or 10 per cent.

This brief treatment of the role of fringe benefits in the compensation structure does not exhaust the wide variety of specific influences exercised by each of the programs. It does suggest, however, the principal ways in which the programs as a whole modify the structure of compensation as portrayed by wage-rate statistics alone. These modifications are of interest in subsequent chapters analyzing the dimensions of the wage structure.

Collective Bargaining and Employee Benefits

Elaboration of the system of employee compensation to include the kinds of benefits discussed in earlier sections of this chapter is generally conceded to be one of the major influences of collective bargaining on American industrial practice. In this concluding section, an attempt is made to appraise the validity of this hypothesis as it applies to the evolution of the compensation system found in the automobile industry. Since much of the recent discourse on the impact of unions and collective bargaining is contradictory and confusing, we have chosen to explore the matter in some detail. This requires that we deal not only with particular developments in the auto industry, but also with some of the broader issues of concept and method which at present are a serious hindrance to progress and understanding in this area.

The prevalent view among economists regarding the influence of unions and collective bargaining in the development of fringe benefits is ably stated in the following quotation:

> The spread of fringes and the growing diversity of the entire system of employee compensation have been changes wrought mainly if not predominantly by unionism —directly through collective bargaining and indirectly through legislation affecting premium pay and social security benefits. Granted that in part fringe benefits are alternatives to wage increases an employer might well have conceded even without any union, the group nature of most of these benefits puts them largely in the category of provisions uniquely attainable through collective bar-

gaining or legislation. Ordinarily, the readily replaceable individual employee is no more able to negotiate his own medical plan with the employer than to achieve a rearrangement of shift hours, if only because to concede him such benefits is normally to run the risk of extending them to the whole group, incurring costs having a scale in excess of the marginal worth of the particular employee. Though there are exceptions to this contention, it seems quite reasonable to conclude that the revolution in wage compensation since 1940 is one of the major economic impacts of the new American unionism.[22]

This view assigns a primary role to unionism. It also assumes that the incidence of unionism is to be measured with reference to the operating results of a nonunion market characterized by individual response. Clearly, the plausibility of this assumption is of critical importance, since it determines whether we interpret the above conclusion as yielding (a) a measure of the *actual* influence of unionism on the system of wage compensation, or (b) simply a measure of the difference in operating results between a unionized market and a (hypothetical) nonunion market. Since we have already expressed skepticism regarding the validity of this assumption, the comments that follow, insofar as they allude to the nonunion market, imply the second kind of measure in which this form of market is treated as a norm. As elsewhere, it is left to the reader to decide whether this construct is a valid standard against which to measure the *actual* consequences of unionism, although we shall raise some issues pertinent to the decision.

In pondering the role of unionism and collective bargaining in the spread and growing diversity of employee benefits, we cannot neglect two sets of facts: (1) that many types of em-

22. George H. Hildebrand, "The Economic Effects of Unionism," in Neil W. Chamberlain, et al., eds., *A Decade of Industrial Relations Research, 1946–1956* (New York, Harper, 1958), p. 131.

ployee benefit programs antedate unionism (and the threat of unionism);[23] and (2) that the economic and social forces giving rise to the union's quest for increased security and leisure also had a profound influence on other groups, including management and government.

The fact that many companies initiated benefit schemes of their own volition (most frequently for salaried workers, but also for hourly-paid workers) signifies of course that there are important exceptions to the competitive hypothesis—as expressed in the quotation above. These exceptions, it is true, are duly noted as "alternatives to wage increases an employer might well have conceded even without any union." However, the fact that they were conceded in the absence of unionism, that they were incorporated in the personnel policies of a number of companies, tends to weaken the contention that they are "uniquely attainable through collective bargaining or legislation."

Even in the absence of organization, employers are not immune to the pressures created by the varied needs and reactions of workers. It is true that these needs may be less effectively asserted and that management's response may be minimal (motivated principally by a concern for stability and efficiency), but the range of practices and programs adopted by numerous companies in preunion times and the rationale

23. See the comments to this effect in Sumner H. Slichter, James J. Healy, and E. Robert Livernash, *The Impact of Collective Bargaining on Management* (Washington, Brookings Inst., 1960), chap. 13–15. On pensions, for example, these authors observe: "It seems reasonable to conclude that unions have contributed substantially to the rapid spread of pensions. Employers, however, initiated the move toward pensions and cannot be cast in the role of antagonists even though they are concerned about costs" (p. 377). Similarly, on vacation and insurance plans, they report: "It would appear from the data [for 1939–40] that many of the early introductions of vacation provisions in union contracts served to bring already-established vacation practices under contract rather than to establish the practice. Impressions from War Labor Board experience are that this point was decidedly significant for insurance programs but less important for vacations" (p. 427).

for such adoptions are a reminder that employers, even in an unorganized and highly competitive environment, may find it desirable and, indeed, advantageous to cater to some of these so-called nonmonetary or nonwage needs.[24] The simple predictive model which underlies the notion that such practices and programs are peculiar to a unionized market, though instructive, is an oversimplification traceable perhaps to an inadequate view of the complex tasks of manpower management and of the adaptability and inventiveness of both managers and workers.

It may be contended, of course, that some or all of these earlier programs were introduced in an effort to forestall organization and are therefore properly regarded as part of the union's influence. Apart from the fact that in many of these situations the threat of unionization appears to have been so remote as to be virtually negligible, this contention is not at all disturbing since it reinforces rather than weakens our main thesis that any workable alternative to unionism must somehow meet the problems and pressures that lead workers to organize. The union is, after all, a device or vehicle that owes its origin to the existence of certain strongly felt needs and its continued survival to its ability to yield some measure of satisfaction of these needs. If the only way to avoid unionism is through the anticipation and voluntary adoption of some reasonable facsimile of its program (however that is to be determined!), then there is really no meaningful alternative to unionism in terms of results (in this case, the compensation system). With or without the union, management is required to respond in similar fashion to workers' problems.[25]

24. While altruism may have played a part in the introduction of some pre-union benefit programs, others were clearly calculated to affect beneficially worker morale, productivity, turnover, and attendance.

25. Whether management can in fact accommodate successfully in ways that produce results differing significantly from bargained results is of course the crux of the problem in assessing union influence. It may well be that non-union forms of accommodation which meet the requirements of a highly industrialized, democratic society exist, but we are frankly skeptical. Cer-

At the same time, it must also be acknowledged that the union's drive for the extension of benefit arrangements post-dated for the most part the establishment of basic governmental programs in the same or related areas, reflecting the sweeping changes in social and economic attitudes ushered in by the depression. The new unionism may have played its part in strengthening these attitudes, but it can scarcely be credited with creating them. Indeed, it was creature rather than creator of the changing social outlook which introduced an era of active support for unionism and its goals.

A major difficulty resulting from the fact that unionism has been part and parcel of this sweeping process of change is that we lack a clear conception of how the organization, policies, and practices of management would have developed over the same period in a nonunion system. It seems quite arbitrary to assume either that no evolution in attitudes and policies would have occurred or that evolution would simply have paralleled what has in fact developed in the presence of unionism. Yet it is usually on one or the other of these two assumptions that our current judgments are based. Even without this difficulty, it is not always easy to establish management's true position relative to various issues. Apart from arguments based on the logical workings of the competitive system, the main case for a substantial union influence in the spread of fringes rests on the strong antagonism often displayed by management toward union demands incorporating such programs. The evidence is simply that most employers must be prodded into granting these concessions against their will and better judgment. The same can be said, however, of wage increases granted under collective

---

tainly, it is dangerous to assume that we can generalize from the experience of a few nonunion firms or markets operating in a unionized environment, though the study of these firms in relation to this environment may yield useful insights. The ultimate test of the validity of any nonunion model in this context is, however, the requirement that it fit the industrial facts of life in such manufacturing centers as Detroit, Pittsburgh, Akron, and Cleveland. This is an exacting requirement and the basis of our skepticism.

bargaining; yet no one argues seriously that wages would not have increased but for unionism. In this connection, it is well to remember that the logic of present-day bargaining casts the employer (with a few notable exceptions) in an essentially defensive role. He seldom initiates wage and benefit improvements, for concessions which are employer initiated typically raise the cost of settlements. In any event, the battle must be waged, at least from outward appearances, if the various constituencies and parties at interest are to remain satisfied with the process.[26] Consequently, while we frequently learn what management is officially opposed to in negotiations, we cannot always ascertain the true extent of that opposition or the degree to which it is dictated by the nature of the bargaining process itself.

Having stated these reservations, the stubborn fact remains that any attempt to assess the influence of unionism and collective bargaining as such must rest largely on speculations and conjectures concerning the relationship between bargained solutions and the solutions generated by nonbargaining models. In this context, the primary assumption underlying the use of any particular nonbargaining model is of course that the model has practical relevance from the standpoint of the operating requirements of the American economy in the mid-twentieth century. The models typically adopted for this purpose have been crude and poorly defined. This is as unfortunate as it is unavoidable for it no doubt reflects the present unsatisfactory

26. As Frank Rising of the Automotive and Aviation Parts Manufacturers Association has stated: "Let's agree that the union can influence management, and that it does. It uses plain economic force, or the threat of that force, to gain some management decisions which it otherwise would not get. I might add that management makes some good decisions on its own, and sometimes has to work quite hard to find a way to let the union take credit for it!" ["Union Influence on Management Decisions in the Automobile Industry— An Industry Point of View," in *Proceedings of the Industrial Relations Research Assn.* (Dec. 28–30, 1954), p. 31.] Unfortunately, these are matters which normally remain hidden to the outside observer.

state of our knowledge in this area.[27] Unhappily, our own judgments are based of necessity on a model of this type, derived primarily from an examination of the relationship between bargained outcomes and the objectives and attitudes of unions and employers. This is a familiar model, but its principal assumptions are seldom recognized explicitly. These are, first, that more than two decades of bargaining with unions have not unduly affected developments in the organization, outlook, and behavior of management (to say nothing of influences on the structure and dimensions of the economy); and, second, that in the absence of unions the compensation system would more or less reflect the objectives of management as expressed in the bargaining process (these objectives being attuned presumably to the requirements of the market). Since these assumptions are open to challenge, the judgments that follow concerning the probable behavior of management and of the compensation system in a nonunion market are frankly vulnerable. The reader must decide whether they warrant acceptance.

On the basis of this crude sort of model, we would judge that of the private benefits listed in Table 3, the union's influence has been greatest in the area of private pensions and SUB and least in the area of insurance. This estimate is at best in the nature of an educated guess; the evidence on management attitudes is fragmentary, and what little there is is not always easy to interpret. For this reason, the evidence and arguments that underlie our judgment in each of the major program areas are developed below.

27. While we would not dispute Hildebrand's summary judgment that "the past decade [1946–56] of research in labor economics has been an unusually fruitful one" or that "one of the most impressive qualities exhibited by this work is the emergence of an informed theoretical empiricism" ("Economic Effects of Unionism," pp. 138–39), the present uncertainty concerning the economic effects of unionism (as witness the studiously vague, often uneasy, and frequently conflicting pronouncements of professional economists in and out of government) suggests that in this area at least our claims to progress are easily exaggerated.

Private Pensions and SUB. In the absence of unionism, it seems reasonable to conclude that private pension plans and SUB plans would not have been introduced by unilateral management decision. This conclusion may appear so obvious as to warrant no additional comment in view of management's reluctance to negotiate pensions in the late forties and SUB in the mid-fifties. But evidence of this nature is not necessarily conclusive for some of the reasons already stated. It is true, for example, that General Motors refused to negotiate pensions with the union until a "court of last resort" had ruled that this was an issue on which bargaining was required by law. In appraising the company's position, however, it is well to remember that GM adopted exactly the same position with regard to insurance, yet it had operated an insurance plan of its own since 1926. We do not infer from this that the company's principal objection to a private pension plan was simply an unwillingness to submit the determination of such a plan to bargaining, though we do suggest that one may legitimately distinguish between a pension plan and a *bargained* pension plan, and that opposition to the latter does not automatically spell disapproval of the former. In GM's case (and in the case of other companies) there is reason to believe that opposition to private pensions reflected in part a general distaste for any further widening of the union's sphere of influence, as well as a concern about the union's notions of fiscal responsibility. Specifically, auto managements appear to have been concerned with the costs of a bargained noncontributory program—especially the cost of funding past service credits and the absence of built-in cost restraints such as a contributory program might provide; with the difficulties likely to be encountered in negotiating programs whose uncertain incidence left room for conflicting subjective judgments; and with inevitable demands by union leaders for joint determination of pension fund investments with the objective, not of maximizing the fund's return or safeguarding its assets, but of financing "socially desirable" projects which could not attract funds in the open market. Considerations such as these might well induce a company to take a firm stand in negotiations against a program of this sort, regardless of its true position and sympathies. Indeed, viewed in the light of customary bargaining behavior, it would be unreasonable to expect otherwise.

While these qualifications caution against the simple assumption that management opposition in bargaining is a sufficient condition to establish the independent effects of unionism, there is, in our view, a more convincing reason for supposing that auto managements would not have installed private pension plans (or SUB) of their own volition—namely, the existence of basic federal programs in these areas. It is not simply a case that management itself has said as much,[28] but also that the very existence of these programs would almost certainly have tended to channel any pressures for improvement in old-age and unemployment security in the legislative direction. It is the existence of these alternative devices, erected by government without any strong affirmative support from organized labor, but in response to a widespread and deeply felt community need, that

28. Ford's treasurer, L. E. Briggs, indicated his company's position after the pension agreement in late 1949: "Our first thought was that over the long pull, the best way of providing for workers after their period of useful service is through federal old-age security legislation. Since these provisions are presently inadequate we decided to enter into a pension agreement this year as part of our contract, setting up proper conditions and safeguards": *Detroit Free Press,* Oct. 5, 1949. It will be recalled that this plan was designed to raise retirement benefits (inclusive of social security) to $100 a month at age 65 for workers with 30 or more years' service. Any increase in federal benefits reduced the private benefit payable to the worker by the same amount.

Similarly, on January 6, 1950, GM's C. E. Wilson told the Chicago Executives Club that adequate, soundly financed federal pensions were the best answer to the old-age security problem. He urged that federal pensions be more closely geared to earnings' levels since the program in existence discriminated against the higher-paid worker. He thought, however, that some supplementation would be necessary in high-wage industries—an observation which no doubt recognized that this was already a fait accompli in the auto industry with the signing of the Ford agreement.

would seem to provide the most convincing argument against employer initiation of private pension and SUB programs. Indeed, it was largely the failure of these basic programs to keep pace with rising real incomes that caused unions finally to seek supplementation at the bargaining table through private programs.

Group and Health Insurance. It appears that the UAW had little to do with the introduction of insurance plans into the industry, though it almost certainly accelerated the pace of their revision and liberalization. Insurance programs were already a common feature in the industry in the late 1920s. GM's program had been established in 1926 when $1,000 of life insurance was made available to employees in return for a monthly contribution of 50 cents. This program was expanded in 1928 to include moderate sickness and accident cash benefits.[29] In late 1929, a survey conducted by the Studebaker Corporation revealed that most auto companies had a basic plan. At the Packard Motor Company, for example, the Packard Aid Association operated a voluntary program which cost participating employees $1.40 a month (deducted from wages) and provided life insurance coverage, graduated from $1,250 to $3,500 according to seniority, and weekly sickness benefits of $12 for the first week of disability and $2 for each working day thereafter (up to a total of $180 during any 12-month period). The Chrysler Corporation's plan, on the other hand, geared benefits and contributions to earnings levels. Weekly contributions of 30 to 80 cents purchased life insurance of $1,000 to $3,000 and disability benefits of $7 to $21 a week for a maximum of 26 weeks for any one disability. Studebaker's own plan was said to be similar. Indeed, plans of one sort or another were reported for all companies in the survey with the single exception of the Hudson Motor Car Company.

Clearly, insurance plans antedated the UAW, and there

---

29. *Welfare and Pension Plans Investigation,* Final Report of the Senate Committee on Labor and Public Welfare (1956), p. 139.

seems no more reason in principle to assume that they were introduced as a result of some vague threat of unionism than that they represented the response of a moderately perceptive employer to a widely recognized and long-established employee need. After all, the practice of mutual aid through the pooling of funds accumulated by periodic dues payments has a much longer history than unionism itself. Moreover, this is the sort of plan that a rational employer might well adopt of his own accord. Many of these early plans had a built-in "service reward" feature which geared benefits to length of service. It is clear that for some companies at least service-connected compensation was part of a deliberate policy aimed at reducing excessive turnover. But even without this feature, sponsorship of a group plan which permitted employees to purchase insurance benefits at rates substantially below the premiums on individual policies enabled a company to secure a measure of employee goodwill at little expense. There is really no reason to assume that a reasonably astute businessman would require much prodding to engage in this kind of undertaking.[30]

However, if the union played at best a minor role in the introduction of insurance plans, their incorporation into collective agreements in 1948 has almost certainly led to a more rapid liberalization and extension of benefits than would have occurred under exclusive management supervision. It is unrealistic to assume of course that no improvements would otherwise have occurred in a period of rising incomes, improving medical services, and sharply increasing medical costs. Indeed, since the major part of the cost of management-sponsored programs

30. This view of unionism's role in the initiation of insurance programs derives support at a more general level from consideration of the true alternatives to bargained health plans. In our opinion, group programs sponsored by employers and/or private insurance companies or, failing that, some form of governmentally directed health program represent the only substitutes that might realistically be expected. Thus, while unionism may have influenced the form of health plan adopted, it has not been responsible for the provision of health protection.

would probably have been met through direct contributions by the participants, the only natural limit to the rate of improvement in such programs is the requirement that a sufficient number of employees elect to participate in order to justify the program and to guarantee the insurability of risks. In actual practice, management's judgment as to the level of benefits the majority of employees would willingly support might impose a lower rate of progress, though periodic surveys and polls conducted by the company on specific revision proposals offer one obvious means of reducing this gap.

It is naturally hazardous to conjecture what program levels this alternative system would have in fact produced. Indeed, our own prediction of lower levels rests mainly on the grounds that the potentiality for expansion is simply less—for while the rate of improvement under this type of system is limited by employee decisions regarding the allocation of earnings (and perhaps still further by some lag in management's response to employee wishes), the same is not necessarily true of the bargained system. The UAW's objective in this area has been twofold: to improve benefit levels and to transfer premium payments to the employer. Its success in the latter can be gauged from the fact that GM employees paid two thirds of the cost of group insurance and the full cost of Blue Cross–Blue Shield in 1947, but only one third and one half respectively of the costs of greatly improved programs in 1960.[31] It is not unlikely that this type of bargained system, which tends to conceal the cost of improvements to employees, acquires a momentum of its own and hence may outrun the rate of development that employees themselves would freely choose to support out of earnings. Unfortunately, there is no way of verifying whether or not this has occurred. Certainly the fact that approximately 99 per cent of eligible employees have elected coverage under existing "voluntary" programs proves nothing considering the method of financing developed under bargaining. Moreover, where

31. GM Corp., "Free Collective Bargaining Works!" (1961), p. 10.

union leadership is aggressively committed to the continuous expansion of such programs (as is certainly the case in the UAW), a considerable part of the union's activities is devoted to the task of persuading members that leadership priorities are sound and worthy of maximum support.[32] Obviously, there are limits to these powers of salesmanship and persuasion, but insofar as union efforts are successful in bringing about some revision of members' preferences, the leadership can be said to create in part the basis for acceptance of its own policies.

These arguments provide grounds for asserting that the potentiality for a more rapid expansion exists under the bargained type of program in autos and that unionism is therefore at least capable of promoting a higher rate of development than could reasonably be expected in management-supervised programs. Beyond that, however, we would simply hazard the guess that part of this potentiality has been realized in the auto industry. This judgment is based in part on the belief that management, typically cautious and conservatively oriented in its approach to decisions in these areas, could not be expected to match the impatient and aggressive drive of the union.

Premium Payments. Premium payments are one aspect of labor's drive for shorter hours (or increased leisure). Initially, overtime payments were intended as an inducement to management to fix and maintain regular working schedules of reasonable length. Shift premiums similarly were intended to discourage or reduce to a minimum the scheduling of work during undesirable hours. Insofar as these were unavoidable,

32. Mention of these possibilities is not intended as a criticism of union policy. Not very much is known about the range of discretion enjoyed by entrenched union administrations in the selection and design of specific policies and programs. Nevertheless, it is generally conceded that union leaders are responsive to a variety of pressures in formulating demands, and there is sufficient evidence of leadership-membership differences in the priorities assigned to various aspects of the employment relationship to warrant the view that, although the union is essentially a service organization, the union leader is far from being simply a passive agent of the membership.

the requirement of premium rates meant that workers were compensated for the extra hardship or inconvenience. Nevertheless, in the years up to 1940, the primary emphasis was on premium rates as penalties designed to prevent overtime work. Since World War II, however, successive improvements in the structure of premium payments have tended to obscure the original aim; premium payments have come to be regarded by most workers as a special form of compensation offering an attractive opportunity for additional income rather than as a protection against long or undesirable hours. This shift in emphasis is reflected in agreement provisions safeguarding the worker's right to overtime. Indeed, penalties have been imposed in instances where management has failed to equalize overtime among the various claimants.

It is generally acknowledged that unions, through bargaining pressure and political agitation, have played an influential role in reducing hours of work. This position rests mainly on the historical observation that employers did not voluntarily reduce hours but, on the contrary, vigorously opposed all union efforts to achieve reductions. It is reinforced by the view that market competition is less effective in reducing hours than in raising wages, since a change in hours, unlike a change in wages, is hardly an appropriate subject for individual bargaining. "It is not possible . . . for individual workers to demand and receive reductions in hours. Efficient factory management requires that working hours be the same for all. The initiative for reducing hours must therefore come from the employer. It is natural that employers should have hesitated to take the initiative in this direction. They could never be completely certain that, in a particular case, man-hour output would rise enough to offset the decline in hours. . . . Even at best, the increase in man-hour output would take some time to appear."[33]

33. Lloyd G. Reynolds, *Labor Economics and Labor Relations* (Englewood Cliffs, N.J., Prentice-Hall, 1959), pp. 218–19. It should be observed that the latter part of this statement refers not to employer reluctance to reduce

As an explanation of why the initiative for reduction of hours came from unions rather than employers, the case presented above is persuasive. By and large, employers were opposed to the movement for shorter hours. We cannot conclude from the evidence of early struggle, however, that the gradual reduction in working hours over the last century or so is uniquely attributable to unionism except in the sense that these changes were accomplished in an environment of union agitation for shorter hours. In the absence of unions, ideas and institutions would certainly not have remained static during a century and more of rapid economic development, and it is inconceivable that a progressive, democratic society would have failed to evolve some mechanism for apportioning increased productivity between income and leisure (if the market mechanism itself offered no solution).[34] We may not be able to visualize the particular form of mechanism that might substitute for unionism, much less predict the rate of reduction that such an alternative mechanism might produce, but assuredly working hours would have declined substantially since the nineteenth century, with or without unions. In assessing the independent influence of unionism, therefore, the relevant comparison is not between the observed downward trend in hours and a zero trend predicated on a set of conditions appropriate only to an earlier stage of economic and social development, but between the observed trend and an alternative downward trend based on a set of conditions

___

hours of work as such, but to an unwillingness to reduce hours and simultaneously raise wage rates so as to maintain weekly earnings.

34. It is important to remember that the shorter-hours drive was part of the general reform movement of the early and middle nineteenth century. The demand was a rallying cry for all groups seeking to elevate the status and well-being of the working population. Unionism, as it happened, emerged as a primary vehicle for translating this desire into effective action, but the goal itself was not peculiarly a union goal, nor was unionism the primary motivating force. See, e.g., George Brooks, "Historical Background," in *The Shorter Work Week,* papers delivered at the Conference on Shorter Hours of Work sponsored by the AFL-CIO (Washington, Public Affairs Press, 1957).

appropriate to successive stages of development in a progressive society.

A system with unions may well have produced a more rapid rate of reduction in working hours than would any alternative system, but so far there is little in the way of convincing evidence. If the choice between income and leisure had been left more to the discretion of employers, it may be argued that the latter would have laid more stress on the income loss suffered by workers as a result of increased leisure and would therefore have favored a more modest rate of reduction.[35] Indeed, it may even be argued that if the choice had been left to workers them-

35. Where daily and weekly hours are excessively long and fatiguing, a reduction in hours unaccompanied by a reduction in weekly earnings need not increase costs since man-hour output may rise sufficiently to offset the fall in hours worked. Employers generally were probably unaware or too skeptical of these possibilities in the nineteenth century and consequently opposed changes or failed to initiate changes that were of benefit to themselves as well as their employees. By overestimating the loss of output attendant on hours' reduction, management was led to resist the desire for shorter hours more vigorously than objective circumstances warranted. This is not of itself evidence that management would have set a more moderate rate of reduction, but it does provide some basis for asserting that management would have pursued a rather cautious approach to the issue, at least in the initial stages. At the same time, most employers were surely aware of the strong undercurrent of discontent with long hours and some of them apparently adopted the concept of hours' reduction as part of their personnel policies. Some shortening of work hours was therefore to be expected, especially as early experiments with the policy proved costless and even beneficial to the companies concerned.

As working hours decline, however, the possibilities for compensating improvements in man-hour output diminish, and real income must be increasingly sacrificed for greater leisure. As this point of trading is reached, employer concern with output and cost effects might be expected to reassert itself and constitute a brake on further reductions—at least to the extent of recognizing such reductions explicitly as substitutes for income improvements. This suggests that employers, left to their own devices, would have stopped short of the levels advocated in recent decades by unions, especially since the union view has tended either to underestimate the real cost of recent and proposed reductions (by unwarranted projections from past experience) or to conceal the true nature of the choice between income and leisure in representations before members and the public.

selves, less stress would have been placed on shorter hours—at least in the past few decades. The prevalence of dual job-holding, the widespread desire for overtime work, and frequent complaints about the inadequacy of earnings opportunities all lend support to the notion that union pressures in this respect may tend to outrun workers' desires. Even among those workers who find the shorter workweek attractive, it appears that many do so not because it means more leisure, but rather because it promises additional income through increased overtime opportunities.[36] This suggests that any system giving greater emphasis to employer or worker preferences would have led to a somewhat less rapid reduction in working hours. This judgment is strengthened perhaps by the notion that unionism served to bring the issue of increased leisure into sharper focus by its persistent agitation for shorter hours. This view has been stated by Chamberlain: "It seems a reasonable judgment . . . that unions have played an influential, if secondary, role in the general reduction of hours in the United States, by helping to mobilize an already present social sentiment in favor of more leisure. Leisure was wanted so that men might cultivate their tastes and interests instead of simply working that they might exist. Rising productivity permitted leisure as one of its fruits. If the will and the means have been the primary factors, the unions have nevertheless been an important instrumental influence by focusing and organizing the sentiment."[37] This assumes, of course, that organized action was not inevitable. But if in the absence of unionism some other instrument of collective protest had emerged, this also might have served to focus and mobilize public sentiment, though not necessarily in precisely the same directions.

On the basis of our alternative model (wherein management attitudes, conditioned by the market, constitute the primary

36. For comments on some of these points, see Brooks, "Historical Background," p. 19; and Reynolds, *Labor Economics*, p. 227.

37. Neil W. Chamberlain, *Labor* (New York, McGraw-Hill, 1958), p. 527.

determinant of employment terms), we would predict a somewhat less rapid reduction of working hours and certainly a less
elaborate structure of premium payments than has been established under unionism. Working hours were reduced substantially in the auto industry during the 1930s. A close observer
of these developments describes the trend and its causes:

> At the beginning of this period, before the influence of
> the government and the union was brought to bear, there
> was a wide variation in the working hours of individual
> companies, but the most typical working week consisted
> of 54 hours. . . . In motor-vehicle manufacturing 71.7
> per cent [of wage earners] usually worked more than 48
> hours and 3.1 per cent more than 54 hours. Prior to the
> depression which began in 1929, a working week of 60
> or more hours was not at all unusual during rush periods.
> Throughout most of the period of the operation of the
> National Industrial Recovery Act the weekly employment
> of production workers in the automobile industry was
> limited to 48 hours, with a long-term average of 40 hours.
> The entrance of the union has resulted in further reduc-
> tions. The 5-day, 40-hour week is now typical. Only a few
> of the early agreements provided for a 44-hour week.
> These had to be revised in October 1939, when the 42-
> hour limitation of the Wage-Hour Act (Fair Labor Stan-
> dards Act of 1938) became effective.[38]

This description underlines the difficulty of disentangling the
effects of the UAW and of unionism generally in a period of
massive dislocation, widespread agitation for reform, and radically new ventures in government regulation. The most that
can be said with assurance is that unionism was a factor among
others in pinning down the 40-hour week and 8-hour day as
the basic working schedules governing auto manufacturing.

38. William H. McPherson, *Labor Relations in the Automobile Industry*
(Washington, Brookings Inst., 1940), p. 69.

Moreover, with regard to premium payments as such, it is clear that employers would have preferred to retain greater discretion in varying the length and scheduling of the workweek to meet demand fluctuations without incurring overtime penalties. The personal interviews conducted by McPherson with auto industry executives shortly after unionization leave no doubt on this score. His findings are forcefully stated in the following paragraphs:

> During periods of "normal" production there is little management opposition to the 40-hour week. . . . In the motor vehicle branch, however, managers appear to be more insistent [than in the parts branch] on the right to operate on Saturday without overtime rates so long as they keep within the 40-hour limitation. Most managers in the industry apparently consider that regular use of the short workday on Saturday is uneconomical, although they frequently used it during rush seasons before the advent of the union.
>
> During periods of peak production there is strong management opposition to the 40-hour week. The overtime differential makes extra work so costly as to be impractical except under very unusual conditions. . . .
>
> Managers are probably more strenuously opposed to the present hour limitations during peak seasons than to any other practice which the union has been able to introduce. They would like to be able to operate 45 or 48 hours a week during 20 weeks each year without paying overtime rates. This would enable them to rely more completely on their best employees, and there would be less need for the temporary hiring of less efficient men, who in any case cannot hope to receive very significant annual earnings in this industry. This flexibility in hours would result in a smaller, more stable working force receiving higher annual earnings at existing wage rates.

Such a change is now impossible owing both to union attitudes and to the Wage-Hour Act.[39]

It is tempting, of course, to regard premium payments as peculiarly a union device. It is not unlikely, however, that the depression and the abrupt change in social outlook that followed it would have produced a form of legislation similar to that embodied in the Fair Labor Standards Act even in the absence of unions. It is also possible that an enlightened management would have installed some form of premium for long or undesirable working hours as part of an equitable system of compensation. Indeed, employers generally might well have been compelled eventually in a high-income, high-employment economy to compensate for these inconveniences (or accept an inferior quality of labor) simply to retain and attract the necessary work force. Beyond that, it is not unreasonable to suppose that as incomes and living standards rise, the premium required to compensate workers for extra inconvenience rises more than proportionately. Although we cannot rule out the existence of premiums in any feasible alternative system, the excess demand for overtime work at present premium rates and the need for "rationing" procedures in contracts indicate a liberalization of the premium structure well beyond operating requirements.[40] At the same time, it is difficult to conceive of management voluntarily initiating (out of a sense of equity or justice) quite the same entangling web of restrictions on its operating efficiency.

Having stated this conclusion, it is necessary, finally, to reserve a word for the origin of some of these hours-of-work benefits in the automobile industry—especially the introduction by Ford of the 8-hour day, with time and a half for overtime,

39. Ibid., pp. 71–72.

40. This conclusion applies with particular force to overtime premiums. It is probably not applicable to shift premiums, for few workers with an effective choice elect to work on second or third shifts. Though exceptions are to be expected, shift work is generally a "chore" which the more junior men reluctantly are compelled to perform.

in 1914, and of the 40-hour week in 1926. These Ford innovations, although unique, deserve some mention for they demonstrate rather dramatically the central issue in measuring union influence.

Reduction in the length of the workday from 9 to 8 hours in 1914 was part of a sweeping revision of Ford labor policies which also introduced the $5-day and a system of sick-leave allowances. The motives inspiring these innovations have been differently interpreted. According to Keith Sward, the change in policy was designed to pacify a disgruntled work force, on the verge of a "spontaneous insurrection," and to thwart an organizing campaign conducted by the International Workers of the World.[41] Allan Nevins, on the other hand, rejects the explanation that the new policies were dictated by self-interest and business expediency and attributes them instead to a combination of profit sharing, efficiency engineering and practical idealism.[42] Fortunately, it is unnecessary for our purpose to attempt to resolve these differences in viewpoint, though in all fairness we would observe that Sward's analysis of early Ford policies bears the stamp of his aversion for the harsh and repressive labor conditions that were to characterize Ford operations in the 1930s. The point we wish to establish here is simply that shorter daily and weekly hours, as well as the practice of premium payments for overtime, were introduced into auto manufacturing by unilateral management decision. If the changes are interpreted as a necessary response to labor unrest and the threat of collective action, spontaneous or otherwise, then the industrial context apparently afforded management little choice.[43] Under the circumstances, there is no more reason to label the change a consequence of unionism (or,

41. *The Legend of Henry Ford* (New York, Rinehart, 1948), pp. 52–56.

42. *Ford: The Times, the Man, the Company* (New York, Scribner's, 1954), pp. 533–40.

43. Why Ford was compelled to choose this particular form of response remains to be explained. Other manufacturers faced with the general threat of unionization in this period were certainly not forced to respond in similar

more correctly, of the threat of unionism) than a necessary condition of doing business. Certainly, it is erroneous to assume that the widespread discontent which alone created the threat of collective action would somehow or other have dissolved or remained dormant if by some magic the IWW had been spirited from the scene. Short of outright suppression, the threat of "spontaneous insurrection" and the mass exodus of workers from the Ford plant could hardly be countered except through some change in the conditions of work. To contend otherwise is to credit the union rather than the factory system (and industrialization generally) as the source of industrial unrest. If, on the other hand, these policy changes are attributed to enlightened self-interest on the part of management, then they reveal a type of behavior and degree of discretion in decision making which are seldom encompassed in the customary image of the nonunion or preunion entrepreneur responding to pressures in the labor market by a more or less mechanical manipulation of wage rates. Either way, the facile explanation that such developments are uniquely or primarily *caused* by unionism is deficient and requires reexamination.

Paid Holidays and Vacations. Paid holidays and paid vacations, which are largely a development of the last two decades, are in a sense simply an extension of the earlier movement toward shorter hours—in this case a reduction in the number of hours worked per year. Indeed, since the late 1930s, the drive for increased leisure has been conducted almost exclusively at this level, except in periods of unemployment when union leaders have proposed reduction of the workday and workweek as one means of combatting idleness.[44]

---

fashion. Indeed, the introduction of the $5-day alone would have guaranteed Ford immunity from pressure.

44. Auto workers have experienced a serious unemployment problem in recent years which can be traced to the combined effects of the recession, rapid technological change, and a leveling-off in the demand for automobiles. Recognizing that recovery of the economy offers only a partial solution in

Paid vacations and paid holidays made their appearance in auto contracts in 1940 and 1947 respectively. Since it is unlikely that all auto managements would have adopted the types of programs developed under collective bargaining on a voluntary basis, we are inclined to regard these benefits, and especially the rate at which they have been liberalized, as primarily a consequence of unionism. However, the significance of these programs in autos lies less in the direction of shortening the work year (a common assumption) than it does in altering the timing of income payments (annual and lifetime) and in redistributing income in favor of senior employees. This conclusion is based on the following considerations.

First, the GM and Chrysler contracts provide for pay in lieu of vacations and not for vacations with pay. Thus, for more than two thirds of the workers engaged in auto manufacturing, the vacation program represents a special type of income payment (disbursed in a lump sum annually) and not increased leisure. Moreover, even in those companies where vacations are provided, they do not necessarily shorten the work year if, as appears common, they merely take the place of layoffs for many lower-seniority workers during slack periods such as model changeovers. For a good majority of the industry's workers, therefore, vacation plans are income- rather than leisure-producing; they redistribute earnings over time and, to some extent, among individuals but do not affect annual hours of work.[45]

---

returning unemployed auto workers to jobs in the industry, the UAW proposed to management in the recent 1961 negotiations a number of methods for creating job opportunities through reduction in hours—including reduction of the workday, workweek or work year without loss of pay, longer vacations, additional paid holidays, and industrial sabbaticals (UAW press release, July 9, 1961). There is no indication, however, that the union pressed this program vigorously at the bargaining table.

45. The fact that most workers in the industry are subject to annual layoff in late summer at the time of model changeovers may be one reason for sup-

Second, on the matter of paid holidays, the union's influence has probably had less to do with the granting of holidays as such than with the payment of wages for existing holidays. We do not know what holidays were actually granted in auto plants prior to unionization, but a review of records and studies pertaining to early negotiations gives no indication that holidays as such were an issue. UAW contracts in the late 1930s did specify, however, time and a half or double time for work on six legal holidays, and this undoubtedly helped to regularize, if not also to extend, the practice of plant shutdowns on these days except in emergency situations. The GM Department of the UAW has summed up the preunion situation at GM plants as follows:

> For years before we had a Union, and for some time after we had a Union, a holiday was pretty much like any other day. If it fell during a busy season you worked like any other day, and for straight time. If it fell during a slack season, management would give you the day off, but when you received your pay check the following week you lost all enthusiasm for holidays because you were one day short and all the grocery money just was not there.
>
> The first time that holidays were given any consideration as being something different than the ordinary day

posing that management would have moved slowly in initiating vacations. However, McPherson's study of management attitudes in the auto and parts industries in 1939 reveals significant differences in viewpoint among company executives. Many felt that paid vacations were desirable because they were already granted to salaried employees or because they would improve labor morale and productivity (the motive, incidentally, that underlay such preunion plans as those at Studebaker and Packard). Others opposed paid vacations because they were too costly. Still others believed there was little logic in their application to wage earners in seasonal industries, since wage earners in such industries already received a vacation in the form of layoff and were already compensated for unstable employment by higher wage rates and/or the receipt of unemployment compensation. (*Labor Relations,* pp. 110–11). This range of attitudes in 1939 illustrates of course the need for caution in generalizing about management behavior.

was in the settlement of the tool and die strike in August of 1939. In that settlement, the corporation agreed to pay double time on a holiday if you worked.[46]

On the basis of these comments, penalty rates on holiday work might be expected to raise the average number of holidays actually enjoyed in a given year, though we have no way of estimating the incremental effect on leisure. *Paid* holidays for wage earners, on the other hand, were largely a development of World War II, when the WLB, in an effort to relieve some of the pressure and tension accumulating under its wage-restraint program, followed a fairly liberal policy in approving "fringe" gains. Consequently, when paid holidays were finally negotiated in autos in 1947, the practice was already well established in other areas of industry. Interestingly enough, if the UAW had had its way, the practice would have been instituted in auto plants only at a later date, for the 1947 auto pattern of 11.5 cents and six paid holidays was based, not on UAW demands, but on a prior settlement between GM and the Electrical Workers' Union. Indeed, in an effort to demonstrate its independence, to avoid the appearance of pattern following rather than pattern setting, the National GM Conference, under Reuther's leadership, initially rejected the company's offer of paid holidays and insisted instead on a straight 15-cent increase. A press statement of April 16 explained the union's position:

> Delegates to the Conference accepted this 15¢ offer, but instructed their negotiating committee to meet with General Motors Corporation in order to have the 15¢ offer applied as a blanket wage increase rather than as an 11½¢ an hour increase plus 6 paid holidays, which the Corporation proposes.
>
> The General Motors Conference took this unanimous action because it feels that the General Motors workers

46. "Educational Outline," UAW-GM National Agreement (June 12, 1955), paragraphs 138 through 143a: Holiday Pay.

should be free to spend the money which the Corporation is offering them in a way which more nearly meets the needs of the General Motors workers who did not ask for paid holidays and do not want any portion of the 15¢ paid for any holidays.

Since the cost to the Corporation is the same, it is difficult for the General Motors workers to understand why General Motors insists that workers take something they did not ask for, while denying them something they did ask for.[47]

This only means of course that the introduction of paid holidays under collective bargaining would have been delayed if GM had capitulated to union pressure. It does not mean that in the absence of unionism GM would have instituted these payments voluntarily.[48]

The results of this analysis of the influence of unionism and collective bargaining on the system of employee compensation in the automobile industry can be summarized briefly. Granted that these are matters of judgment which cannot be stated with precision, we conclude nevertheless that the UAW has been responsible for establishing the present systems of private pen-

47. This reference is to the UAW's demand for a comprehensive social security program embracing hospital-medical care and pensions. Interestingly enough, Ford's offer to allocate part of the 15-cent increase to a contributory pension program was also rejected. It was rumored at the time that defeat of the Ford proposal was engineered by Reuther in order to embarrass an opponent on the UAW Executive Board who, as leader of the Ford Department, had been largely responsible for negotiating the plan.

48. GM's response to the Union's demand for a 15-cent increase is nevertheless worth noting. As Harry Anderson, the vice-president in charge of personnel at GM, explained the company's position to Reuther on April 24, 1947: "The proposal to pay for six holidays not worked is the first offer of this nature in the automobile manufacturing industry. As most of our operations are closed on the holidays enumerated, we feel that seniority employees should be paid for such days, thus assisting in stabilizing employment and increasing earnings."

sions and supplementary unemployment benefits in auto plants. In the absence of bargaining, there was little reason for management to adopt either of these plans, largely, we believe, because of the prior existence of federal programs in these areas. Even under collective bargaining, the programs adopted would have differed if management preferences—as revealed in negotiations, addresses, and personal interviews—had been given more weight. Apart from a more gradual liberalization of benefit levels in both programs, management would have preferred in the pension area a system that was contributory, that related contributions and benefits to earnings levels, and that gave less emphasis to the crediting of past service and to the extension of improvements to present retirees. As for SUB, Ford's view was that total unemployment benefits should be related to area wage levels in order to preserve incentives to seek work in low-wage areas. In the case of GM, which abhorred the notion of SUB, the accumulation of a separate fund for each worker was apparently favored over the pooling arrangement negotiated at Ford.

With regard to other benefit programs, the independent influence of the union is less clear-cut. In the insurance area, the UAW doubtless brought about an expansion of group and hospital-medical plans, but it cannot be credited with initiating them in the majority of companies nor with the full range of improvements developed since the 1930s. Without the union, insurance plans would have been a feature of the industry's compensation system. The main difference is that company-sponsored plans would have been less elaborate and would have placed stronger reliance on the contributory principle.

Paid vacation and paid holiday plans also bear the stamp of collective bargaining. In the auto industry, however, these programs have had very little effect on the annual working hours of the majority of employees. This follows from two sets of facts. First, the vacation provisions covering most workers in the industry either grant pay in lieu of vacation (which is simply the equivalent of a bonus geared to seniority) or are designed so that vacations merely take the place of layoffs. Second, paid holidays have been largely a substitute for the unpaid holidays already granted in preunion times. Insofar as the union has had some influence in this area then, it has been mainly in the direction of altering the form of annual and lifetime income payments to employees. We cannot rule out the possibility, of course, that some companies would have established paid vacations and paid holidays—especially the latter—of their own volition. Nor can we deny that some managements might have found it advantageous to install service-connected benefits (similar in effect to pay in lieu of vacation plans) as a means of promoting work-force stability in the tight labor market that characterized the postwar years. We would judge, however, that the union's aggressive drive to expand these programs in the last decade or so has established benefit levels beyond those of any alternative system that management itself might have proposed.

Finally, we conclude that unionism, apart from producing a somewhat sharper reduction and more rigid scheduling of working hours, has created a structure of premium payments much higher than would otherwise have developed. Shift premiums represent the only exception to this generalization. If it is assumed that premium prices for long or undesirable hours would reflect in the union's absence the requirements of the labor market, then the present need for rationing such hours clearly indicates that the prevailing prices are excessive. Thus, management could certainly have met its operating requirements at lower premiums. Even without the market test, it is difficult to visualize what rationale besides union pressure could have produced the present high structure of premium rates.

Fringe Benefits and the Occupational Structure
of Compensation

The purpose of this appendix is to make explicit the assumptions underlying conclusions stated in the text concerning the role of selected fringe
benefits in the occupational structure.

Group Insurance. Under the group insurance programs in force in
auto plants, employee benefits and contributions are geared directly to
wage levels. Table 5 gives the schedule of benefits and employee costs
in effect at Ford in the period 1958–61. Since the effective rate range of

TABLE 5. Schedule of Insurance Benefits and Employee Costs
at Ford, 1958–1961

Basic hourly rate		Life Insurance	Accidental Death and Dismem- berment	Monthly Total and Perma- nent Disability	Weekly Accident and Sickness Disability	Em- ployee's monthly cost
Under $2.25		$4,000	$2,000	$ 80	$48.00	$3.44
$2.25 and under	2.45	4,400	2,200	88	52.80	3.79
2.45	2.65	4,800	2,400	96	57.60	4.13
2.65	2.85	5,200	2,600	104	62.40	4.47
2.85	3.05	5,600	2,800	112	67.20	4.80
3.05	3.25	6,000	3,000	120	72.00	5.15
3.25	3.45	6,400	3,200	128	76.80	5.50
3.45	3.65	6,800	3,400	136	81.60	5.85
3.65	3.85	7,200	3,600	144	86.40	6.20
3.85 and over		7,600	3,800	152	91.20	6.55

the Ford plan, which is typical of group insurance practice in the industry,[1] embraces all but a very few occupations at the extremes of the wage-rate structure, it is clear that the integration of group insurance into the compensation structure does not affect appreciably the pattern of relative (wage) differentials among occupations.

Paid Vacations and Paid Holidays. With the exception of Studebaker, where vacation pay is based on a percentage of earnings (graduated by seniority), vacation payments in the industry are as shown in the accompanying schedule.

Seniority	*Vacation Pay*
1 but less than 3 years	40 hours
3 but less than 5 years	60 hours
5 but less than 10 years	80 hours
10 but less than 15 years	100 hours
15 years and over	120 hours

In addition, each company provides the equivalent of seven full holidays with pay. Since payments under both programs are based on the employee's wage, exclusive of overtime and shift premiums, their incorporation into the compensation structure leaves relative differentials unaffected.

Premium Payments. These payments include time and a half for work in excess of 8 hours daily and 40 hours weekly and for Saturday work as such, double time for Sunday and holiday work, and premiums of 5 and 10 per cent for second and third shift work respectively. In the absence of evidence that certain occupations (e.g. the skilled trades) enjoy a more or less permanent advantage over others because of greater overtime opportunities (i.e. that earnings differentials and rate differentials consistently diverge), it may be assumed that the inclusion of premium payments as part of employee compensation does not change the structure of relative returns to the various occupational groups.

Private Pension and Hospitalization Plans. Pension benefits in the auto industry are related to seniority and not to earnings. Under the Ford plan in effect up to 1961, the basic benefit for an employee retiring on or after September 1, 1958, at age 65 and with at least 10 years' service, was $2.40 per month for each year of service before 1958, plus

1. The only significant deviation from the pattern is found in the Studebaker agreement which provides for uniform benefits and employee contributions. However, this agreement covers less than 1 per cent of the industry's workers.

$2.43 per month for service in 1958, plus $2.50 per month for each year of service after 1958. Benefits for early retirement and total and permanent disability retirement were calculated on a similar flat-rate basis. Under Blue Cross–Blue Shield, benefits vary with marital status and number of dependents but not with wage levels. Up to 1961, auto companies paid one half the subscription rate for the classification of coverage (self only, self and spouse, or self and family) elected by the employee. Since there is no relationship between benefits and earnings under either program, we may assume that the benefits have the same dollar value at all occupational levels.

Supplemental Unemployment Benefit Plan. The impact of the SUB program on occupational differentials is difficult to assess. Shortly after the program was introduced, one analyst noted how it would affect the skilled-unskilled differential:

> Skilled, highly paid employees were unhappy about the settlement in general, because the benefits bought by the SUB nickel will go primarily to less skilled and lower seniority workers at the Big Three. Skilled employees generally have the best chance of not being laid off and also the best re-employment opportunities. Usually they are high-seniority workers, thus further increasing their retention rights.
>
> As the last to be laid off, a high-seniority, skilled employee might be caught with a Trust Fund position permitting only partial or short-term benefits. Even if the fund were in a strong position, the skilled worker making over $2.25 in Missouri or $2.75 per hour in Michigan would not get his full 65% because of the $25 maximum on supplements. The SUB nickel therefore has the effect of further narrowing the skilled-unskilled wage differential in the automobile industry.[2]

This analysis suggests that the compression of skill differentials brought about by SUB exceeds that of a flat-rate increase. Whether this is so, however, depends largely on the layoff experience of the various skill groups—a matter about which we have no direct information.[3] In

2. Edward D. Wickersham, "Repercussions of the Ford Agreement," *Harvard Business Review* (Jan.-Feb. 1956), p. 65.

3. Insofar as junior workers benefit more than senior workers from SUB, this is simply the reverse of the situation with respect to vacations and may be treated (in the initial stages) as a form of personal (intraoccupational) differential. The value of the program is inversely related to seniority for all occupations. Insofar as skilled workers of given seniority (including minimum

support of this view it is certainly true that many skilled workers would have preferred in the high-employment year of 1955 a 5-cent wage increase or perhaps an individual security plan similar to that adopted in the flat-glass industry and advocated by General Motors. Indeed, separate craft unions in the industry representing electricians and patternmakers insisted on a 5-cent wage increase in lieu of SUB. It is also true that the $25 maximum on supplemental payments prevented the highest-paid workers from realizing a combined unemployment benefit equal to the stated percentage guarantees. The effect of the maximum

TABLE 6.   SUB Payments for a Single Worker in Michigan and Missouri, 1956

	Michigan		Missouri	
	Amount due from Trust Fund		*Amount due from Trust Fund*	
Hourly rate	*65% guarantee*	*60% guarantee*	*65% guarantee*	*60% guarantee*
$1.75	$ 8.77	$ 5.86	$12.77	$ 9.86
2.00	12.97	9.66	17.97	14.66
2.25	18.17	14.46	23.17	19.46
2.50	23.24	19.14	25.00(28.24)	24.14
2.75	25.00(28.44)[a]	23.94	25.00(33.44)	25.00(28.94)

a. The figures in parentheses denote what payments would have been made from the SUB fund in the absence of the $25 maximum.

Source. These figures are taken from a UAW pamphlet entitled "Guaranteed Payments by State for Workers at Various Wage Levels and with Various Size Families under Ford and General Motors Supplementary Benefit Plan Agreements with UAW-CIO" (n. d.), pp. 11, 14.

---

seniority) are less subject to layoff than production workers of similar seniority, then production workers can be said to benefit more from SUB than skilled workers. This we are inclined to believe is true, though we hesitate to make any more positive judgment. At the same time, it is likely that certain low-paid unskilled workers in custodial occupations (janitors, sweepers, elevator operators) have relatively stable employment experience and consequently do not receive much benefit from SUB. If this is so, the range of differentials is not compressed, though certain production worker groups may secure a relative advantage.

was not great in states such as Michigan and Ohio where there are heavy concentrations of auto workers, but it was substantial in those states with relatively low unemployment compensation levels. Table 6 indicates the guaranteed payments for a single worker in Michigan and Missouri over a range of wage levels covering all but the highest-paid occupations. The figures in parentheses denote what payments would have been made from the SUB fund in the absence of the $25 maximum. These estimates indicate that the effect of the benefit maximum is to compress the upper part of the compensation structure. For the majority of occupations, however, the benefit formula clearly tends to widen differentials.[4]

It is possible that layoff experience since 1955, revision of the maximum benefit amount to $30 in 1958, and the addition in the same year of separation pay allowances geared to wage levels and seniority, have caused skilled workers to reassess the value of SUB. We have no evidence one way or the other. All things considered, however, the most reasonable assumption is perhaps that the SUB program has an effect on the compensation structure roughly similar to that of a flat wage increase.

Public Programs. If governmental programs are considered a part of the compensation structure, then the net effect of these programs on relative differentials between occupations is clearly one of contraction. Both the federal retirement program and the federal-state unemployment compensation system gear benefits partially to earnings. However, since benefit maximums are relatively low at the same time that auto wage levels are relatively high, the majority of auto workers, provided they meet the qualifying requirements, can expect the same benefits at time of layoff and approximately the same benefits at time of retirement. Under the federal retirement program, which relates benefits to earnings and marital status, the formula for computing benefits is designed to yield larger retirement incomes per dollar of contribution to lower-paid workers. The effect of this formula is shown in the accompanying schedule.

4. One obvious consequence of SUB is the reduction of geographic differentials. As of August 1957, the average benefit paid to Ford workers in Michigan was $12.58 and in Missouri $22.66. These differentials offset differences in state benefit levels. Ford's original proposal to the UAW sought to continue geographic differences in layoff benefits by relating the percentage guarantees to average earnings in the labor market area rather than to Ford wage levels. But this provision, designed to preserve the laid-off auto worker's incentive to actively seek re-employment in relatively low-wage areas, was opposed by the union and omitted from the final agreement. (*Proceedings, Special Meeting of the UAW National Ford Council,* June 14, 1955.)

Average Monthly Earnings After 1950	*Monthly Retirement Benefit*
$200	$ 84
250	95
300	105
350	116
400	127

Since the method of computing benefits limits current federal pensions to a maximum of approximately $120 per month (the maximum rising gradually over time to $127) and since the earnings of most auto workers will entitle them to pensions in excess of $100, there is little differentiation on the basis of wage levels. However, insofar as modest benefit differences do exist, our assumption that public programs simply maintain absolute differentials between occupations tends to overstate the degree of contraction.

CHAPTER 3

The Wage System and Personal Differentials

Personal differentials are the differences in earnings among workers in the same occupation in the same establishment. This chapter examines the behavior of such differentials under collective bargaining. To set the stage for the discussion, however, it is well to review first the over-all dimensions of the industry's wage structure and the nature of plant wage systems.

The Structure of Wages

The over-all character of the wage structure in autos is portrayed in Table 7 which gives the distribution of workers by earnings class for selected years in the period 1934–57. The unique features of this wage structure are the high degree of wage compression and the sharp reduction of wage dispersion over time. Despite a more than threefold increase in wage levels since 1934, the earnings of more than 50 per cent of the industry's workers have remained within a narrow range of 20 cents and those of over 80 per cent of the workers within a spread of

TABLE 7.   Per Cent Distribution of Production Workers[a] by Average Hourly Earnings in Automobile Manufacturing Plants, 1934–1957

1934		1940		1950		1957	
Average hourly earnings (cents)	Workers	Average hourly earnings (cents)	Workers	Average hourly earnings (cents)	Workers	Average hourly earnings (cents)	Workers
Under 45	2.0%	Under 62.5	1.8%	Under 130	0.6%	Under 200	0.1%
45 and under 55	6.3	62.5 and under 72.5	2.4	130 and under 140	4.2	200 and under 210	3.4
55 65	33.0	72.5 82.5	12.3	140 150	11.4	210 220	9.8
65 75	19.7	82.5 92.5	25.2	150 160	39.1	220 230	39.9
75 85	18.3	92.5 102.5	29.0	160 170	22.5	230 240	23.0
85 95	11.1	102.5 112.5	17.7	170 180	8.4	240 250	8.0
95 105	6.3	112.5 122.5	7.5	180 190	4.7	250 260	1.4
105 115	1.8	122.5 132.5	2.0	190 200	4.5	260 270	1.6
115 and over	1.5	132.5 142.5	1.2	200 210	2.5	270 280	3.4
		142.5 152.5	0.5	210 220	1.3	280 290	4.7
		152.5 162.5	0.2	220	0.4	290 300	1.9
		162.5 and over	0.2	230 and over 230	0.4	300 and over	2.8

a. The 1934 statistics include a small number of office workers (less than 7% of total) which results in a slight downward bias in the distribution.

Sources. N. A. Tolles and M. W. La Fever, "Wages, Hours, Employment and Annual Earnings in the Motor-Vehicle Industry, 1934," *Monthly Labor Review* (March 1936), p. 532; Harold R. Hosea and George E. Votava, "Wage Structure of the Motor-Vehicle Industry," *Bulletin no. 706* (U.S. Dept. of Labor Statistics, 1942), p. 19; H. M. Douty, "Wages in the Motor-Vehicle Industry, 1957," *Monthly Labor Review* (Nov. 1957), p. 1323.

40 cents. These developments are summarized in the dispersion indexes in Table 8. For the period as a whole, relative wage dispersion fell sharply from 30 per cent to only 6 per cent, and even absolute dispersion declined from 20 cents to only 14 cents.

TABLE 8. Wage Dispersion in Automobile Manufacturing, 1934–1957

	1934	1940	1950	1957
Interquartile range (cents)	20	18	14	14
Median (cents)	69	96	159	230
Relative dispersion $\left(\dfrac{\text{interquartile range}}{\text{median}} \times 100 \right)$	30%	19%	9%	6%

Sources. These measures of absolute and relative wage dispersion are calculated from the original distributions presented by the Bureau of Labor Statistics (see sources in Table 7). The inclusion of a small number of office workers in the 1934 tabulations is not believed to have affected dispersion measures significantly for that year.

The distinctive character of these developments is revealed in a comparison with other industries. Of the 31 industries surveyed by the Bureau of Labor Statistics between 1950 and 1955, automobile manufacturing had by far the lowest dispersion index—9 per cent in a distribution which otherwise ranged from 15 to 62 per cent with a median value of 28 per cent.[1] Moreover, for 17 of these industries for which data were available covering roughly the postwar period (1945–47 to 1952–55), the change in relative wage dispersion was moderately downward while absolute wage dispersion rose rather sharply.[2] Similar data are not available for autos, but the trend in the

1. L. Earl Lewis, "Wage Dispersion in Manufacturing Industries, 1950–55," *Monthly Labor Review* (July 1956), p. 781.
2. Ibid., p. 785. The median values of these changes were —13 per cent and +38 per cent respectively.

absolute dispersion index over these years was certainly downward rather than upward. In short, the auto wage (or earnings) structure is distinctive on two counts: the high degree of earnings compression in recent years and the sharp decline in dispersion since World War II.[3]

The high concentration of earnings in auto manufacturing has been attributed to a number of factors: the large proportion of the work force (approximately 50 per cent) engaged in highly mechanized and fractionalized assembly operations which require only a minimum of skill; the absence of incentive methods of wage payment; the heavy concentration of production in a few large firms with primary locations in the same geographic area; company-wide bargaining with the same industrial union; and specific company and union wage policies—especially the wage system developed at Ford prior to the depression and the UAW's preoccupation with the wage needs and problems of lower-paid workers after the depression.[4] While all of these factors have probably contributed in some degree to the relatively narrow earnings distribution existing

3. It is not our intention to suggest here that the behavior of the wage structure in autos differed radically from that of other industries. Instead, we have sought to establish merely the existence of a highly concentrated structure and a relatively high rate of wage contraction. Clearly, the measures of dispersion used here for convenience have their shortcomings and should be interpreted with caution. They do not take account, for example, of changes in the distribution outside the interquartile range—changes which would be reflected in dispersion measures such as the standard deviation. Certainly, employment of the latter measure would indicate a moderate widening of absolute wage dispersion in the auto industry between 1950 and 1957. It is enough for present purposes, however, to note these deficiencies; for while dispersion indexes based on the standard deviation and coefficient of variation would yield more precise comparisons between industry distributions, they would not alter our conclusion concerning the distinctive character of the auto wage structure.

4. See Lewis, "Wage Dispersion," pp. 780–86; H. M. Douty, "Wages in the Motor-Vehicle Industry, 1957," *Monthly Labor Review, 8* (Nov. 1957), 1323–24; Charles R. Walker and Robert H. Guest, *The Man on the Assembly*

in auto manufacturing in recent years, it is not an easy matter to document their separate effects. Union influence did not make itself felt, of course, until the late 1930s and consequently was not a factor in the initial establishment of a concentrated wage structure. Early Ford policies, on the other hand, do appear to have exercised a compressive influence, though we cannot determine from available information how lasting these effects were or how widespread their impact on the wage scales of other producers.[5] All things considered, however, it is our judgment that the compressed structure of earnings found in the industry in the early 1930s reflects primarily the existence of a large number of relatively undifferentiated assembly and related jobs in a highly concentrated industry, in terms of both the number of firms and their geographic location.

While we can only guess at the reasons for wage compression

Line (Cambridge, Harvard, 1953), pp. 84–85; Sumner H. Slichter, James J. Healy, and E. Robert Livernash, *The Impact of Collective Bargaining on Management* (Washington, Brookings Inst., 1960), p. 599.

5. In 1913 Ford management adopted a new job classification and rate system which substituted 8 basic wage rates for the 69 found in the company's plant and classified all workers into 6 basic categories. These categories were further subdivided into three groups on the basis of skill ratings. The minimum hourly wage for laborers was set at 26 cents and the maximum rate for skilled mechanics at 54 cents. The introduction of the $5-day in January 1914, however, appears to have reduced these skill differentials radically. Nevins reports that by April of that year 200 Ford men received $7 a day, 1,000 received $6 a day, and the remaining 15,000 received or would soon receive $5 a day. Thus, while the basic hourly rates remained in effect, qualified workers were paid a "profits" share that adjusted their earnings to one of the three basic day rates. See John R. Lee, "The So-Called Profit Sharing System in the Ford Plant," Annals, American Academy of Political and Social Science, 65 (May 1916), 300; Nevins, *Ford: The Times, the Man, the Company*, pp. 546–48. Sward (*Legend of Henry Ford*, p. 58) takes a less charitable view of the $5-day innovation, but he nevertheless corroborates its compressive effects on the wage structure when he concludes: "Even though the company was paying better than average for its common labor, it was correspondingly less generous with its workers who were skilled or semi-skilled."

prior to the 1930s, the explanation for further concentration since that time is relatively straightforward. The sharp reduction of relative dispersion between the 1930s and 1950s is due mainly to the practice of granting equal cents-per-hour increases to all employees regardless of wage level. Indeed, approximately four fifths of the reduction up to 1950 can be explained on this basis.[6] The remainder, reflecting the reduction of absolute dispersion during the 1940s, is the effect principally of the elimination or narrowing of various forms of personal differential (merit spreads on production jobs, incentive payments, extended "learning" periods at rates substantially below job rates, and rate discrimination on the basis of sex and color) and, to a lesser extent, of the development of greater wage rate uniformity among plants, companies, and geographic areas.[7] These factors explain the behavior of the dispersion indexes since the 1930s. A significant trend in the earnings distribution which is concealed by the indexes, however, is the clear tendency toward bimodality (see Table 7). The formation of a secondary mode in the upper tail of the distribution can be traced to the influence of special wage adjustments for the skilled trades (mainly tool-and-die and maintenance craftsmen) and to the increasing importance of these trades in the industry's

6. If the interquartile range had been preserved during this period, the index of relative dispersion would have stood at 13 per cent in 1950 instead of 9 per cent as was actually the case.

7. The constancy of the absolute dispersion index in the 1950s is the result simply of the application of general cents-per-hour wage adjustments to a wage structure already highly stable. In the 1955 negotiations, the annual improvement factor was changed from a cents-per-hour to a percentage basis—2.5 per cent with a 6-cent minimum. This change has tended to increase absolute rate dispersion, but up to 1957 the effect of the minimum was to confine the impact of differential increases to the upper wage brackets. The 1955 GM agreement, for example, applied the A.I.F. increase to hourly wage rates, exclusive of the cost-of-living allowance, and limited per-cent adjustments to rates of $2.60 and above. Since the 1957 earnings data in Table 7 include a cost-of-living allowance of 16 cents, it is clear that the change in the formula brought gains to only a small proportion of workers in the high-wage brackets, leaving the interquartile range unaffected.

work force. We shall have more to say about this and related matters in our discussion of occupational wage differences, but we may note at this point the role of special wage adjustments in shaping the earnings distribution during the last decade or so. The data in Table 9 show typical wage adjustments by source in the period of 1948–58.[8]

TABLE 9. Wage Increases by Source for Selected Classifications, 1948–1958

	Average production classification	*Average maintenance classification*	*Average die-making classification*
Annual improvement factor	$0.46	$0.47	$0.49
Cost of living (incorporated in rates)	.22	.22	.22
Other special adjustments	.02	.23	.23
Current cost-of-living allowance	.22	.22	.22
Total increase (1948-58)	$0.92	$1.14	$1.16

Source. General Motors Corp., "Ten Years of Industrial Peace at GM" (1958), p. 23.

Clearly, the expanding differential between production workers and skilled craftsmen during the last decade has been effected almost entirely by special skilled trades increases. Since the 1958 negotiations resulted in another special increase of 8 cents for these groups, more recent earnings distributions would show this trend more markedly.[9]

8. General Motors Corporation, "Ten Years of Industrial Peace at GM" (1958), p. 23.

9. The future course of the earnings distribution will depend naturally on the rate of wage change, shifts in the occupational composition of the work force, the formula adopted for general wage changes, and the negotiation of any special wage adjustments. For the near future, however, it is reasonable

Up to this point, we have been concerned with identifying the factors underlying the trend in the earnings distribution of workers in the industry; we have not sought to establish the role of the union. To evaluate the latter, it is necessary to consider the part played by unionism in the elimination or reduction of personal rate differentials as well as the union's influence in the bargaining process on the form of wage increases granted in the industry. This is the objective of subsequent chapters, but we may anticipate here a few of our findings.

The reduction of personal differentials is largely an effect of unionism. While we can only guess at the way these rate differentials would have behaved over the last 25 years or so in the absence of bargaining, a careful weighing of union and management attitudes, as reflected in negotiations and in statements of wage policy, suggests that the union has been primarily responsible for the elimination of rate ranges on production jobs, the narrowing of the spread between starting rates and job rates, the shortening (and regularization) of qualifying periods, and the virtual abandonment of sex differentials, and has been partly responsible for the sharp decline in the use of incentive payments. It is likely that some reduction of personal differentials would have occurred in any case, but certainly not to the extent experienced under unionism.

The more significant reduction in relative dispersion, due mainly to a sequence of cents-per-hour increases, is more difficult to appraise. The secular trend toward narrower wage struc-

---

to expect that the earnings distribution will reflect with even greater precision the effect of superimposing two fairly distinct wage distributions representing essentially the unskilled and semiskilled production groups, on the one hand, and the skilled nonproduction groups, on the other. If the wage-escalation provisions of current contracts are continued, the behavior of the industry's wage structure will depend importantly on the degree of inflation experienced. With stable prices and rising wage levels, the percentage annual improvement factor (2.5 per cent with a 6-cent minimum) will tend increasingly to preserve the relative spread in rates. Rising prices, on the other hand, will produce a further narrowing, since cost-of-living adjustments are applied to all rates in equal cents-per-hour amounts.

tures is too pervasive a phenomenon to be ignored. Most types of differentials have tended to decline in recent years and for reasons largely unrelated to unionism. Nevertheless, it is our view that, in the absence of bargaining, the wage structure would have been somewhat wider and production workers' earnings, especially, would not have undergone such severe compression. Had management been permitted to pursue its own wage policy, subject only to the restraints of the market, wage changes would almost certainly have taken the form of differential adjustments from time to time. This would not necessarily have altered the long-term relationship of the skilled craftsman's rate to that of the unskilled production worker, but it would clearly have provided a wider cents-per-hour spread within production groups as a whole.

In short, it is our view that the distribution of production workers' earnings, far from narrowing in absolute terms during this period, would actually have widened in the absence of collective bargaining. Relative dispersion, it is true, would have declined in line with economy-wide movements, but perhaps at not more than half the rate realized under bargaining.

Plant Wage Systems

The wage system in auto plants consists of a set of job classifications and related wage rates. These classifications are essentially the occupational categories into which the thousands of separate jobs in auto manufacturing are grouped for administrative purposes. They may be narrow or broad in coverage—i.e. they may apply to one specific machine or operation or, alternatively, to a wide variety of operations that are similar from the standpoint of function, skill, effort, working conditions, and so forth.[10] The scope of each classification is defined

10. The local wage agreement for one body plant, for example, lists 64 distinct operations under the general classification "Assembler Specified Hardware," 67 under the general classification "Assembler General," and 17 under the general classification "Assembler Miscellaneous." In the stamping plant of

either by the specific language of the local wage agreement or by established plant practice.

Prior to unionization, job classifications and rates were determined unilaterally by management. With the advent of collective bargaining, existing classifications and rates, together with descriptions of the various types of jobs in the bargaining unit, formed the basis for the negotiation of plant wage agreements. In early bargaining sessions, the adjustments made in classification and rate relationships were apparently substantial in a number of plants. More recently, however, the wage systems have been reasonably stable and relatively free from attempts at radical revision. Nevertheless, the fact that the parties are not committed to formal job evaluation principles has occasionally given rise to serious trouble—especially in the determination of rates for new or changed jobs. Since this issue and the related problem of adjusting the wage system to rapid technological change have been the principal sources of friction between the parties in this area during the last decade or so, they are discussed below.

Once agreement is reached, wage scales in auto plants are frozen for the duration of the contract and wage disputes are limited to the rates on new jobs. In each company the collective agreement provides a procedure for the handling of such disputes. Thus, the GM agreement contains the following "new job" provisions:

> *Paragraph 102:* When new jobs are placed in production and cannot be properly placed in existing classifications by mutual agreement, Management will set up a new classification and a rate covering the job in question,

---

another company, the "Production Worker" classification covers 17 distinct operations such as bending fixture operator; burr, file, buff or grind; drill press—light; riveting—hand and machine; shear operator—scrap; stamper and packer—stock; and stock handler.

and will designate it as temporary. A copy of the temporary rate and classification name will be furnished to the Shop Committee.

Paragraph 102a: As soon as possible after machinery and other equipment have been installed, and in any event, within 30 calendar days after a production employe has been placed on the job, the Shop Committee and Management shall negotiate the rate and classification, and when negotiations are completed, such classification and rate shall become a part of the local wage agreement. . . .

This method of administering plant wage structures serves, on the one hand, to promote stability during the life of the contract and, on the other, to preserve the flexibility necessary for appropriate adaptation to change—in methods, machinery, materials, etc.[11]

11. The benefits flowing from these arrangements have been summed up by GM management as follows (General Motors Statement Re: UAW Demand to Change Paragraph 102, 1955):

The Local Wage Agreements which have come to exist under the National Agreement provisions serve a real and vital purpose. Under a wage agreement, the work performed in the plant is codified into classifications and a rate of pay agreed upon for each classification of work. The wage agreement brings stability and continuity into the conduct of the business and especially into the relationship between employes and the Management. It is the contract or gauge by means of which the wages paid employes are computed.

In the event a significant change in the method of performing an operation is made, so that the job content for which the classification and rate was negotiated no longer exists, or in the event an operation not included in the wage agreement is placed into production and such operation cannot be placed into an existing classification in the wage agreement, the parties must establish a new classification to cover such work. This is done by negotiation and agreement.

Under the procedures which have existed since 1942, the plant relationship has been favored by a general stability in the plant classification and wage structures. In the relatively few situations in which a dispute

The unique feature of provisions for handling rates on new jobs is, however, the explicit limitation on the powers of the umpire or arbitrator. Under auto contracts, the umpire is empowered to determine whether or not a job is properly classified (in line with the local wage agreement and established plant practice) and whether or not a job is in fact a "new job" (and therefore subject to negotiation and agreement), but he may not establish a new classification or wage rate. It follows that failure to reach agreement on the rate for a new job leaves the union free to strike provided it has complied with certain simple procedural requirements such as the exhaustion of prescribed grievance steps, authorization of the strike by the International Union, and prior written notice to the company of intention to authorize. This arrangement originated with management. When GM agreed in 1940 to the installation of a permanent umpire system, it insisted that disputes relating to rates on new jobs and work standards be excluded from the umpire's jurisdiction. This same restriction was carried into the Ford and Chrysler agreements when these companies, at the urging of the War Labor Board, introduced umpire systems in 1943. If the union was displeased initially with this restriction on arbitration, it soon learned to live with the arrangement and indeed to appreciate its usefulness. More recently, it has been management—especially at Ford and Chrysler—that has expressed serious doubts concerning the desirability of contract provisions that permit the union to strike legally during the life of the contract, while the union now stubbornly refuses to accept any extension of the umpire's authority in these areas.

The union's refusal to arbitrate new job rates can be traced in part to its reluctance to abandon the "strikeable issue" as a

has arisen over the proper classification of a job, the issue has been resolved by the Impartial Umpire. Both the Union and the Corporation were beneficiaries of this stability, for certainly nothing could be more disruptive of relationships or conducive to controversy than an unstable classification and wage structure in the plants.

bargaining tactic[12] and perhaps as a safety valve under the long-term contract. It also reflects, however, recent technological developments in the industry. Ever since the introduction of automation into auto plants in the early 1950s, the union has expressed dissatisfaction with the restrictions that existing "new job" provisions and umpire rulings imposed on its scope for bargaining classification and rate changes. The importance the union attaches to this matter is indicated in the following excerpts from a report to the membership in late 1954, dealing with the impact of automation on plant wage systems:

> Because of the extreme changes in factory methods caused by automation, existing classifications and wage structures are becoming increasingly obsolete. In new plants the dramatic effect of automation is clearly visible. There the "new job" principle can be invoked more easily to secure new classifications and improve wage rates. In existing plants, however, where automation is installed on a piecemeal basis, it is more difficult both to pin down the

12. Ford's decision in 1955 to seek extension of the umpire's authority over disputes involving new job rates (as well as production standards and health and safety issues) was prompted by the union's use of the "strikeable issue" to force additional concessions from management in the 1953 "living document" negotiations. In these negotiations, reopening the five-year auto contracts two years prior to their expiration date, the UAW compelled Ford not only to meet the pattern already established at GM but to better it in a number of respects. As events indicated, these extra concessions were the price of settling a serious strike over new job rate and health and safety issues at the company's Canton forge plant which was threatening to close down the whole of Ford's assembly operations. The union naturally protested the charge that it had employed the "strikeable issue" as a bargaining tactic, but the evidence is hard to deny. When the company first refused to reopen its agreement, the union made clear its strategy. It informed the company on December 3, 1952, that local unions were being requested "to register their dissatisfaction within the framework of the contract." At the same time, local unions were instructed to refuse to cooperate with the company and to be more vigilant on new job rates, health and safety, and production standards. This threat was not lost on management officials; refusal to settle would be met through grievances which allowed the union to strike legally—as it did in the Canton plant.

degree and kind of change requiring action, and to negotiate the necessary new classifications and rates. In such situations the Union should be alert to obtain new classifications and rates even on semi-automated jobs. Our members must be prepared to continue the fight for the upward revision of rates based on new classifications for automated jobs. Management must be brought around to acceptance of the principle that automated and semi-automated jobs require new classifications and rates whether in new plants or old.

Any efforts by management to extend existing classifications to cover these new automated and semi-automated jobs should be resisted by the Union. It is important, also, that the issue not be left to umpire or arbitration determination. Umpires and arbitrators should have no role in the determination of new classifications and wage rates because there are no objective criteria which they can apply. Since these new operations will be the basis for the wage and classification structure of the factory of the future, the Union must maintain maximum freedom to exert its full influence in the shaping of that structure.

The new classifications and rates should be established in recognition of the changed nature of jobs in which increased responsibility offsets by far any reduction in physical effort and manual dexterity accompanying automation. This increased responsibility, in most cases, flows from the much larger investment represented by the equipment under the individual worker's control. . . . [But] even where there is no increase in such investment, the individual worker becomes responsible for a much larger volume of output. Automated equipment is a signpost of changed jobs in the factory requiring the negotiation of new classifications carrying higher rates reflecting the increased investment per worker. . . . The union demands and expects that where different work requirements, investment, and output provide the obvious proof that a change has occurred new classifications and rates will be negotiated.[13]

It was presumably to lay the groundwork for such a policy that the union sought in its negotiations with GM in 1955 to alter the "new job" procedures of the contract. The provision which the union sought to substitute for Paragraph 102 (see p. 92) was worded as follows:

> When new or changed equipment, operations, methods of operation or products are placed in production, management shall within two weeks notify the shop committee. The Union may then investigate the job. Thereafter, if the parties fail to agree within thirty (30) days to place the job within an existing classification in the wage agreement, Management within two more weeks will set up a new classification and a rate covering the job and will designate it as temporary.[14]

If granted, this demand would have broadened considerably the union's right to bargain the classification and rating of changed jobs. It would have required that management report all method and equipment changes to the union, that all jobs affected be open to investigation by the union, and that the fact of disagreement itself (rather than past practice and the classification descriptions in local wage agreements) determine the existence of a new job and hence management's obligation to bargain. As management noted in its reply, the union's proposal would eliminate the wage agreement as an effective instrument of stability in the relationship, since minor changes in equipment, job content and job method—changes which are daily occurrences in auto plants—would provide the basis for invoking the "new job" procedure. In short, it was manage-

13. *Automation: A Report to the UAW-CIO Economic and Collective Bargaining Conference* (Nov. 12–13, 1954), pp. 16, 18.

14. *UAW-CIO Proposals for 1955 GM Contract Revisions,* submitted to General Motors Corporation, March 29, 1955.

ment's conclusion that the proposed procedure would compel more or less continuous negotiation of classifications and rates, and would make it "next to impossible to operate the plant, determine costs, or compensate employes correctly."[15]

GM's arguments against a change in "new job" procedures reveals, incidentally, the value to management of broadly defined job classifications—and, for that matter, of relatively little wage-rate discrimination among low-skilled production workers. As the company noted in its rejection of the union's demand:

> During fifteen years of experience . . . the parties have proven the value of using general job classifications which are unaffected by minor job changes which do not affect the basic structure of the classification. The value of such a system is found in the fact that minor or insignificant changes in a job do not alter the basic skills sufficiently to warrant a change in the wage rate of the job. Thus, equity would dictate that the rate of the job remain the same even if for some reason it seemed advisable to call the job by some other classification name. General classifications have therefore prevented innumerable disputes and much paper work in changing job titles for no significant purpose at all.

This suggests that the relative lack of wage-rate discrimination in auto plants may be explained in part by the need for a reasonably stable classification and rate structure—a structure that can accommodate without undue strain continuous minor changes in job content and conditions as well as the frequent reassignment of workers between roughly similar jobs requiring only the most elementary skills. In the context of more or less continuous change, broad classifications and a relatively undifferentiated rate system appear as a highly rational arrangement.

15. General Motors Statement Re: *UAW Demand to Change Paragraph 102* (1955).

Perhaps the most interesting and certainly the most instructive set of bargaining developments occurring in the area of plant wage-classification systems in recent years has been in the Ford Stamping Division. Since the clash of policies in this instance reveals the nature of some of the classification and rate problems confronting management and the union in adjusting to rapid technological change, it will serve our purpose to explore these developments in some detail.[16]

The Ford Motor Company has stamping plants at Dearborn, Buffalo, Cleveland, and Chicago. When the company first introduced automation into its Buffalo plant, it decided that efficient maintenance of the equipment necessitated a breakdown of traditional skilled-trades jurisdictions. This was desirable because of the variety of skills required, the costliness of waiting and "down-time" on automated lines, and the company's conviction that it could train workers who were not journeymen to perform competently the necessary duties of all-around maintenance on automation equipment. Accordingly, prior to recognition of the union at the plant, management established the single classification of "Automation Equipment Maker and Maintenance," covering the trades of die maker, machine repairman, welder, millwright, pipefitter, tinsmith, and hydraulic specialist. The rate given to this classification was that of die maker, the highest rate of any of the skilled trades involved. At the same time, the company instituted the new classification of "Automation Tender" to cover production workers formerly classified as heavy-press operators. This new production classi-

16. The discussion below is based mainly on the following sources: Ken Bannon and Nelson Samp, "The Impact of Automation on Wages and Working Conditions in Ford Motor Company–UAW Relationships," in *Automation and Major Technological Change,* The Industrial Union Dept., AFL-CIO (April 22, 1958), pp. 13–20; and Slichter et al., *Impact of Collective Bargaining,* pp. 272–75. The latter study does not reveal either the name of the company or the location of the plants in which these events took place. Identification is not, however, a difficult task, thanks to the paper by Bannon and Samp, the director and assistant director, respectively, of the UAW's Ford Department.

fication carried a rate 5 cents above the old rate for press operators. In the opinion of Slichter and his colleagues, "there can be little doubt that this latter move was designed, in part, to instill in the production workers satisfaction with the program that would override any possible dissatisfaction on the part of the craft groups whose separate orthodox identities were being destroyed."[17] These writers also report that the union, once recognized, made no attempt to eliminate the new maintenance classification. This is probably true as far as actual negotiations were concerned. However, the international union did try to mobilize the members' support for a fight against the crossing of trade lines but was unsuccessful "in view of the rate of pay they were enjoying."[18]

In 1955, when Ford opened its new stamping plant in Cleveland, it incorporated the classification and wage-rate system adopted earlier in the Buffalo plant. In subsequent negotiations, the UAW's Ford Department again sought support for preservation of the separate skilled trades classifications—this time with limited success. In the agreement finally reached, the new maintenance classification was eliminated, and each worker was classified according to his trade. However, an automation maintenance department was established with a single rate range for all crafts; and it was agreed that craftsmen in the department would cross trade lines in their work. The international union's attitude toward this arrangement was summed up by its spokesmen as follows: "Our efforts to convince the workers affected of the deterioration of skilled trades standards fell on deaf ears."[19] As at the Buffalo plant, the attraction of the 5-cent increase for production workers was a crucial factor in gaining local acceptance of the plan. The compromise solution meant, however, that management had less freedom to train nonjourneymen in all-around maintenance of automation equipment.

17. Slichter et al., p. 272.
18. Bannon and Samp, p. 19.
19. Ibid.

Shortly afterward the union was confronted with a similar situation at the Chicago stamping plant. Management had installed a single classification and rate covering the seven skilled trades. However, in subsequent negotiations, completed in late 1956, the union was successful in eliminating the new classification and the practice of crossing trade lines.[20]

The most notable development in the stamping division occurred, however, in the 1955 negotiations when management sought to introduce the new maintenance classification into its older Dearborn plant. In its proposal to the union in May of that year, the company offered to eliminate base rate differentials between the Cleveland plant and the Dearborn and Buffalo plants provided the union would agree to continue the "Automation Equipment Maker and Maintenance" classification at Buffalo and extend it to Dearborn. As the union reports it, "the skilled tradesmen [at Dearborn] refused and were supported by the production workers, 50 per cent of whom would have been eligible for an increase of 5 to 15 cents an hour."[21] Another version of what appears to be the same negotiations indicates, however, that the production workers endorsed the company's proposal, only to have it rejected by the skilled tradesmen who, in this instance, had the right to vote separately on the matter by virtue of the fact that they belonged to a separate unit within the local. As Slichter explains the situation:

> The parent local or the international union could have intervened, yet chose not to do so in spite of the fact that the rejection meant an annual loss of more than a quarter of a million dollars for the production employees. A representative of the heavy press operators explained, "The matter is out of our hands. We like the five-cent increase, but the international is leaning over backward not to

20. *Report of UAW President, Walter P. Reuther, to the 16th Constitutional Convention, UAW* (April 7–12, 1957), p. 10-D.
21. Bannon and Samp, p. 20.

offend the skilled workers." The recent loss of the pattern makers to the Pattern Makers League and a threat by the tool and die unit to break away undoubtedly explains the caution of the international on any action that might alienate the member craft employees.

Although internal union political considerations are the principal reason for the UAW's resistance to an extension of the plan, the union tries to rationalize its position on other grounds . . . But there has been a political capitulation by the officers to the craft identification interests of the skilled group minority within the union.[22]

Interestingly enough, while the union has opposed any broadening of skilled trades classifications in automated plants, it has actually sought simplification of the classification structure for production jobs. Thus, in the 1956 negotiations at the Ford Chicago stamping plant, the union hailed the signing of a new and simplified classification and rate agreement for production workers at the same time that it successfully frustrated the company's attempt to install the new maintenance classification. Although this plant was comparable in manufacturing methods and processes to the one at Dearborn, the union noted that in contrast to the 315 classifications existing in the latter and "as part of our program for a broader exercise of seniority" the Chicago agreement included only 101 classifications.[23]

In summary, the union's main drive in this area, except in the case of the skilled trades, has been to "automate" the wage and classification system. As Jack Conway, Reuther's administrative assistant, expressed it: "Just as old machinery becomes obsolete in the new technology, so do wage rates, job classifications, seniority groupings, and wage payment methods. These too must be modernized, and the task is not easy."[24] To set the

22. Slichter et al., p. 27.
23. Bannon and Samp, p. 19.
24. Jack Conway, "Labor Looks at Automation," *Business Topics* (June 1955), 7.

stage for such modernization, the union has sought to overcome in negotiations the restrictions imposed on its freedom of action by long-standing contract provisions and umpire rulings. Moreover, it has repeatedly emphasized the importance of barring umpires from any role in the classification or rating of automated jobs on the grounds that there are no "objective criteria" to apply. It is clear, however, that the union's objection to arbitration is based not so much on the absence of "objective criteria" as on the existence of criteria which reflect the traditional factors of skill, effort, and job conditions rather than, as the union would now have it, the level of job responsibility as measured by the investment or output per worker. It is less a matter, therefore, that there are no rules to the game than that the union wishes to change the rules in order to enlarge its opportunities for wage improvement.

Management, for its part, has been concerned mainly with preserving a stable wage and classification system and preventing an upward whipsawing of wage rates. The union's seizure of the automation issue is regarded as little more than an opportunistic attempt to secure additional concessions on the wage front. In essence, the companies argue that automation does not call for any substantial revision of the wage-classification system (although, as in Ford's case, there may be a willingness to trade concessions), that present contract procedures are adequate for handling such adjustments as may be required, and that the annual improvement factor already provides the mechanism for adjusting wages to productivity advances due to technological change.[25] The union, on the other hand, has sought to refute the "productivity" argument by drawing the following distinction between the improvement factor and higher pay for automated jobs:

25. The pertinent language in auto contracts reads as follows: "The annual improvement factor provided herein recognizes that a continuing improvement in the standard of living of employes depends upon technological progress, better tools, methods, processes and equipment, and a cooperative

The compensation for increased productivity represented by the improvement factor, payable to all workers, can in no sense be considered to be compensation to the individual worker whose specific job has been raised to higher levels of responsibility by the introduction of automation . . . The union demands and expects that where different work requirements, investment, and output provide the obvious proof that a change has occurred, new classifications and rates will be negotiated. But it should be equally clear that these adjustments are separate and distinctly different from the general wage increases which are the result of the operation of the Annual Improvement Factor provisions of our contracts.[26]

In this case, the union has chosen a rather weak prop on which to rest its argument. Individual rate adjustments are not in fact "separate and distinctly different" from general wage adjustments of the annual-improvement-factor type. Rather they represent an alternative (or competing) method of sharing gains in productivity among workers. Insofar as wages are to be adjusted to reflect specific productivity gains, the distribution may take the form of upgrading and of individual wage rate adjustments or of a general wage increase (such as the annual improvement factor), or of some combination of the two. The union may argue of course that the current annual improvement factor reflects only part of the gain to which workers are entitled as a result of technological and organizational improvements and that the remainder is reserved for individual rate adjustments. Or it may simply refuse to be bound by any specific

attitude on the part of all parties in such progress. It further recognizes the principle that to produce more with the same amount of human effort is a sound economic and social objective. Accordingly, . . . each employe covered by this agreement shall receive an annual improvement factor increase of two and one-half (2½) per cent of his straight time hourly wage rate . . . or six (6) cents per hour, whichever is the greater . . . "

26. *Automation: A Report,* pp. 17–18.

productivity figure. Whatever the contentions of the parties, however, it should be clear that both forms of wage increase are chargeable against productivity advances and that the notion of a (noninflationary) wage increase geared to productivity gains embraces of necessity both forms of adjustment and accords them equal weight in terms of their cost impact.

Personal Differentials

With respect to personal wage differentials, there is virtually unanimous agreement that the influence of unionism has been substantial,[27] though it is often difficult to disentangle this influence from that of other forces, particularly company and government policies. In the discussion below we consider the ways in which collective bargaining appears to have affected this type of differential in the industry's wage structure.

Job Rates. Equal pay for equal work, based on notions of equity and the desire to eliminate favoritism and competition between workers, is the central motivating force of union wage-structure policy. This aspect of policy receives its most forceful expression within individual establishments where the union has insisted on the substitution of uniform job rates for the personalized rates established and maintained by management. Since detailed wage statistics are lacking, we cannot estimate the actual magnitude of personal differentials at the time of unionization. Nevertheless, the extent of personalized rate setting in the preunion period is suggested in an early study published in 1940, one year before the organization of Ford.

> Employees of the same sex doing similar work in the same plant may be paid at different rates. These differentials are due chiefly to variations in the employee's length of service and his versatility. Versatility is likely to increase with length of service because transfers are fre-

27. See Clark Kerr, "Wage Relationships—the Comparative Impact of Market and Power Forces," pp. 175, 181; Reynolds and Taft, *The Evolution of Wage Structure,* p. 193.

quently necessary in this industry to permit changes in the volume of production and retention of high-seniority men during periods of extensive layoff.

Prior to unionization, these differentials frequently were not standardized, and foremen had considerable latitude in setting the rates of their individual workers. This is still the case in the Ford Motor Company, where increases above the hiring rate are based upon ability, experience, and length of service, each case being treated individually without the application of any fixed standard or regulation.[28]

The effect of unionization was the fairly rapid elimination of this lack of standardization in job rates. Already in 1940, differentials within an occupation in organized plants were based on length of service, and in many collective agreements standard job rates had been introduced. In such agreements, the only permissible differentials were those between the hiring rate, the probationary rate, and the standard rate. The typical spread between these rates was 10 cents (the union having opposed wider spreads), and the normal time taken to reach the standard rate was two or three months. As McPherson concluded from his study of this aspect of wage structure: "Individual differences among employees who have passed the probationary period are now fewer in number and smaller in extent than before union recognition. Some firms have gradually standardized the rate on each job by applying any wage increases only to the employees receiving the lowest rates on each job until regular employees doing the same type of work were all on the same rate."[29]

The earliest evidence of the union's impact on personal differentials in the plants of the individual auto manufacturers is found at Studebaker, the first company to recognize the union.

28. McPherson, *Labor Relations in the Automobile Industry,* pp. 81–82.
29. Ibid., p. 83.

No details are available, but the task the union faced and the extent of its accomplishment by 1937 is suggested in the following passages drawn from the official history of Studebaker Local No. 5:

> The wage structure in the plant [in 1935] was a source of constant irritation to the Union because there were nearly a hundred different wage rates and no one seemed to know why. Piecework prices were established differently in almost every department and few people knew just how they were determined.

> The Union had almost from the beginning insisted that these matters must be settled by negotiation and that the the number of wage rates should be greatly reduced and standardized so that people doing similar work throughout the shop would have the same classification and receive the same base pay. While under receivership, the Company had consistently refused to take action on such a plant-wide program but had settled a few cases here and there strictly on a departmental basis. The Union pressed hard for a structure that could be understood by everyone, and the Company reluctantly listened to their demands and started talking on the subject.

> This system was the result of 80 years of practice and the complications that were encountered seemed endless and grew worse as they proceeded until it seemed they would never succeed in unraveling the chaotic pattern, but the Union's determination never lessened even though it took nearly two years to complete the job. . . .

> By April of 1937, the big job of overhauling and streamlining the cumbersome and outmoded wage structure in the Studebaker plant had been completed and was ready for presentation to the membership for ratification.[30]

30. "A Brief History of the Labor Movement of Studebaker-Local No. 5, UAW-CIO" (Studebaker Local No. 5, Education and Publicity Committee, 1953), pp. 32, 36.

This new wage structure was ratified on May 21, 1937, and Local 5 was able to claim that it was the first Auto Workers' local to achieve a contract and a union-negotiated wage structure. "The news spread like wildfire until practically every Local in the country took up the fight to win similar gains for themselves."[31]

Progress in this area was slower, however, in the plants of the Big Three. This is attributable partly to later organization and partly to stronger management resistance. Some movement toward the reduction of personal differentials was of course accomplished in individual plants of these companies during the early years of organization; and it is certain that the "inequity fund" of over $5 million negotiated at GM in 1940 was applied partly to this objective. But many of the most significant gains were registered during World War II. In 1942 the UAW had sought a number of wage improvements at General Motors. Since the parties could reach no agreement on the issues, the case was certified to the War Labor Board. Included in the union's demands were a number of wage-structure proposals, the most important of which called for the elimination of rate spreads among production workers doing the same or comparable work and equal pay for women. The company opposed the elimination of such spreads on the grounds that there were substantial differences in merit and ability between operators. It also opposed the elimination of the sex differential, contending that the lower rates for women reflected legitimate differences in job content since women were seldom able to perform the full range of job assignments required of men. The Board, however, was sympathetic to the union's position. In its directive of September 26, 1942, it provided that new employees were to be hired at a rate no lower than 10 cents below the rate for the job classification, with automatic increases of 5 cents at the end of 30 days and 5 cents at the end of another 60 days. In addition, it gave support to the principle of equal pay for women.

31. Ibid., p. 36.

These were significant gains. According to the union, the Board's decision resulted in wage increases and back pay awards for female employees which alone amounted to several million dollars.[32] At the same time, the limitation on hiring rates and the provision for automatic rate progression meant that workers would no longer have to remain at the starting rate for the job for periods up to six months (even though, as the union claimed, they were often already producing at an efficient level within the first week).[33] The impact of this ruling on prevailing company practice was revealed in GM's complaint to the Board that the new provision would grant some workers an automatic 25-cent increase. As the union reported it, GM had hired 6,000 new men at its Delco-Remy plant in Anderson, Indiana, at a 75-cent starting rate to be increased over a period of 18 months to $1.00—the regular rate for the job. Since the Board's order was retroactive, the company was required to advance immediately to the $1.00 rate those workers who had already been on the job for three months.[34]

By the end of World War II, other auto manufacturers had been brought into line with the Board-directed GM policy on hiring rates. Ford was apparently the last holdout; but in November 1945 it, too, agreed that all employees would in future be hired at 10 cents below the minimum regular rate for all jobs.[35]

32. R. J. Thomas, President, UAW-CIO, "Automobile Unionism, 1943," Report submitted to the 1943 Convention of the UAW-CIO (Oct. 1943), p. 80.

33. Recalling the pre-1942 experience in 1955, the union had this to say about GM's hiring practices: "It was not so many years ago that even a sweeper's job had a merit spread. You hired in at whatever rate management wanted to fix and then you moved to top rate of the job on merit. 'Merit' of course was entirely up to the foreman's judgment. Not too many workers got top rate. Some were still asking for top rate after 20 years on the job": "In GM Forward-Forward-Forward in '55" (UAW-CIO, 1955), p. 21.

34. *Minutes, International GM Council, UAW-CIO* (Sept. 26, 1942), p. 32.

35. R. J. Thomas, President, UAW-CIO, "Automobile Unionism, 1946,"

UAW demands for the elimination of personal differentials were not satisfied, however, by these provisions which restricted the spread between hiring and job rates and required automatic progression to the minimum job rate within a period of 90 days. Differences in earnings still arose between workers doing the same work, owing to the existence of merit ranges on many jobs, production as well as nonproduction. Accordingly, demands for the elimination of merit spreads on all production jobs were pressed in the postwar period. By early 1948 this objective had been secured for all practical purposes at GM. It should be noted that management itself credited this change to the union—a change which it felt removed all incentive for superior work.[36] In its 1948 negotiations with Ford, the union tackled this same problem of rate ranges on production jobs, citing its earlier successes in other firms. As it wrote the company in June of that year:

> Your competitors provide that workers in all classifications except the skilled trades classifications advance to the rate of their respective jobs within 90 days after hire. Ford workers in many classifications are subject to the operation of a system under which workers on the same job are paid rates varying by as much as 20 cents per hour. The placing of individual workers within the rate ranges applicable to their jobs depends on the arbitrary whims of supervision. These merit spreads tend to promote corruption and favoritism. They deprive many workers of the earnings to which they are entitled on the basis of work performed.[37]

Again the union was successful. By 1950 single rates for all

Report submitted to the 1946 Convention of the UAW-CIO (March 23, 1946).

36. *Minutes, GM-UAW Negotiations* (April 8, 1948), pp. 61–62.

37. UAW-CIO press release, June 25, 1948.

production jobs had been established in the plants of auto manufacturers.[38]

In recent years, the issue of merit ranges has been confined to the skilled trades—i.e. maintenance and tool-and-die craftsmen. These nonproduction groups comprise a fifth to a quarter of all employees in auto company work forces. From time to time union officials have proposed that the rate ranges for these crafts also be eliminated or reduced; but the main drive, supported by the craftsmen themselves, has been to substitute automatic progression for merit and ability.[39] In this, the union has met with only partial success. It has not been able to secure any reduction in the 20- to 21-cent merit ranges established by the War Labor Board in 1942.[40] On the other hand, it has made some progress on the issue of automatic progression. In the plants of the Independents, skilled workers move up automatically through the rate range and, at Chrysler, they progress automatically to the midpoint of the range. At Ford and GM, however, "merit" remains the criterion for movement within the rate ranges for skilled crafts. This means that as far as nonproduction jobs are concerned, there remains in effect a personal rate system. These jobs have no production standards, are not machine paced, and consequently afford some opportunity for relating rates to individual performance. Even where

38. "Wage Structure: Motor Vehicles and Parts, 1950," *Bulletin No. 1015* (Bureau of Labor Statistics, U.S. Dept. of Labor, 1951), pp. 3–4.

39. See, e.g., *Proceedings, 4th Skilled Trades Conference* (1955), p. 31. UAW leaders have opposed merit spreads on all jobs but have bowed to the desire on the part of skilled workers for the preservation of rate ranges. This system is traditional in the skilled trades and is reportedly preferred as a symbol which gives recognition to craftsmanship and artistry.

40. In the 1955 negotiations with GM, for example, the union asked that the skilled rate spreads be reduced to the prewar maximum of 15 cents. Management opposed this demand on the grounds that the prewar spread had been 10 per cent and that percentagewise therefore there had been no widening of the range. It also contended that if skilled workers at the minimum were moved up, as the union proposed, "it will give the least deserving people a nickel increase": *Minutes, GM-UAW Negotiations* (June 11, 1955), p. 547.

automaticity is not recognized officially, however, union pressures and policing of the system, along with the difficulties of objectively measuring relative performance, have introduced an element of automatic progression. A worker who is not advanced in line with others becomes a case requiring explanation. This appears to have produced a system in which the top rate in the range is now the normal expectation; and indeed, in stable times, the large majority of skilled workers are to be found at this rate.

Method of Wage Payment. So far in our discussion of personal differentials we have made no mention of the method of wage payment in the industry. There is, however, one aspect of union wage policy that may have significantly influenced personal earnings differentials through its impact on wage payment methods—namely, the uncompromising stand adopted by the UAW against the use of incentive plans. Piece-rate plans, especially of the individual or small-group variety, normally produce much larger earnings differentials among workers doing the same or comparable work than do hourly-rate systems. Consequently, insofar as the union has been responsible for eliminating incentive methods of wage payment in the industry, it has also been responsible for the reduction of personal differentials that typically accompanies the move to hourly-rate systems.

In preunion days, the great majority of workers in the auto industry were compensated under some form of incentive plan. Most of the plans in existence during the 1920s were group incentives; but since these proved inequitable and unsatisfactory they were discontinued in a large number of plants and replaced by individual piece-rate systems. The decade of the 1930s, however, witnessed a rapid reduction in all forms of incentive payment. The majority of the industry's assembly plants apparently shifted to an hourly-rate system in 1934. According to one observer, "This change was made at the specific request of the workers, expressed in most cases through the works councils then in general use in the industry."[41] With the entry of the UAW into auto plants in 1937, the trend away from piece rates was continued, so that by the end of World War II only a small proportion of the industry's work force (less than 15 per cent) was employed in plants with incentive wage systems. In the years following the war, the only company-wide incentive plans in operation were those at Studebaker and Kaiser-Willys, though there were perhaps a dozen plans or more in individual plants belonging to the Big Three. By the mid-1950s, however, most of the remaining plans, including the company-wide plans, had been discontinued, so that in 1957 less than 2 per cent of the industry's production workers (mainly in forging occupations and in some light machine and assembly work) were paid on an incentive basis.[42]

The elimination of incentive plans in auto plants is widely interpreted as a consequence of unionism.[43] This judgment rests in large part on the rough coincidence between the rise of the UAW, an organization militantly opposed to wage incentives, and the demise of piece-rate systems, the traditional method of wage payment in the industry. It is fortified by the knowledge that much of this change apparently took place under union pressure, exerted on some companies directly through bargaining, on others indirectly through the threat of organization. Given the evidence, there seems little reason to question the conclusion that worker dissatisfaction, expressed through collective action or the threat of collective action, was a primary influence in the changeover from piecework to hourly rates in a number of plants in the mid-1930s.

41. C. B. Gordy, "Measured Day Work Replaces Incentives in the Automobile Assembly Industry," *Society for the Advancement of Management Journal* (Nov. 1936), p. 163.

42. Douty, "Wages in the Motor Vehicle Industry, 1957," p. 1323.

43. See, e.g., McPherson, *Labor Relations in the Automobile Industry,* p. 94; Sumner H. Slichter, *Union Policies and Industrial Management* (Washington, Brookings Inst., 1941), p. 287; Van Dusen Kennedy, *Union Policy and Incentive Wage Methods* (New York, Columbia, 1945), p. 94.

While the case for union influence is strong on these grounds, however, some doubts have been expressed regarding the extent of auto management's commitment to the incentive method—and hence the degree of opposition actually encountered by labor in the changeover. These doubts stem largely from the fact that, although many of the unions in manufacturing officially favored the abolition of all incentives, the automobile industry was the only industry in which widespread changes in method occurred. Kennedy, a careful student of these developments, could find no obvious explanation for this unique experience, although he suggested that "the high degree of rationalization in automobile production, the fact that in many phases of production the pace is governed by lines and conveyor systems, and the fact that labor costs are such a small proportion of total costs are undoubtedly among the factors which have made automobile manufacturers less resistant to hourly methods of wage payment."[44] In their recent study, Slichter and his colleagues have carried this view even farther with the observation that "automobile companies, with their particular production conditions, were one of the first management groups to question the incentive philosophy, and as a result bargaining on this issue did not in fact involve any great divergence of views."[45] If this judgment is correct—if management was in fact only mildly committed to wage incentives and therefore not strongly motivated to fight the issue—it has important implications, for it weakens our confidence in the claim for a clear and unambiguous union influence. At least, the possibility of voluntary abandonments, either in the 1930s or in later years, cannot be so easily dismissed. To evaluate this issue, however, it is necessary to explore in reasonable detail the attitudes reflected on both sides and the extent to which they represent divergent philosophies.

The UAW's opposition to incentive methods of wage pay-

44. Kennedy, *Union Policy and Incentive Methods,* p. 95.
45. Slichter et al., *Impact of Collective Bargaining,* p. 493.

ment is one aspect of the drive against "speedup," accounted a major factor in the initial organization of the union. The union has viewed these methods, on the whole, as devices employed by management to speed up operations, pitting worker against worker and emphasizing efficiency at the expense of health and safety. The force of popular opposition within the membership was perhaps not fully realized, however, until incentives became a factional issue within the UAW during World War II. In this period a great many plants in the nation, spurred by patriotic motives, government pressure for increased output, and the opportunity to improve earnings in the face of wage controls, installed some form of incentive plan. Within the UAW's jurisdiction, such plans were also considered in local situations and in a few cases adopted. The pressures became insistent, however, only upon Russia's entry into the war, when left-wing groups within the union launched a drive for a return to piecework in the plants of the major companies —a drive, incidentally, that coincided with the demands of some firms, such as GM, for the reintroduction of incentive payments. Sensing the sentiment of the general membership and recognizing no doubt an opportunity to enhance his own standing in the union, Walter Reuther, then a UAW vice-president, immediately came out in staunch opposition to all incentive proposals, insisting that "the introduction of incentive plans in our industry will create further chaos and confusion and will not solve the basic wage problem nor increase overall production."[46] That he struck a responsive chord and established once and for all the outright rejection of incentives as official UAW policy is clear from the following account of the episode:

> In the UAW, George Addes [secretary-treasurer and leading contender with Reuther in the struggle for control] . . . introduced a proposal for incentive pay, including

46. UAW-CIO press release, April 13, 1943.

piecework. Reuther was shrewd enough to sense that this was unthinkable to union men because it involved a self-imposed speedup. When he opposed it, a labor observer wrote in the *Detroit News* of May 9, 1943, "As of today Reuther is the fair-haired boy of the rank-and-file."[47]

After Reuther's election to the presidency of the UAW in 1946, the issue of speedup and incentives again became a focal point in the struggle between contending factions. At the 1947 convention, Reuther's report to the membership accused the Addes-Thomas-Leonard group of circulating false and malicious propaganda to the effect that the UAW president was in favor of speedup and piecework. After presenting evidence to refute the charges made against him, Reuther reiterated his stand on incentives: "The UAW-CIO grew out of the fight against the speedup in our industry and that fight continues. Better working conditions and higher wages can and must be won out of the profits of the industry and improved technology and not out of a work pace that destroys the health and shortens the lives of our workers. Militant and aggressive opposition to piecework and speedup must continue to be the corner-stone of our basic union policy."[48] This has remained the official union position, reaffirmed in resolution after resolution, up to the present.

But if the union's position was thus clear and unequivocal, what can be said of management's? The attitute of the companies is best understood by examining briefly what transpired in key negotiating sessions during the first decade or so of bargaining.

In its earliest negotiations with General Motors, the UAW demanded the abolition of all piecework. This the company

47. Eldorous L. Dayton, *Walter Reuther: Autocrat at the Bargaining Table* (New York, Devin-Adair, 1958), p. 146.

48. *Report of the President, Walter P. Reuther, to the 11th Convention, UAW-CIO* (Nov. 9, 1947), Part 1, p. 41.

refused to do. As Alfred P. Sloan later advised the company's stockholders, "It was agreed that wage payment plans may be adopted, changed or modified, as may be directed by the workers directly involved."[49] Mr. Sloan stated what was apparently the company's position at that time—namely, that it had no particular preference for one method of wage payment over another, that several plans were in operation in different plants, and that local management had full authority to negotiate such matters. Less than two years later, however, Vice-president C. E. Wilson took a less moderate view of the issue. In the course of a major address in 1939, he stressed the importance to management of payment by results:

> An employer in working out his labor relations must keep this principle in mind. Some theories have been advanced that all employees should be paid the same wage. This has been proven by experience to be a false philosophy. To pay the same rate per hour to employees who did different amounts of work, even though they are engaged in the same or similar occupations, has also been found to be unsound. An employee with greater ability or ambition should be able to earn more money and to advance in the organization. . . . The proper recognition for work, merit and ability in the operation of a factory must not be interfered with.[50]

This prewar statement of policy, endorsing a method of wage payment that preserved work incentives, was to become a cornerstone of GM's bargaining program in the war and early postwar years. Whatever the company's motives in "voluntarily" eliminating incentive plans in a number of its plants

49. Alfred P. Sloan, Jr., President, General Motors Corporation, "The Story of the General Motors Strike," submitted to stockholders (April 1937), p. 9.
50. C. E. Wilson, "Essentials in an Employer's Labor Policy," in *Addresses on Industrial Relations,* Bulletin No. 9 (Ann Arbor, Bureau of Industrial Relations, Univ. of Michigan, 1939), p. 10.

in the mid-1930s, experience under unionism brought with it the desire for greater freedom in determining wage methods— especially in extending incentives.

The first move by the company came in 1943 when, as we have noted, some firms were establishing incentive plans as a means of raising output and wages. In that year, GM submitted to the union a demand for a change in the agreement which read as follows: "That the Union withdraw its opposition and lend its support to individual piece work or other incentive methods of pay when it has been determined by management that the introduction of such incentive method of pay will increase the production of war materials. Any change in the wage payment plan will be negotiated with the shop committee before being placed in effect. The Corporation is satisfied that the introduction of incentive pay will increase war production from ten to twenty-five per cent without increase of manpower."[51] With Reuther leading the GM locals and, at the same time, the struggle against piecework within the union, it is not surprising that the demand came to naught. As the war drew to a close, however, it was obvious that many auto managers favored a return to incentive methods, and it was inevitable that the issue would be tested in early negotiations.

In March 1945, the Automotive Council for War Production, speaking on behalf of the automotive industry, issued the challenge in a statement before the Senate War Investigating Committee. This statement denounced the unions for inhibiting output through policies that deadened incentives. Attention was drawn to the "glaring inequality" of a wage system that permitted no differential in pay "between the workers who do an honest day's work and the drones and militant hotheads who are destroying the industry's productivity," to collective bargaining agreements that no longer allowed recognition and reward of workers on the basis of merit and ability, and to the marked decline in productivity experienced in plants with

51. *Minutes, GM-UAW Negotiations* (March 22, 1948), p. 44.

hourly-rate systems as contrasted with plants on incentive. The Council urged, therefore, that "wherever applicable, an incentive plan to reward merit, ability and productivity of the individual worker is an important step toward increasing output, reducing cost and conserving manpower."[52]

At the bargaining table GM took up the issue in the first postwar round of negotiations. The company asked the UAW leadership to withdraw its opposition to piecework and to honor its agreement that wage-payment plans were a matter for local determination.[53] The company's negotiators claimed that the employees and shop committees in certain plants wanted to install piecework but were prevented from doing so by union officials. This was not disputed by the UAW's chief negotiator who informed management that local determination was limited to the issue of continuing existing plans and did not include the extension of such plans into plants already operating on an hourly basis.[54] In these negotiations, it is clear that the company's demand was more than a tactical maneuver; many local plant managers (if not also local unions) were anxious to make the switch from hourly rates to incentives but found their efforts frustrated by the International Union's mandate. As Vice-president Harry Anderson explained the situation at a meeting of GM plant managers and personnel directors on January 24,

52. George Romney, Managing Director of the Automotive Council for War Production, "Manpower Problems and their Effects on War Production," a statement before the Senate War Investigating Committee (March 9, 1945), p. 13.

53. The pertinent provisions of the GM-UAW agreement were the following:

Paragraph 90: Wage payment plans are a matter of local negotiation between the Plant Managements and the Shop Committees, subject to appeal in accordance with the Grievance Procedure.

Paragraph 91: Any change from an incentive plan to an hourly rate method of pay is a matter for local determination and any such changes must be made on a sound and equitable basis which does not increase average production costs, and which provides for maintaining efficiency of the plant.

54. *Minutes, GM Council, UAW-CIO* (March 15, 1946), p. 33.

1946: "In the local negotiations at the various plants, many of you have demanded that the local union negotiate some form of incentive pay. At some of the plants, the local union has admitted that their hands are tied by the mandate of the International. In spite of the fact that for the time being you may not make any progress along this line, it is a good idea if you want incentive pay to make the demand for incentive pay locally and keep it a live issue."[55]

In the 1948 negotiations, GM again sought a relaxation of the International's opposition to the extension of incentive plans in individual plants. It submitted a document to the union expounding the virtues of this type of wage system (in terms of the gains to be expected in productivity and earnings) and proposed the establishment of local plant committees to consider the desirability of a changeover to piecework. The union's response was to label the corporation's plan "a plea for speedup."[56] It was argued that since the steel shortage imposed a ceiling on auto production, higher productivity would not result in greater output but simply in longer and more frequent layoffs. It was also argued that incentive pay systems transferred part of the risks of doing business, including the costs of managerial inefficiency, from management to labor. Finally, the union challenged the company's insinuation that its opposition did not reflect the will of the membership. It reminded management that the UAW "was born in the fight against speedup" and that the corporation itself had "in a last desperate effort to head off unionization, 'voluntarily' abolished its speed-up system in some plants."

As a counterproposal to the company's demand the union asked for deletion of Paragraphs 90 and 91 from the contract

55. For a bitter attack on UAW wage policies at this time, see the talk, "Wages and Economic Efficiency," delivered by A. T. Court of the General Motors' Labor Economics Section to members of the Academy of Political Science, May 1946.

56. UAW-CIO, "Sweat Today—Starve Tomorrow" (Research and Engineering Dept., April 8, 1948).

(n. 53) and the substitution of the following clause: "Any plant now working on an incentive pay plan, and who desire to change to an hourly rate plan will be permitted to do so. The method of carrying out this provision will be negotiated locally."[57] Management, for its part, opposed deletion of Paragraph 91 on the grounds that the company needed some assurance that efficiency would not suffer in the changeover from an incentive to an hourly-rate method of wage payment. Indeed, the difficulties encountered in controlling costs and restoring plants to normal operating efficiency following such changeovers were the principal reason for management's renewed interest in incentives. A representative of the Fisher Body Division (the last stronghold of piecework operations in GM) noted how this experience had affected management's thinking: "Up to that time, our top management people were sympathetic toward changeover from piece work to day work, as evidenced by the plants that we had on day work. And at one time they changed plants over themselves to day work believing that that maybe was a better method of wage payment. But it is only because of the performance which your people gave in the plants which put them [management] in the position they are in today with respect to the incentive system of wage payment."[58] To management, this was the critical issue in changeover for which, so far, there had been no satisfactory solution. It rejected the union's answer that the company retained the right to discipline workers who failed to do their jobs, pointing out that discipline against slowdown or the failure to meet production standards was much less necessary under piecework and that the use of discipline under these circumstances usually meant a squabble with the union.

Concurrently with GM's drive to weaken the union's resistance to the extension of incentive methods, negotiators for Ford

57. *Proceedings, GM-UAW Negotiations* (March 18, 1948), p. 44; (April 8, 1948), p. 63.
58. *Proceedings, GM-UAW Negotiations* (March 18, 1948), p. 73.

were likewise seeking to promote the greater use of incentive systems in that company's plants. On June 21, 1948, for example, Ford Vice-president John S. Bugas proposed in a memorandum to the Ford UAW Negotiating Committee "that we agree to extend incentive practices in the company, and that we establish a joint committee to study this matter further." We do not know with what determination this subject was pursued by the company in the actual negotiations, but we do know that it resulted—as at GM—in no modification or relaxation of the international union's stand on incentives.

Since 1948 the question of how workers are to be compensated has receded as an issue in national negotiations between the UAW and the Big Three, though it remained alive in local negotiations in individual plants still operating on an incentive basis. In February 1948 the UAW reported that nine GM plants were on piecework and that only a minority of these wished to retain the system, primarily because it yielded higher earnings.[59] It was not until 1955, however, that the union was able to report the elimination of piecework in most of these plants.[60]

In the case of the Independents, matters were somewhat different. Both Studebaker and Willys continued to operate under incentive plans up to the early 1950s, with the apparently full approval of the local memberships concerned. Indeed, the elimination of these systems in 1954 came at the insistence of management and had to be won over worker opposition—a fact that is not surprising in view of the high earnings–low effort experience under both systems. It is unfortunate that little is now known about the precise operating characteristics of the plans in these two companies, making it impossible to explore their specific shortcomings. Nevertheless, it may be instructive to note briefly the sorts of problems that plagued the Studebaker incentive plan.

59. *Minutes, National GM Conference, UAW-CIO* (Feb. 24, 1948), pp. 382, 417.
60. Report of Reuther, 16th Convention, p. 2-D.

The principal difficulties faced by Studebaker in the operation of its incentive wage system appear to have been the maintenance of a satisfactory relationship between the earnings of incentive and nonincentive workers and the prevention of an upward drift in piece earnings relative to base rates. These two problems were interrelated and derived in large part from the difficulties involved in setting appropriate piece prices (or work standards) and in revising these prices as conditions warranted. We shall consider each of them in turn.

The problem of the differential in earnings between production and nonproduction workers at Studebaker had been one of long standing. Indeed, it was considered by the emerging union in 1934 to be "the most critical wage problem in the shop." Accordingly, one of the first acts of the union was to approach management for some relief on the issue. This early attempt to correct the "inequity" by raising the day rates of nonproduction (nonincentive) workers was unsuccessful, although later in the same year the union won a 5-cent plant-wide wage increase. By 1935, however, the problem of the earnings' differential had become so acute, the discrepancy in pay so large, that the union membership voted "to instruct the Company to take enough money from the piecework prices to give the day workers a 5¢ per hour increase."[61]

This unorthodox solution, prompted by a threatened split in the union, appears to have met the issue for a time. In the early war years, however, the problem re-emerged in virulent form. In August 1942 the hourly earnings of Studebaker production workers averaged $1.24 compared with $1.14 for nonproduction workers. By June 1943 the respective averages had risen to $1.49 and $1.16. In ten months, therefore, the differential had increased from 8.8 to 28.5 per cent. The union convinced the company that something had to be done to reduce this growing earnings spread between the two groups. Accordingly,

61. "A Brief History of the Labor Movement of Studebaker-Local No. 5, UAW-CIO" (Studebaker Local No. 5, Education and Publicity Committee, 1953), pp. 27–31.

on August 12, an agreement was entered into "to correct presently existing inequalities between the straight-time hourly rates of nonproductive (hourly rated) employees and the straight-time hourly earnings of the productive (piece work) employees and to do so without any increase in the net labor cost of production." This improvement in earnings for hourly-rated employees was to be accomplished by raising efficiency above a base level established from payroll records (measured in terms of "standard" hours required) and passing the resulting savings along to the remaining indirect labor force. The plan was successful, and the savings thus realized permitted the payment of a bonus to nonproduction workers from November 1943 to the end of the war.

With the discontinuance of this wartime plan, the earnings differential between production and nonproduction workers again became a source of great dissatisfaction. Hourly-rated workers, in particular, felt the squeeze of rising living costs and reduced overtime payments. It was decided, therefore, under pressure 'from the union, to reinstate the incentive plan for indirect labor. The wartime plan, which had proved beneficial in that it had yielded earnings increases without raising costs, was not judged a suitable model for a permanent peacetime plan. Instead, a different method of bonus payment was adopted which geared the incentive earnings of indirect labor to the production groups served.[62] This plan, effective October 1946, was short lived. It yielded a 12 per cent incentive during the first three weeks, but by mid-December it had proved so

62. It was felt that the great majority of nonproduction workers performed work of a nature that could be related directly to output and, indeed, that varied directly with the rate of output. These nonproduction workers were grouped in appropriate departments and a group piece price established for each group. The remaining nonproduction workers (e.g. powerhouse and plant protection employees), whose work did not vary with the rate of output, were placed in a general plant group and earned premiums based on the average premium earned by all nonproduction groups for which piece prices had been established.

unsatisfactory that it was eliminated and a 15 per cent increase over base rates granted in its stead. "The principal reason for discontinuing the program," writes Dubin, "was the fact that production fluctuated so widely between departments as to create wide weekly changes in the pay for non-production workers. Thus, sweepers in the same classification, but working in different departments to whose output their incentive bonus was tied, might have as much as ten cents an hour differential in their hourly pay."[63]

In the late summer of 1947, as a result of negotiations begun in the spring, a new incentive plan was installed which the union described as a "more workable agreement." This plan appears to have been more successful. However, the 1950 negotiations found the parties again engaged in discussion of a "liberalized non-productive incentive plan," which suggests that the issue of the earnings inequity between direct and indirect labor was a continuing one. Indeed, when incentives were finally eliminated at Studebaker in 1954, the system then in vogue seems to have awarded a 15 per cent incentive bonus to hourly-rated workers for hours worked on any day during which the final passenger assembly line produced finished units yielding piecework earnings in excess of classification rates. This premium was to be paid on all hours worked in any week during which the final line yielded such piecework earnings for half or more of that week.[64]

The behavior of the earnings differential between piecework and hourly-rated jobs was not, as we have noted, the only problem arising under the Studebaker incentive system. Throughout the postwar period, a more serious difficulty confronting management (and one that was never really solved under the incentive plan) was control over the upward drift in incentive

63. Frederick H. Harbison and Robert Dubin, *Patterns of Union-Management Relations,* p. 140.
64. Supplemental Agreement between the Studebaker Corporation and Local No. 5, UAW-CIO, July 28, 1952.

earnings caused by loose piece prices. The evidence here is fragmentary, but sufficient to indicate the essential nature of the problem.[65] The Studebaker piecework system had been designed originally to yield earnings 10 per cent above base rates which were approximately equal to Detroit hourly rates. In return the company expected a production rate 10 per cent above the Detroit level. While it is very doubtful that man-hour productivity at South Bend ever exceeded Detroit levels, management at Studebaker was apparently satisfied with the prewar situation. In 1941, the last year of peacetime production, piecework earnings were 9.2 per cent above base rates. The wartime behavior of incentive earnings is not known in any detail, except for the fact that average hourly earnings for production workers rose from $1.24 to $1.49 between August 1942 and June 1943. The over-all trend in earnings is revealed, however, in the statistics in Table 10.[66] This trend reflects, of course, the incentive premium introduced in late 1943 for nonproduction workers.

While a variety of factors may have contributed to the relatively sharp increase in earnings at Studebaker during the war period, there can be no doubt that the incentive system played a prominent role. Certainly it was the major factor accounting for the large postwar difference in earnings (approximately three times the size of the prewar differential) between Studebaker and the rest of the industry. The company's own statistics confirm this, for while management sought to extend the prewar incentive system (especially the prewar earnings potential) into the postwar period, it soon admitted that the plan had miscarried badly because of an inability to control piece prices and manpower assignments. As a result, incentive premiums in the spring of 1947 averaged 27.5 per cent above base rates and

65. The points made below are developed more fully in chap. 6, which deals with competitive relations. Discontinuance of the incentive plan in 1954, the merger of Studebaker with the Packard Motor Company, and the accompanying changes in personnel make it difficult, if not impossible, to reconstruct the detailed character or performance of the plan.

66. Harbison and Dubin, p. 137.

ranged as high as 50 per cent for some workers. Seven years later, when the incentive plan at Studebaker was finally abolished, it was yielding average hourly earnings 18 per cent above competitors' levels in Detroit. These figures might signify some improvement in the operation of the incentive system in the intervening years. This does not necessarily follow, however, for evidence of how the system performed in the early 1950s suggests that much of the slack was taken up in the form of excess manpower and a slow over-all work pace. Loose incentive standards were reflected as much in more leisurely operations as in higher earnings.

TABLE 10.   Average Hourly Earnings—Studebaker and the Auto
and Parts Industry, 1941–1946

Period	Studebaker (cents)	Auto and parts industry (cents)	Studebaker as per cent of auto and parts industry
1941 First half	105.8	99.8	106
Second half	114.3	108.6	105
1942 First half	122.6	115.6	106
Second half	123.9	118.2	105
1943 First half	138.0	122.2	113
Second half	147.8	124.6	118
1944 First half	160.9	126.3	128
Second half	163.9	127.8	128
1945 First half	167.3	128.2	130
Second half	149.3	123.0	121
1946 First half	147.0	128.0	115
Second half	159.2	137.1	116

Source. Harbison and Dubin, p. 137.

This brief discussion serves to indicate some of the difficulties experienced by one company in the administration of its incentive plan; and it is always possible that Studebaker's troubles, although extreme, were symptomatic of the kinds of difficulties confronting other plant managements attempting to administer incentive plans in the face of strong union opposition. However, the complex set of forces known to affect the results of incentive systems, and the existence of marked differences in labor-relations performance during this period (discussed in chapters 6 and 7), caution against drawing any ready generalizations from this one company's experience about the practicability of wage incentives in the industry as a whole.

Having examined the circumstances underlying the change-over from incentive to hourly-rate methods of wage payment in the industry, what may we conclude about the influence of unionism and collective bargaining? In our view, the evidence supports the following judgment. The UAW was instrumental in eliminating a number of piecework plans in the industry during the 1930s, although to some extent it appears simply to have hastened a trend that was already developing. Earlier studies reveal that a growing number of company officials had little, if any, strong commitment to incentive plans as such and that some changeovers almost certainly took place which were unrelated to union pressures, direct or otherwise. It is true that a fairly strong and widespread preference for piecework emerged in the 1940s; and one suspects that, with less firm resistance on the part of the international union, some expansion of incentive plans would have occurred in plants belonging to the Big Three. However, opinion among managers as to the relative merits of alternative payment methods was clearly divided, and much of central management's effort in negotiations was designed to return the determination of payment plans to the local level.

We are inclined to regard the resurgence of interest in incentive plans in the 1940s as a quite natural reaction to the strain of adjusting, under already difficult war and postwar conditions, to union rules and policies which, in management's view, were throttling efficiency. Under the hourly-rate systems as originally established, merit ranges had continued to provide a (limited) means of rewarding ability and preserving incentives. However, the erosion of these ranges and the gradual destruction of any

personalized rate system, in conjunction with the greater difficulty of maintaining effort through discipline in the unionized
plant, must surely have encouraged some managers to see in
incentive systems a remedy to the "efficiency" problem. Needless to say, this desire to change back to incentives indicates
only that some managers preferred this kind of system *under
collective bargaining*. It does not necessarily follow that the
same preferences would have prevailed in an alternative (nonunion) system. Indeed, the desire for changeover, even under
collective bargaining, might well have been satisfied by the
reintroduction of adequate merit ranges in an hourly-rate system, had this been thought a realizable objective.

Whatever the motivation for management's renewed interest
in piecework in the war and immediate postwar years, it is
significant that incentives have not been a prominent bargaining
issue, except in a few individual plants, since 1948. In part, this
decline in enthusiasm may reflect a certain resignation to union
opposition—to insistent demands urging the abandonment of
incentives and to the reduction of their effectiveness through
the imposition of strict standards and the pressure of "incentive" grievances. But while we cannot discount the force of the
international union's resistance, it is difficult to avoid the conclusion that management's acceptance of measured day work
(i.e. a combined system of hourly rates and production-standard
controls) reflects a growing realization that incentive plans in
practice are not necessarily superior from the standpoint of efficiency. Where work is machine paced, where schedules fix within narrow limits the number of pieces to be produced in each
time period, and where methods, materials, and processes are
subject to frequent change, incentive systems tend to lose their
effectiveness. This change in management attitude, brought
about by the logic of production conditions, appears to be the
main cause of declining sentiment in favor of incentives. Otherwise it is difficult to explain why this has ceased to be an important issue in negotiations and why company officials in a posi-

tion to observe the relative merits of the two wage systems in actual operation are no longer interested in extending incentives.[67]

In short, the UAW has played a role in the abandonment of wage incentives, partly through direct pressure for their elimination, partly through influencing management's thinking toward a more critical evaluation of their operating results, and partly through curbs on local-union discretion. What would have happened in the absence of collective bargaining (or, for that matter, in the context of a less violently "negative" union policy) is of course a speculative matter. It seems reasonable to suppose, however, that wage incentives under these conditions would have been less readily (or less rapidly) abandoned in at least some of the plants and would have continued to occupy a place in the industry's wage system, though not in the wage system of each plant or company. Certainly we see no compelling reason to assume that wage incentives would have continued to play the same prominent role as in the 1920s or early 1930s or that management's views would have remained the same as in earlier years. It is clear, however, that the notion of payment by results—of rewarding merit, effort, and ability —is deeply embedded in management's wage philosophy and would have found greater expression in the wage system in the absence of bargaining. In some plants this might have taken the form of piece rates; in others, of merit ranges or other forms of personalized payment in an hourly-rate system. In this way the different preferences of individual managers and plant work groups would have been accorded wider recognition in the industry's over-all wage system. With greater freedom to experiment and to test the merits of different kinds of wage plans, the system too, in all probability, would have exhibited less internal

67. It is true that production personnel in at least one of the larger companies have occasionally advised the use of incentive plans in new plants, but this advice has not been acted upon since top management officials are convinced that experience in the industry argues against it.

stability (or rigidity). At any rate, it is most unlikely that management as a whole would have embraced of its own volition the type of wage system developed under bargaining—a system that has virtually removed all personal rate differentials within the various production occupations.

The union's influence on personal differentials can now be summarized. We have argued that the main thrust of the union's drive to eliminate incentives coincided with a growing management sentiment that questioned the validity of such payment methods in the technological environment characteristic of large-scale auto production. In this sense, the UAW was riding a trend, already under way, and based fundamentally on the logic of the industry's production conditions. By reinforcing the trend, the union undoubtedly increased the tempo of change, forcing the pace of adjustment in some plants and spreading the movement more rapidly to lagging firms. This quickening of the transition to new payment methods has probably had the effect of eliminating piecework plans that otherwise would have remained in operation in certain segments or pockets of the industry—most likely in those activities subordinate to or supporting the basic manufacturing and assembly processes. Such plans would constitute, in our judgment, only a minority of the changeovers since the depression. Nevertheless, insofar as a number of incentive plans had to be abandoned under union pressure, the union must be credited in these instances with reducing the range of personal differentials. Needless to say, this conclusion is applicable only to incentive plans that actually did result in differential earnings for workers in the same occupation. It would not apply in the case of a group bonus plan which apportioned piece earnings uniformly among all workers in the same establishment.

When this "incentive" effect is added to our earlier findings concerning the role of the union in modifying the hourly-rate system—i.e. the elimination of rate ranges on production jobs, the reduction of the spread between starting and job rates in all production classifications, and the establishment of shorter probationary periods and of automatic rate progression—it is clear that the union's over-all influence has been to reduce substantially and, in most respects, eliminate the range of personal differentials in auto plant wage structures.

This conclusion is limited, however, to the union's impact on wage-rate (or earnings) differentials. When the concept of wages is broadened to take account of major fringe benefits, the analysis in chapter 2 indicates that the UAW has been responsible for creating or enlarging a variety of personal "benefit" differentials. In particular, it has been responsible for the establishment (or, more correctly, the *widening*) of what might be termed the "seniority differential"—a form of personal differential based on length of service. Since unionism did not originate the idea of service-connected benefits, it is not to be credited with the full range of developments in this area. We have argued, however, that unionism has been largely responsible for the establishment of private pension programs which, at the time of their introduction, represented a substantial transfer of income from lower- to higher-seniority groups.[68] This is equivalent in principle to a wage increase graduated by length of service, as far as the current work force is concerned. The same is true of vacation plans that take account of prior service, although here the union's independent influence is much less easily established. For the majority of the industry's workers, existing vacation plans are in the nature of service

68. It is well to note that, even if we concede that management in a high-wage industry such as autos would have been prompted (in the absence of unionism) to offer its employees a private plan to boost (inadequate) public benefits, there is every reason to believe that such a plan, apart from being voluntary, would have embraced the contributory principle and would have tended to relate each worker's prospective benefit rather closely to his actual contribution. It is our view that this is a much less likely alternative than is management's support for an improved federal program. The point to be made, however, is that neither alternative affects the validity of our conclusion with regard to the union's influence on the "seniority differential."

bonuses. Since the possibility cannot be ruled out that individual companies would have installed (in some cases, reinstalled) such bonuses, or even bona fide vacation plans, their existence cannot be attributed entirely to the union. Indeed, the only judgment that can be made with reasonable assurance is that vacation benefits have been raised more rapidly by the union's aggressive demands for improvements. In short, the "seniority differential" created by such plans is wider under bargaining than it otherwise would have been. The union's influence on these two major benefit programs—private pensions and vacations—has produced, therefore, a significant widening of personal differentials based on length of service.

Clearly, then, if the broader concept of wages is adopted, the union's over-all impact on personal differentials is a mixed one. It is well to remember, however, that the wage discrimination associated with new (or revised) benefit programs which credit past service applies only to the current work force and is, in this sense, temporary.

CHAPTER 4

Occupational Differentials

Occupational differentials are defined as the differences in wages paid to workers in different occupations in the same establishment. Therefore, unlike other dimensions of the wage structure which focus on the issue of "equal pay for equal work," the occupational dimension raises the issue of "unequal pay for unequal work"—a more intriguing but less tractable kind of problem. Occupational wage movements have been investigated extensively in recent years and, as a result, our understanding of this aspect of wage behavior has improved significantly. Nevertheless, some major points of controversy remain, including the actual influence of unionism.

The most significant development in the general movement of occupational differentials over time has been the gradual but steady contraction of the skill structure of wages. This compression, which has been under way for several decades in most of the highly industrialized countries of the West, has been characterized as "an important, massive and highly controversial social phenomenon."[1] It is this phenomenon that economists

1. Clark Kerr, "Wage Relationships—The Comparative Impact of Market

have sought especially to explain; and it is around this phenomenon that much of the current debate revolves. Actually, the main issues in dispute are concerned less with the specific forces involved than with the relative emphasis to be accorded each. Thus, there is considerable agreement that among the main secular influences at work have been maturing industrialism, the spread of public education, and a rising egalitarian philosophy.[2] There is also fairly wide agreement that, in the period since the beginning of World War II, this secular trend toward a narrower structure has been reinforced by the short-run factors of high-level employment and inflation. A force of a more controversial nature, however, has been the rise of industrial unionism. While some economists have tended to discount the importance of this influence entirely or to relegate it to a decidedly minor role, others would accord it a prominent place among the forces shaping this aspect of the wage structure.

The main reasons for rejecting industrial unionism as a significant factor in the narrowing of occupational differentials are (1) the virtual universality of the narrowing tendency, (2) the presumed adequacy of alternative explanations couched in terms of market forces, and (3) the apparent absence of any significant correlation between the type of union organization and the rate of decline of differentials. These are impressive arguments, but they have so far failed to dislodge the contrary view which rests essentially on the claim that institutional necessities (i.e. the pressures implicit in the composition and power structure of union membership) can and do affect the behavior of skill differentials through their influence on the character of wage adjustments.

Given the nature of these continuing differences in view-

---

and Power Forces," in John T. Dunlop, ed., *The Theory of Wage Determination*, p. 178.

2. See Lloyd G. Reynolds and Cynthia H. Taft, *Evolution of Wage Structure*, pp. 358–59; George H. Hildebrand, "The Economic Effects of Unionism," in Neil W. Chamberlain et al., eds., *A Decade of Industrial Relations Research, 1946–1956*, pp. 121–24; Kerr, "Wage Relationships," pp. 187–88.

point, it is evident that the issue of union influence is not to be resolved by abstract argument but only by a careful examination of occupational wage developments in the appropriate decision-making units in the economy. This is the principal task of the following analysis which focuses on the behavior of occupational differentials in automobile plants.

The Pattern of Occupational Differentials

The work force in auto plants can be divided into two more or less distinct groups—production workers and nonproduction workers. In the former group, which comprises roughly two thirds of all wage earners in the industry, the key occupations (or job classifications) from the standpoint of rate-making are those of assembler and machine operator. These occupations are important for a number of reasons: they include a large proportion of a company's workers and hence are a major determinant of the level of wages and labor costs;[3] they comprise operations that are well known and common to a number of industries and are therefore appropriate guides in relating the auto plant wage scale to the local wage structure; and they are a strategic point of contact with the labor market in that much of the company's recruitment and turnover takes place at these levels. Other production jobs, normally filled by in-plant upgrading and transfer, have their rates set in relation to these primary rates on the basis of a comparison of skill requirements, job content, etc.[4]

The nonproduction group comprises chiefly the custodial operations and the tool room and maintenance departments. Tool room and maintenance workers—the skilled trades—con-

3. Thus, one company estimated that almost 50 per cent of its wage earners in late 1957 were minor assemblers, major assemblers, or machine operators.

4. Inspection is closely related to production from the standpoint of rate making. Since the inspector must know the operation he checks, he should be paid at least the rate for that operation and, in fact, he often receives a slightly higher rate.

stitute approximately 15 per cent of the work force.[5] The strategic jobs in rate setting in the skilled trades are the tool and die maker in the tool room trades and the electrician and machine repairman in the maintenance trades. These maintenance crafts have become increasingly important in automobile manufacturing during the last decade with the development of electronics and the trend toward more complicated and expensive machinery. Generally speaking, the electrician's rate is the highest rate paid in maintenance, with other crafts receiving either the same rate or 5 to 10 cents less. Similarly, the tool-and-die-maker's rate is typically 5 or 10 cents above that of the skilled machine operator (shaper, grinder, lathe operator), but it is lower than that of, say, the die sinker—a job requiring two years of training beyond that of die maker. At the other end of the wage scale are the custodial jobs such as janitor and sweeper which carry the lowest rates for unskilled (male) help.

Given the wage rates for these key job classifications in auto manufacturing, the wage structure for the vast majority of occupations in the industry is closely defined by reason of well-established rate relationships. Consequently, in tracing the general behavior of occupational differentials, it is sufficient to focus attention on a relatively small number of strategic job rates.

In Table 11 we trace the movement of average hourly earnings in selected occupations over the period 1922–57. Because of variations in coverage and sample size, and possible bias in the reporting of wage data (particularly in the depression years), small differences in the wage movements for specific occupations in the period prior to 1940 are not necessarily significant. The data do provide, however, a rough measure

5. One of the Big Three companies reported that the proportion of skilled workers among wage earners in its plants was almost 18 per cent in late 1957, while another reported a ratio of about 13 per cent in mid-1955. The typical situation is believed to be closer to the lower of these two figures, though in recent years the proportion of skilled workers has tended to rise in response to automation and rapid technological change.

TABLE 11.   Average Hourly Earnings in Selected Occupations in
the Automobile Industry, 1922–1957

Occupation	1922[a]	1928[a]	1930[a]	1932[a]	1934	1940	1950	1957
Janitor, sweeper	$	$	$	$	$	$0.77	$1.37	$2.07
Laborer, material handler	0.495	0.589	0.589	0.575	0.613	0.85	1.48	2.17
Assembler, chassis and final[b]	0.647	0.758	0.681	0.570	0.720 ⎫			
Assembler, motor and transmission	0.661	0.762	0.725	0.632	0.745 ⎬ 0.94		1.60	2.27
Machine operator, I	0.659	0.751	0.713	0.634	0.714 ⎫			
Machine operator, II	0.700	0.792	0.774	0.667	0.754 ⎬ 0.96		1.62	2.29
Punch press operator	0.715	0.746	0.717	0.646	0.693	0.96	1.62	2.30
Sprayer, paint	0.723	0.824	0.733	0.615	0.783	1.01	1.67	2.39
Electrician						1.03	1.85	2.81
Tool-and-die maker	0.769	0.919	0.887	0.785	0.899	1.19	1.97	2.95
Patternmaker, wood and metal						1.22	2.11	3.40
Industry average	$0.662	$0.756	$0.733	$0.638	$0.730	$0.97	$1.63	$2.37

Relative Average Hourly Earnings (Material handler = 100)

Janitor, sweeper						91	93	95
Laborer, material handler	100	100	100	100	100	100	100	100
Assembler, chassis and final	131	129	116	99	117 ⎫			
Assembler, motor and transmission	134	129	123	110	122 ⎬ 111		108	105
Machine operator, I	133	128	121	110	116 ⎫			
Machine operator, II	141	134	131	116	123 ⎬ 113		109	106
Punch press operator	144	127	122	112	113	113	109	106
Sprayer, paint	146	140	124	107	128	119	113	110
Electrician						121	125	129
Tool-and-die maker	155	156	151	137	147	140	133	136
Patternmaker, wood and metal						144	142	157

Relative Average Hourly Earnings (Assembler, motor = 100)

Tool-and-die maker	116	121	122	124	121	127	123	130

a. Includes some workers in the automotive parts division.
b. Unweighted average of earnings for assemblers, axle, chassis, and final.
Sources. Bureau of Labor Statistics: "Wage Structure of the Motor-Vehicle Industry," p. 17; "Wage Structure: Motor Vehicles and Parts, 1950," *Bulletin No. 1015* (1951), pp. 6–7; "Wage Structure: Part 1, Motor Vehicles," *Report No. 128* (July 1957), p. 13.

of the general dimensions of the wage structure in the prewar years and are indicative of broad tendencies in the behavior of skill differentials during that period. The wage data covering the period since 1940 are, on the other hand, quite reliable.[6]

The principal developments in the occupational wage structure are easily summarized. Viewing the period as a whole, there has been a gradual but steady evolution toward a narrower pattern of differentials. If we consider only those occupations for which wage data are continuously available, the extent of this narrowing since the 1920s is indicated by the reduction in the over-all range of earnings (as represented by the laborer-tool maker differential) from 55 to 36 per cent and by the even greater contraction of the range for unskilled and semiskilled jobs (the laborer-paint sprayer differential) from 46 to 10 per cent. This trend toward a generally narrower structure has been interrupted or modified, however, by two other developments: the temporary, sharp compression of the rate range in the depression and the tendency for skilled trades rates to rise relative to the rates for most other occupations since the depression.

The data in Table 11 reveal the abrupt contraction of occupational differentials during the depression. It is our view, however, that this peculiar behavior is mainly a reflection of the difficulties of charting wage movements accurately in a period of violent change. The sudden reduction in differentials between 1930 and 1932 and the equally sharp recovery between 1932 and 1934 are entirely due to the relative stability of the common laborers' earnings. While workers in other occupations experienced a decline in hourly earnings of approximately 10 cents in the first two-year period and a roughly similar increase in the second two-year period, laborers' earnings by comparison fell less than 2 cents and rose again by

6. This can be judged from the more detailed rate data for two of the major auto manufacturers presented in Tables 12 and 14. The wage movements portrayed in these tables are typical of rate developments within all companies.

less than 4 cents. It is possible, of course, that the rates for unskilled labor were largely maintained during this period of rather sharp wage reductions for higher-paid groups. This, after all, was not an uncommon occurrence during the depression.[7] However, the deep cut in earnings suffered by other relatively low-paid workers such as assemblers and machine operators, and the absence of any reference to the use of this type of wage policy in the industry during the depression, cast doubt on the accuracy of the earnings figures for common labor. In any event, if skill differentials are based on the earnings of any other occupation, an entirely different wage pattern emerges which gives little evidence of any abrupt change during the depression years.

Of much more significance to the present study is the developing pattern of wage relationships within and between the two main groups of hourly rated workers in the industry—the production workers and the skilled tradesmen. Tables 12 and 13 show the major trends in this pattern since approximately the time of union entry into the industry. Within each group, relative differentials have declined by about 60 per cent.[8] Between 1940 and 1960, all production workers regardless of wage level received the same absolute increase of $1.52. As a result, dingmen's rates rose only 127 per cent compared with 152

7. Although economists are agreed that skill differentials will tend to widen in periods of prolonged depression as long as wage levels are left to the free play of market forces, the failure of differentials to widen and the fact that in some cases they even narrowed during the early 1930s, have suggested the existence of what may be termed a "socially determined minimum wage"— i.e. a wage floor which, by force of law, social custom, or trade union policy is not easily breached. If this social minimum is close to the prevailing wage rates for low-paid workers, effective downward wage pressures will tend to compress the structure of differentials. See Melvin W. Reder, "The Theory of Occupational Wage Differentials," *American Economic Review* (Dec. 1955), pp. 833–52; P. W. Bell, "Cyclical Variations and Trends in Occupational Wage Differentials in American Industry since 1914," *Review of Economics and Statistics* (Nov. 1951), pp. 329–37.

8. The exceptional behavior of the rate for patternmakers is explained later in this chapter.

TABLE 12. Relative Occupational Wage Rates in a "Big Three" Assembly Plant in Detroit, 1937–1958

Occupation	Feb. 1937	Dec. 1940	June 1942	Jan. 1946	Apr. 1947	May 1948	Aug. 1950	June 1953	Sept. 1955	Oct. 1958
Nonskilled				*(Major assembler = 100)*						
Janitor	79	80	79	82	84	87	88	90	90	92
Conveyor loader	84	85	87	89	89	90	91	92	93	94
Checker	89	90	91	92	93	94	94	95	95	96
Asembler, minor	95	95	96	96	96	97	97	97	98	98
Assembler, major	100	100	100	100	100	100	100	100	100	100
Boring-mill operator	105	105	104	104	104	103	103	103	102	102
Grinder, crankshaft	111	110	109	108	107	106	106	105	105	104
Metal finisher	117	115	113	111	111	110	109	108	107	106
Tool room										
Lathe operator	117	122	133	129	127	125	126	128	130	129
Grinder	117	127	138	133	130	128	129	130	132	132
Tool-and-die maker	126	132	143	137	134	131	132	133	135	134
Patternmaker	126	132	143	137	134	131	132	147	154	151
Maintenance										
Millwright	105	112	116	118	120	118	120	122	125	125
Electrician	111	117	121	121	123	121	123	125	127	127
Tool room and maintenance				*(Millwright = 100)*						
Millwright	100	100	100	100	100	100	100	100	100	100
Electrician	105	104	104	103	103	103	103	102	102	102
Lathe operator	110	109	115	110	106	105	105	104	104	104
Welder	110	113	119	113	109	108	108	106	106	106
Tool-and-die maker	120	118	123	116	112	111	110	109	108	108
Patternmaker	120	118	123	116	112	111	110	120	123	121

Source. Derived from Table 14.

TABLE 13. Wage Increases for Selected Occupations in a Typical Assembly Plant in Michigan, 1940–1960

| | Wage rates | | | | | | Wage rates plus fringe benefits[a] | | |
| | | | | Absolute and relative increases | | | | | Absolute and relative increase |
Occupation	Aug. 1940	Mar. 1950[b]	Mar. 1960[b]	1940–1950	1950–1960	1940–1960	Aug. 1940	Mar. 1960[b]	1940–1960
Tool-and-die[c]									
Diemaker	$1.30	$2.02	$3.35	$0.72 55%	$1.33 66%	$2.05 158%	$1.38	$4.16	$2.78 201%
Boring mill operator	1.25	1.97	3.29	0.72 58	1.32 67	2.04 163	1.33	4.09	2.76 208
Grinder operator	1.20	1.92	3.23	0.72 60	1.31 68	2.03 169	1.28	4.02	2.74 214
Shaper operator	1.15	1.87	3.17	0.72 63	1.30 70	2.02 176	1.22	3.95	2.73 224
Maintenance[c]									
Welder, gas and arc	1.20	1.92	3.23	0.72 60	1.31 68	2.03 169	1.28	4.02	2.74 214
Electrician	1.15	1.87	3.17	0.72 63	1.30 70	2.02 176	1.22	3.95	2.73 224
Millwright	1.10	1.82	3.11	0.72 65	1.29 71	2.01 183	1.17	3.88	2.71 232
Carpenter	1.05	1.77	3.04	0.72 69	1.27 72	1.99 190	1.12	3.80	2.68 239
Nonskilled									
Dingman	1.20	1.76	2.72	0.56 47	0.96 55	1.52 127	1.28	3.43	2.16 169
Power hammer	1.15	1.71	2.67	0.56 49	0.96 56	1.52 132	1.22	3.38	2.16 177
Paint spray, sheet metal	1.12	1.68	2.64	0.56 50	0.96 57	1.52 136	1.19	3.34	2.15 181
Inspector, sheet metal finish	1.10	1.66	2.62	0.56 51	0.96 58	1.52 138	1.17	3.32	2.15 184
Diesetter, double	1.09	1.65	2.61	0.56 51	0.96 58	1.52 139	1.16	3.31	2.15 185
Balancer, finish crankshaft	1.06	1.62	2.58	0.56 53	0.96 59	1.52 143	1.13	3.27	2.14 189
Grinder, camshaft	1.03	1.59	2.55	0.56 54	0.96 60	1.52 148	1.10	3.24	2.14 195
Assembler, conveyor, engine	1.00	1.56	2.52	0.56 56	0.96 62	1.52 152	1.07	3.20	2.13 199
Checker, receiving & shipping	0.97	1.53	2.49	0.56 58	0.96 63	1.52 157	1.04	3.17	2.13 205
Handtrucker	0.85	1.41	2.37	0.56 66	0.96 68	1.52 179	0.92	3.03	2.11 229
Elevator operator	0.75	1.31	2.27	0.56 75	0.96 73	1.52 203	0.81	2.91	2.10 259

See p. 143 for notes.

per cent for assemblers. Similarly, within the skilled crafts, wage increases over the period were in the narrow range of $1.99 to $2.05, so that diemakers' rates rose 158 per cent compared with 190 per cent for carpenters. Since the relative increases to the skilled trades exceeded those of the production workers by a substantial margin, the differential between the average craftsman and the average production worker has, at the same time, widened substantially. Indeed, the only non-skilled workers to receive relative wage increases as large as or larger than the average skilled craftsman are those in the low-paid, nonproduction jobs such as elevator operator, janitor, and hand trucker.[9]

Table 13 also shows the behavior of "compensation differentials"—i.e. wage rates plus fringe benefits—over the same 20-year period. The use of this broader concept of wages, as we

a. The value of fringe benefits for each occupation in 1960 is computed in accordance with the assumptions adopted in chap. 2. Programs that are assumed to be of equal dollar value to all workers (i.e. the private and public retirement and unemployment compensation programs and hospitalization insurance) are incorporated by adding 29.3 cents to all wage rates. Programs, on the other hand, that yield benefits scaled to wage rates (i.e. group insurance, vacation and holiday pay, and premium payments) are incorporated by multiplying each wage rate by the ratio of the average value (cost) of the programs to the average wage rate and adding the result to the wage rate. The 1940 data assume a value of 4 cents for federal programs (the approximate value in 1939) and of 3% for vacation pay, group insurance, and premium payments.

b. Rates include 13 cents cost-of-living allowance.

c. Maximum rates only. Merit ranges for the skilled trades were increased from 15 to 20 cents during World War II.

Source. The data were drawn from the files of the UAW Research Department. The 1960 rates are extrapolations of late 1957 rates, taking account of improvement factor increases in 1958 and 1959, the special skilled trades increase of 8 cents in 1958, and the transfer to base rates of 15 cents of the cost-of-living allowance in 1958.

9. It should be noted, however, that the patternmaker (a highly skilled and highly paid craftsman) has gained even relative to the janitor. The figures in Table 14 show that the patternmaker-janitor differential was 65 per cent in late 1958, as compared with 60 per cent in early 1937.

TABLE 14. Occupational Wage Rates in a Typical "Big Three" Assembly Plant in Detroit, 1937–1958

Occupation	Feb. 1937	Dec. 1940	June 1942	Jan. 1946	Apr. 1947	May 1948	Aug. 1950	June 1953[a]	Sept. 1955[b]	Oct. 1958[c]
Nonskilled										
Janitor	$0.75	$0.80	$0.89	$1.075	$1.19	$1.35	$1.45	$1.72	$1.85	$2.21
Conveyor loader	0.80	0.85	0.97	1.155	1.27	1.40	1.50	1.77	1.90	2.26
Checker	0.85	0.90	1.02	1.205	1.32	1.45	1.55	1.82	1.95	2.31
Minor assembler	0.90	0.95	1.07	1.255	1.37	1.50	1.60	1.87	2.00	2.36
Major assembler	0.95	1.00	1.12	1.305	1.42	1.55	1.65	1.92	2.05	2.41
Boring mill operator	1.00	1.05	1.17	1.355	1.47	1.60	1.70	1.97	2.10	2.46
Grinder, crankshaft	1.05	1.10	1.22	1.405	1.52	1.65	1.75	2.02	2.15	2.51
Metal finisher	1.10	1.15	1.27	1.455	1.57	1.70	1.80	2.07	2.20	2.56
Tool room[d]										
Lathe operator	1.10	1.22	1.50	1.685	1.80	1.93	2.08	2.45	2.66	3.12
Welder	1.10	1.27	1.55	1.735	1.85	1.98	2.13	2.50	2.71	3.18
Tool-and-die maker	1.20	1.32	1.60	1.785	1.90	2.03	2.18	2.55	2.77	3.24
Patternmaker	1.20	1.32	1.60	1.785	1.90	2.03	2.18	2.82	3.15	3.65
Maintenance[d]										
Millwright	1.00	1.12	1.30	1.535	1.70	1.83	1.98	2.35	2.56	3.01
Electrician	1.05	1.17	1.35	1.585	1.75	1.88	2.03	2.40	2.61	3.07

a. Includes 5-cent cost-of-living allowance.
b. Includes 7-cent cost-of-living allowance.
c. Includes 10-cent cost-of-living allowance.
d. Maximum rates only. Rate ranges for the skilled trades were increased from 15 to 20 cents during World War II.
Sources. Rates for 1937–55 supplied by UAW. Rates for 1958 computed by applying to 1955 rates the annual improvement factor increases for 1956, 1957, and 1958; the 8-cent increase for skilled trades in 1958; and the 15-cent cost-of-living allowance added to base rates in 1958.

might expect, tends to accentuate the narrowing of differentials within each of the basic groups and reduces slightly the relative gap between the wages of skilled tradesmen and production workers. These minor modifications do not, however, affect any of our conclusions based on the behavior of wage rates alone. Whether broadly or narrowly defined, wage relationships among occupations show the same clear pattern of development within and between groups.

Having identified the major trends in occupational differentials during the period since the late 1930s, we are now in a position to inquire into the effects of unionism. First, we examine the nature of general wage changes in the industry with a view to determining the union's influence, if any, on the type of adjustments granted. Second, we explore, with the same objective in mind, the conditions under which the wage levels of the skilled trades have risen relative to the wage levels of virtually all other occupations in the industry.

The Pattern of General Wage Adjustments

General wage increases negotiated in the automobile industry have progressively narrowed the occupational wage structure. Up to 1955, all such increases took the form of across-the-board, cents-per-hour wage adjustments which had the effect only of maintaining absolute differentials in rates between occupations. This is clearly illustrated in Table 15 which shows the pattern of general wage improvements negotiated at General Motors since 1940.[10] Since wages more than

10. The first multiplant wage adjustment negotiated at GM was on August 5, 1939, after a successful tool-and-die-workers' strike. The agreement did not result in a general wage change, though it did provide for the upward revision and formalization of pay scales for tool and die makers and for certain maintenance classifications. GM workers were granted a 5-cent wage increase in November 1936 and a similar increase in February 1937, but these were not determined through collective bargaining. ["General Motors Corporation, 1939–1949," Wage Chronology No. 9, Monthly Labor Review (Sept. 1949), pp. 259–60.]

TABLE 15.   General Wage Adjustments at General Motors,
1940–1955

Effective date of GM-UAW agreement	*General wage provision*
April 28, 1941	10 -cent increase
April 28, 1942	4 -cent increase
March 19, 1946	18.5-cent increase
April 24, 1947	11.5-cent increase
May 29, 1948	11 -cent increase (This two-year agreement introduced the wage-escalation provisions which are now a familiar feature of auto and other industry contracts. Of the 11-cent increase, 6 cents was added to base rates and 5 cents was designated a cost-of-living allowance, to be adjusted quarterly in accordance with changes in the BLS Consumer Price Index. The annual improvement factor, payable on May 29, 1949, was set at 3 cents.)
May 29, 1950	4 -cent increase (This five-year agreement raised the improvement factor, payable on each anniversary date through 1954, to 4 cents.)
May 29, 1953	5 -cent increase (This agreement reopened the 1950 contract, raising the improvement factor to 5 cents and incorporating 19 cents of the 24-cent cost-of-living allowance into base rates.)[a]

a. The only significant deviations from the GM pattern occurred in the late 1940s. On May 31, 1948, Chrysler granted a straight 13-cent increase and on Aug. 28, 1950, a 10-cent increase. Ford and other companies followed Chrysler's lead in 1948; but in late 1950, as inflationary pressures brought sizable cost-of-living increases to GM workers, the industry generally adopted the wage-escalation provisions of the GM contract.

doubled during this period (1940–55), the preservation of absolute differentials through cents-per-hour wage increases obviously meant a contraction of relative differentials in excess of 50 per cent.

The year 1955 marks, however, the transition to a new type of formula for general wage adjustments in the industry. In the agreements of that year, the annual improvement factor was changed to a percentage basis with a fixed cents-per-hour minimum. As a result, annual wage adjustments during the last six or seven years have been governed by the provision that "each employee . . . shall receive an annual improvement factor increase of two and one half (2½) per cent of his straight-time hourly wage rate . . . or six (6) cents per hour, whichever is the greater."[11] The effect of this new formula on occupational differentials was not very great initially for, as the rate levels in Table 14 indicate, only workers in a few of the higher-paid occupations qualified for increases above the minimum.[12] With rising wage levels, however, the number of workers eligible for adjustments above the 6-cent minimum has increased, and this trend will continue as long as the formula is maintained in its present form.

The fact that the skilled trades have not suffered a deterioration of their relative wage position during this period of flat-rate general increases has been due mainly to the negotiation of a series of special cents-per-hour wage adjustments which, while contributing to compression within the skilled trades wage structure itself, have more than preserved the percentage rate differential between tradesmen and production workers. These special wage increases for the skilled trades are discussed in a later section of this chapter. For the moment our concern is with the general wage adjustments outlined above and the extent of the union's influence upon the character of these

11. *Agreement between General Motors Corporation and the UAW-CIO* (June 12, 1955), p. 66.
12. Indeed, the Bureau of Labor Statistics estimated that the average increase under the formula in its first year of application approximated 6.1 cents; and even the union, which could be expected to err on the high side, reported an average increase of only 6.2 cents: "Ford Motor Company," Wage Chronology No. 14, *Monthly Labor Review* (Oct. 1955), p. 1152; UAW press release (June 6, 1955).

adjustments. The central question is whether, in the absence of unionism, the same pattern of wage change would have occurred.

Although there is probably some truth in the observation that unions during the 1940s and early 1950s were too preoccupied with urgent problems of wage level to give much, if any, attention to questions of wage structure, negotiations between the auto companies and the UAW indicate that, in this industry at least, issues of structure were by no means neglected. On the contrary, union policy quite consciously favored a reduction in relative differentials through flat-rate increases, and there is evidence that at least some of these increases were accepted only with reluctance by employers. During the early years, union negotiators repeatedly stressed their concern for the low-paid worker and the need to raise the lower end of the wage scale. Their desire was largely to accord this worker a decent standard of living, though frequently the case was buttressed by the claim that such action would provide a firmer base for the wage structure as a whole. Undoubtedly this sentiment was more strongly felt, and the objective more vigorously pursued, by some union leaders than by others.[13] Yet all shared an essentially common viewpoint, and certainly no union leader urged a wage policy that would promote the expansion of absolute differentials between the various skill classes. Management, on the other hand, although it avoided any open break with the union over the form of wage increase, clearly favored a wage-adjustment policy that would foster a somewhat wider wage structure.

13. In early 1947, GM Vice-President Harry Anderson recalled how, in the 1937 negotiations, two of the five union representatives "had argued that all people working for GM should be paid the same rate of pay whether or not he be a janitor or the most highly skilled tool and die maker": "Collective Bargaining and Labor Agreements," a talk delivered in Cincinnati, Ohio, Feb. 6, 1947. We can be sure that this extreme view was confined to only a small minority of unionists in the early years and was never seriously pursued in any major bargaining session.

The question of occupational differentials was raised indirectly in the first "wage structure" agreement between GM and the UAW in 1940. In June of that year, the parties agreed to a wage equalization fund of $5 million to be used for the elimination of wage inequities in the corporation's plants. In the ensuing local plant negotiations, the corporation apparently sought to channel the funds toward the skilled trades, whereas union officials insisted on bringing up the rates of lower-paid workers. The union reported the issue and its resolution as follows:

> GM attempted, during the plant wage negotiations, to give the skilled workers the majority of the increases in most of the outlying plants, and in some of the bigger metropolitan units. The corporation knew that because of increased industrial activity skilled workers would be in great demand and that they would have to grant these workers increases later on. The corporation attempted to anticipate future wage demands on the part of skilled workers by granting them increases that should have gone to workers throughout the plants in other classifications.
>
> Our union prevented the misuse of the equalization fund by working out a provision whereby the rates which existed within established brackets would not come out of the over-all plant fund. Such adjustments, it was agreed, would be considered merit increases and would be granted in addition to the equalization increases. . . . Almost every plant received more than its original allotment and the total increase, including merit increases, brought the fund close to $7,000,000, which was substantially more than the corporation had agreed upon in the 1940 contract.[14]

However, the union's victory was only a partial one. In the nego-

14. R. J. Thomas, president, "Automobile Unionism (1940–41)," a Report submitted to the 1941 convention of the UAW-CIO, Buffalo, N.Y., (Aug. 4, 1941), pp. 31–32.

tiations the union committee had pressed strongly for a wage increase for the lowest-paid classifications of janitor and sweeper, but without success. As Reuther reported to delegates from the GM locals, the company had adamantly refused to raise the rate for these occupations, and union negotiators had agreed that it would be unwise to force the issue in view of the wage increases already secured for workers in other occupational categories. He promised, however, that janitors and sweepers would receive special consideration in future wage demands.[15]

Concern for raising the rates of the lowest-paid classifications was widespread throughout the union at this time. Numerous resolutions were adopted directing the organization's officers to press for higher wages for such groups. In the June 1941 agreement at Chrysler, minimum job rates (applicable to the lowest-paid occupations) were increased only 5 cents when all other rates were raised 8 cents. This, and similar developments, were protested at the 1941 convention. As a result, special efforts were made during the war years to promote the wage interests of the lower-paid groups. In requests to the War Labor Board in late 1943, the Chrysler Department urged a wage increase for all workers earning less than $1.05 while the GM Department demanded that the minimum wage rate of 89 cents be raised to at least $1.00.[16] The principal justification for this demand, apart from the higher cost of living, was the insufficiency of earnings to ensure the standards of health and efficiency reflected in wartime family budget estimates.[17] At the same time, the Little Steel formula, which limited wartime wage

15. *Minutes of Proceedings, International GM Council, UAW-CIO* (Dec. 7–8, 1940), pp. 3–4.

16. Thomas, "Automobile Unionism, 1943" (Oct. 4, 1943), p. 91; UAW-CIO, "Wage Stabilization and Postwar Security," a partial brief submitted to the National War Labor Board by the General Motors Department (Nov. 1943), pp. 37–38.

17. *UAW-CIO's Reply to General Motors Corporation's Position on Union Demand for Cost-of-Living Adjustment,* in matter of UAW-CIO and GMC, NWLB, Case No. 111–4665–D (Feb. 3, 1944), p. 10.

increases to 15 per cent above the levels prevailing on January 1, 1941, was attacked by union officials because, among other things, it implied the desirability of maintaining relative differentials. Reuther's statement to the WLB in late 1943 summed up the official UAW position: "Any cost of living adjustment which is predicated upon a percentage basis tends to intensify wage differentials and inequities, for it gives the lower paid workers who need the greatest increase, the least increase."[18]

The union's commitment to flat-rate increases as the only fair and proper method of wage adjustment was continued into the postwar period. In its spectacular demand on GM in 1945, the union's proposal was publicized as a 30 per cent wage increase (with no change in prices). However, at the September conference of GM locals, Reuther argued that a percentage increase was unwise and recommended that the union seek instead a straight cents-per-hour adjustment.[19] In the negotiations, this objective was clearly spelled out to management. When, on November 16, GM offered a wage increase of 10 per cent, Reuther asked if the company would be willing to grant the increase on a flat cents-per-hour basis. GM's chief negotiator replied that an increase of this sort would narrow skill differentials, but the union disagreed: "Personally, our feeling in the matter is that a percentage treatment of wage classifications tends to destroy proper relationship much more quickly than does a flat increase, and certainly from any basis of equity tends to give the fellow that needs the least increase the most, and the fellow that needs the most increase the least, if you are talking about purchasing power. . . . We want a penny increase; the GM Conference voted unanimously; they realize that raising the base rate is an important factor in maintaining high standards in their trades and gets higher wages in general." This was not management's position, however, and it registered its

18. UAW-CIO, "Wage Stabilization and Postwar Security," p. 4.

19. *Proceedings, International GM Conference, UAW-CIO* (Sept. 14–15, 1945), pp. 31–32.

disapproval in a simple and straightforward dissent—"You see, that isn't our philosophy."[20]

In preparation for the 1947 negotiations, the two leading factions in the union declared themselves in favor of cents-per-hour wage increases and against percentage increases. In late 1946, Secretary-Treasurer George F. Addes, Reuther's chief opponent on the Executive Board, submitted a list of policy proposals to the International Policy Committee, one of which stated that "all applications of wage increases shall be in dollars and cents and not in percentages."[21] A few months later, Reuther, now president of the union, endorsed the same policy of flat-rate increases as a matter of equity and simple justice.[22] On this point at least, the factions were agreed.

The pattern increase in 1947 was 11.5 cents, reached first at GM on April 24. In the following year, after GM and Chrysler had settled for 11 cents and 13 cents respectively, Ford abandoned its "hold-the-line" policy on wages and offered the union a 14-cent increase on rates of $1.50 or more and an 11-cent increase on rates below $1.50. In a memorandum to the union negotiating committee, the company's spokesman noted that "this form of increase will erase many of the inequities in our present wage structure of which we are aware and to which you have already called our attention."[23] In reply, the union asked for a 14-cent general increase and the establishment of a 2-cent equalization fund to be used to bring skilled trades rates into line with "prevailing levels" and to correct certain other rate inequities.[24] Apparently both parties recognized the

20. *Proceedings, GM-UAW Negotiations* (Nov. 16, 1945), pp. 642–43.

21. Proposals for the Implementation of the UAW-CIO Wage Equalization Policy to be Submitted to the International Policy Committee by Secretary-Treasurer George F. Addes, Oct. 7, 1946.

22. *Proceedings, National Wage Conference* (UAW-CIO, 1947), p. 137.

23. Memorandum from John S. Bugas, vice-president in charge of industrial relations, Ford Motor Company to Ford UAW-CIO National Negotiating Committee, June 21, 1948.

24. UAW-CIO press release, June 25, 1948.

need for some "stretching" of the occupational structure. However, the company's proposal of a bracket increase would have increased the absolute spread in production rates, whereas the union's demand sought instead a special wage concession for the skilled trades which could be sold to the membership as something "extra"—i.e. something not gained at the expense of other (larger) groups. The agreement subsequently reached followed the Chrysler pattern of 13 cents across the board.

In the first postwar recession year of 1949, bargaining shifted from the wage front to pensions. The first pension plan was concluded at Ford on September 28 and guaranteed $100 a month (inclusive of federal social security payments) to workers at age 65 with 30 years' service. This guarantee of a flat-rate sum clearly favored the lower-paid worker. It was also in line with union policy. As Reuther informed the delegates from GM locals, the issue of relating benefits to wage levels had been introduced in the Ford negotiations (presumably by management), but the idea of graduated benefits had been rejected— a stand that Reuther himself considered sound.[25]

More recently the UAW has adopted a less positive attitude on the issue of absolute vs. percentage wage increases, though it was not until 1955 that this change in attitude was to be reflected in auto contracts. However, before considering this reorientation in wage policy and the reasons behind it, it is worth noting briefly an exchange of views on the wage issue at Studebaker in the fall of 1950 which illustrates the divergent positions of the parties and the kinds of institutional pressures to which union leaders respond in a vigorously democratic union.

The 1950 negotiations at Studebaker concerned, among other things, revision of the company's incentive plan for nonproduction workers. Under the old plan, which had been in effect for two and a half years, the incentive bonus had

25. *Proceedings, National GM Conference, UAW-CIO* (Nov. 10–11, 1949), p. 59.

amounted to 15 per cent of hourly base rates. When management indicated that it intended to continue the 15 per cent bonus in the revised plan, the union, surprisingly enough, asked that the formula be changed so as to channel a greater part of the bonus to workers in the lower-paying jobs. Management quite naturally questioned the wisdom of this proposal and pointed to the dangers involved in taking money away from the higher-paid groups. The union negotiators explained, however, that in seeking abandonment of the percentage bonus they were simply "trying to get that lower guy up a bit," that they could not expect to please everyone but only the majority, and that the lower-rated workers on the line (the bulk of the work force) were pressing hardest on the union for effective wage action. Nevertheless, the union committee, impressed perhaps by the company's arguments, finally sought management's approval for submission of the two plans—a 15 per cent bonus or a flat dollar bonus—to a vote of the membership.[26]

Since the union's proposed bonus formula raised certain "payroll" questions, the company was reluctant to commit itself immediately but promised to prepare a position for the following afternoon. At the next day's session, management explained that the only practical way of introducing the cents-per-hour (incentive) formula was on a quarterly basis, with current payments geared to hours worked in the previous quarter. It agreed to the union's request to place the matter before the membership, but reminded negotiators that the plan, in management's view, showed poor judgment. Data were presented to show that while the new formula would raise the earnings of the lowest-paid worker by about 3 cents, it would cost the tool maker and other skilled craftsmen more than a nickel.

After a short recess to consider the company's plan, the union committee informed management that it had decided to stay with the 15 per cent incentive after all. Perhaps the quarterly

26. *Minutes of Meeting between Studebaker Corporation and Local 5, UAW-CIO,* (Sept. 6, 1950), pp. 7–18.

feature acted as a deterrent. Or possibly the committee had re-assessed the risks involved in its proposal to cut the earnings of skilled and other higher-bracket workers. Relinquishment of the cents-per-hour formula did not mean, however, that the interests of lower-paid workers were not to be advanced in the settlement. On the contrary, the parties had already discussed a flat wage increase that would automatically narrow the structure of occu-pational rates and earnings. Moreover, there had also been a discussion of individual rate (inequity) adjustments in which the company's representative, although strongly opposed to a union request for higher rates at the bottom of the wage scale, had nevertheless agreed to so recommend if all other wage mat-ters could be settled. This discussion incidentally revealed that Studebaker's lowest rates in South Bend were already far above Detroit levels and its skill differentials much more compressed than elsewhere in the industry—a revelation that certainly bears witness to the success of earlier union efforts to improve the wage lot of lower-paid workers.[27]

It is thus clear from the record that the UAW, at least in the period up to the early 1950s, was embarked on a program de-signed to raise the relative wage standards of workers at the lower end of the industry's wage scale. It was, moreover, a program that had been consciously adopted by the leadership. Since then, UAW wage policy has undergone some modifica-tion, partly because of increasing pressures from the skilled trades and partly as a result of management initiative in pro-posing a new formula for annual wage adjustments. The skilled trades problem is dealt with in the next section of this chapter, but here we may note that beginning in 1951 successive annual skilled trades conferences were to demand—each year with greater impatience and resentment—that the UAW abolish its policy of flat-rate increases and negotiate on a percentage basis. In the pursuit of this objective, they no doubt found an ally in

27. *Minutes of Meeting between Studebaker Corporation and Local 5, UAW-CIO* (Sept. 7, 1950), pp. 23–24.

management. Ford officials were probably the most outspoken in their support of percentage adjustments.[28] Nevertheless, the view was widely shared; representatives of other companies have stated emphatically that they would have granted fewer cents-per-hour increases in the postwar period but for the steadfast opposition of the union to any other form of increase.

It is significant that the changeover in the annual improvement factor in 1955 from a cents-per-hour to a percentage basis was a management innovation. In its approach to negotiations in that year, the union was apparently seeking no more than an upgrading of the cents-per-hour amount of the formula to take account of higher wage levels. Indeed, preliminary conferences had already been held with General Motors and Ford when Reuther explained to convention delegates that the union's objective was a cost-of-living escalator that would protect the buying power of the cents-per-hour amount of the factor against inflation.[29] When GM seized the initiative, however, and offered the union (as part of its "income security" proposal) an improvement factor increase of 2.5 per cent with a 6-cent minimum, the stage was set for the transition to a new type of annual wage-adjustment formula.

Although the improvement factor finally adopted in the 1955 agreements was precisely what GM had offered the union in its initial proposal, it does not follow that management's wage preferences had been fully realized. The 6-cent minimum, to be sure, had its origin in a company proposal, but it was a con-

28. Thus, in a speech at the Industrial Relations Center at Princeton University on Sept. 16, 1953, John Bugas declared that when Ford considered the pros and cons of the 5-year contract in 1950, it foresaw—not without misgivings—that successive applications of the 4-cent improvement factor would narrow skill differentials. In emphasizing the company's apprehension over this development, Bugas told his audience that Ford had always argued for per cent increases that would maintain proper differentials: Notes, Industrial Relations Library, Ford Motor Company.

29. *Report of the President, Walter P. Reuther, to the 15th Constitutional Convention, UAW-CIO* (March 27–April 1, 1955), p. 23. See also *UAW Administrative Letter, 6,* No. 20 (Dec. 2, 1954).

cession made necessary by the presence of the union. In 1955, GM and Ford were both anxious to establish a method of wage adjustment that would maintain relative differentials. However, they were forced to recognize that the 5-cent improvement factor in the old (expiring) agreement set the lowest acceptable wage increase for any new settlement with the union. Indeed, Ford had sought in each of its two proposals to establish the minimum at this level, and GM negotiators later claimed that they too had intended to offer a 5-cent minimum and had changed to 6 cents only after remarks by UAW officials had convinced them that a 5-cent increase would be rejected.[30] The improvement factor formula of 1955 was therefore a compromise: the percentage component reflected management's preference, but the 6-cent minimum, which has limited the expansion of absolute differentials in recent years, was largely an effect of unionism.

To summarize this part of the analysis, it appears that wage differentials among production jobs—and, for that matter, among skilled occupations—have been narrowed as a direct result of union policy. This conclusion follows from the fact that the UAW has been responsible for the industry's exclusive reliance on cents-per-hour changes as the method of general wage adjustment up to 1955 and for the high cents-per-hour minimum in the improvement factor formula of recent years. Unfortunately it is not possible to measure the precise degree of compression attributable to the union factor alone, for other broad forces operating throughout the economy were modifying the structure of differentials in the same direction. The pervasive influence of these forces has been shown in other studies[31] and is demonstrated perhaps in the decline of auto

30. *Minutes, GM-UAW Negotiations* (June 9, 1955), p. 507. In this connection, it is well to remember that GM's offer of May 17 was intended to divert the union from its drive for a guaranteed annual wage or employment plan. This objective explains the company's interest in proposing *acceptable* terms of settlement.

31. See Harry Ober, "Occupational Wage Differentials, 1907–1947,"

plant differentials during the period prior to union entry. Whatever the narrowing effect of these nonunion forces, however, the industry's occupational wage structure would clearly have undergone less compression in recent decades in the absence of unionism.

The UAW policy on general wage changes was designed deliberately to raise the living standards of low-paid workers. To union leaders imbued with the equalitarian philosophy of industrial unionism, this was a matter of simple justice. It happened also to be consistent with the political realities confronting the UAW leadership, for such a policy catered to the interests of numerically preponderant groups in the membership—surely an important consideration in an organization characterized by a high degree of "grass roots" democracy, bitter factionalism, and considerable political instability.[32] At least through the 1940s, therefore, the "political factor" was an important influence in the formulation of union policy. The critical task of leadership was above all to maintain majority support, and policies were perforce subordinated to this objective. Under the circumstances it is not surprising that the more skilled and highly-paid production workers should have suffered a significant deterioration in relative wage position. These workers who, as union and management officials alike admit, have been "penalized" during the last two decades, have lacked strategic strength within the union and hence the wherewithal to express their dissatisfactions effectively. In this respect their position differs radically from that of the skilled craftsmen who, despite minority status, have become an increasingly influential force within the union organization.

Monthly Labor Review (Aug. 1948), pp. 127–34; H. M. Douty, "Union Impact on Wage Structures," *Proceedings of the Industrial Relations Research Association* (Dec. 28–30, 1953), pp. 61–76.

32. For an excellent analysis of the differences between the UAW and other labor organizations, such as the Steel Workers, see Philip Taft, *The Structure and Government of Labor Unions* (Cambridge, Harvard, 1954), pp. 213–26.

The Skilled Tradesman–Production Worker Differential

The issue of the impact of unionism upon the differential between skilled craftsmen and production workers is a complicated one, for while union policy, especially in the early years, has been oriented toward the wage interests of lower-paid workers, the union has had to accommodate increasingly to pressures from the skilled trades for more effective representation of their special interests. As a result, the UAW "program" —to use the term loosely—has consisted simply of a series of moves designed to meet two distinct sets of interests (skilled craftsmen's and production workers') which often appear in conflict. In short, there has been no simple, clear-cut, consistent policy, but instead a highly pragmatic and flexible approach—a set of responses governed by the logic of organizational requirements. This becomes clear when one examines what may be called "the skilled trades problem" of the UAW.

At the outset it is well to recognize that the increasing accommodation to skilled trades interests on the part of UAW leaders stems not only from growing dissatisfaction and threats of secession, but also from an awareness of the dramatic changes being wrought in the mass-production industries and of the challenges these changes pose for industrial unionism. Within the ranks of organized labor, the UAW has been among the first to realize that the preservation of industrial-union power and influence depends importantly on the union's ability to adapt its structure and functions to the shifting occupational composition and changing needs of the factory work force.[33] Especially significant is the fact that automation and related technological change is steadily eroding the traditional base of union power. Office, technical, and engineering occupations are expanding largely at the expense of production and maintenance jobs,

33. See, in addition to Reuther's convention reports, the remarks by James Stern, assistant to UAW Vice-president Leonard Woodcock, in "Automatic and Major Technological Change" (Industrial Union Dept., AFL-CIO, April 22, 1958), pp. 10–15.

particularly the former. The need to organize these rapidly expanding groups—or else accept a dwindling influence in the industry—has lent a special urgency to the union's efforts to satisfy the skilled trades; for on the union's ability to serve these interests well rests much of its claim as the appropriate agency to represent the particular needs of office and technical personnel. This consideration, in conjunction with the fact that skilled tradesmen constitute a rising proportion of UAW membership and have access to alternative means of representation in the form of craft unions, has placed these trades in a very strong position. It is within this context that the union's handling of the "skilled trades problem" is to be understood.

The Skilled Trades Problem. Although the skilled trades problem within the UAW reached critical proportions only in the mid-1950s, the problem itself is of long standing and dates from the early years of the union. Already in the late 1930s skilled groups within the membership were agitating for an improvement in auto company rates to the higher levels prevailing in the building and mechanical trades;[34] and in early 1941 the UAW's GM Council, in recognition of the special problems facing tool-and-die and maintenance workers, was urging the International Union to grant skilled groups greater representation rights as a means of contributing to better understanding and improved cooperation within the union.[35] The 1941 convention witnessed a concerted effort by the skilled trades to air their grievances and gain union support for a program of improvement. In a resolution submitted to convention delegates, the Greater Detroit Maintenance Workers Council documented the specific complaints: that the wages of maintenance workers in the UAW were not commensurate with the skill and responsibility their jobs demanded; that UAW wages were below the levels of compensation gained by other labor organizations for similar work; that companies were undermining the position of craftsmen by the employment of

34. UAW press release, June 29 and July 9, 1939.
35. *Minutes, International GM Council, UAW-CIO,* Feb. 11–12, 1941.

"maintenance helpers" on skilled jobs; and that supplementary contracts for the skilled trades were necessary in all plants to meet these special needs and problems.[36] The Council requested that the International Executive Board establish forthwith a joint Maintenance and Tool and Die Committee for the purpose of drawing up an appropriate supplementary contract which would be served immediately on the large automobile companies.

Although sympathetic to the grievances of the trades and their desire for redress, President R. J. Thomas and other UAW officials opposed the idea of a supplementary agreement on the grounds that it would tend to fragment the industrial union structure. They warned convention delegates that supplementary agreements were a "divisive influence" that would encourage other groups to seek similar treatment. The Maintenance Council insisted, however, that there was no other solution. First-class maintenance journeymen were earning less on the average than skilled production workers. Moreover, some of the workers classified as "helpers" had been in that category for years and were really first-rate mechanics employed at laborers' wages. These were serious problems, yet Council members had found it difficult, if not impossible, to secure relief under prevailing bargaining arrangements. "In some cases, the regional directors and their organizing staff contended it was impossible to negotiate higher wages for one group of workers and the only negotiations that were practical at the present time under an industrial union were blanket increases in pay."[37] It was felt, therefore, that a supplementary contract, negotiated preferably at the beginning of the peak production period for skilled workers, was the only remedy. The Council warned that if the union ruled otherwise and neglected these problems, it was courting disunity and possible defections to the AFL crafts.

The resolution finally adopted by the convention instructed

36. *Proceedings, Sixth Annual Convention, UAW-CIO* (Aug. 4, 1941), pp. 529–30.

37. Ibid., p. 532.

the International Executive Board to set up a joint Maintenance and Tool and Die Contract Committee whose function was to draw up a set of proposals containing (1) wage standards for UAW maintenance workers that compared favorably with those established by other labor organizations (i.e. the AFL building trades unions); (2) wage standards for tool-and-die makers in captive shops (i.e. shops of the major auto companies) that equaled the levels prevailing in job shops (estimated to be 30 to 40 cents higher); and (3) the steps necessary for eliminating all maintenance helper classifications and establishing apprenticeship programs. Negotiations on these proposals were to begin immediately with the Big Three and agreements were to carry the same expiration date as the present contracts with the respective employers. In this way the union would seek to meet the skilled trades complaints, but through the usual channels.[38]

Union difficulties with the skilled trades were intensified as the war progressed. With critical shortages of skilled help developing, it was inevitable that management would upgrade production workers into skilled trades departments to meet emergency needs, and journeymen feared that this influx of new workers would dilute and oversupply the trades. Their fears were eased, however, when the union signed agreements with the major companies designed to regulate the flow of upgraders into tool-and-die departments. These agreements typically provided that upgraders and trainees, after a brief probationary period, would be paid the minimum rate of the skilled classification to which they were transferred. Production workers with the necessary experience and qualifications were invited to file applications for transfer, and as vacancies arose for which no journeymen were available, qualified applicants

38. It is interesting to note that shortly thereafter this same convention unanimously approved another resolution to raise the wages of nonproduction workers at the other end of the wage scale (i.e. janitors, sweepers, material handlers, et al.) to "a standard compatible with that now paid production workers." (Ibid., p. 576.)

from production departments would be brought in. Upgraded employees would retain and accumulate seniority in their own production groups and would be given seniority status in the upgraded group for purposes of layoff and rehire in line with their date of entry into the group. When the supply of upgraders was exhausted, trainees (with no experience) could be transferred or hired into the skilled department. To guard against automatic movement into journeyman status, however, trainees and upgraders were to be placed in classifications so identified. To prevent their displacing journeymen, it was provided that before the hours of regular journeymen could be reduced, upgraders and trainees would be moved to other units in the plant.

While the upgrader-trainee agreements allayed for the time being the journeymen's fears that their trades would be flooded as a result of the emergency, the problem of wage "inequities" remained. A wage differential between the job shops doing contract work for the auto companies and the captive shops belonging to the companies was, of course, traditional in the industry. It was justified on the grounds that job shops provided less steady employment and made greater demands on skill. This explanation had never satisfied the skilled trades themselves, and it was to prove even less acceptable in the war years. In early 1942, skilled tradesmen were already complaining that, because of the differential of 20 to 30 cents, upgraders and learners in job shops were earning more than experienced tool-and-die makers in the captive shops.[39] To make matters worse, job shops were also bidding up journeymen's rates, thereby increasing the size of the differential. This was possible in spite of the wage stabilization program for, unlike the captive shops, the job shops had no formal rate maximums and hence no predetermined rate ceilings. At the same time, the auto companies were reluctant to raise their own skilled rates since this would tend to distort the wage structure and create pressures for compensatory increases in a large number of other

39. UAW press release, Feb. 16, 1942.

classifications. When the union requested increases for skilled workers in the captive shops, therefore, employers informed the War Labor Board that they would not grant any wage adjustment to the skilled trades unless ordered to do so by the Board.[40] The Board recognized the dilemma facing the companies, but found that stabilization of the tool-and-die wage structure was urgently necessary. It fixed maximum wage rates for job-shop employees and issued directives for wage adjustments in the captive shops. These directives, handed down in September-October 1942, granted a 4-cent general wage increase to all auto company employees and additional increases of 6 cents per hour to skilled tool-and-die makers and certain maintenance occupations, such as electrician and machine repairman. In addition, a fund of 1.5 cents an hour was provided for distribution among other maintenance occupations.[41] To forestall any pressures for additional adjustments arising out of these special increases, the Board announced that its action "will be understood to have no effect upon the rates of the wages paid to employees in other departments of the companies." It also announced that these increases restored the traditional wage differential between the job shops and captive shops.[42]

The failure to include other skilled maintenance classifications in the special increase was denounced, however, by the UAW. On November 5, 1942, the union informed GM and Chrysler managements that it was not prepared to negotiate on the 1.5-cent fund since it was protesting the Board's decision.[43] When this protest was denied, GM and the UAW

40. UAW press release, Sept. 21, 1942.

41. "General Motors Corporation, 1939–1949," Wage Chronology No. 9, *Monthly Labor Review* (Sept. 1949).

42. Quoted in John W. Riegel, "Wage Stabilization and Adjustment Policies of the National War Labor Board," *Personnel Management in Wartime Industries,* Bulletin No. 14 (Bureau of Industrial Relations, Univ. of Michigan Press, 1943), pp. 126–27.

43. UAW press release, Nov. 5, 1942.

reached an agreement on the fund whereby 5,000 tool-, die- and pattern-makers and 3,500 maintenance workers were granted additional increases of 5 cents and 6 cents respectively.[44] The maintenance trades refused, however, to accept the Board's decision as final. They continued to press for wage adjustments. In August 1944 the union reported that representatives of more than 50,000 maintenance workers would meet with the Director of the Office of Economic Stabilization and members of the War Labor Board to discuss the issue.[45] On December 1, it was further announced that Reuther was seeking, on behalf of 16,-000 maintenance workers in GM plants, an increase of 10 to 11 cents to restore the traditional rate relationship destroyed by the WLB's 1942 decision granting 15 cents to tool-and-die makers and only 4 cents to the majority of maintenance workers. These efforts eventually bore fruit. On April 17, 1945, by order of the Board, maintenance workers were granted a 5-cent increase, retroactive to October 6, 1944. It was not until the 1947 negotiations, however, that the remaining 5 cents was won by maintenance workers, and the "historic differential" between maintenance and toolroom trades restored.

These special wartime adjustments for skilled craftsmen provided only temporary relief. At the war's end there were two critical issues raised by journeymen in the plants of the auto companies. The first of these was the captive shop-job shop differential already referred to—an issue that was to plague the UAW throughout the 1940s and 1950s. The second was the upgrader-trainee program. With the war ended, the skilled trades were pressing hard for a dismantling of the program, an end to the use of helpers in maintenance departments, and the establishment of apprenticeship programs. One result of these pressures, aimed at protecting and improving the status of the skilled worker, was a flare-up of resentment among production workers. Many of the latter felt that the International

44. UAW press release, Jan. 12, 1943.
45. UAW press release, Aug. 29, 1944.

Union was bowing too readily to skilled trades demands. In resolutions submitted by a number of local unions to the 1947 convention, it was claimed that international policy discriminated against upgraders who had acquired the skill and ability to work in the skilled trades, that upgraders were not represented in the UAW's Skilled Trades Department which was responsible for recommending policies affecting the trades, and that the concept underlying the international's policy smacked more of craft than industrial unionism and could only foster disunity in the organization.

The question of what to do about upgraders and trainees was to trouble the International Union for some time. In his report to the 1947 convention, the Director of the Skilled Trades Department noted the difficulties and frustrations encountered by the leadership in its attempts to find a solution that would satisfy both skilled journeymen and upgraders.[46] With the issue so unsettled and apparently threatening a split in the union, the convention directed the International Executive Board to establish a joint committee of five journeymen and five upgraders to review the situation and make recommendations to the Board. The committee's recommendations, assigned to the Skilled Trades Department for implementation in the spring of 1948, sought in essence to close off the upgrader route to the skilled trades. Present upgraders who, in the joint opinion of management and the union, had the necessary qualifications would be given journeyman status, either immediately or after a shortened apprenticeship program; but all future skill needs would be met through expanded apprenticeship programs. According to the Skilled Trades Department, reporting a year later, "In several plants where this policy has been negotiated and accepted, the friction and differences between the various groups heretofore in existence have, in most cases, been eliminated or greatly alleviated. . . . Today many of the local union officers realize that the answer to the skilled trades problems is

46. *Report of the President, Walter P. Reuther, to the 11th Convention, UAW-CIO*, Part 2 (Nov. 9, 1947), p. 19.

not upgrading, but establishing apprenticeship training standards which assure the apprentice of proper training."[47]

To be successful, it was not enough that the new policy satisfy divergent interests within the union; it had also to prove acceptable to employers, and it was only to be expected that the latter would insist on certain guarantees, especially against artificial scarcities. The GM negotiations illustrate how management approached both the issue and the union's proposed solution at the bargaining table.

In 1948, management at GM was sympathetic to the journeymen's desire for protection against unnecessary skill dilution and summarized its own approach to skill requirements as follows: (1) all-around journeymen, if available, should be hired first; (2) replacement and expansion needs should be met, where possible, through apprenticeship training; (3) requirements unmet by (1) and (2) should be filled through upgrading. It was the company's view that any practical program should take account of the equities of present journeymen and upgraders and also of the future needs of business. The union's proposal, however, made no provision for any future upgrading arrangements, and since management anticipated substantial model changes, it was apprehensive lest a shortage of skills should impose delays in the preproduction stages. Accordingly, while GM was willing to expand its apprenticeship programs, it was unwilling to eliminate the upgrader agreement. It could see no reason to delay work, say, on a major tooling program because of a skill shortage when it was prepared to use some of its own production employees, at higher rates, for essentially single-purpose machine operations. In addition, management noted that 18 per cent of GM's skilled employees were already 55 years of age or over, which meant that replacement alone was a large problem.[48] It reminded union negotiators that, while the upgrader-trainee program

47. *Report of the President, Walter P. Reuther, to the 12th Convention, UAW-CIO* (July 10, 1949), p. 94.
48. *Proceedings, GM-UAW Negotiations* (March 18, 1948), pp. 110–14.

had been formalized by agreement in 1941 to meet the serious wartime shortage of skills, this method of training predated the union's entry into the industry and was the traditional channel to journeyman status. Management could see no reason why an industrial union should seek to eliminate this avenue to the skilled trades. In its opinion, the union's position could only be characterized as "a craft union bellyache in an industrial union."

GM negotiators were also critical of the feature in the union's proposal providing for joint decision on the question as to which upgraders met the necessary trade qualifications. This was a management responsibility, guaranteed in Paragraph 9 of the contract (covering the right to hire), and the company was unwilling to qualify its right in this respect. It rejected the union's claim that the provision was intended only to protect workers against unfair treatment and favoritism, since other union actions—particularly the refusal to agree to increases in the apprentice-journeyman ratio in cases of established need—suggested that the real motive was control over the supply of skilled help. Union spokesmen did not dispute the point. Instead they maintained that if the trades were now refused fair treatment, journeymen would surely refuse to cooperate in the training of others during any future emergencies in order to protect themselves against flooding of the market. The union admitted that most of the present skilled tradesmen had achieved journeyman status through on-the-job training, but it added that the men themselves now recognized that this route led to overcrowding and intermittent employment. As the director of the GM Department informed management negotiators: "What we do here, it seems to me, has to have within it implicit recognition that we are guarding against an oversupply."[49]

The outcome of these negotiations was a compromise. The agreement permitted the union to claim that both parties were committed in principle to the elimination of upgraders and

49. *Proceedings, GM-UAW Negotiations* (May 19, 1948), p. 15.

trainees as a long-term proposition; but in fact GM had retained its freedom to meet skilled needs flexibly at the local level—at least for the time being.

In the 1950 negotiations, the union continued to press for a solution to skilled trades problems—i.e. higher rates in the captive shops and a more effective measure of control over the supply of skilled workers. It was successful only on the wage issue. Skilled maintenance and tool-and-die workers received an extra 5-cent increase and pattern makers an extra 17-cent increase. GM refused, however, to be further restricted in meeting its skilled trades requirements. Indeed, it felt that the union had already gone too far in limiting the supply of skilled help. In a memorandum of May 4, it reviewed the nature of its current manpower deficiencies and reminded the union that efforts to increase the number of apprentices (in line with probable replacement needs) had been frustrated at both the national and local levels. In a second communication on May 10, the company presented figures to show that without the upgrader program, skill requirements would be "woefully unfulfilled." It insisted, therefore, that the 1948 agreement be continued with only minor modifications.

The question of maintenance helpers was also made an issue in the 1950 negotiations. The union based its case for the elimination of such helpers at GM on the following arguments: (1) helpers are performing skilled maintenance work at rates 10 cents below the minimum journeyman rate; (2) there is currently no limit on the period of time for which management can employ a worker as helper at this low rate; and (3) the employment of helpers is unnecessary since the present skilled trades section of the contract permits management to engage an unlimited number of maintenance mechanics in on-the-job training. To ease the transition, the union indicated its willingness to allow management discretion in granting journeyman status to all helpers who merited it. Management, however, refused to go along, partly because the union's proposal would simply compel the company to pay journeymen's rates on the type of work performed by helpers, and partly because its present practices were in full accord with the September 1945 Memorandum of Understanding which committed the corporation to abolish helpers in the apprenticeable trades only.

The upshot of these discussions was a written agreement which clarified the status of helpers along the lines indicated by management. Where apprenticeship plans were instituted and were deemed to meet plant requirements, helper classifications would be eliminated—with the proviso, however, that helpers might still be used as necessary during periods of "model change and plant rearrangements." Helpers who had already acquired, or could through additional training acquire, the necessary skills and ability, were eligible for reclassification as journeymen. Finally, present helpers who did not undertake additional training had their status protected under the agreement.[50] It was clear from these provisions that GM, while recognizing the desirability of apprenticeship training where feasible, had no intention of accepting undue restrictions on its freedom in the manpower area.

Despite the failure of the UAW to secure strict adherence to apprenticeship training as the sole source of skilled help in auto plants, the Skilled Trades Department was able to report in 1951 that the International Executive Board's policy had been "the means of alleviating and eliminating the friction and differences which caused much trouble between the skilled trades journeymen and upgraders."[51] This partial solution of the upgrader problem was no sooner realized, however, than the outbreak of the Korean war reintroduced the problem of skill shortages and the need for some arrangement whereby production workers could move into the skilled trades. With compa-

50. *Agreement between General Motors Corporation and UAW-CIO,* May 29, 1950, Appendix B.

51. *Report of the President, Walter P. Reuther, to the 13th Convention, UAW-CIO* (April 1, 1951), p. 202.

nies demanding another upgrading program, the International Union, mindful of the difficulties encountered under its earlier policy, moved promptly to formulate a plan which would limit upgrading strictly to the period of the emergency. This plan was incorporated into the union's proposed Changeover Agreement and circulated to all local unions.

The Changeover Agreement stipulated that where skilled workers were not available, production workers could be transferred to the skilled trades departments for the period of the emergency, provided certain conditions were met. These conditions called for the establishment of an approved apprenticeship program and for the definition of a journeyman as any person who holds a UAW-CIO journeyman classification, has served a bona fide apprenticeship, or has had ten years of practical experience. Workers in production departments with adaptable skills were to be given an opportunity to transfer to work in the skilled classifications before the hiring of new nonjourneymen employees for such work. These changeover employees were to be used only on basic machines in tool-and-die and machine repair departments and only to assist journeymen in maintenance departments. They were to be compensated at not less than the minimum rate of the skilled classification to which they were assigned, and they were not to acquire seniority within skilled departments, but only within the changeover group and within their former production group. As further protection to journeymen, the agreement provided that before the regular hours of skilled workers were reduced (in the event of a reduction in force), changeover employees and other nonjourneymen workers (such as bench hands who had not served an apprenticeship) would be transferred back to their former classifications or laid off. Changeover employees were to be clearly designated as such and were required to sign a waiver indicating consent to all terms of the agreement. The final provision read as follows: "This agreement shall terminate upon conclusion of the national emergency and/or upon violation of any term hereof by the company or upon refusal of the company to hire available UAW-CIO journeymen at the prevailing rate, while changeover employees are being used."[52]

The Changeover Agreement was clearly designed to pacify the skilled trades by protecting them in advance against any permanent increase in the supply of journeymen. It came at a time when the International Union, despite extra wage increases and other gains, was being widely criticized for its neglect of skilled trades interests. This criticism found expression in mounting threats of secession and occasional defections to other unions. Indicative of both the growing unrest and the rising influence of the trades within the union was the convening of the first International Skilled Trades Conference in March 1951, just a few weeks before the UAW unveiled its new upgrader program. The purpose of the conference, authorized reluctantly at the request of the skilled workers, was "a complete airing of the problems confronting these workers within [the] International Union."[53] The resolutions adopted at the conference for submission to the UAW convention (scheduled for the following month) bear witness to the widespread resentment felt by skilled workers toward the "industrial union" policies of the UAW. The more important resolutions were the following:

1. When overtime hours are required in any plant, journeymen shall be given the opportunity to work first and, if they refuse, upgraders or changeover employees shall be allowed to work. (The alleged purposes of this resolution were to prevent management from obtaining cheaper labor for work on overtime days and to avoid another split within the union.)
2. All future wage increases shall be negotiated on a per-

52. *UAW-CIO Administrative Letters, 3,* No. 11 (March 21, 1951).

53. *Minutes, International Skilled Trades Conference* (March 3–4, 1951), p. 4.

centage basis instead of a cents-per-hour basis. (This change in wage policy was deemed necessary to restore a proper differential between skilled workers and production workers and to re-establish the traditional position of skilled workers in the auto industry as the highest paid in the apprenticeable trades.)

3. A skilled trades conference shall be called three months prior to each UAW convention. (In this resolution, skilled trades delegates expressed concern with the timing of their conference which was less than a month prior to the convention. They noted pointedly that as a minority group in most local unions, their desires were seldom recognized; that Regional Wage-Hour Councils were nonlegislative bodies and therefore not always effective; that it had taken over two years of constant pressure to have the present conference authorized; and that the time available between the conference and the convention was too short "to do justice in selling the [skilled trades] resolves" to convention delegates.)

4. Summer Schools sponsored by the UAW shall include a presentation and clarification of skilled trades problems and UAW skilled trades policies. (This educational program was aimed at dispelling the "considerable misunderstanding and friction" existing between production workers and skilled journeymen.)

5. All local agreements and memorandums relating to skilled trades problems shall be referred to the International Skilled Trades Department before being submitted to the local union for acceptance. (This resolution stemmed from the complaint that many local agreements in large corporations such as GM violated international policy and were detrimental to skilled trades interests. A companion resolution asked that no agreements whatever involving skilled workers

be negotiated without the assistance of a representative of the Skilled Trades Department. This was to protect against the application of "production worker" clauses, such as transfer and seniority provisions, to the skilled trades.)

6. Every effort shall be made by the International Union to replace paragraphs 127 and 130 of the GM agreement with the new Changeover Agreement.[54] (The 1950 "upgrading" provisions of the GM contract, according to this resolution, allowed management to "build for itself an over-abundant supply of manpower" and were therefore unfair to journeymen and newly graduated apprentices.)[55]

The response of the International Union to these intensified pressures for action was to expound the advantages of industrial unionism over craft unionism for auto workers, to underline its concern for the particular problems of the skilled trades, and to stress the special efforts expended on their behalf. Of the 20 resolutions adopted at the 1951 Skilled Trades Conference, all were unanimously approved by the International Executive

54. The sections referred to in the agreement between GM and the UAW (May 29, 1950) read as follows:

(127) Employees who were upgraders or trainees and who are presently being given further training in skilled trades classifications shall be eligible to be reclassified to the classification in which they are being trained when such training has been completed. For the purpose of layoff and rehire from the skilled group, the seniority status of such employes in the skilled classifications to which assigned will be computed by crediting them with 50% of the time elapsed since the date of entry into that or related skill classifications.

(130) Where qualified journeymen are not available either through new hires or from graduated apprentices, employes may be given such training as will qualify them to satisfactorily perform the assigned work, following which they shall be eligible to be reclassified in their skilled classification with the seniority status as provided in paragraph 127 above when they are assigned to work.

55. *Minutes, International Skilled Trades Conference* (March 3–4, 1951).

Board and assigned to the Skilled Trades Department for implementation. In January 1953, this Department reported that 18 of the 20 resolutions had been fully carried out, while the remaining two were "in process of compliance."[56] It also reported the rapid growth of apprenticeship programs which would forestall any future reliance on temporary expedients such as the Changeover Agreement.

On the question of higher wages for the skilled trades, the UAW sought to exploit the war-created shortage of skilled help in the machine tool industry by urging the creation of a panel by the Wage Stabilization Board to consider steps to relieve the shortage and prevent the pirating of skilled tool makers by high-wage firms. A tripartite committee was established, but the union was unable to secure a majority in support of its move for a uniform national rate for tool-and-die makers. Labor and public members of the special study panel did recommend, however, the establishment of seven basic wage areas with prescribed rate ranges for jobbing and captive shops in each area. According to the *Journal of Commerce* (October 11, 1951), the maximum rates recommended by the panel were far in excess of prevailing levels. Tool makers in Detroit, for example, could expect to gain from 25 to 50 cents per hour—an increase that would certainly destabilize plant wage structures and create pressures for similar increases on the part of maintenance (and production) workers. A concerted effort by employers, however, resulted in the Board's rejection of the special panel's recommendations.[57] The UAW immediately

56. *Report of the Skilled Trades Department to the Second Skilled Trades Conference, UAW-CIO* (Jan. 17–18, 1953), p. 10.

57. In an attempt to curb wage increases in "random-rate" shops, the panel's industry members proposed restrictions on wage increases allowable under General Wage Regulation 5. This regulation permitted merit increases up to 6 per cent a year in shops where no rate maximums existed. Since most of the jobbing shops had no formal rate structure (i.e. no rate-range maximums), these employers were free to grant increases to skilled workers. The Board rejected this proposal also (*Wall Street Journal,* Nov. 1, 1951).

appealed the Board's decision, but the appeal came to naught, and the skilled wage problem remained to plague the union. As Reuther stated on November 30, 1951, "Had the panel recommendations . . . been adopted, the wide inequities between wage rates in the tool and die 'job' shops and the auto industry-owned 'captive shops' would have been reduced and a more equitable and realistic wage pattern established, thus removing one of the basic causes of skilled manpower problems."[58] Rejection of the recommended increases was, of course, the responsibility of the WSB; nevertheless, many skilled workers also blamed the International Union for its failure to achieve results and demanded more vigorous action.

During the succeeding months, the UAW stepped up its drive for a special wage adjustment for the skilled trades. A resolution to this effect was placed before local delegates to the GM conference in September 1952. The purpose of the resolution, as explained by the Director of the GM Department, was to increase rates in the captive shops in line with increases permitted in job shops under Regulation 5, thereby re-establishing the proper wage relationship. The conference was advised that the best union strategy for exerting pressure on the company was for skilled workers to refuse to train nonjourneymen in skilled trades work. To increase support for the resolution among "production" delegates, UAW officials assured them that a breakthrough in skilled rates would soon be followed by adjustments for other workers.[59] Many of the delegates remained unconvinced of the desirability or propriety of singling out the skilled groups for special treatment. Nevertheless, the resolution was approved.[60]

58. UAW press release, Nov. 30, 1951.
59. *Proceedings, International GM Conference, UAW-CIO* (Sept. 12–13, 1952), pp. 138–41, 271–74.
60. Similar pressures were being exerted, of course, at other companies. At Ford, the union had been pressing for a wage adjustment for the skilled trades since late 1950. This was necessary, the union argued, "in order to retain and attract more workers and also to erase the inequity between Ford

Meanwhile the skilled trades workers themselves placed the UAW leadership unmistakably on notice. In a strongly worded resolution on wage inequities, they denounced the widening gap in the captive shop–job shop differential, the loss of wage position relative to production workers (which, apart from equity considerations, was destroying the attractiveness of learning a trade), and the policy of cents-per-hour wage increases. They complained, moreover, that the International Executive Board had repeatedly promised skilled trades committees that these wage inequities would be adjusted, but had failed on most occasions to follow through. It was not enough to be told by the Board that no other union had done more for the skilled trades, for all the evidence on wage benefits secured by the UAW and other unions proved quite the contrary. The Skilled Trades Conference therefore appealed to the Board to adopt the following policy:

1. That all spread rates and rate maximums be eliminated as soon as possible.
2. That percentage wage increases be negotiated instead of cents-per-hour increases.
3. That a stronger effort be made to obtain wage increases for skilled workers in captive shops.
4. That such efforts be continued until auto workers have again reached their historical position as the highest paid in the trades.
5. That a strong drive be made to obtain a substantial increase within the next six months.[61]

---

and the jobbing shops." The union was particularly incensed that Ford, by its own acknowledgment, was paying employees of other concerns working under contract in Ford plants as much as 70 cents more per hour than Ford workers were receiving for similar work. "Yet, while admitting this and the inability to hire skilled help because of the low wages, the Company refused to correct the evident inequity": Letter, UAW National Negotiating Committee to John S. Bugas, vice-president, industrial relations, Ford Motor Company, Dec. 3, 1952.

61. *Minutes, International Skilled Trades Conference, UAW-CIO* (Jan. 17–18, 1953), pp. 32–34.

The debate on this resolution from the conference floor was predictable. As the UAW official responsible for skilled trades affairs, Vice-President Gosser, director of the Skilled Trades Department, expressed strong accord with the resolution except for that part comparing the UAW's performance unfavorably with that of other unions. At the same time, a production worker expressed what was no doubt the majority sentiment among nonskilled UAW members when he called for a general wage increase, complaining that "the biggest amount of our people should not be deprived of a decent standard of living just to make everything fine for the skilled trades workers."[62] Among spokesmen for the skilled workers themselves, however, the only criticisms voiced were that the resolution did not go far enough in documenting skilled trades problems and in demanding requisite action on the part of the International Union.[63] Indeed, there was talk of a mass exodus from the UAW unless the skilled trades program was more vigorously implemented. Like it or not, UAW officials were compelled to bow to these demands.

Subsequently, in May 1953, the union was successful in reopening its long-term contracts (1950-55) with the auto manufacturers. As part of the settlement, skilled workers were granted a special 10-cent increase, with an additional 10 cents for patternmakers and die sinkers. In an address supporting the settlement, Reuther commented on the "difficult and complex" problem of accommodating the needs and interests of both skilled workers and production workers in a single organiza-

62. Ibid., p. 38.
63. Other important resolutions passed by the conference were the following: No outside contracting of work in any plant without prior written approval of the local union; premium pay for work on Saturday and Sunday as such and on holidays for skilled workers engaged on seven-day operations; mandatory acceptance and effectuation of all skilled trades policies by local unions and their officers; greater emphasis by the union on direct wage increases; and the negotiation of supplementary contracts for the correction of contract provisions permitting transfer of workers between the skilled trades.

tion and frankly admitted the UAW's "craft union bellyache." Although the Korean War had created a severe shortage of skilled help and hence the opportunity for getting some improvement in skilled trades rates, Reuther found at least partial justification for the special increase on grounds of equity: "In some sense there was an historic inequity which had developed in certain skilled trades groups as it related to production. It was not as great as the 10 cents reflects. That improves the relative historic position of the skilled trades workers."[64] He told his audience, however, that while the union would do what it reasonably could to meet the problems of the skilled trades, it would grant no special privilege to any group nor be stampeded by any threats of secession. Apparently Reuther's objective was to placate both groups within the union for it was already evident that the skilled workers considered the 10-cent increase inadequate (in view of the size of the job shop-captive shop differential), whereas the production workers considered it unfair.

It was only natural, of course, that the special treatment accorded the skilled trades should have repercussions elsewhere within the union. Many production workers felt that the International Union was a captive of this strategically placed minority group and demanded a return to the principles of industrial unionism. Other workers in more or less borderline classifications sought recognition as skilled tradesmen. In addition, special groups such as the foundry workers attempted to promote their own particular programs along lines similar to those followed by the skilled trades.[65] The skilled craftsmen themselves might still be dissatisfied, but others in the union envied their privileged status.

Whatever difficulties these counterpressures created for the

64. *Proceedings, International GM Conference, UAW-CIO* (May 28, 1953), p. 76.

65. *Minutes, 8th Foundry Conference, UAW-CIO*, 1953; *9th Foundry Conference, UAW-CIO*, 1954.

union, they did little to diminish the growing influence of the skilled trades with the UAW leadership. At the 1955 Skilled Trades Conference, Joseph McCusker, a member of the International Executive Board and of the Board's Skilled Trades Committee, assured the delegates on this point. He reminded them how the resolutions passed by earlier skilled trades conferences had received unanimous Board approval and been adopted as international policy; and he all but promised that the same favorable action could be expected on resolutions passed by the current conference. Indeed, the delegates were advised that the only obstacles to adoption of the skilled trades program were to be found in the membership: "Our difficulty is not in convincing the leadership of the International Union of the justice and need for your program. Our difficulty is in the democracy that exists in our . . . Union, that we have to sell and convince the membership, both skilled and unskilled, of the need of the program and how not only the skilled workers can gain, but the production workers can gain by upholding the skilled trades standards."[66]

If the problem of satisfying skilled workers proved troublesome in the early 1950s, however, it was to grow much more serious as the decade wore on. In the 1955 settlements, which saw the substitution of a percentage annual improvement factor for the cents-per-hour factor and the establishment of the first SUB plans in basic industry, skilled tradesmen again received a special wage increase amounting to 8 cents an hour. Dissatisfaction with the settlement was immediate and violent throughout the skilled trades. The wage increase was regarded as woefully inadequate, and strong objections were raised against the SUB plan which most skilled workers regarded as a program developed primarily for the benefit of production workers.[67]

66. *Proceedings, 4th Annual International Skilled Trades Conference, UAW-CIO* (Jan. 20–22, 1955), p. 9.
67. We have already noted that this reaction to the SUB plan reflected in part the stable employment experience enjoyed by skilled workers up to that

The extent of unrest was apparent in the numerous walkouts and in the anxious efforts of the union's leadership to crush the incipient revolt. The *Detroit News*, for example, reported that nearly 10,000 skilled workers at Ford's large River Rouge plant had absented themselves from work in protest over the agreement;[68] and the *Detroit Times* mentioned an unconfirmed report that secret negotiations were being conducted to grant Ford's disgruntled tradesmen an additional 5 cents.[69] A few days later these tool room and maintenance workers terminated their walkout at the Rouge plant, but vowed they would fight for membership rejection of the contract.[70]

Even more threatening to the union leadership, however, were the numerous moves to secede from the UAW and set up independent skilled locals.[71] The main challenge came from the newly formed Society of Skilled Trades, an organization that by late 1955 claimed a membership of 50,000 in Michigan.[72]

---

time. Many skilled workers would have preferred the 5-cent wage increase negotiated by "splinter" unions of skilled craftsmen in the industry in lieu of SUB.

68. June 7, 1955.

69. June 8, 1955.

70. *Detroit Times*, June 9, 1955.

71. There were many references to such actions in the press. The *Detroit Times* (June 13) reported that skilled workers at GM's Flint facilities, angered by the union's failure to secure an adequate wage increase, had established a committee to consider the possibility of setting up a separate local within the UAW or an independent union. The *Wall Street Journal* (July 19) noted that some 2,000 UAW skilled tradesmen had voted to seek permission from the NLRB to form an independent organization to be called the "Society of Industrial Skilled Trades of North America." On November 4, the *Detroit News* announced that the independent Detroit Die Sinkers Lodge 110 had won an election at GM's Oldsmobile Forge plant in Lansing and that die sinkers at Chevrolet Forge in Detroit had voted to withdraw from the UAW and join the same independent organization. The UAW itself announced that on September 16, after the suspension of three union officials of Chrysler Local 212 for "efforts to foster dual unionism and eventually a separate union," it had been forced to send telegrams threatening disciplinary action to skilled workers at Chrysler's Automotive Body Division who had walked out in protest over the suspension.

72. *Detroit News*, Oct. 3, 1955.

The purpose of this new organization was to establish an independent skilled trades union that would preserve the status and serve the interests of the skilled craftsman. As its acting president explained: "It is understandable why we are short-changed in the UAW contracts. The UAW is a democratic organization and subject to majority rule. We are in the minority and the UAW leaders are compelled to follow the dictates of the majority.[73] There is no doubt that many skilled tradesmen shared his view.

Meanwhile, other journeymen, less anxious to quit the UAW, agitated within the union for reconsideration of skilled trades demands—particularly the need for greater representation, improved bargaining rights, and higher wages. At a special conference of the trades, convened in early November to discuss grievances with the International Executive Board, representatives of the skilled workers emphasized their dissatisfaction with the union's wage performance and warned Board members of the probable consequences of any further neglect of skilled trades' interests. UAW officials were successful, however, in quashing one resolution calling for the immediate reopening of auto wage contracts[74] and in marshalling support for another condemning the societies and other groups who sought "to promote dual unionism by attempting to break the teamwork and cooperation between skilled and production workers in the UAW-CIO."[75]

Whatever comfort the UAW leadership may have drawn from such support, the situation remained critical, and some affirmative action in the interests of the skilled trades was urgently needed. Dissident skilled groups had already petitioned or were about to petition the NLRB for representation elections among the crafts. The Board refused to entertain these "craft severance" petitions because a contract was already in existence.

73. *Detroit Free Press,* Nov. 7, 1955.
74. *Detroit Times,* Nov. 6, 1955.
75. UAW press release, Nov. 5, 1955.

But it promised reconsideration of the petitions, if so requested, at the time of contract expirations in mid-1958. On reconsideration at this later date, the Board again denied the petitions, ruling that "requests of severance elections must be co-extensive with the existing bargaining unit from which a union seeks to detach specified categories of workmen."[76] As one writer has speculated on the results of these actions: "The Board's denial of craft severance thwarted what might have developed into a sizable local-independent movement in the automobile industry. If immediate elections had been ordered, the Society of Skilled Trades predicted that one hundred thousand skilled workers would have withdrawn from the UAW."[77]

The breathing spell afforded the leadership by the NLRB's decision was not wasted. On November 30, 1956, the International Executive Board, after lengthy deliberations, adopted a policy statement on the skilled trades which became the basis of recommendations to the Skilled Trades Conference in mid-December. In his address to the conference, Reuther assured the skilled trades that their problems would receive full and sympathetic attention. In anticipation of the inevitable grumblings that the new international policy represented a full capitulation to the crafts, Reuther also sought to assure nonskilled members that what the Board proposed was not a departure from the industrial union principle but merely a refinement of the industrial union structure to enable the leadership to take care of special problems.[78] Whether this latter assurance rested on a valid distinction is certainly debatable. In any event, it is clear that the Executive Board had simply done what it had to do in order to stave off a mass revolt of the skilled trades.

The new program called for the elimination of merit spreads in all skilled classifications and for the addition to present maxi-

76. General Motors Corporation, 120 NLRB 1215.

77. Leo Troy, "Local Independent and National Unions: Competitive Labor Organizations," *Journal of Political Economy* (Oct. 1960), p. 496.

78. *UAW Administrative Letter, 8,* No. 23 (Dec. 28, 1956).

mums of a "very substantial wage increase." The new rates were then to be regarded as guaranteed minimum rates "beyond which advances could be made but with no maximum limit." The objective, of course, was to place workers in captive shops on a par with those in job shops. Nonskilled workers were assured that this demand would not be at their expense. A much more signicant policy change, however, dealt with representation and bargaining rights. It was proposed that skilled workers be allowed to vote separately on matters pertaining only to their trades, that "under prescribed circumstances" they be permitted the right to strike action, and that they be given "direct representation of their own choosing as part of all local shop bargaining committees and of all national bargaining committees." Finally, the Board called for an expanded apprenticeship training program with a higher hiring age limit for applicants from the production force displaced by automation and technological change.

There can be little question that this new program was adopted with serious misgivings by the UAW leadership. However, the issue of craft vs. industrial unionism was real and immediate: skilled workers were determined to win some measure of independence—a separate identity; and the only question was whether this would be accomplished within the UAW or through the medium of outside craft unions. UAW officials apparently had little choice. They recognized the danger inherent in the new program that other groups might similarly seek a separate identity, and they were anxious to avoid any extensive fractionalization of the membership. On the other hand, it is doubtful if any other single minority group had the necessary leverage within the union to compel such action; and the new program was likely to aid the union in its drive to convince the growing numbers of office and technical workers in the industry that the UAW was capable of serving their particular interests. In addition, if special groups voted separately in the ratification of contract terms, the International Union would be in a stronger position to meet any subsequent complaints about the contract by these same groups.

The new program had to be approved, of course, by the UAW as a whole, and for this hurdle the Executive Board prepared carefully. The change in the bargaining structure was portrayed as an evolutionary advance in the principle of industrial unionism:

> Collective bargaining will continue to be more complex as the technology in our industries becomes more complex. Our Union has the responsibility of finding new and effective tools, tactics and techniques for dealing with these new and increasingly complex problems. The Union is a living body and collective bargaining is a living process. Nothing is static and progress is possible only in terms of change. What represented an effective approach to collective bargaining at the beginning of our Union is no longer realistic or effective for new approaches must be made to new problems.
>
> Without in any way weakening or compromising the principles of industrial unionism, which is the source of the strength and the solidarity of our Union, we must find ways to refine the principle of industrial unionism in order to meet new problems, to meet the problems common to all the workers in our Union and yet at the same time to be able to deal satisfactorily with special problems within our Union. No member of our Union has a right to special privilege, but every member of our Union who may have a special problem because of the nature of his work, has a right to have this special problem dealt with effectively. . . .
>
> In essence, our policy suggests that we make provisions in the structure of our collective bargaining machinery to assure that skilled trades groups, office workers, technicians and engineers, in plants in which there are sizable groups of workers in these classifications, be permitted

direct representation in the negotiation and administration of our bargaining agreements and with the negotiation of supplementary agreements dealing with their special problems on which they have the right to act.

This policy . . . will also enable the Union to meet the problem of raids by craft unions under the current policies of the National Labor Relations Board and also will enable the Union to carry out more effectively the task of organizing unorganized workers, the white collar and clerical field and the thousands of technicians and engineers working in industries under our jurisdiction.[79]

At the 1957 convention, the Resolution Committee brought out both a majority and a minority report on the Board's recommendations. The majority report contained the Board's program and supporting arguments. The minority report, on the other hand, expressed the view that the new program smacked of surrender of the "industrial union" principle. It found the wage demand for the skilled trades unrealistic; and it insisted that strike votes by skilled workers should require ratification by the local union involved. Otherwise, the report noted, there would be a further breach in the relations between skilled and production workers.[80]

The new program caused considerable debate on the convention floor (as it had previously in the Executive Board), but the resolution embodying the majority report was finally accepted. The responsibility for stating the Executive Board's case for the change in policy fell to Vice-President Leonard Woodcock. His presentation was forceful and direct: the convention could accept the program and thus give the International Union the tools necessary for safeguarding its strength or it could reject the program and resign the UAW to a future

79. *Report of UAW President, Walter P. Reuther, to the 16th Constitutional Convention* (April 7–12, 1957), pp. 56–58.

80. *Proceedings, 16th Constitutional Convention, UAW* (April 7–12, 1957), p. 277.

of diminished influence and effectiveness. Woodcock first underlined the shifts taking place in the labor force as a result of automation and technological change, and dramatized their portent in the following appeal:

> It is an inescapable fact that if we cannot achieve the organization of professional and technical and engineering employes, and also office workers, this Union will become an increasingly less effective force. . . . In the early days of May of this year . . . there will be a most important National Labor Relations Board election. Two thousand engineers and technicians employed in the Minneapolis-Honeywell Regulator Company in Minneapolis, who have voted to join UAW, based upon the fact that we are proposing to make this change, will decide whether or not they want this Union. If we pass what is being proposed here, then we are reasonably sure that those 2,000 engineers and technicians will join themselves to our Union. Every engineer in American is looking at this election. If we win, we can begin to do the job that has to be done. Give us these tools, and we will have the chance to organize these other workers.[81]

With respect to the skilled trades themselves, Woodcock warned the delegates that the right of self-determination for skilled tradesmen in the auto industry was not a matter to be settled by convention decision. "The inescapable fact is that the law of the United States . . . gives these workers in little bits and pieces the right to go down the craft road, to separate themselves out." Again, to demonstrate the crucial consequences of the convention's action, Woodcock drew attention to two "extremely important" pending NLRB elections (at the Fisher Body stamping plants in Marion, Indiana, and Mansfield, Ohio) in which tool room workers would vote separately for the International Association of Tool Craftsmen (Society of

81. Ibid., pp. 280–81.

Skilled Trades) or the UAW as their bargaining agent. He predicted that the outcome of these elections would depend largely on the adoption or rejection of the new skilled trades policy proposed by the UAW leadership.

Finally, in an appeal to the self-interest of production workers, Woodcock noted that a companion resolution, unanimously approved at the Skilled Trades Conference, provided for lifting the age limit under apprenticeship programs for workers already in the industry in order to permit production workers to become qualified journeymen. "This is an important, a vital matter to the production workers, because as plants become more and more automated within the production and maintenance units, there are less job opportunities for production workers. There tend to be more job opportunities for skilled trades. As men are displaced on the production line we have to have the mechanism within our own organization to move them across into the place where the job opportunities are. If the skilled trades have moved out into separate craft unions, then that opportunity is gone for everybody."[82]

Arguments such as these convinced the majority of delegates that the new skilled trades policy was necessary. Intracorporation councils were revamped in order to accommodate the new bargaining arrangement. The National General Motors Council replaced its nine regional subcouncils with eleven functional subcouncils, each consisting of plants performing similar work. One of these new subcouncils was Tool-Die and Maintenance, another Design-Engineering-Model Maker-Pattern Shops. Similarly, the bylaws of the National Ford Council were amended to provide for eight functional subcouncils, for the election (by skilled trades delegates) of a bona fide journeyman to serve on the national negotiating committee, and for four resolutions committees to report out proposed contract demands on matters affecting skilled trades workers, assembly plant workers, manufacturing plant workers, and parts depot workers.

82. Ibid., p. 282.

It is too early to judge the effects of this radical change in the union's internal structure. In his 1959 report, Reuther stated that the special procedures had "worked fairly well" in the 1958 negotiations. Nevertheless, the International Executive Board proposed shortly thereafter that the skilled trades structure be integrated more closely into the union's collective bargaining machinery in order to strengthen the representation rights of the trades. A new skilled trades policy was accordingly adopted in early 1959 with this objective in mind.[83] The new policy eliminated the regional skilled trades subcouncils and established nine "functional" subcouncils representing skilled workers from various sections of the union's jurisdiction—General Motors, Ford, Chrysler, Jobbing Shops, Agricultural Implement, Aircraft and Missiles, Parts Industry, Independents, and Miscellaneous. It also established a Skilled Trades Advisory Committee composed of representatives elected by each of the functional subcouncils. The duties of this nine-man Advisory Committee are to assist the Board "in developing policies and programs essential to the advancement of the welfare and best interests of all skilled trades workers in the UAW, taking into consideration differences that may exist between different sections of our Union." At the same time, the Annual Skilled Trades Conferences, bringing together delegates from all UAW locals, are to be continued "to facilitate a broad, representative discussion of skilled trades problems, policies and programs."

This new attempt to strengthen further the bargaining rights of the skilled trades was prompted perhaps by the difficulties encountered in the 1958 negotiations. At the outset the companies made clear to the UAW that they had no intention of altering their bargaining procedures to suit the union's new bargaining structure. The union might adopt any ratification system it chose, but as far as management was concerned, there was only one national contract with the union, and that con-

83. *Report of UAW President, Walter P. Reuther, to the 17th Constitutional Convention, UAW* (Oct. 9–16, 1959), pp. 343–46.

tract, as in the past, would be accepted or rejected in its entirety. Given this stand by management, it is difficult to see how the separate bargaining rights accorded the skilled trades could make much difference. Since the NLRB has ruled that the issue of unit redetermination is bargainable but not strikeable, any strike by the skilled workers is automatically a contract strike (even if production workers have voted to accept the contract) and, hence, the employer may legally shut out all workers in the bargaining unit.[84] The result, in essence, is a company-wide strike but without majority ratification—a prospect that union leaders would hardly welcome with equanimity.

The procedures adopted in 1959 may well reflect the union's awareness of this weakness in its earlier plan. This would explain the attempt to improve the bargaining effectiveness of the skilled trades, not through the establishment of new bargaining units as in 1957, but more directly through an increase in their effectiveness within existing bargaining units. In any event, it is doubtful if the new policy has so far produced any significant change in the bargaining position of the skilled trades.

Insofar as a subsidiary goal of the new bargaining structure was to enhance the union's chances of organizing office workers, engineers, and technicians in the industry, there is again no evidence of its effectiveness. Indeed, the Minneapolis-Honeywell election in May 1957, which Woodcock had referred to as a strategic test of the union's drawing power, resulted in defeat for the UAW (1,300 "against" and 568 "for"), despite the convention's endorsement of the new skilled trades program. Nevertheless, UAW officials remain convinced (or, at least, hopeful) that time is on their side. Reuther recognizes the task of organizing the white-collar worker as a "most formidable challenge" requiring an intensification of effort in

84. For a discussion of the significance of the skilled trades amendments of 1957, see Muriel Beach, "The Problems of the Skilled Worker in an Industrial Union: A Case Study," *I.L.R. Research, 6* (New York State School of Industrial and Labor Relations, Cornell Univ., 1960–61), 8–15.

the formulation of programs designed especially to appeal to such workers. He sees in present business trends, however, changes that reduce the gulf in experience and outlook between the white-collar and blue-collar worker—changes that are awakening the white-collar worker to a clearer realization of the need for collective action.[85]

Whether the new bargaining structure and any subsequent revisions will resolve the UAW's dilemma of adequately representing the skilled trades (and other special interest groups) without a fuller abandonment of the principles of industrial unionism remains to be seen. The perceptive remarks by James Stern, assistant to UAW Vice-President Leonard Woodcock, pose both the challenge and the opportunity:

> Union bargaining programs increasingly are designed to give recognition to the apparent desires of engineers, technicians and office worker members to keep their identity separate from that of production workers. Many such groups are advocating separate local unions, separate contracts with separate representation and separate demands. Automation, however, changes relations among engineers, technicians and production workers in such a manner as to make their work more closely related. . . . The cohesive bond among these groups must be kept strong by acceptance of basic principles. Yet these principles cannot be so numerous and all-encompassing that they deprive each group of its right to determine within the over-all framework, the specific objectives and strategy for reaching them. . . .
>
> In the next few years automation will contribute to a lessening of the difference that exists in the working conditions and methods of wage payment of production workers as opposed to white collar workers. The automated factory of the future will be based on a rigidly controlled environ-

85. See, e.g., Report of Reuther to the 17th Convention, pp. 339–40.

ment. The factory may be as clean as the office. Wage payment on an hourly basis may become inappropriate. Blue collar workers may wear white collars and receive monthly salaries. Demands for separate units and differential treatment will diminish under these circumstances.[86]

Stern's guarded optimism about the future strength of existing industrial unions in manufacturing is further tempered, however, by his recognition of the problem posed by divergent group interests and the possibility that other (newly created) organizations will emerge in the engineering and technical fields.

All things considered, the future strength and stability of the UAW would seem to depend in part on its ability to win greater support from the skilled workers currently within its ranks. It is not enough to have defeated the threat of possible mass defections through the technical rulings of the NLRB (which incidentally illustrate in rather dramatic fashion the conflict in public policy between the stability of bargaining relationships and the principle of self-determination). A more positive solution is required if the union is to demonstrate its worth to those growing groups of workers it feels it must organize if it is to continue to play a vigorous and influential role in the affairs of the industry, the labor movement, and the nation as a whole. Indeed, at a more immediate level, it may be that the UAW, if it fails to develop a workable plan for the skilled groups themselves, "will experience internal dissension or may split apart at the seams and discover that the 'forever' of its theme song 'Solidarity Forever' was in reality a period of slightly more than twenty years."[87] Whatever else the recent changes imply, it is clear that the simple, undifferentiated "industrial unionism" of past decades is today inadequate. Such central principles as

---

86. *Automation and Major Technological Change,* A Panel Discussion at a Conference held under the auspices of the Industrial Union Dept., AFL-CIO (April 28, 1958), pp. 13–15.

87. Beach, "Problems of the Skilled Worker," p. 15.

"majority rule" have been substantially modified. Increasing fractionalization is leading toward a federation of special groups with differing interests and objectives, concerned with preserving their separate identities. Where these developments will lead cannot be discerned at present. They confirm, however, Reuther's own observation that, "The Union is a living body and collective bargaining is a living process. Nothing is static and progress is possible only in terms of change." In the skilled trades amendments, the UAW has demonstrated a capacity for remarkable change and a willingness, it would seem, to move further along radically new paths as objective circumstances require. In this willingness to experiment may lie the key, if there is one, to successful adaptation to a new environment.

The Skilled-Unskilled Differential. In the first section of this chapter dealing with the behavior of occupational differentials, we observed that the wage position of skilled tradesmen has not deteriorated relative to that of production workers. Indeed, it was noted that certain trades (such as patternmaker and die sinker) have even enjoyed larger percentage increases than the average unskilled *nonproduction* worker. In the section just completed, we examined the circumstances under which these developments came about and presented evidence on the forces shaping union wage policy. This information does not permit us to state categorically how unionism (through collective bargaining) has affected the skilled-unskilled differential, but it does provide the basis for formulating a reasonable judgment.

Since the union's inception, skilled tradesmen within the UAW have agitated for a fuller recognition of their status and a more adequate representation of their special craft interests. In the plants of the auto companies, discontent among skilled workers was evident even before the beginning of World War II. The wartime emergency, with its sudden upsurge of demand for skilled help, merely accentuated dissatisfactions. The absence of formal rate maximums in job shops permitted an increase in the captive shop-job shop differential at a time when job shops were offering steady employment. To the skilled tradesmen in the captive shops, this meant that their wage position was worsening precisely during a period when one of the main reasons for the traditional differential (i.e. less security of employment in the job shop) had disappeared. Concurrently, companies were augmenting the supply of skilled help by upgrading competent production workers through special training programs. This influx of upgraders and trainees not only eased the pressure of short supply, but also made skilled tradesmen apprehensive about the future when employment opportunities returned to normal. Special wage adjustments during the war offered a temporary palliative to the trades, but by the war's end dissatisfaction among skilled workers had reached a new peak.

In the postwar period, the International Union was under severe pressure from the skilled trades to abandon its "industrial union" policies and give some measure of protection to skilled interests. The partial solution or handling of one problem seemed only to lead to other problems of a more critical nature. There was the upgrading program, the perennial problem of the captive shop-job shop differential, the use of maintenance helpers, and such other issues as subcontracting and premium payments on seven-day operations. In addition, skilled workers complained of a deterioration of their wage position relative to that of production workers—a claim that we have shown to be spurious over the period as a whole.[88]

In the years following World War II, discontent among skilled tradesmen in the UAW has grown continuously and has been manifest in rising pressures for reform in the structure as well as in the programs of the union. Despite the counterpres-

88. There was, it is true, some narrowing of the differential in the late 1940s, but this only partially offset the widening that had occurred as a result of special wartime increases. Moreover, beginning in 1950, the narrowing trend was reversed. Hence, at no time since the war has this skill differential declined to the level existing in the late 1930s (see Table 13).

sures exerted by production and other unskilled workers and the natural reluctance of most UAW officials to abandon traditional principles, this force for reform has proved irresistible. Union leaders have been compelled to beat a retreat, to accommodate increasingly to the skilled workers' desire for a separate identity and a larger role in the formulation of union policy. This responsiveness stems largely from the open revolt of the 1950s (which only the combined efforts of the union, the companies, and the NLRB could quell) and the rising numerical importance of the skilled crafts under the "new" technology. It reflects, in addition, the realization that failure to serve the interests of these trades will blunt the union's campaign to organize the expanding force of white-collar, technical, and engineering workers in the industry.

The special efforts of the union on behalf of the skilled trades may be grouped into two related categories. The first category consists of direct pressures for wage adjustments over and above the general wage increases. Indeed, during the 1950s, these special adjustments were a consistent feature of contract settlements—5 cents in 1950, 10 cents in 1953, 8 cents in 1955, and 8 cents in 1958.[89] Management, for the most part, does not appear to have fought these adjustments too strenuously, presumably because of its own concern for the preservation of "proper" rate relationships. It has steadfastly refused, however, to eliminate (or reduce significantly) the gap between rates in its own captive shops and in job shops (and "outside" construction) on the grounds that the captive shops offer steadier and

89. It is interesting that no additional wage increase was granted to the skilled trades in 1961. This may be due to the overwhelming importance of the "job security" issue in these negotiations or to the fact that job shops, because of the slackening of production schedules, no longer provide as attractive an alternative to employment in the captive shops; or it may simply signify that wage levels have now risen sufficiently so that the annual improvement factor of 2.5 per cent (6-cent minimum) operates largely to maintain occupational differentials. At any rate, the union's main drive in the skilled trades area appears to have related mainly to issues of contracting out, upgraders and trainees, maintenance helpers, etc.

more secure employment and make lesser demands in terms of all-around skills. The UAW leadership itself seems resigned to the continuance of these differentials, although naturally it must press for their elimination. As a representative of the UAW Competitive Shop Department explained, the auto companies not only refuse to equalize the rates but are able to make their refusal effective through "farming out" work to job shops, thus maintaining some downward pressure on their own (captive shop) rates. This same technique can be presumed to apply with equal force in the maintenance-construction field. Hence, the union's persistent demands for some agreement that will limit management's discretion to "contract out" skilled trades work.

The actual difference in rates between captive shops and job shops in the Detroit area as of January 1957 is shown in Table 16. It is clear from the data that job shop rates average substantially higher than captive shop rates. The median rates for tool-and-die makers, for example, are $3.43 and $2.90 respectively. Since the rates used in this table are shop maximums and since merit spreads in job shops are customarily larger, a comparison of shop minimums would show a smaller differential. But even in this case the difference is substantial; median minimum rates are $3.12 for job shops and $2.70 for captive shops. This average differential of 40 to 50 cents has not been disturbed in recent years and there is no reason to believe it will be reduced significantly in the near future. Consequently, we can expect continued agitation on the part of skilled workers in the auto companies for wage equalization regardless of what happens to the skilled-unskilled differential.[90]

The second aspect of UAW skilled trades policy, which supplements and reinforces direct pressures for wage increases, consists of measures to control the supply of skilled workers

90. It might be noted that the entire wage structure is higher in job shops than in captive shops so that occupational differentials are approximately equal in the two types of shops.

while maintaining or raising the demand for their services. The drive to abolish the use of upgraders, trainees, and helpers, opposition to the crossing of jurisdictional lines, the restrictions sought on subcontracting, and the limits imposed on apprenticeship training fall into this category. Each is designed to

TABLE 16. Wage Rate Distributions in Captive and Job Shops in the Detroit Area for Specified Occupations, January 1957[a]

Diemaker			Electrician			Janitor, sweeper		
Rate bracket	Number of captive shops	Number of job shops	Rate bracket	Number of captive shops	Number of job shops	Rate bracket	Number of captive shops	Number of job shops
$2.60–$2.69	1		$2.10–$2.19	1		$1.50–$1.59	1	
2.70– 2.79	1					1.60– 1.69		
2.80– 2.89	14		2.50– 2.59	2		1.70– 1.79		
2.90– 2.99	28	1	2.60– 2.69	5		1.80– 1.89	1	
3.00– 3.09	8	1	2.70– 2.79	34	1	1.90– 1.99	22	
3.10– 3.19	1	2	2.80– 2.89	3		2.00– 2.09	13	
3.20– 3.29		1	2.90– 2.99	3		2.10– 2.19	3	2
3.30– 3.39	9		3.00– 3.09		2	2.20– 2.29		
3.40– 3.49	9		3.10– 3.19	1	1	2.30– 2.39		4
3.50– 3.59	6		3.20– 3.29			2.40– 2.49		3
3.60– 3.69	5		3.30– 3.39		1			
3.70– 3.79	2		3.40– 3.49		1	3.10– 3.19		1

a. All rates are shop maximums and include the cost-of-living allowance.

Source. Data compiled from *UAW Tool, Die and Maintenance Survey* compiled by the Wage-Hour Division of the Competitive Shop Dept. for the Skilled Trades Dept. (April 1, 1957).

reduce the relative supply of skilled help. It is unlikely, however, that these policies have had much effect to date, largely because of the countermeasures adopted by the companies. Thus, management has refused to allow serious encroachments on its right to contract out skilled work, has pressed with some measure of success for more liberal apprentice-journeyman ratios, and has avoided active bidding for skilled help in periods of shortage. The ability to "farm out" skilled work to job shops and building-maintenance contractors and the practice of advertising extensively in other areas for scarce skills provide, of course, a safety valve against union pressure tactics and render practicable any tacit "antipirating" arrangement. In addition, auto mangements are aware that selective increases granted to specific occupation groups, even when justified by market considerations, often become the basis for "inequity" demands by other groups in the work force. These equitable comparisons, through which wage raises granted to meet specific scarcities tend to become generalized, create in turn a bias in favor of meeting such scarcities through upgrading, job breakdown, contracting out, etc. Moreover, if the scarcities are in part due to restrictive union policies, management's resentment may well fortify the search for alternatives.

On the basis of these and other considerations, what may we conclude about the impact of unionism on skill differentials—especially the differential between skilled workers and production workers? In our judgment, it is most unlikely that unionism has exercised a narrowing influence, save perhaps temporarily in the immediate postwar years (i.e. 1945–49). In fact, a case can be made that it has been responsible for some widening of these differentials since the late 1930s. This contention is supported by the following evidence.

First, if accepted interpretations of the general trend in skill differentials are valid, we should have anticipated some decline in such differentials in auto plants. Instead, the skilled trades in this industry have experienced an improvement in wage position relative to production-worker classifications—including assembly and related occupations where much of the industry's work force is concentrated; and there is not even much evidence of an over-all worsening of skilled trades wages in relation to the lowest-paid nonproduction jobs such as material handler and janitor. In addition, the economic attractiveness of a skilled trades career (journeymen's claims to the contrary notwithstanding) has been enhanced by substantial improvements in the wage status of apprentices since World War II. Hence, it cannot be argued that the relative wage gains for skilled craftsmen were necessary in order to compensate for earnings sacrificed during early years in training. The gain in apprentice wage levels is shown in Table 17 which is based on data supplied by

TABLE 17. Comparison of Wage Rates for Selected Occupations, 1941–1958

Year	Apprentice (starting rate)	Toolmaker (minimum rate)	Assembler	Sweeper
1941	$0.90	$1.30	$1.15	$0.95
1946	1.08	1.58	1.33	1.13
1950	1.375	1.875	1.575	1.375
1955	1.955	2.485	2.005	1.805
1958	2.325	2.91	2.335	2.135
Increase 1941–58				
Dollars	1.425	1.61	1.185	1.185
Per cent	158	124	103	125

one of the larger companies. This gain, which has raised the starting rate for apprentices from below the sweeper's rate in 1941 to approximately the same rate as the major assembler in 1958, has come about through the participation by apprentices in the special increases granted the skilled trades—5 cents in 1950, 10 cents in 1953, 5 cents in 1955, and roughly 4 cents in 1958.[91] The fact that the starting apprentice rate is now on a par with the basic production rate represents a significant

91. The 1955 increase for apprentices was 3 cents below that for journeymen. The 4-cent increase in 1958, when journeymen received 8 cents, took the form of a training incentive payment which, for tool room apprentices, ranged from $38.21 for the first 1,000-hour shop period to $107.01 for the eighth.

improvement in the career earnings of the skilled craftsman. Not only has his skill premium been rising, but even during his earliest period of training (i.e. his first 1,000 hours), he now earns the equivalent of the production worker—the major alternative employment opportunity in the industry.[92]

Second, in spite of the fact that skilled tradesmen comprise a minority (albeit an important and growing minority) in the UAW, it is abundantly clear from the record that this strategically situated group has assumed an increasingly commanding role in the union's program. Although the wage impact of policies designed to regulate the supply of skilled help and to "protect the integrity of the trades" has probably been of little significance to date (largely on account of management's opposition), the vigor, extent, and direction of the union's over-all skilled trades' program, including persistent direct pressures for wage increases, has ensured at least that tradesmen's interests have not been slighted.[93] These groups have received (and will no doubt continue to receive) a disproportionately high share of the union's total effort on behalf of its membership.

These considerations suggest that the influence of unionism has been in the direction of maintaining and probably of widening the skilled-unskilled differential. There are, however, additional factors to consider before bringing in a final verdict —factors that, in the main, might be held to provide the counterargument to the position adopted here.

92. This situation in autos, incidentally, affords an interesting contrast to the findings of a survey conducted by the Machinists Association where a majority of respondents among local and national representatives felt that the reduction of the skill differential had diminished the incentive to become an all-around machinist. "Many of the respondents emphasized that the starting wages of apprentice machinists are only about half the journeymen's wage and less than the wages of unskilled workers. For many able workers, the wage advantage they would enjoy ultimately as skilled machinists apparently does not seem large enough to warrant the temporary sacrifice of income entailed by entering apprenticeship": National Manpower Council, *A Policy for Skilled Manpower* (New York, Columbia, 1954), pp. 260–61.

93. The strongest criticism of UAW skilled trades policies came from tool-and-die manufacturers during the Korean War when stepped-up defense pro-

It was noted that management itself has expressed a preference for the maintenance of a "proper" wage relationship between skilled rates and production rates. This attitude reflects in part concern for the preservation of incentives, in part the desire to avoid the risks of multiple unionism. These motives were not sufficiently strong to cause employers to initiate special wage adjustments for the skilled trades, but company spokesmen have intimated (in and out of negotiations) that the union experienced no great difficulty in securing at least some of the special wage adjustments granted since 1950. In addition, it is a matter of record that the percentage annual improvement factor introduced in 1955 was a management innovation. Granted the employers' interest, however, in preventing undue narrowing of the skilled trades-production worker differential, the fact remains that pressures for a still wider differential have come from the union and have been met with firm resistance. This is most evident in management's adamant refusal to eliminate the captive shop-job shop differential, long a primary aim of UAW wage policy and a major source of discontent among skilled auto workers.

It may be argued, incidentally, that the continued existence of the captive-job shop differential (and the maintenance-construction differential, too, for that matter) is an indication that craftsmen's rates in auto plants have simply kept pace with the market. Two points should be noted, however: first, the job shop (and construction) rates referred to are themselves "bar-

---

duction created a shortage of tool-and-die makers in such centers as Detroit. Chester A. Cahn, managing director of the Automotive Tool and Die Manufacturers Association, was expressing an industry view when he assailed the UAW in 1952 for hampering tool shop production in Detroit by its restrictive manpower policies. As examples, he cited the eligibility requirements for a UAW journeyman card of ten years in the industry, efforts to control upgrading, resistance to the hiring of qualified machine hands, and the threats of discipline against craftsmen holding more than one job. (*Detroit News,* June 8, 1952.) The UAW was also charged with hampering apprenticeship programs through its efforts to restrict apprentice-journeyman ratios to 1:10. (*Journal of Commerce,* Aug. 7, 1952.)

gained" rates;[94] and second, while the absolute differential appears to have no more than doubled in the last twenty years or so, wage levels have almost trebled over the same period, so that the percentage differential between rates in the two types of establishments has declined by about a third. At least in a relative sense, therefore, captive shop workers have improved their wage position under collective bargaining.

These two points take on added significance when it is considered that, because of the reliance of many job shops on orders from auto manufacturers, rates in these shops are more sensitive to upward wage pressures. In periods of skill shortage in auto labor markets, all companies resort to advertising and (subject to whatever restrictions the union may impose) to the combined use of apprentices, upgraders, trainees, and helpers as a means of augmenting supply. However, auto manufacturers have an additional advantage in that they may transfer part of their own skill demands to job shops by stepping up outside contracting. This ability to transfer part of the wage pressure to other employers, along with a natural reluctance to destabilize the wage structure by granting increases to special occupational groups beyond specified contract rates, probably accounts for

94. The problem of locating the so-called "market" or "natural" rate is difficult enough in a nonunion labor market since there exists typically a wide range of rates for any one occupation. In a large, highly unionized market such as Detroit, where numerous organized and unorganized shops exist side by side, the problem is even more perplexing, for such a market is likely to be characterized by the existence of two rate ranges (union and nonunion) which are overlapping and more or less interrelated. The absence of wage data for unorganized job shops in Detroit makes it impossible to compare rate ranges. However, if we accept at face value repeated claims by the UAW Skilled Trades and Competitive Shop Departments that the operation of unorganized job shops in the Detroit area poses a serious and continuing threat to UAW wage standards, then it is erroneous to cite rates in organized job shops as an appropriate measure of "market" rates. Of course, even on the assumption that these "bargained" job shop rates do represent a reasonable approximation of "market" rates, the problem of identification remains, owing to the range of variation of such rates about their median value (see Table 16).

the fact that active wage bidding for skilled help during periods of scarcity has been confined to job shops. Moreover, even in normal times when supply is adequate, job shop operators, because they work to contract on fixed delivery schedules, are more vulnerable to union-wage and other pressures. In these circumstances, the strike is a potent weapon; it threatens the company with loss of orders and the penalties that often accompany failure to meet delivery schedules, including destruction of the business. Thus, it is not surprising that a captive shop-job shop differential has remained in effect; and while there are undoubtedly limits to the width of this differential at any time (set, for example, by the dissatisfaction of captive shop workers expressed through a high quit rate or intensified union wage pressures), one may as legitimately inquire why the differential is no wider than it currently is as why it has not been further narrowed. Indeed, given the force of equitable comparisons under collective bargaining, it might be argued that the special vulnerability of job shop rates to union pressures has had the effect of pulling up captive shop rates as well.

In short, the relative behavior of captive and job shop rates provides no firm ground for rejecting the judgment that the net tendency of unionism in auto company plants has been to widen the rate differential between production work and the skilled trades.

Finally, it may be argued that the trend toward a wider wage gap between skilled tradesmen and production workers since 1950 is attributable to shifts in the skill mix of the work force—i.e. the relative increase in the demand for tool-and-die and certain maintenance craftsmen—brought about by automation and related technological change. This explanation in terms of conventional market forces is appealing but it is surely not adequate. Except for the Korean emergency and the production boom of 1955, there has been little evidence of a general shortage of skilled help during the last decade. More important, there have been no signs at any time of a shortage of applicants (apprentices, production-worker upgraders, trainees, helpers) for work or training in skilled trades departments. On the contrary, the union's main problem has been to limit the flow of labor into the skilled trades—a clear indication that the skill premium is excessive. Beyond that, of course, it is difficult to justify any conventional market explanation for wage behavior in the industry in recent years when unemployment in the principal auto center (the Detroit area) has fluctuated between 6.4 and 19.5 per cent of the labor force, and has fallen below 8 per cent in only 13 months out of the last 48. Since competitive market forces cannot account for recent wage-level changes in auto plants, there is reason to question their adequacy in explaining wage-structure movements. In our view, a more reasonable interpretation would stress the role of institutional factors, especially the union. The improvement during the last decade in the relative wage position of the skilled trades may reflect in part a natural reaction to the narrowing produced by union wage policy in the immediate postwar years. This reaction has been reinforced and extended, however, as a result of the increasing influence of skilled craftsmen within the union and in the formulation of union policy. In other words, the rising importance of the skilled trades has had its impact on the skill differential not so much through the direct pressure of short supply as through a reorientation of the union's wage program.

In summary, our attempt to measure the influence of unionism upon occupational wage relationships in the auto industry leads to the conclusion that unionism has narrowed certain differentials but not others. Its major impact has been to compress wage differences *within* each of the two major work groups—production workers and skilled tradesmen. This does not mean that the relative wage positions of various jobs within the production group would otherwise have been preserved, for there is reason to believe that the actual skill requirements on a number of the higher-paid production jobs have declined since the 1930s, or at least that the skills involved have become less scarce. Developments such as these, in conjunction with secular influences at work during recent decades, would have produced some narrowing of the relative structure of wages. Nevertheless, in the light of differences in union and management wage philosophies—revealed in management's criticism of the union's insistent demands for flat increases, its apprehensiveness about the effects of wage-leveling on incentives and morale, and its promotion of differential increases—it is reasonable to conclude that in the absence of collective bargaining (or of a union so steadfastly dedicated to cents-per-hour wage adjustments), wage compression would have been less acute, and absolute differentials would have undergone at least a modest expansion. On the other hand, the net influence of unionism on wage differentials between skilled tradesmen and production workers appears to have been in the other direction. The effect in this instance should not be exaggerated, but the weight of evidence points to the conclusion that unionism has increased the skill premium beyond what it would otherwise have been.

CHAPTER 5

Interplant Differentials

Personal and occupational differentials, the subject matter of the last two chapters, are the basic dimensions of the *intraplant* wage structure. In this final chapter on wage relationships, attention is focused on wage-level differences between plants —i.e. on the *interplant* wage structure. Since our purpose is to evaluate the influence of unionism upon such differentials, we shall first examine the nature of union wage objectives in this area and second, the behavior of plant wage levels within and among the various firms. One aspect of union wage policy that merits special attention in our discussion is the recent interest of the UAW leadership in profit sharing. Because the implications of the union's profit-sharing proposal are at present vague and uncertain, however, we have chosen to discuss this matter separately in the concluding section of the chapter. It is perhaps well to remind the reader that the emphasis at this point is still on wages as employee compensation. The more complex issue of interfirm cost differences and the union's effect on competitive relations is treated at length in chapters 6 and 7. In a sense, therefore, the present discussion rounds out the study of wage structure and provides an introduction to the examination of competitive relations in the industry.

Union Policy

The principle of the standard rate, of "taking labor out of competition," applies as much to wage relationships among plants as within plants. This drive for interplant wage uniformity is especially insistent in industries where all firms are unionized, compete in the same product market, and have major facilities located in or near the same labor market. Since this is largely the situation in auto manufacturing where, in addition, the entire industry output is concentrated in only a few firms which bargain with the union on a company-wide basis, it is not surprising that wage equalization among auto plants has long been a basic goal of UAW policy.

During World War II, in furtherance of this objective, the UAW campaigned unstintingly for an industry-wide wage agreement that would apply the principle of equal pay for equal work to all firms within the union's jurisdiction. In its drive it sought to enlist the support of the War Labor Board through a series of appeals that simultaneously criticized the Board's handling of wage disputes on an individual basis and enumerated the advantages of an industry-wide approach to the issue of wage stabilization. The union's view of wartime wage policy was most effectively stated by Walter Reuther, then director of the UAW's General Motors Department. In the fall of 1943, Reuther noted that the fundamental weakness of the wage stabilization program was the "continuation of gross wage differentials and inequalities" resulting from the Board's policy of handling wage cases as "individual and unrelated problems."[1] To remedy the weakness, Reuther proposed the establishment of a tripartite wage commission which would survey the indus-

1. "Wage Stabilization and Post-War Security." Partial brief submitted to National War Labor Board by General Motors Dept., UAW-CIO (Nov. 1943), p. 4.

try, delineate logical subdivisions based on type of product, and create through job evaluation a basic wage agreement that would establish the pattern of rates for each subdivision by job classification throughout the entire automotive, aircraft, and allied industry—i.e. throughout the union's basic jurisdiction.

In support of its demand for an industry-wide wage agreement, the union advanced the following arguments. (1) Industry-wide wage stabilization, by eliminating gross wage inequalities among workers doing comparable work, would remove a major source of labor unrest and boost morale and productivity. (2) The creation of a master wage pattern for the industry would greatly simplify the problem of wage adjustment. Instead of settling thousands of individual plant wage disputes, the Board would be required only to decide adustments to the pattern which would then apply uniformly to all plants. This would eliminate the bottleneck of dispute cases before the Board and remove a source of frustration that has led to unauthorized strikes. (3) An industry-wide wage agreement would contribute to employment stabilization by reducing the high rate of turnover that results when workers shop around for higher-paying jobs. (4) Industry-wide wage stabilization, aside from its wartime advantages, would ease the transition to peacetime production by protecting employment opportunities in the older, established production centers against the "unhealthy and socially-destructive competition" of new facilities in low-wage areas. In short, the case for industry-wide wage uniformity was based on considerations of equity, security, industrial efficiency, and industrial peace.

The one aspect of the wage stabilization program that UAW leaders found most alarming was the "area wage-bracket system." Under this system, the War Labor Board, by order of the Director of Economic Stabilization, was directed to establish wage-rate brackets for each occupational group and labor market area based on the "various rates found to be sound and tested going rates." All rates falling within the established brackets were regarded as stabilized rates. Since an area bracket system, narrowly defined, ran counter to the goal of rate uniformity, the UAW protested its application to the automobile industry on anything other than an industry-wide basis. Union officials pointed out the gross injustice of wage differentials between workers in different parts of the country employed on identical work and often by the same employer. They claimed that narrow "area" brackets, based on local rate averages, threatened destruction of the high-wage standards achieved in UAW plants and prevented the union from securing uniform corporation-wide wage rates "in derogation of long-established practice in collective bargaining between the UAW and the automobile . . . companies."[2] This bracket system not only frustrated the union's efforts to spread established rates within a corporation to new plants, but it even encouraged certain management representatives to apply the same (area) method of rate setting to new jobs in existing plants, thereby creating differentials between plants that had formerly paid the same rates.[3] Finally, the union insisted that this "vicious" policy was not only disrupting the pattern of wage relationships, but was actively encouraging decentralization of operations. As President R. J. Thomas stated in his report to the 1944 convention, "by the very simple process of moving a plant 75 or 100 miles, . . . the General Motors Corporation, with WLB sanction, has been able to pay rates anywhere from 15 cents to 30 cents below the original location."[4]

Despite persistent wartime pleas for industry-wide wage stabilization, little was accomplished along that line during

2. R. J. Thomas, president, UAW-CIO, "Automobile Unionism (1944)," *A Report submitted to the 1944 convention of the UAW-CIO* (Sept. 1944), pp. 44–45.

3. "Wage Stabilization and Postwar Security," p. 16.

4. "Automobile Unionism (1944)," p. 67. The insidious effects of the area bracket system were outlined by Reuther in a report (*The Area "Bracket Racket"*) delivered at a conference of GM locals in May 1944. Noting that the bracket racket denied equity to the workers and destroyed "that degree of

the war years. Accordingly, the objective remained a prominent feature of the UAW's postwar program. Both major factions in the union made wage equalization the backbone of wage policy, though Reuther criticized the opposition (i.e. the administration up to March 1946 and the controlling group on the Executive Board until November 1947) for its failure to formulate objectives clearly and especially for its lack of an over-all plan for coordinating local-union activities under strong centralized leadership. The name calling and political maneuvering that characterized the period did not divert the union, however, from its preoccupation with wage-structure objectives. On this point at least all groups were united. At the March 1946 convention, delegates called upon the International Union for a more vigorous program to organize the unorganized and eliminate substandard wage contracts in the industry. Less than a month later, the International Executive Board adopted a policy statement which set as the union's basic objective the establishment of "industry-wide bargaining and national wage agreements" and as an interim goal the elimination of all wage inequities within each plant and corporation under contract.[5] On October 18 and again on December 9, Reuther submitted tentative drafts of wage policy to the International Executive Board for its approval. The emphasis in both drafts was on the need for interplant uniformity: "An industry-wide wage agreement based on the principle of equal pay for equal work without regard to products being manufactured or the geographic

---

stability and uniformity which we have established in our industry wage pattern through the processes of collective bargaining," Reuther concluded that the policy was an invitation to "post-war economic catastrophe" and faced the union with its most challenging problem in the transition to a peacetime economy.

5. "Statement of Policy for the UAW-CIO," April 19, 1946. At the convention, the resolution calling for Executive Board action was described as the most important resolution coming before the delegates. In the floor discussion, criticism centered on corporations that were setting up "runaway" plants in low-wage areas and on the transfer of work and contracts away from such high-wage markets as Detroit and Toledo. [*Proceedings of the 10th Conven-*

location of the plant is the most important economic objective of our union. . . . We must replace our present system of carrying on hundreds of isolated and uncoordinated wage negotiations . . . with wage conferences of the entire industry where the full power of our union can be expressed and translated into an industry-wide agreement for our entire membership. . . . The maximum degree of stability will not be achieved until a rational overall wage program which will take labor out of competition is effected."

Steps to implement the union's wage program were outlined in both drafts. In addition, Reuther advocated that the Executive Board's International Policy Committee, assisted by appropriate union departments, draw up a set of minimum contract standards for the industry covering wage rates, overtime, shift differentials, vacation pay, holiday pay, rest periods, paid lunch periods, veterans' provisions, nondiscrimination clauses, and health and safety provisions. No agreement that failed to meet these minimum standards was to be approved. At the same time, Reuther informed all local unions (by letter of November 8, 1946) of the ratification procedures that had been adopted by the Board for the purpose of enforcing the new contract standards.

It is unnecessary to detail the evidence of the union's strong commitment to the policy of equal pay for equal work throughout the postwar years. Suffice to note that there has been continuous advocacy and unanimous support of the policy throughout the organization, as well as continuous pressure at the bargaining table for its implementation. Indeed, the objec-

---

tion, UAW-CIO (March 23–31, 1946), pp. 42–46.] In its deliberations on the resolution, the International Executive Board was reported to have given top priority to the task of wiping out all intraplant and interplant inequalities in companies under contract. "Not until wage inequalities in already organized plants have been eliminated and not until unorganized shops have been brought into the union can the workers be assured both of their wage standards and the security of their union": UAW-CIO, *Research Report, 6*, no. 5 (May 1946).

tive of equal rates is strongly embedded in the organizational structure of the union. For the membership as a whole, the responsibility for promoting a standardized wage structure rests primarily with the Competitive Shop Department. This department, established in the early 1940s, has two divisions—the Organization Division and the Wage-Hour Division. The former trains organizers, assists in the prosecution of strikes, aids existing locals in organizing drives, and directs generally the organizational activities of the union. The Wage-Hour Division conducts wage surveys, compiles wage and contract statistics for industry subdivisions such as tool and die shops and foundries, and is responsible for coordinating and directing the work of the numerous Wage-Hour Conferences and Councils which represent important segments of the membership and have as their primary function the standardization of wages, hours, and working conditions. Since its inception, the Competitive Shop Department has actively encouraged the closest cooperation among all departments and regional offices of the union in its drive to extend organization and establish uniform wage structures within competing groups of plants. Within the automobile companies themselves, however, wage equalization is mainly the responsibility of the intracorporation councils representing the local unions in each corporation.

The union's drive for interplant wage uniformity is based mainly on considerations of equity and security. As a matter of simple justice, workers doing the same job and using the same skills should receive the same compensation, regardless of the financial condition of the employing company or the location of its facilities. Differing wage levels for comparable work in competing plants leave the low-paid worker dissatisfied and the high-paid worker insecure. Their existence encourages "runaway" shops and decentralization, penalizes the more liberal employer, and renders the task of general improvement in wage conditions more difficult. Underlying union policy is the belief that competition, to be socially constructive, should be based on superior management, better engineering, and more efficient methods of processing and distribution—not on lower wage scales.[6] In defense of its position, the UAW has noted on numerous occasions that other prices do not vary according to geographic location or "ability to pay." Thus the prices of automobiles are the same regardless of where they are produced or sold; the prices of consumer goods (and hence living costs) are fairly well standardized among areas; and, most important, the prices of other productive factors (capital, raw materials, and parts and accessories) are uniform for all producers in all locations. With price uniformity the rule, why, asks the union, should the price of labor services vary? In pursuit of the equal-pay objective, therefore, the union has a strong and unambiguous motivation.

While the standard rate is a fundamental cornerstone of trade union wage philosophy, most unions have found it necessary in practice to reconcile this principle with differences in "ability to pay." In the majority of industries where differences in size, efficiency, or location introduce significant cost differences, the union concerned has been forced to modify its application of the standard rate to take account of such variations. Normally this has meant granting some wage (or other) relief to firms of demonstrated poor profitability and financial condition in order to safeguard employment opportunities. In these circumstances, wage equality is modified by considerations of cost equality; stability requires uniformity of unit costs rather than standardization of hourly earnings. The dilemma posed for the union is obvious—equity concepts suggest that equalization of earnings is the appropriate policy target, but stability, in terms of the preservation of prevailing employment patterns, is better served by equalizing unit costs. Each union must, on the basis of its

6. See, e.g., the testimony of Walter P. Reuther before the Senate Committee on Labor and Public Welfare, Feb. 21, 1947.

experience and the character of the industry and membership it serves, select its own particular compromise between these two objectives in formulating wage policy.

As far as basic policy for the automobile industry is concerned, Reuther has stated the UAW's position as follows: "For ourselves, we of the UAW are willing, as we have been willing for the past 12 years, to be bound by the policy first enunciated in 1945, that demands for wage increases and other economic gains in administered price industries should be confined within the limits of ability to pay, without price increases, of an efficient firm functioning under full employment conditions."[7] This statement expresses simply the manner in which the UAW's leadership, at least in principle, has resolved the dilemma of the "standard rate" vs. "ability to pay" in the face of wide variations in the fortunes of competing firms. Wage demands, to be sure, take account of ability to pay—not the ability of each firm, however, but only the the efficient firm operating under conditions of full employment. This signifies, in effect, that while profitability is an important consideration in establishing wage demands, differences in profitability are merely measures of differences in the effectiveness of management. The approach thus permits the union to recognize the relevancy of profitability and financial condition without compromising its dedication to the goal of wage equality. The emphasis on "an efficient firm" avoids the embarrassing problem of low profits and even of losses in less fortunate companies, while the stress on "full employment conditions" makes actual measures of ability irrelevant except under the most advantageous circumstances.

The clear implication is, of course, that the less efficient firm deserves no special dispensation—and, indeed, union officials have stated so quite emphatically on a number of occasions. In a wartime discussion of Hudson's financial difficulties, for

---

7. U.S. Senate, "Administered Prices," *Hearings before the Subcommittee on Antitrust and Monopoly of the Committee on the Judiciary,* 85th Congress, 2d Session (1958), p. 2427.

example, UAW President R. J. Thomas is reported to have announced that if Hudson could not afford to meet the rates paid by other companies "it was high time they quit the business and [left] it to those who could and did pay high wages."[8] Similarly, in the 1948 negotiations at General Motors, when a question was raised regarding differences in profitability, the following exchange took place:

> *Management Representative:* In your union if—this is a hypothetical question—if a pattern were established by a manufacturer at a certain level, would you expect a lesser wage increase from an organization that had no profits? *Union Representative:* No, we think that if there is going to be a competitive economy, the inefficient producer has got to be pushed out of business. We don't think that inefficiency in management should be subsidized out of workers' living standards. We do think that wage levels throughout the entire economy, the purchasing power of wage and salary workers generally, should be based on the ability of the economy to pay.[9]

This policy that labor should not be called upon to subsidize inefficient producers still commands general approval within the UAW leadership. Up to now, the union has insisted that industry standards be met in each of the auto companies regardless of financial condition. It is true, of course, that the union has permitted certain deviations from the pattern settlement in recent years—notably in the case of the Independents in the mid-1950s. But while these developments are significant and may foreshadow a reorientation of union wage policy, they have not as yet signaled an abandonment of the standard rate. Pattern concessions are considered in detail in chapter 6 and there is therefore no need to enter into an extended discussion

8. Reported by GM Vice-President Harry Anderson in *Proceedings, GM-UAW Negotiations* (Nov. 9, 1945), p. 558.
9. *Proceedings, GM-UAW Negotiations* (April 30, 1948), p. 85.

at this point. It should be noted, however, that the pattern concessions granted to date have been adustments toward rather
than away from the prevailing industry standard—i.e. they have
had the effect of reducing interfirm differentials already in
existence. This type of adustment is obviously distinguishable
from the pattern concession granted to a firm already paying no
more than the standard.

It should be understood, of course, that the reference here is
to union policy as it has been applied to the automobile companies. Elsewhere within its jurisdiction the union has frequently
allowed smaller companies to deviate from the industry wage-
benefit standard in cases of demonstrated need. This is the clear
implication, for example, of Levinson's study of pattern bargaining by the UAW, though the study itself is concerned more
with the pattern of wage settlements (i.e. increases) than with
the structure of wage levels.[10] Nevertheless, Levinson's main
conclusion concerning the determinants of the pattern of settlements confirms our own findings regarding adherence to the
industry standard in the case of the automobile companies. Thus
Levinson writes: "Many of the large companies . . . were faced
with serious financial difficulties during some part of the period
covered, yet no, or very minor, modifications of the pattern
appeared in the negotiated settlements. It seems clear, therefore, that in large units in general, and in the large automobile
firms in particular, the broader economic considerations took
precedence over the narrower problems of individual firms."[11]
We would simply add to this observation the distinction that
should be drawn between a below-pattern and below-standard
concession. In Levinson's study, the concessions made to American Motors and Studebaker-Packard would presumably be

10. Harold M. Levinson, "Pattern Bargaining by the United Automobile
Workers," *Labor Law Journal* (Sept. 1958), pp. 669–74.
11. Ibid., p. 671. By "broader economic considerations" is meant the threat
posed by a below-pattern settlement to the union's bargaining position in subsequent negotiations and the fact that such a settlement merely transfers production and employment from high-wage to low-wage firms.

included with other pattern deviations actually resulting in sub-standard wage-benefit levels. In these two companies, however, this was not the case, for in both instances the contract remained above standard even after concessions were granted. Indeed, it was recognition of this initial superiority of contract terms that finally prompted UAW officials to support limited relief for the Independents during the crisis of the mid-1950s; and even then the widespread publicity given by the union to the continuing above-standard provisions of these contracts did little to prevent other employers from pressing for similar concessions and local unions from protesting the action that had given rise to such pressures.

In short, there is no reason to date for supposing that the UAW has abandoned strict adherence to the principle of the standard rate in negotiations with the automobile companies. There is, however, one important qualification to be added. It is possible to detect in recent years a gradual shift in the thinking of UAW officials which may yet be translated into effective action at the bargaining level. In 1958, the UAW offered the industry a profit-sharing proposal which, if seriously intended, represents a rather dramatic shift in wage policy and a significant modification of the standard-rate principle. Since the role of profit sharing in the union's bargaining program is unclear at this time, it seems advisable to postpone any detailed comment on the issue to the final section of the present chapter.

Having explored the nature and basis of union policy, our purpose now is to investigate the impact of this policy on the pattern of interplant wage differentials. Collective bargaining is of course a process of joint determination; consequently, the actual behavior of differentials must be appraised from the standpoint of management's as well as the union's wage objectives. It is primarily where these wage objectives are in conflict and a compromise is required that we have an opportunity to observe any independent union influence. Naturally, the objectives themselves—as we have had occasion to note in earlier chapters—must be realistic in the sense of being consistent with minimum market requirements. If management, for example, adopts a stand for bargaining purposes that would fail in any case to call forth the necessary labor supply, then with or without the union the objective is unattainable, and it would obviously be erroneous to credit the union under these circumstances with a result that is unavoidable even in its absence.

Intrafirm and Interfirm Differentials

In general, auto managements have opposed the union's drive to eliminate interplant differentials. They have also taken exception to the phenomenon of pattern bargaining. In the discussion below, we shall look first at developments within each of the major companies (i.e. at intrafirm wage differences) and then at wage relationships among the various companies.

Intrafirm differentials. Although most companies with widely scattered operations take the view that wage scales should reflect community wage levels, the strongest advocate of this position in the auto industry has been General Motors. In 1937, Alfred P. Sloane, Jr., stated the corporation's basic policy in this area, and the same policy has been reiterated by GM officials in every negotiating session since that time. As Sloane explained it to the company's stockholders:

> The Corporation is engaged in many different industries. It is conducting operations in over fifty communities, situated in fourteen different states. Each different industry and each different community . . . has a different set of operating conditions. For instance, the wage scale varies basically. Continuity of employment varies greatly in one industry as against another. Naturally, this has an influence on the wage scale. The cost of living varies. This should likewise be reflected in the wage scale. The geographic separation of the Corporation's various operations sometimes involving thousands of miles, requires an en-

tirely different treatment in the various phases of its operations, as compared with a manufacturing unit entirely within one community.[12]

Unlike its competitors, GM insisted from the very beginning on contractual recognition of the fact that wage scales were a matter for local negotiation and should reflect, among other things, "the general level of wages in the community."[13]

We have unfortunately no early record of the extent of intrafirm wage differentials at GM and therefore must rely on general impressions. In the union's view, however, the company's original wage system was chaotic. We get some notion of this from the union's description of the task of allocating the $5,000,000 wage equalization fund negotiated in June 1940:

> There had been no uniform wage policy in GM such as existed in the Chrysler Corporation. Each GM plant had its own wage policy. As a result inside the GM corporation, among plants that were organized and were covered by a single contract, there was in some cases a wage spread as high as 50 cents per hour on the same job. . . . After several months of plant negotiations, the union finally worked out a series of readjustments which served to correct most of the injustices. In the process, some plants received average wage increases ranging from three to eight cents an hour. In several Eastern plants many workers received as much as 40¢ per hour increase.[14]

12. Alfred P. Sloane, Jr., president, General Motors Corporation, "The Story of the General Motors Strike," submitted to stockholders (April 1937), p. 5.

13. The specific provision of the GM-UAW contract read as follows: "The establishment of wage scales for each operation is necessarily a matter for local negotiation and agreement between the Plant Managements and the Shop Committees, on the basis of the local circumstances affecting each operation, giving consideration to the relevant factors of productivity, continuity of employment, the general level of wages in the community, and the wages paid by competitors."

14. Thomas, "Automobile Unionism (1940–41)," p. 31.

While there is reason to believe that a substantial portion of the equalization fund was used to correct personal rate inequities and to erect a more rational job classification and rate structure within individual plants, these comments suggest that some leveling between plants also occurred, if only as a by-product. In any case, the correction of intraplant inequities represents the logical first step in the drive to standardize interplant wage rates. It is noteworthy that in the process of apportioning the fund, the union met with some internal criticism: "There was naturally some feeling in the plants where the wage increases were small that a blanket wage increase would have been preferable. This might have presented an easy way out of a complicated problem, but it would not have advanced the goal of the union to achieve a sane wage policy in GM. The GM department's basic reason for establishing the . . . fund . . . was to bring wage rates for comparable work into line and to create a wage structure in GM whereby we would be in a position to move forward for a large blanket increase."[15]

Whatever the effect of the 1940 adjustments, it is clear that interplant differentials at GM remained substantial in the war and postwar period. In the spring of 1945, when Reuther reported to delegates from the GM locals the need for equalizing wage rates on an industry-wide basis, he noted particularly the large differentials that existed between GM plants doing comparable work. To cite just two examples: in Indiana, the Anderson Delco plant paid male rates 10 to 22 cents higher and female rates 31 to 43 cents higher than the Bedford plant, while in Michigan, Detroit Diesel paid rates up to 25 cents above those in Grand Rapids Diesel.[16] In his brief to the corporation on October 26, 1945, Reuther therefore asked that part of the

15. Ibid.

16. *Minutes, International GM Conference, UAW-CIO,* March 30–31, 1945. To illustrate the effect of the WLB's area bracket system, Reuther called attention to the fact that GM's Terre Haute and Kokomo plants, both of which were engaged in radio electronic work, had differentials of 10 to 16 cents in 1945 compared with a prewar differential of 7 cents.

30 per cent wage increase sought by the union be devoted to eliminating all interplant differentials.[17] He estimated that a fund approximately equal to 3 to 4 per cent of existing wages would be required to eliminate interplant inequities, while about 1 per cent would take care of intraplant inequities.[18] In all, this suggests a cost of 5 to 6 cents an hour per employee.

With no progress made in this direction in the first two post-war rounds of wage settlements, the union renewed its efforts for inequity adjustments in 1948. At the GM conference preceding negotiations, local delegates voted the elimination of inequities a *must* in any new agreement.[19] The announced policy of the International Executive Board was that inequity adjustments were to be sought outside the basic 30-cent wage demand. As Reuther explained this aspect of policy, the international union did not want to level rates at the expense of workers in the higher-wage plants.[20] In his view, the union had no right to ask Detroit workers to finance wage increases elsewhere; otherwise, differentials could have been eliminated years earlier. This claim is, of course, open to dispute, but it does indicate a dilemma for the union. In the immediate postwar years, despite the increases won in successive negotiations, unions had difficulty in maintaining real wages in the face of rapid inflation. Under these conditions, differential wage treatment that further depressed the real income of workers in higher-wage plants was likely to cause considerable resentment —hence the union's emphasis on adjustment funds as something "additional" or "extra" after all workers had already received the basic increase to which the economic situation entitled them.

In the actual negotiations in 1948, union spokesmen in-

17. UAW-CIO, *Purchasing Power for Prosperity* (GM Dept., Oct. 26, 1945).

18. *Minutes, National GM Conference, UAW-CIO* (Sept. 14–15, 1945), p. 28.

19. *Minutes, National GM Conference, UAW-CIO* (Jan. 17, 1948), p. 133.

20. Ibid., p. 109.

formed company officials that the union's goal was not necessarily to standardize wage rates at the highest level prevailing
for each job classification, though they indicated that they were
not prepared to accept wage cuts for any large number of
employees.[21] According to union calculations, the cost of eliminating differentials on a corporation-wide basis was about 8
cents; but GM's estimate, based on the union's demands, was
closer to 11 cents.[22] In any event, GM was unwilling to accede
to the union's demand, insisting that plant rates take account
of differing community wage levels.

The failure of the union to do much about interplant differentials at GM was a source of annoyance within the UAW. In
some instances, criticism was leveled against the union as well
as the corporation. Delegates demanded action and not words
in response to the perennial "equal pay for equal work" resolution. It was not until 1955, however, that the union was able
to report any progress at GM.

The UAW's principal demand in 1955 was the guaranteed
annual wage. In an attempt to defeat this drive, General Motors
offered the union on May 17 an attractive package of benefits
including, among other things, a 2-cent fund for the correction
of inequities. This strategy backfired when Ford later switched
from its first offer, closely resembling GM's, to a second offer
containing its supplementary unemployment benefit plan. The
inequity fund remained on the bargaining table, but management soon made it clear to the union that it was intended primarily for the adjustment of *intra*plant inequities.[23] Thus, when
the union asked GM negotiators in early June to "relax more"

21. *Proceedings, GM-UAW Negotiations* (March 18, 1948), p. 20.
22. *Minutes, National GM Conference, UAW-CIO* (April 27, 1948), pp.
38–39.
23. The 2-cent fund in its initial form included a 5-cent increase earmarked
for the skilled trades. In the final settlement, GM agreed to match Ford's
special increase of 8 cents for skilled workers and to provide 2 cents per production worker for the correction of other inequities.

on their area-rate theory and to eliminate the "red flag" clause in the contract tying plant wage rates to community wage levels, the latter replied that they were not prepared to abandon this criterion. "Our inequity fund emphasizes intraplant inequities except with regard to the skilled trades. We used some of the money to wash out intra-city inequities such as those at AC-Flint. But as between cities that's another problem. Some Chambers of Commerce don't even want us in their towns. In divisions like Chevrolet and B-O-P we are trying to level out on similar operations. To level out corporation-wide, however, would cause as big a headache for you as for us. Bedford as a matter of fact may go out of business if they get Saginaw rates."[24]

Actually, the company did make one or two additional concessions on interplant differentials. On June 11 it announced to union negotiators that within the central foundry group it had raised the rates at Danville, Illinois, to the level of Defiance, Ohio. It admitted that it was prepared to move on the rates of both of these plants again, but it refused to meet the union's demand for rate equalization with its Saginaw, Michigan, plant on the grounds that this entailed selecting the highest rates across the country as the standard.[25] Finally, GM agreed to eliminate the differential, in most cases amounting to 10 cents, between outlying parts warehouses and parts warehouses attached to Chevrolet assembly plants.[26] As a result of these negotiations, UAW officials were able to report to the national conference of GM locals that the union had made some progress toward the reduction of differentials in foundry and parts plants and had eliminated from the contract the reference to local community wage levels as a criterion in rate setting. Nev-

24. *Minutes, GM-UAW Negotiations* (June 8, 1955), p. 477.
25. Ibid. (June 11, 1955), p. 526.
26. Letter from N. J. Ellis, General Director of Industrial Relations, Chevrolet Division, to E. S. Patterson, GM Dept., UAW, June 20, 1955.

ertheless, as Reuther reminded the delegates, "the day must come in GM where we have one national wage agreement that covers every plant with uniform rates."[27]

Since 1955 the union has continued to press for wage equalization at GM, but progress has been limited. In September 1957, the union conducted eight-day strikes at two new GM plants in Mansfield, Ohio, and Marion, Indiana, which resulted in wage advances approximating 10 cents per hour. In announcing the settlements, UAW Vice-President Leonard Woodcock also stated the union's objective: "Successful ending of two authorized strikes at new Fisher Body Stamping plants . . . brought wage rates as high as any paid for similar classifications in any GM plants. . . . Wage advances approximated ten cents per hour and covered all classifications. . . . In this way, the workers in Mansfield and Marion . . . won the fight to guarantee that General Motors work will not be moved into new areas at cut rates."[28] Despite modest advances of this sort, however, the basic issue remains. In the 1958 negotiations the union again demanded wage equalization at Detroit levels and the corporation again refused. GM reportedly estimated that it would have cost the company 6.2 cents per hour per worker to satisfy the union's request.[29] The final settlement, which provided a 0.5-cent inequity fund (based on approximately 247,-000 workers) for allocation among the various local unions, must therefore be regarded as little more than a token contribution toward company-wide wage equalization.

Differences in job titles and possible differences in job content make it difficult to measure the actual range of interplant rate differentials at GM in recent years. However, a 1957 survey of key rates in 35 plants engaged primarily in assembly operations and in 67 tool and die shops gives some notion of rate dispersion within the corporation for essentially similar

27. *Minutes, National GM Conference* (June 21, 1955), p. 379.
28. UAW press release, Sept. 30, 1957.
29. *New York Times,* Sept. 28, 1958.

TABLE 18. Rate Dispersion for Selected Occupations in General
Motors Plants, 1957

Assembly operations (35 plants)

Janitor, sweeper		Assembler (general)		Dingman (finish)		Material Handler (trucker, stock laborer)		Electrician	
$1.87	35	$2.07	1	$2.27	2	$1.92	2	$2.51	2
		2.12	32	2.32	6	1.94	1	2.56	4
		2.14	1	2.37	9	1.97	19	2.61	14
		2.17	1	2.42	5	1.98	1	2.63	1
				2.47	10	1.99	6	2.67	14
				n.a.	3	2.00	2		
						2.02	4		

Tool-and-die operations (67 plants)

Janitor, sweeper		Laborer		Electrician		Toolmaker		Pattern-maker	
$1.83	1	$1.85	2	$2.51	2	$2.67	4	$2.89	1
1.84	3	1.87	13	2.56	8	2.70	2	2.91	1
1.85	1	1.89	1	2.58	1	2.72	6	3.10	1
1.87	49	1.90	1	2.59	2	2.78	24	3.12	2
1.92	2	1.92	19	2.61	27	2.84	5	3.18	2
1.94	1	1.94	2	2.67	26	n.a.	26	3.21	1
1.97	1	1.96	2	n.a.	1			3.24	4
n.a.	9	1.97	8					n.a.	55
		2.02	1						
		2.04	1						
		2.07	1						
		n.a.	16						

Sources. Assembly rates are from the *Wage Manual* compiled by the
UAW General Motors Department (June 11, 1957); tool-and-die rates are
from *UAW Tool, Die and Maintenance Survey* (April 1, 1957). All rates
are the maximum rates in each plant.

work (Table 18). These data indicate that the degree of dispersion in plant wage levels is generally not very great. At the same time it is clear that the cost of eliminating interplant differentials is modest if median rates are chosen as the standard, but quite substantial if the highest rates in the various classifications are instead selected.

The issue of interplant wage differentials in the other major auto companies can be treated more summarily, for in these firms the union's objective has long since been realized.[30] In the case of Ford, a major step in the direction of eliminating interplant (or geographic) differentials was taken in 1941 when the company signed its first agreement with the union. Whatever the company's motives in abruptly signing the most liberal contract in the industry after years of bitter antiunionism, Ford agreed from the beginning to equalize rates in its *assembly* plants throughout the nation at the Detroit level. According to company spokesmen, management did not dispute the union's arguments in support of equal pay in 1941 and approached the bargaining table prepared to accede to the union's demand. It was not until the 1950s, however, that management agreed to establish a similar rate equality in its manufacturing operations.

During the years immediately following World War II, the new Ford management,[31] aware that concessions granted in 1941 had placed the company at a competitive disadvantage, refused to yield to pressures for rate uniformity in its manufacturing plants. In spite of its firm opposition at this time, however, Ford's determination to resist wage equalization does not

30. Wage equalization has not been an issue at American Motors and Studebaker-Packard. With the mergers in the mid-1950s and the consolidation of automotive facilities shortly thereafter, these smaller companies have not confronted the union with the kind of interplant wage problems encountered in the widely scattered operations of the Big Three manufacturers.

31. The reference here is to the management team organized by Henry Ford II when he assumed control in 1946 and began the massive job of rebuilding the tottering Ford empire.

appear to have matched that of GM. By the early 1950s the union was reporting steady progress toward its goal.

The first major breakthrough at Ford was announced by the UAW Ford Department in its report to the April 1951 convention:

> We have established complete rate and classification schedules for the Canton, Ohio, and Monroe, Michigan, plants. In both instances these schedules were established on the basis of the wages paid nationally rather than on the area in which the plant is located. Many of the inequities which have existed in individual plants likewise have been corrected and eliminated. New rates and classifications were established for over 200 new types of work. In every instance these met the national pattern.[32]

Two years later, the same union department noted that Ford had completely reversed its position that area rates should apply in the establishment of rate and classification structures in new plants. This claim was based on submissions entered by the company before the Wage Stabilization Board requesting approval of wage rate schedules, based on Detroit levels, for the new Kansas City aircraft plant, the Cincinnati automatic transmission plant, the Cleveland engine and foundry plants, the Richmond parts depot, and the Chicago aircraft engine plant. As the director of the Ford Department added, "in all instances, the area rates were considerably lower."[33]

Finally, in 1955, as part of its counterproposal to the union's demand for a guaranteed annual wage, Ford offered the following changes:

1) Eliminate the Green-Island Plant differential, contin-

---

32. *Report of Reuther to the 13th Convention, UAW-CIO* (April 1, 1951), p. 150.

33. *Report of Reuther to the 14th Convention, UAW-CIO* (March 22–27, 1953), p. 122.

gent on modification of the local fatigue allowance agreement to reduce the allowance in line with changed conditions and to permit the use of countervailing relief in lieu of the allowance. This will involve increases varying from five cents (5¢) to twenty cents (20¢) an hour. . . .

2) Eliminate the base rate differential between Cincinnati and Livonia plants, contingent on the Union's agreeing to separate seniority groups for machining and assembly operations at Cincinnati. . . .

3) Eliminate the base rate differential between Cleveland Stamping Plant and Dearborn and Buffalo Stamping Plants, contingent on the Union's agreeing to continuance of the Automation Equipment Maker and Maintenance classification at Buffalo Stamping Plant and its extension to the Dearborn Stamping Plant.[34]

This first Ford offer was soon superseded by the company's SUB proposal. Nevertheless, wage differentials between the Buffalo and Cleveland stamping plants, the Cincinnati and Livonia plants, and the Green Island and Rouge plants were eliminated in the final settlement.[35] With these adjustments, the UAW could now claim elimination of all geographic wage differences at Ford.

It is important to note that Ford management, though less strongly committed to geographic differentials than GM, would prefer to base plant wage scales on local area wage levels. Indeed, it is the company's practice to set rates at new plants initially in line with "going rates" as revealed in community wage surveys. The company anticipates that these rate scales will be rejected by union negotiators and it does not expect therefore to be able to maintain below-Detroit rate levels in these plants. Yet the company is anxious to avoid condemnation

34. Ford Motor Company, *Outline of Company Proposal to UAW-CIO on Economic Matters* (May 26, 1955), pp. 3–4.

35. UAW-CIO, National Ford Dept., *The Bargaining Spotlight*, June 1955.

by other local employers concerned with the impact of Detroit rates on the local wage structure. By setting lower rates initially, the company meets its obligation to other employers and transfers responsibility for violating local wage standards to the union.

At Chrysler, virtual uniformity of plant wage levels was also accomplished by the mid-1950s, the major steps being taken in the 1950 and 1955 negotiations. While the union complained of many inequities in the company's wage structure during the 1940s, the principal inequity was a 9-cent differential between Chrysler's Detroit plants and its three Indiana plants at Kokomo, New Castle, and Evansville. In line with industry policy at the time, Chrysler refused to accede to union demands for a reduction of these differentials in the first three postwar rounds of negotiations. In 1950, however, at the end of the protracted pension strike, the company agreed to reduce the differential by 3 cents. As the union announced in its report of the settlement to Chrysler workers, the reduction was the first progress the union had been able to make at the company in this direction in 12 years of striving. As an indication of management's reluctance to move on the issue, the union noted further that Chrysler had "refused to make any concession whatsoever with respect to the area wage differential until the 94th day of the strike."[36] There was, however, no evidence of a recurrence of these difficulties in 1955 when, after the inequity adjustments at Ford and GM, Chrysler agreed to eliminate all remaining differentials between Detroit and non-Detroit plants. It was estimated that this concession, which established a uniform national wage scale at Chrysler, brought increases of 4 to 9 cents to 16,000 hourly-rated and salaried workers in six different states.[37]

36. "What Chrysler Workers Won," letter from Walter P. Reuther to all Chrysler workers (undated).
37. UAW press release, Sept. 1, 1955.

Chrysler's opposition to union efforts to eliminate area differentials was based on the belief, shared by other companies, that plant wage levels should reflect local market conditions. It was reinforced, moreover, by a strong reluctance to level area differences as long as these were preserved in competing companies. Chrysler management already felt that the company was at a disadvantage (compared with General Motors) since its facilities were more heavily concentrated in the high-wage Detroit area. Its decision to eliminate area differentials in 1955 was strongly influenced therefore by its recognition that Ford had already adopted a national wage policy and that GM was apparently moving in the same direction. Interestingly enough, Chrysler did not agree to eliminate a differential of approximately 26 cents between Detroit and a small Louisiana plant on the grounds that this would upset the local wage structure and bring very strong protests from other employers in the area. Apart from this exception, however, Chrysler had by 1955 committed itself to a uniform corporation-wide wage structure.

Interfirm differentials. The structure of interfirm wage differences and its behavior over time can be summarized as follows. If Detroit area rates are made the basis of comparison, variations between firms have been relatively minor for the majority of occupations throughout the period of collective bargaining. Moreover, insofar as there are differentials between the plants of different firms (which are not to be attributed to differences in geographic location), they do not vary in the same direction for all occupations, suggesting that average differentials are not significant. Certainly, no one firm pays uniformly higher rates than any other firm. There is of course strong pressure under collective bargaining for a more rational ordering of classifications and wage rates; and it is likely therefore that the elimination of personal differentials and the numerous individual inequity adjustments have created a more uniform job classification and rate structure for the industry as a whole. Nevertheless, there is little evidence in the wage data for the last 20 years or so that would justify a conclusion that hourly rates have at any time differed substantially between firms. Except for the one occasion to be noted below, reasonable rate uniformity among companies has been the rule since at least the 1930s;[38] and such interfirm differentials as still exist are primarily a reflection of differences in the geographic location of facilities.

Within this generalized picture of interfirm wage relationships, it is to be observed that individual companies have from time to time deviated from industry standards. This has occurred for two reasons—differences in the timing of unionization and differences in the method of wage payment. The former was responsible for some temporary widening of interfirm *rate* differentials, most notably as a result of the wage lag at Ford up to 1941, while the latter was responsible for substantial *earnings* differentials between firms with incentive plans such as Studebaker and other firms with hourly-rate systems. We shall comment briefly on each of these types of deviations.

The fact that Ford was not organized until the spring of 1941 apparently permitted that company to enjoy a temporary wage advantage over its unionized competitors. According to UAW statistics, Ford wage rates in 1940 were 10 to 15 per cent below those of GM, Chrysler, and other organized companies. Indeed, in March 1941, the UAW announced (in its *Research Bulletin,* Issue no. 7) that average hourly wage rates in five unionized auto companies ranged from $1.035 to $1.067 compared with a Ford average of $0.90. One may question, of course, the reliability of comparisons issuing from a partisan

38. In this connection, the following comment by Harbison and Dubin (*Patterns of Union-Management Relations,* pp. 195–96) is pertinent: "General Motors or Ford set the pace in the auto industry before the appearance of the UAW and other unions. The principal difference today is that wages are determined by joint union-employer deliberation in the power centers rather than by unilateral managerial discretion. To some degree, furthermore, the patterns set may be more rigidly followed throughout the industry as a result of the actions of the unions involved."

source. In this case, however, the comparisons were soon verified. When Ford agreed in June 1941 to match the highest wage rates paid in each industry in which it operated, the result was to raise the average wage rate from 95.8 cents to $1.16.[39] A year later, in late 1942, when the War Labor Board awarded a 4-cent general increase to GM and Chrysler workers, it denied a similar adjustment to Ford workers on the grounds that the latter had already received increases in basic rates of 25 to 28 per cent since the summer of 1941.[40]

While stepped-up defense activities were undoubtedly creating wage pressures in auto labor markets in 1941 and while Ford's first contract with the UAW clearly raised the company's wage rates to the top of the industry wage structure, it is unquestionably true that the initial impact of unionism (i.e. during the period 1937–41) was to raise competitors' rates above the Ford level, thereby creating a temporary differential. Since that time, Ford has contended that its wage rates are excessive by industry standards, though the WLB's decision in 1942 and the special inequity funds negotiated at GM since that time have been acknowledged as reducing, if not quite eliminating, Ford's wage disadvantage.

Interfirm differences in *earnings* resulting from the retention of incentive methods of wage payment have been of much greater significance. It should be recognized, however, that the very sizable differentials developed at Studebaker and Willys-Overland during the war and postwar periods are to be attributed largely to a deterioration of the incentive systems in both companies (see chapter 6). For present purposes, it is sufficient to note that, in Studebaker's case, the incentive system which had been designed in the mid-1930s to produce an average

39. *Business Week* (Dec. 6, 1941), p. 94.
40. *Business Week* (Oct. 24, 1942), p. 98. These estimates are in line with the union's. On Oct. 18, 1954, Ken Bannon, Director of the UAW National Ford Dept., placed the average increase at 20.4 cents with "typical" increases of 26 cents for major assemblers, 23–38 cents for electricians, 11–26 cents for die makers, and 7–17 cents for janitors.

earnings level 5 to 10 per cent above base rates (i.e. Detroit hourly rates) was yielding earnings of 20 per cent or more above in the war and postwar years. Indeed, the average differential between Detroit and South Bend was 18 per cent in the fall of 1954 when the company, on the verge of closing down, managed to eliminate its piecework system. The data in Table 19, drawn from the Studebaker and UAW files, indicate the spectacular growth and eventual elimination of the South Bend-Detroit *earnings* differential.

TABLE 19. Average Hourly Earnings for Selected Occupations in South Bend and Detroit, 1937–1955

| | *1937* | | *1945* | | *1954* | | *1955* | |
| | *South* | | *South* | | *South* | | *South* | |
Occupations	*Bend*	*Detroit*	*Bend*	*Detroit*	*Bend*	*Detroit*	*Bend*	*Detroit*
Janitor, sweeper	$0.63	$0.75	$1.07	$0.89	$2.08	$1.75	$1.905	$1.78
Assembler, conveyor	0.99	0.95	1.40	1.12	2.44	1.98	2.055	1.98
Electrician	0.93	1.10	1.46	1.40	2.59	2.46	2.355	2.46
Toolmaker	1.03	1.20	1.67	1.60	2.79	2.61	2.53	2.61
Welder, arc and gas	1.06	1.10	1.51	1.27	2.51[a]	2.13[a]	2.155	2.13

a. Rates for acetylene welder.

Apart from these particular developments which have given rise to temporary deviations from industry rate or earnings standards, interfirm wage differences have been of little significance. This is illustrated in Table 20 which gives comparative rates for selected occupations in the various firms as of 1947 and 1955, the only years for which such data are available. The most notable feature of the 1947 statistics is of course the high earnings levels produced under the Studebaker and Willys incentive systems. These have already been discussed. The 1955 statistics, on the other hand, reveal a fairly uniform

TABLE 20. Hourly Rates in Selected Occupations in Major Auto Companies, January 1947 and April 1955

Occupations	G.M.	Ford	Chrysler	Hudson[a]	Packard[a]	Studebaker[b]	Nash[c]	Willys[d]
January 1947								
Common labor, sweeper	$1.075	$1.08[e]	$1.075	$1.085	$1.105	$1.346	$1.085	$1.100
Milling, general	1.295	1.33	1.305	1.355	1.235	1.719	1.365	1.752
Assembler, bench	1.295	1.28	1.255	1.275	1.265	1.722	1.295	1.674
Assembler, conveyor	1.325	1.33	1.305	1.305	1.305	1.722	1.325	1.688
Grinder, crankshaft	1.425	1.46	1.455	1.485	1.445	1.590	1.435	1.555
Welder, arc and gas	1.425	1.43	1.455	n.a.	1.445	1.746	1.435	1.663
Electrician	1.585	1.63	1.565	1.595	1.545	1.737	1.485	1.505
April 1955[f]								
Material handler	1.90	1.855[e]	1.83	1.83	1.89	1.955	1.96	
Milling, general	1.97	1.955	1.98	1.98	1.97	2.055	2.03	
Drilling, general	1.97	1.955	1.98	1.98	1.97	2.005	2.03	
Punch press, light	1.97	1.955	1.93	1.93	1.97	2.005	2.06	
Assembler, major	2.00	2.005	1.98	1.98	1.99	2.055	2.02	
Grinder, external	2.00	2.035	2.03	2.09	2.03	2.055	2.13	
Checker, receiving	2.00	2.005[e]	1.88	1.92	1.97	1.955	1.96	
Sprayer, enamel	2.10	2.105	2.13	2.13	2.14	2.105	2.15	
Electrician (top rate)	2.46	2.505	2.46	2.46	2.46	2.355	2.38	
Toolmaker (top rate)	2.56	2.605	2.61	2.61	2.61	2.53	n.a.	
Patternmaker, bench (top rate)	2.88	2.875	2.88	2.81	2.85	2.63	2.75	

a. Rates do not include 3 cents at Hudson and 3.5 cents at Packard received in lieu of holiday pay.
b. South Bend, Ind. Data for 1947 represent earnings rather than rates.
c. Kenosha, Wis.
d. Earnings data rather than rates.
e. Midpoint of 10-cent range.
f. Hourly rates include 6-cent cost-of-living allowance.
Source. UAW wage surveys.

pattern of rates, except for a tendency toward a more compressed rate structure at Nash and Studebaker, the only two companies located outside the Detroit area.[41] We would speculate that this narrower rate structure is the product of local labor market conditions and localized bargaining. The Nash and Studebaker facilities are located respectively in Kenosha, Wisconsin, and South Bend, Indiana. Compared with Detroit, these are low-wage markets, and it is reasonable to suppose therefore that market forces have exerted little, if any, upward pressure on the rates for specific occupations. This means, in effect, that there is more room for institutional forces to shape intraplant wage relationships. Given this permissive condition and the fact that, up to 1955, bargaining with these companies was conducted by local union officials directly responsible to the membership, it is not unlikely that political considerations weighed heavily in the formulation of wage policy and in the shaping of a wage structure which favored the lower-paid, numerically preponderant groups. Otherwise it is difficult to explain the difference in wage structure between Studebaker and Nash, on the one hand, and Detroit-based Hudson and Packard, on the other.

Outside of these locational differences, the wage scales of the various companies are quite similar. If account is taken of intrafirm (or geographic) differentials, then GM appears to enjoy a slight wage advantage over its competitors. If, in addition, correction is made for differences in employee benefits, then the smaller companies would be raised to the top of the interfirm wage structure. Again, however, we would add that whatever the disadvantages suffered by these firms up to 1955, the margin has been greatly reduced in the last six or seven years as wage and benefit levels have been more closely aligned with Detroit standards.

Analysis of the pattern and behavior of interplant wage

41. Willys ceased passenger-car production in 1955 and hence was omitted from the wage survey from which these data are drawn.

differentials suggests that unionism has had the following effects. It has been successful in eliminating all geographic differences in plant wage levels at Ford and Chrysler and has made modest progress toward the same goal at General Motors. This leveling of rates in outlying plants cannot be explained in terms of market forces or employer preference. Management feels strongly that plant wage scales should be based on local community standards. Moreover, it has experienced no difficulty in staffing and operating outside-Detroit plants at below-Detroit wage levels. There is thus no reason for the equalizing of rates beyond the obvious one of strong union pressure.

With regard to interfirm differentials, the union has probably been responsible for developing, through inequity adjustments, a more uniform ordering of jobs and rates within each company and hence among the several companies. In addition, it must be held responsible for the early temporary widening of interfirm *rate* differentials that resulted from the uneven pattern of unionization and—if we may anticipate a later finding—for part of the spreading *earnings* differential that resulted from the deterioration of the Studebaker and Willys incentive systems. Finally, by insisting on Detroit standards in other lower-wage labor markets, the union has almost certainly altered the pattern of interfirm wage relationships, mainly to the disadvantage of Nash (now American Motors) at Kenosha and Studebaker at South Bend and to the slight advantage of GM which alone has resisted the union's drive for wage equality.

Profit Sharing

In 1958 the UAW made a surprising proposal to the auto companies when it requested, among other things, the negotiation of a profit-sharing plan. If seriously intended, this proposal marks a sharp break with traditional wage objectives. If successfully implemented, it means compromise, if not abandonment, of the principle of equal pay for equal work. In this concluding section, we examine the meaning of the profit-sharing proposal and its implications for union wage policy and inter-firm wage relationships.

The UAW's "new approach" to bargaining was officially un-veiled before a special UAW conference convened in January 1958 to ratify the bargaining program for negotiations in the spring. The International Executive Board's recommendations, approved by the convention, called for a "two-package" pro-posal to be served on management—a basic minimum demand consisting of a general wage increase, the elimination of wage inequities, and improvements in pensions, SUB, and health insurance; and a supplementary demand providing for the shar-ing of profits above a specified return on investment. As the union itself described the mechanics of its profit-sharing pro-posal:

> We propose that the corporations meet, as the minimum cost of doing business, basic wages to workers, basic salaries of corporation executives, basic profits of 10 per cent on net capital before taxes to stockholders, and that, having met these three basic obligations . . . there be an equitable three-way sharing of the profits over and above the 10 per cent.
>
> Taking into account the fact that profits retained by the corporations after payment of bonuses to their execu-tives will be subject to the corporate profits tax, we pro-pose that one-half of all profits above 10 per cent on net capital before taxes be retained by each corporation for its stockholders and executives.
>
> We propose that one-fourth be allocated to all wage and salaried employees other than executives eligible to participate in the executives bonus plan. . . .
>
> We recommend that the remaining one-fourth be allo-cated by the corporations to consumers. This we make as a

recommendation rather than as a collective bargaining demand, because the corporations have persistently insisted that prices are not subject to collective bargaining.[42]

The union's leadership was quick to point out that this seemingly radical demand was in fact based on "conservative" practices introduced by the industry itself. Thus, the basic formula for measuring "extra" profits was no more than an extension of the principle adopted by GM and Ford for computing executive bonuses, while the recommendation for consumer rebates borrowed directly on an idea originally advanced by Henry Ford and later endorsed by American Motors' President George Romney. The union justified this "unusual approach" partly on traditional grounds—the growing imbalance between productive power and purchasing power and the union's inability, despite years of striving, to influence the "irresponsible" pricing policies of the larger corporations. More noteworthy, however, was the expressed desire to offer some measure of relief to the overburdened smaller companies. For the first time, the union explicitly recognized the dilemma confronting it in pursuing the "standard rate" in the face of large differences in "ability to pay":

> The uneven economic situation as between large, wealthy corporations and smaller, less favorably situated companies confronts the UAW and other trade union groups with a serious collective bargaining problem. If our collective bargaining demands are tailored to fit the more favored economic position of the larger corporations, they create serious problems for corporations less favorably situated. If, on the other hand, our demands are tailored to fit the economics of the less favorably situated companies, then we give the large corporations a still greater advantage and further intensify the im-

42. *UAW Administrative Letter, 10,* no. 1 (Jan. 13, 1958).

balance out of which the economic problem originally developed.[43]

In stating the dilemma, the union was careful to avoid any forthright admission of the desirability of relating employee compensation to each firm's profitability or "ability to pay." It is clear, however, that the 1958 proposal represented a significant movement in this direction for, while the basic demands to be served on all companies were geared to economy-wide productivity improvements and were to be pressed regardless of a company's profitability and financial condition, the supplementary demand was designed to produce variations above that minimum level in accordance with the actual profits realized in each individual firm. The union explained its purpose as follows: "It does not require a less favored company to meet a fixed demand based upon the economics of a more favored company, nor does it permit a more favored company to escape its obligation to workers and consumers by taking refuge behind the economics of less favored companies."[44] Whatever the explanation, however, the new program clearly marked a sharp break with traditional UAW wage principles in the industry.

The response of the companies to the union's new approach was immediate. It was also violent. Spokesmen for the Big Three called the proposal extravagant, inflationary, unrealistic, and foreign to the concepts of the American free enterprise system.[45] The most devastating attack was mounted by Ernest R. Breech, Ford's board chairman. In an address on January 23 which coincided with the meeting of delegates to the special UAW convention, Breech noted that "as a propaganda device, the Reuther proposal is a natural, because it appears to offer almost everybody something for nothing; as a working proposi-

43. Ibid.
44. Ibid.
45. UAW press release, Jan. 14, 1958.

tion, it is fanciful and full of fishhooks."[46] Turning first to the "fishhooks," Breech pointed out (1) that the consumer-rebate aspect of the plan would lead inevitably to a one-company industry since consumers would naturally purchase the product of the most profitable firm; (2) that profit sharing in this form would encourage union demands for participation in the full range of business decisions from expenditures on advertising and research to plans for capital expansion; and (3) that the union's plan provided for the sharing of profits only, leaving the burden of losses to other groups.

Ford's deep aversion for the plan, however, was revealed less in the listing of its flaws (a strong enough indictment) than in Breech's scathing assault on union leadership, on the "inexorable law of union politics" which compelled leaders such as Reuther to press for ever greater gains regardless of the condition of industry or the needs of the nation. Expressing his own "sad disillusionment" over Reuther's failure to display any sense of public duty, Breech pictured the UAW leader as caught in the vise of his own ambitions and the drive of power-hungry rivals to supplant and surpass him. Under the circumstances, it was altogether unrealistic and unreasonable to expect of the union leader actions motivated by the least concern for the public interest.[47]

46. "Union Monopoly vs. the Public Interest," an address by Ernest R. Breech, chairman of the board, Ford Motor Company, delivered at the annual meeting of the Nashville, Tenn., Chamber of Commerce, Jan. 23, 1958.

47. This frank denunciation of a union bargaining proposal well in advance of negotiations marks a sharp departure in the strategy of the auto companies. Up to 1955, the companies were generally of the opinion that exchange of views should be confined to the bargaining table since the public airing of disputes hardened attitudes and hampered the process of settlement. This sudden reversal in 1958 reflects partly the depths of management's aversion for the UAW proposal. It may also be attributed, however, to a growing belief that earlier policies designed to promote a more harmonious and cooperative relationship had not achieved their purpose. Restraint in responding to "unsound" union proposals and a reluctance to antagonize the

In the months that followed, these and other criticisms of the UAW's profit-sharing proposal were repeated and amplified by other company spokesmen. Theodore Yntema, Ford's financial vice-president, attacked the recommendation for price rebates on the grounds that it would destroy the weaker firms and accentuate cyclical fluctuations.[48] George Romney of American Motors, on the other hand, was particularly incensed by the implications of Reuther's plan for management's "right to manage." In the light of later developments, Romney's position on this issue in 1958 deserves special mention. Noting, as did other industry officials, that the close relation of an employee's compensation to his productive contribution was an eminently sound wage principle, Romney denied that this was the intention of the UAW plan. As he testified before a congressional subcommittee in early 1958:

> Inherent in Mr. Reuther's proposal is that the union shall not only have a share in the profits, but shall also share in determining how these profits shall be made and distributed. . . . This profit proposal of the UAW opens up to collective bargaining everything affecting profits and the distribution of profits, because that is the area being dealt with by the proposal, and it would mean that the union could take the position if it wanted to . . . that if

union's leadership by engaging in public debate had not served to soften the violence or frequency of union attacks on management but had simply reserved the field of propaganda to the union.

Breech himself drew attention to a related reason for management's past silence—namely, the union's power to punish frank talk. As he concluded in his address: "They [the union] do this by closing down key plants through intermittent strikes attributed to grievances that normally would not cause a strike. . . . It will be interesting to see if some key Ford plants are not pulled down in the near future because of my speech here tonight. I have chosen to take this course . . . despite that possibility, because of the overwhelming importance of this issue not only to the Ford Motor Company but to the Nation as a whole."

48. U.S. Senate, "Administered Prices," *Hearings*, pp. 2726–27.

wages were not high enough for purchasing power in some given year . . . probably depreciation rates ought to be reduced, so that you could pay out more in the form of wages. . . .

I, therefore, say that the profit-sharing proposal as put up by the UAW opens the door against the precedents that we have been through, of using it as an entering wedge to actually invade ownership rights. I realize I will be told that is not the intent. We have been told that about a lot of things in the past. It is not a question of the intent at the time. The objective is to get a concession, and once the concession is secured then you drive as much through that door of concession as you can get, and this profit-sharing proposal opens the door to actual sharing by the union of the ownership rights of the enterprise in determining whether the capital shall be maintained or whether it shall be used up or how it shall be used.[49]

It was readily apparent from these unrestrained assaults on the union's proposal that the industry was united in its rejection of the UAW's brand of profit sharing. If necessary, leading producers were prepared to meet the issue head on. The question that concerns us here, however, is the extent of the union's own commitment and the implications of the proposal for union wage-structure policy.

It is doubted in some quarters that the union's profit-sharing proposal was intended as a serious bargaining demand. Slichter and his colleagues, for example, suggest that it was probably nothing more than a temporary public relations and bargaining strategy;[50] and their suspicion appears to have been shared by a number of company officials. The UAW's plan was subjected, of course, to critical scrutiny by management; but it was

49. Ibid., pp. 2916–17.
50. *The Impact of Collective Bargaining on Management* (Washington, Brookings Inst., 1960), p. 441 n.

also hinted that the union's purpose was mainly diversionary. Both Breech and Romney had labeled it an attempt to focus public attention on the profit performance of the most successful companies. Romney, to be sure, applauded the union's belated recognition of the differences in profitability among auto companies ("this is the first time the UAW officially has departed from its traditional everyone-must-meet-the-pattern approach"), but he was quick to add that the size of the union's minimum basic demand on all firms precluded any practical application of its new-found philosophy.[51] He no doubt expressed the sentiment of other managers when he concluded: "The second part [i.e. profit sharing] is designed to create a maximum pressure on General Motors and Ford, to focus public discussion on their economic facts without regard to the application of final results to all automotive companies. . . . How many other companies . . . are so vulnerable as General Motors to such a profit-sharing, price-rebate proposal? . . . What could be more likely to force maximum 'basic economic concessions' by General Motors and Ford? The key to the success of the union's program for 1958 is building public sympathy for its broad objectives by arousing resentment against the immediate targets."[52]

Perhaps the strongest reason for viewing the union's proposal with skepticism, however, was supplied almost a decade earlier by the union itself in a research report entitled "What's Wrong With Profit-Sharing Plans?".[53] In this report, the UAW condemned profit sharing as "poison for workers" and exposed in detail the fatal pitfalls and weaknesses of all such plans. Only two of these weaknesses need be noted here.

1) Profit sharing undermines collective bargaining: "You

51. U.S. Senate, "Administered Prices," *Hearings,* p. 2951. Ford estimated the cost of the union's basic demand at 35 to 45 cents per hour (ibid., p. 2716).
52. Ibid., p. 2951.
53. UAW-CIO, *Facts for Action, 1,* no. 6 (April 1949).

have the fact that under profit-sharing there is no longer any industry-wide or even local standard for jobs and wage rates. Pretty soon, community competes with community for whatever work there is, and workers in one plant find themselves competing against workers in other plants to see who will be willing to work the hardest. Instead of stable collective bargaining, you get anarchy. . . . Before profit-sharing came into these plants, the workers were standing shoulder to shoulder for decent production standards and a fair deal for all."

2) Profit sharing is inconsistent with price reductions: "Labor's position on the need for price reductions has been stated over and over again. It was defended by GM workers in one of the longest strikes in UAW-CIO history. Profit-sharing and cost-savings sharing plans are in direct opposition to that position. What happens to that position if workers permit their pay to be used by management as an argument against cutting prices? . . . Since the days of Gompers, both AFL and CIO leaders have consistently argued for a square deal in the pay envelope without the nightmare of bonuses, accounting reports, trick computations and speed-up that come with the dream of a split of the company's profits."

This uncompromising denunciation of the profit-sharing concept certainly lends credence to the view that the union's proposal was little more than a play for public sympathy and support. Before reaching a verdict, however, it is necessary to take account of more recent developments, including the union leadership's own denial of the charges leveled against it.

Reuther himself attempted to scotch the notion that his profit-sharing proposal was simply a tactical device used to divert attention to high-profit firms. In his report to the 1959 convention, he emphasized that profit sharing would continue high on the list of UAW bargaining priorities and confidently predicted that, as with other pioneering demands which had met initially with "violent and bitter rejection," profit sharing would be incorporated eventually into collective agreements with the auto companies.[54] He also sought to disassociate the 1958 proposal from earlier profit-sharing plans and from organized labor's traditional opposition. Thus he argued that UAW members were now sufficiently loyal both to the organization and to trade union principles not to allow themselves to be "misled into permitting their working conditions to deteriorate by beguiling promises of their employers that, if they submit to speed up or other abuses, profits, and consequently the amount of their shares in profits, will be enlarged." He further argued that the UAW's version of profit sharing was not in any sense a substitute for security and an adequate wage structure, but was rather a supplement to these basic objectives. Reuther's main argument, however, was that "blind adherence to the trade union movement's traditional opposition to profit sharing . . . simply does not make sense" in the light of the nation's need for a more balanced distribution of income.[55]

The International Union was of course duty bound to support and justify its own program in the first general postmortem conducted on the 1958 negotiations. However, there are other considerations that lend support to the view that profit sharing was a genuine demand.

54. *Report of Reuther to the 17th Convention, UAW* (Oct. 9–16, 1959), p. 51.

55. Ibid., pp. 52, 62. Reuther again made no direct reference to the fact that acceptance of the union's plan would have meant abandonment of the principle of "equal pay for equal work," the cornerstone of UAW wage-structure policy. He did note, however, that the profit bonus would have yielded 16 cents an hour for GM workers and nothing for Ford and Chrysler workers in 1958 and 48 cents, 63 cents and 25 cents respectively in the first half of 1959 (ibid., p. 61). In his *Administrative Letter* of Jan. 13, 1958, Reuther did try to distinguish the profit-sharing differentials from traditional inequities: "The fact that our supplementary economic package will provide greater gains from the more profitable corporations . . . does not mean that we will subsidize managerial inefficiency through substandard wages and conditions. . . . Substandard wages and wage inequities must be eliminated and all

First, the UAW leadership had already acknowledged by the mid-1950s the need for a new approach to bargaining. This conviction apparently stemmed from the painful readjustments forced on both the union and the less profitable manufacturers as a result of intensified competition after the Korean War. The nature of the new approach was not revealed publicly, but it is significant that the program discussed within the union at the time closely resembled that ultimately adopted in 1958. The trend in administration thinking was reflected, for example, in a talk given by UAW Vice-President Leonard Woodcock in May 1956 to delegates attending the National GM Conference. Calling attention to the fact that past union bargaining policy had compelled financially weaker companies to exceed the GM-Ford pattern and had thus contributed to monopoly, Woodcock emphasized the need for a complete reversal of the union's approach. "We must turn the situation around so that General Motors and Ford, who now pay the least, will pay the most. One way to do this is to have a bonus arrangement for the workers as they have for the executives. This would not create a pattern precedent, yet would put more money into the nation's blood stream, ease monopoly situations, help prevent General Motors from drowning in the fat of its own profits. Nor would it be a substitute for normal economic demands. . . . It would be, just as for the executives, on top of the regular standard wage."[56] These remarks, delivered by a principal officer of the union before representatives of a major segment of the membership, indicate that the profit-sharing idea had already been discussed

---

our members, wherever they work, must be given the reasonable increase in their living standards and other gains called for in our basic minimum economic demands." However, this merely relabels differentials: the new policy provided for interfirm wage variations above a minimum level; it meant subsidizing inefficiency to the extent that it required higher compensation from the more efficient and more profitable companies; and it created exactly the kind of inequities that past union policy had unequivocally condemned.

56. *Summary of Proceedings, National GM Conference, UAW* (May 24–25, 1956), p. 6.

and even tentatively endorsed by leading UAW officials in the spring of 1956. It was not, therefore, something concocted hastily in the few weeks or months preceding the special 1958 collective bargaining conference. Moreover, with the exception of the price-rebate feature—which in 1958 took the form of a recommendation only and was certainly public-relations inspired—the type of program vaguely suggested by Woodcock conforms to the basic formula officially adopted by the union. Indeed, the notion of a simple bonus arrangement patterned after the executive bonus plan is no doubt a more accurate reflection of the union's true intentions.[57]

Second, while some scholars have expressed doubts concerning the union's interest in profit sharing, others have found the proposal entirely consistent with the union's basic motivations and philosophy. This is certainly the position taken by Montgomery and his colleagues when they contend that the union's plan and management's violent reaction to it are logical developments of the union's effort, on the one hand, to extend its "frontier of control" beyond traditional business-union objectives, and management's determination, on the other, to resist such encroachments on the "right to manage." The essence of this view is expressed in the following statement: "The profit-sharing proposal clearly harmonizes, in its basic motivations, with the broad ideological and philosophic approach adopted by the UAW. Rejection of that proposal by the industry . . . is fundamentally consistent both with its 'labor relations' versus 'employment relations' approach to collective bargaining and its conception of the economic realities it must face."[58]

The discussion so far indicates that a case can be made for

57. It is noteworthy that the plan adopted at American Motors in 1961 (discussed below) takes this form. It is also significant that this type of plan is consistent with the union's professed interest in weakening monopolistic tendencies, whereas its 1958 proposal, if accepted, would clearly have threatened the survival of the weaker firms.

58. Royal E. Montgomery, Irwin M. Stelzer, and Rosalind Roth, "Collective Bargaining over Profit-Sharing: The Automobile Union's Effort to Extend Its Frontier of Control," *Journal of Business* (Oct. 1958), p. 331.

either point of view. If the issue of the union's intent is to be resolved, therefore, we must look to actual bargaining behavior for additional clues. Unfortunately, the 1958 negotiations offer little guidance. The union's position had been so weakened by heavy unemployment, a slow car market, and excessive inventories, that it was compelled to order its members to continue at work for three months during the summer without contracts. Economic circumstances were simply not conducive at this time to the testing of a new principle for which management had already expressed such abhorrence. The events of 1961 appear at first glance to offer somewhat clearer evidence, but a close examination of these negotiations introduces new elements of uncertainty. Profit sharing was not featured explicitly in the union's bargaining program. This is not conclusive, however, for employment problems in the form of widespread layoffs, short workweeks and technological displacement necessarily focused attention on the security issue. Moreover, the union's program did not specifically exclude profit sharing since the approach to bargaining in 1961 stressed the problems to be solved rather than the techniques to be employed in their solution. The impression conveyed by UAW officials was that the union was flexible and open minded as to the methods adopted and resolute only as to the specific problems requiring solution.

The key development in the 1961 negotiations came on July 28 when, after only three meetings at the national level (two of which were at the beginning of the month), American Motors offered the UAW its profit-sharing proposal. As the *New York Times* later reported (September 10), this offer "dropped a bombshell that reverberated through the executive offices of General Motors, Ford and Chrysler." American Motors' proposal, patterned after the UAW's 1958 formula for calculating "extra" profits, was rather surprising in view of the fears entertained by Romney in 1958 regarding the impact of this type of plan on management's "right to manage." These earlier fears were apparently minimized in 1961, however, by company insistence on a strong management-rights clause as part of any profit-sharing settlement. Moreover, whatever risks remained, they were undoubtedly outweighed by the prospect of breaking with the tradition of "pattern" settlements and by management's desire to move toward a more cooperative relationship with the union.[59] The company's initial offer sought to substitute a 7-cent wage increase for the wage escalation features of the current UAW contracts, but this was a change that union officials refused to countenance. Their response was described as "polite, but not too cordial";[60] and union attention was returned to the Big Three, particularly General Motors. When, on August 22, however, these three companies presented almost identical offers which the union considered grossly inadequate, the pressure was transferred back to American Motors and that company given four days to settle under a UAW threat that otherwise it would be forced to accept the Big Three settlement on a strict pattern basis. This pressure, which carried with it the promise of relief from certain unduly restrictive or costly contract provisions, was effective.[61] Agreement in principle was announced by the parties on August 26.

In return for substantial concessions beyond the Big Three offer, AMC was able to secure important changes in local work rules—principally a sound work-standards clause at the Milwaukee plant, a reduction in washup time from 10 to 5 minutes, and a more flexible seniority system. Although the actual cost of the settlement is unknown, major provisions called for continuation of the annual improvement factor and cost-of-living escalator, full company payment of improved hospital-medical insurance, liberalization of pensions and group insurance, short

59. Edward L. Cushman, "The American Motors–UAW Progress Sharing Agreement," *Proceedings of the Industrial Relations Research Association* (Dec. 28–29, 1961), pp. 315–24.

60. *New York Times,* Sept. 10, 1961.

61. As George Romney explained the situation to reporters: "We were confronted with working out a contract agreement in principle by Friday [Aug. 25] based on American Motors facts, or a UAW threat to force us to accept the Big Three settlement on a pattern basis": Verbatim transcript of press conference on Aug. 30, 1961, with George Romney, American Motors' president, and Walter P. Reuther, UAW president.

workweek benefits, SUB improvements (including an increase in weekly benefits to about 75 per cent of take-home pay), and the payment of moving allowances to workers transferred between plants of the company. The novel feature in the AMC agreement was, however, the provision for financing some of these improved benefits through the profit-sharing or progress-sharing plan. This plan sets aside for worker compensation 15 per cent of the before-tax profits remaining after the deduction of 10 per cent of the company's net worth. Two thirds of the employees' profit share are to be used to provide benefits; the other third is placed in AMC stock in each worker's name. The amounts accruing to workers under this plan will depend, of course, on realized profits during the next three years, but the UAW estimates that the formula would have yielded the equivalent of 29.9 cents per man-hour in 1959, 23.7 cents in 1960, and 9.6 cents in 1961.[62] Improvements in the pension and insurance programs have first claim on the part of the profit-sharing fund to be devoted to employee benefits. If the fund is inadequate to meet these claims, then the improvement factor payment will be reduced in the amount necessary to finance these two programs on an actuarially sound basis.[63] The transfer of the employees' insurance contribution to the profit-sharing plan is calculated to increase the workers' take-home pay by 5 cents per hour. Offset against these gains were the union's concessions on local work rules. The reduction in cost brought about by these changes is not known, but as Romney told reporters on August 30, "It's not as great as we hoped it might be but . . . it's a very substantial element in this whole package."[64]

62. "Highlights of the 1961 National Agreement between the UAW and American Motors Corporation" (UAW, Aug. 26, 1961).

63. Any surplus in the fund, after pension and insurance claims are met, are to be allocated on the basis of "mutual determination" at the end of the year.

64. In the same press conference Reuther, too, indicated that the union had made certain concessions to the company. It had agreed, for example, to the

The liberal settlement granted by American Motors in exchange for concessions in local working rules gave the UAW the necessary leverage to pry additional benefits from the Big Three. Both parties, it is true, stated that the settlement was not a pattern. Romney, in particular, stressed that the agreement was uniquely tailored to the facts of American Motors:

> The . . . proposed contract is not intended as a pattern for either General Motors or Ford. . . . Neither of these companies could offset similar fringe benefit cost increases through the same local working agreement cost reductions because they do not have the same unduly restrictive seniority clauses, paid-time-not-worked problem or other costly working agreement provisions that we have in our present contract that are eliminated in our proposed agreement. . . .
>
> We have consistently deplored applications of Big Three patterns, or more, to us in the past. We continue to

introduction of more flexibility into the seniority system since the rigidity of former provisions had made it difficult and costly to adjust schedules in the event of curtailed production. But Reuther also emphasized that the union had objected to the removal of certain other "plus" items on the grounds that these items were not unreasonable and rather than being eliminated should be spread to other companies. "We think the problem is that we haven't done our homework with other companies. . . . Take the coffee break. They [AMC] have a 10-minute coffee break in their plants. We don't think that is unreasonable but we do recognize that that is a serious competitive problem when their competitors don't have it. And we intend to be knocking on their doors."

To prevent any misinterpretation of the union's concessions on work rules, Reuther reminded reporters of the over-all superiority of American Motors' contract provisions and of the union's willingness to accept these same provisions without change at General Motors. His explanation proved less than satisfactory to the workers concerned, however; at the Kenosha plant, which employed 12,000 workers or about one half of the UAW's membership at AMC, the new agreement was rejected by a vote of 1,507 to 1,444. The International Executive Board, after weighing the risks involved, decided to order a second vote at Kenosha. This vote, which was preceded by an extensive two-week "education" campaign, affirmed the agreement by a two-to-one margin—6,700 "for" and 3,200 "against": *Wall Street Journal,* Nov. 6, 1961.

oppose pattern settlements, whipsawing tactics and the persuasion of power instead of the power of persuasion. We believe our future union relationships are more likely to be based on economic facts than on economic force as a result of this agreement. We believe this has been very true through the course of these negotiations. . . .

We believe collective bargaining should occur on the basis of the separate and distinct facts of each separate enterprise between parties as equal as possible in collective bargaining power and sharing common basic interests.[65]

But whatever the company's view of the matter, it was plain to all observers that the settlement—obviously beneficial from AMC's standpoint in view of the accompanying cost reductions —had in fact established a very liberal pattern of improvements which larger companies would find it hard to refuse.[66] Reuther said as much in explaining the union's next move to the press: "We have told the companies—I told General Motors this morning—we would be very happy to travel the progress sharing route. . . . But we are not going to threaten to strike over that. We think this is something they ought to be willing to do because it makes a lot of sense because this is the sensible way to meet these kinds of problems. But what we are going to insist upon is that the benefits that accrue from this kind of approach be also afforded the workers in other sections of the industry where the economic facts make these things possible." In short, AMC's settlement established the pattern of benefits for the industry though not necessarily the method of financing.

Under ordinary circumstances, the Big Three might have refused to meet the expensive package negotiated at American Motors; but given the prospect of a 7,250,000 car market for 1962 (after several quite disappointing sales years) and per-

65. Verbatim transcript of press conference, Aug. 30, 1961.
66. It was equally apparent that whipsawing and the "persuasion of power" —traditional instruments of bargaining in the industry—far from being absent, had played an important role in the negotiations.

sistent pressures from Washington for a peaceful settlement, the Big Three were highly vulnerable. They might still have argued for a lower settlement, basing their case on the *net* cost of the AMC agreement and the higher fixed-cost commitment implicit in the traditional method of financing employee benefits, but the likelihood of a firm stand was slight indeed. During the days immediately following the AMC agreement, GM negotiators continued to press their August 22 proposal. But this was to be expected; the contract deadline was not until September 6 and an early capitulation on economic benefits would simply have encouraged the union to push for additional gains in such areas as production standards, compulsory overtime, work by foremen, and union representation—all areas where the union claimed the company was behind the rest of the industry. In an effort to break the deadlock, the UAW formally proposed to GM on September 2 the contract negotiated at AMC, including a 10-minute rest period and 5 minutes' wash-up time. On the following day, professing its inability to understand the company's rejection of the profit-sharing concept, the union submitted an alternative proposal calling for the same gains but financed in the traditional fashion. Again, one day before the strike deadline, it proposed arbitration of all unsettled issues, but on terms that were certain to prove unacceptable.[67] Finally, however, after an extension of the deadline to September 11, the parties reached an agreement incorporating the gains already secured at American Motors, but without profit sharing. Similar settlements followed at Ford and Chrysler, though in the case of GM and Ford, local disputes shut down operations for a period of approximately two weeks.

With this experience in mind, what can we now say of the union's intentions with respect to profit sharing? Acceptance of the plan at American Motors and its offer to General Motors indicate that the union was certainly not averse to the idea. Indeed, these developments may be interpreted as evidence of

67. UAW press releases, Sept. 2, 3, and 5, 1961.

a genuine, positive interest. It is always possible, of course, that Reuther accepted the plan at AMC in order to gain more liberal concessions than were otherwise obtainable. He may also have felt that the plan would help overcome worker resistance to a tightening of work rules since workers could anticipate a share of the profits realized from any cost reductions. Furthermore, his offer of profit sharing to GM clearly ran little risk of acceptance. But mere opportunism does not provide a wholly satisfactory explanation of the union's behavior. For one thing, the Big Three offer of August 22 was made well in advance of the contract deadline, and experience in the industry indicates that early management proposals are usually subject to some upward revision in the closing stages of negotiations.[68] More important, however, is the fact that the success of the UAW's strategy depended less on the profit-sharing concept than on the high-cost working rules existing in AMC's local contracts and the company's obvious impatience to be rid of them. With or without profit sharing, the necessary leverage was surely present: either raise the Big Three offer in return for substantial cost savings at the work-rule level or accept the Big Three pattern when established with no relief on work rules. Faced with this choice, the temptation to yield would seem well-nigh irresistible, especially to a management grown accustomed over the years to independent action.[69] Thus, while profit sharing may well have made possible a somewhat higher level of bene-

68. This offer, it should be understood, already committed the companies to the annual improvement factor, a modified cost-of-living escalator, short workweek benefits, moving allowances, increased jury pay, more liberal vacation allowances, and improvements in SUB, pensions, and insurance. ["The General Motors Proposal for Three Years of Industrial Peace with Security and Economic Progress for GM Hourly Employees" (General Motors Corp., Aug. 22, 1961).] The AMC agreement consisted largely of further improvements in the components of this "package" offer.

69. Romney's independence was already well established in his barbed criticisms of the "gas-guzzling dinosaurs" produced by the Big Three and in his proposals for restoring effective competition to the auto industry. We can assume, therefore, that he was not constrained, as would have been others, in his dealings with the union by concern for the reactions and opinions of his fellow managers in other companies.

fits and a more palatable settlement from the standpoint of the workers, it is questionable whether the plan itself was a necessary condition for the negotiation of a satisfactory contract.

If the union's demand for profit sharing is not to be dismissed, then, as little more than a public relations or bargaining strategy, does this mean that the union is prepared to abandon the principle of equal pay for equal work in favor of a wage structure geared partially to profitability? One can only speculate—and speculation in this area is always dangerous, for bargaining policies, however rationalized, are grounded less in any unified theory than in the particular needs and circumstances of the moment. We would hazard the opinion, however, that to the union's leaders profit sharing represented a useful experiment with intriguing possibilities under prevailing circumstances. It was a fresh approach—no small consideration in view of the popular image of unionism as an aging institution largely devoid of vigor, initiative, and new ideas; it had an obvious public relations appeal;[70] and it promised additional leverage in bargaining for more traditional concessions. If successfully implemented, moreover, it offered a partial remedy to a major union irritant of long standing—the impregnability of GM's profits in the face of the union's determined campaign to effect some measure of private or public control. Finally, the plan's implications for the extension of union influence into areas of decision making so far reserved to management must be accounted an additional inducement. For these reasons we are inclined to accept the union's claim of serious intent.

It is pointless, however, to argue the extent of the union's

70. Despite repeated disclaimers that wage pressures play a role in inflation, union leaders are increasingly sensitive to mounting public concern on this point. The UAW leadership was no doubt influenced in its adoption of the profit-sharing idea by the belief that this form of demand would prove more acceptable to the public on the grounds that wage benefits accrued only after profits were actually realized and hence could not possibly affect product prices. This argument, indeed, featured prominently in the union's publicity campaign. Ironically, the union was simultaneously advising the public that auto companies had evaded the corporate profits tax by passing the burden on to consumers.

commitment to profit sharing and its consequences beyond this initial willingness to endorse and accept such plans. Commitment is a matter to be determined only by experience. It is abundantly clear that the union's leadership recognized and evaluated the risks in advance; and certainly it sought to anticipate criticisms through a carefully prepared program designed to minimize the conflict between the new policy and traditional union principles and, at the same time, to justify departure from past principles on the grounds that new challenges and opportunities compelled a fresh approach. If the membership accepts the dubious distinction drawn between the wage inequities of the past and the earnings differentials introduced under profit sharing, then the new policy may be continued indefinitely. If, as seems more likely, differential earnings generate widespread dissatisfaction and strong wage pressures among workers in the less prosperous companies, the policy will be either modified or abandoned in the absence of union ability to satisfy these pressures.[71] Since the earnings differentials to be expected under the AMC-UAW type of plan are substantial, it is doubtful that such a policy could survive in the long run the kinds of stresses to which it would inevitably give rise. We cannot rule out, of course, the possibility of ingenious adaptations, forged in experience and as yet unforeseeable. At the same time, it must be recognized that neither GM nor Ford is likely to accede to profit sharing as long as the decision is left to private bargaining. It is true that the union can point to past successes in other areas

71. Ford Vice-President Theodore Yntema probably exaggerated the consequences of the UAW's profit-sharing proposal in 1958 when he testified as follows: "There will be inordinate pressure in all companies in an industry to match the wage-plus-profit share in the most profitable company. . . . In the union book, the correction of inequities overrides all other considerations. If the principle of equal pay for equal work is to be pursued, as I am sure it will be, we would see a wage inflation the like of which we have never known." (U.S. Senate, "Administered Prices," *Hearings,* p. 2727.) Nevertheless, the pressure of equitable comparisons which the union has so carefully nurtured up till now is surely not to be satisfied by the simple stratagem of renaming interfirm wage differentials "supplements" to the standard wage.

such as pensions and SUB following years of strong resistance and denial. But these are doubtful precedents. A more realistic parallel is probably to be found in the union's long but vain struggle to secure some measure of control over product pricing.

In any event, the UAW is at present launched on a new three-year experiment at American Motors which is likely to determine the future role of profit sharing in the union's bargaining program. This arrangement would seem to serve the union's purpose well: it provides an opportunity to try out the new approach on a strictly limited basis and offers at the same time a flexible bargaining strategy for 1964. If AMC's operations are profitable under the new contract, we can expect the union to exploit this experience fully in pressing for substantial gains elsewhere. If the experience is adverse, however, the union can and will revert quite naturally to traditional appeals based on "excessive" profit levels at GM and Ford. So far, the profit-sharing idea seems therefore to be working to the union's advantage, but its future role will depend importantly on the result of the present experiment and the contribution of that experiment to the basic union drive for higher wage and benefit levels throughout the industry.

CHAPTER 6

Competitive Relations: The Independents

The most interesting feature of pattern bargaining in the automobile industry during the last two decades has been the negotiation of pattern-plus settlements in the plants of the independent producers. These smaller and weaker firms have not only met but have actually exceeded the pattern of labor standards established in contracts with the Big Three companies. Thus, to the competitive disadvantage of size has been added the burden of more liberal collective agreements. In this and the following chapter, we shall investigate the nature and extent of these labor-cost differentials and attempt to identify their causes. It is unfortunate, of course, that we cannot measure the size of these differentials directly by comparing the actual cost situations in individual firms. Cost information is simply not available, and we are forced to rely therefore on much cruder estimates derived from an analysis of the labor-relations experience of the various firms. Measurements reached in this fashion are inevitably imprecise since they combine quantitative elements and qualitative judgments. Nevertheless, they offer in this instance sufficient insight into the structure and composition of cost differences in the industry to justify their acceptance as a legitimate basis for judging the role of unionism in shaping competitive relations. The labor-relations experience of the independent companies—the Studebaker-Packard Corporation, Willys Motors, Inc., and the American Motors Corporation—is examined below.

Studebaker-Packard Corporation

It is generally recognized that throughout the war and postwar period the Studebaker Corporation (later the Studebaker-Packard Corporation, after the merger with the Packard Motor Company in late 1954) paid substantially higher wages than the remainder of the industry.[1] Less well known, but certainly of equal importance in appraising the company's competitive position, were the labor-cost effects of inferior production standards, higher shift differentials, more liberal relief allowances, and the like. It was these impediments to efficient operations, in combination with higher wages, that placed Studebaker at a substantial cost disadvantage in the years following World War II. The extent of the disadvantage was not fully revealed, however, until the return of intense competition in the industry in the early fifties when, for a variety of reasons (including excessive labor costs), the corporation found itself highly vulnerable and close to bankruptcy.

Management at Studebaker was apparently already aware of the problem of relatively high unit labor costs in the early postwar years, for certainly it expressed its concern with loose work standards and the overmanning of operations on numerous occasions. During the 1947 negotiations, for example, the company approached the union negotiating committee with a proposal for eliminating excess manpower and improving the level of efficiency in its plants. In an effort to ensure full and

1. See, e.g., Harbison and Dubin, *Patterns of Union-Management Relations*, p. 137; Arthur M. Ross, "The External Wage Structure" in Taylor and Pierson, *New Concepts in Wage Determination*, pp. 192–93.

proper consideration of its proposal, the company carried its case directly to the union membership in a letter addressed to all Studebaker employees. The company's statement, reproduced in part below, explained the general nature and purpose of Studebaker's incentive wage system as well as the reasons for management's dissatisfaction with its postwar performance.[2]

> For many years the Studebaker plant in South Bend has been the only large plant in the automobile industry operating under a piece-work system. Under this system Studebaker now pays its employees the same base rates per hour as are generally paid by the industry in Detroit, plus a premium for production obtained through added effort. (In Detroit the base rate generally is the earned rate.) As a result, Studebaker producers have been and today are the highest paid automobile workers in the country.
>
> In the Detroit plants work standards are high. A good day's work is required to earn the base rates. In the past it has been generally agreed that Studebaker workers could, through added effort, produce on an average at a rate approximately 10% above the Detroit work standard and thus earn approximately 10% more in premium pay. In 1941 piece-work earnings of Studebaker producers on the average topped base rates by 9.18%.
>
> By agreement between the union and the management, piece-work prices and manpower assignments on 1947 models were to be so set that producers could, through added effort, earn approximately 10% above base rates. Unfortunately, these piece-work prices and manpower assignments had to be set at a time of confusion and uncertainty in the automobile industry and in our own plants. As a result, some were too high and some were

2. Letter by H. S. Vance, chairman of the board, and Paul G. Hoffman, president, The Studebaker Corporation, to all Studebaker employees, Sept. 8, 1947.

too low. The piece-work prices and manpower assignments that were too low later were corrected. Those that were too high remained in effect, and in some instances premium payments ran as high as 50% over base rates. During the last week in April, premium payments on the average were 27½% over old base rates, due largely to the fact that in numerous instances manpower assignments were too high in many departments. The over-all effect of these maladjustments was that the company was paying for much more manpower than was reasonable to turn out the production scheduled.

The company also outlined the steps it had taken in an effort to remedy the situation. In early February it had advised the union negotiating committee that the incentive system could not be continued unless the union agreed to its request for a general review and overhaul of manpower assignments and piecework rates. Later, when the union committee had demanded the Detroit pattern increase of 11.5 cents (and six paid holidays), management had offered to match the pattern immediately by adding the increase to classification base rates, but it had protested any change in piecework prices pending the aforementioned review. As management noted in defense of its position: "Since May 1, earnings of all Studebaker workers have continued substantially above those of Detroit workers. In the case of producers, earnings have averaged approximately 17½% above the new base rates which are, in effect, the Detroit earning rates."[3]

In the negotiations, which lasted throughout the summer, management sought to promote a program that would (1) provide all production workers with an opportunity to earn approximately 20 per cent above the new base rates (or twice the incentive premium previously agreed to), (2) provide all non-production workers with an opportunity to earn up to 12 per

3. Ibid.

cent above the new rates, and (3) permit tighter work standards but without any reduction in the number of employees. The company estimated that the revised work standards would eliminate excess manpower of approximately 10 per cent of the work force, but it proposed to absorb the displaced workers by increasing passenger car schedules from 62 to 70 units per hour and truck schedules from 17 to 20 units per hour. The results to be expected from the program were summarized as follows: "The net effect . . . is that the money saved by the company through the elimination of excess manpower will be used to help equalize the opportunity for premium earnings throughout the plant. Under this proposal the great majority of producers should enjoy increased earnings and all nonproducers will receive a substantial increase in pay."[4] In addition, management offered to submit to impartial arbitration any of its decisions on manpower assignments and work standards challenged by the union, with the understanding that the arbitrator's rulings would be final and binding on both parties.

This and similar efforts to tighten up on manpower requirements during the late 1940s met with little success for in the September 1950 negotiations the problem of excess manpower again occupied management's attention. Concerned with its cost position, management sought union agreement on a plan designed to ease the situation. The following exchanges during the bargaining session of September 6 point up the seriousness of the problem as well as the union's reaction to management's proposal. Mr. Vance, Studebaker's board chairman, is arguing for a change from group to individual piecework to facilitate the elimination of surplus manpower.

> Mr. Vance (m): Let's be frank about this thing. We can't tie up here to a five-year wage agreement [the industry pattern] unless we open the door to getting out some of the excess manpower in this plant. . . . I told

4. Ibid.

you on several occasions several weeks ago that we weren't going to reach any wage agreement here until we had found a solution to this problem of excess manpower. We discussed this question of transferring these group rates into individual rates at some length here two or three weeks ago.

Mr. Hill (u): If you've got a direct problem . . . why don't you tell us how many people are involved in this question of excess manpower in the plant and say to us that you're going to take them out? Then we can fight it out on that basis.

. . .

Mr. Vance (m): You may ask why we want to change from this $27.00 computation divided by a thousand [group piecework] to the .027 computation [individual piecework] if it amounts to the same thing. . . . We want to do it simply for this reason . . . that if we are on individual piece rate it is possible to adjust these man assignments in this plant without disturbing every piece rate every time it's done, and it's possible to do it over a period of time, largely by not replacing men as they leave in the natural course of things. . . . If you want to know the truth of the matter, that's why I'm interested in it.

. . .

Mr. Hill (u): If you're going to sit over there across the table and arbitrarily tell us that you are going to put individual piecework in wherever there's group work now, then we're in the midst of a dispute right now.

Mr. Vance (m): Can you suggest a better way to resolve this problem? . . .

Mr. Hartman (u): . . . I think we went through this before when George Hupp was president. At that time, as I recall, this Committee told you that if you saw that there was too much manpower in these departments, then it was up to you and your supervision to study that, and it was up to you fellows to take it out. If you people find any spots where there's too much manpower, then that's your job . . . it isn't ours.

Mr. Vance (m) . . . This is a very serious matter . . . it's a problem we've had before us for three or four years, and we've talked about it repeatedly, as you know.

Mr. Hill (u): And you're making a peculiar approach to the problem. You have said to us that you've got too many people in the plant. You're saying to us that you propose to take those people out of the plant by setting up a system . . . that is certainly opposed to the principles of our Union . . . the principle of all Unions.

Mr. Vance (m): What principle?

Mr. Hill (u): Speed-up.

Mr. Vance (m) This isn't speed-up. Do you say that taking the inefficiency out of this plant is speed-up? . . . Do you want to see this business shrink down, and this employment cut down here? . . .

Mr. Hill (u) No . . . we've told you many times that we'd be very foolish to sit here and see our jobs leave for lack of ability to compete . . . [but] I haven't seen you suffering too much from that position yet. I haven't seen you lose a dollar here.

. . .

Mr. Vance (m): No . . . because we've had a seller's market since 1946, and that doesn't mean a damn thing as far as the long run is concerned. . . .

Mr. Hill (u): What you are asking us to do is to tighten up our belts and to put out more work, but still your profits are surely not suffering.

Mr. Vance (m): They will suffer, and suffer severely.

. . .

Mr. Hanna (u): How much in dollars and cents do we

have to take out of this car as far as labor is concerned?

Mr. Vance (m): I don't know the precise amount, . . . but I would say that at the present time, of the excess price that we are over competition, somewhere around 40 dollars of it is due to labor inefficiency in this plant . . . 40 dollars in list price . . . that's 30 dollars in cost. . . .

. . .

Mr. Hartman (u): I don't think it's fair to hold up these raises [i.e. the Detroit pattern of increases for 1950] until we say that we agree with you on setting individual piecework on every job in this plant. If you're going to hold up the wages on account of that, then I think we should be told that, so we can make a report [to the membership] . . .

Mr. Vance (m): Well, suggest some better way of doing it.

Mr. Hartman (u): I think that's your job . . . if you've got too many men in the plant, then you find them and take them out . . . that's your job, not ours.

. . .

Mr. Hill (u): You're already doing it. I don't know why you bring up the subject here. You're saying to us that you want to take 2,800 people out of the plant here . . . is that right?

Mr. Vance (m): No. I said we had to take somewhere around that figure . . . I don't know what the precise figure is . . .

Mr. Horvath (u): Mr. Vance, since 1946 we've talked out this situation several different times, and at those times we told you that your supervision was overmanned, and you told us that if you were overmanned in supervision that you were going to take them out. We told you, then, that if you took out your excess manpower on different jobs you have around this plant on salary and treasurer's payroll, then you naturally can come to the workers and ask to have them cut down on theirs, too . . . that hasn't been done . . . there hasn't even been an attempt made to have it done. It's just like we showed you people the other day . . . in one department of 120 people you've got 17 supervisors.

Mr. Vance (m): Listen, Louie, if we have any excess supervision we want to get it out.

Mr. Horvath (u): I think that's where you should take it out first, and then come back to us and say: "Look what we did . . . now you clean your house."[5]

As part of its plea for an improvement in the manpower situation, management also requested the union's cooperation in correcting loose work standards. This request only brought to light, however, a further restriction on management's freedom of action. The union's position was that the request for assistance was unnecessary since the company already had the right to retime operations under Article XVII of the contract. This article referred, however, to the method of establishing piecework prices on new or changed operations and not to the retiming of operations whose standards were found to be in error. Moreover, it was plain that the union considered Article XVII to bar the revision of any established standard, no matter how improper, unless it followed on a change in the materials, tools, or processes of the operation. As Mr. Vance ruefully complained to the union negotiating committee, "You're taking the position that if we once set a piece rate or having set one at some time prior to the execution of this agreement, no matter how bad it is, that it has to go on forever."[6]

5. *Minutes of Meeting between Studebaker Corporation and Local No. 5, UAW-CIO* (Sept. 6, 1950), pp. 18, 20–22, 25–30.

6. *Minutes* (Sept. 7, 1950), p. 6.

Although overmanning was the major obstacle to efficient operations at Studebaker in the postwar period, other practices also proved burdensome. One such set of practices was the seniority arrangements governing transfers and promotions. The union at Studebaker had always exercised a high degree of job control through what it described as the best seniority clause in the industry. This clause, dating back to the original labor agreement, placed seniority on a plant-wide basis. It had never proved satisfactory to management, however, for its virtually unlimited "bumping" and transfer rights (whereby any worker threatened with layoff or desirous of a change of job could displace any other worker of lower seniority) made it a source of constant confusion in the plant and a major hindrance to effective utilization of the work force. Although the union is reported to have exercised an intelligent restraint in this area up through 1946[7] and apparently agreed in 1947 to some restrictions on the exercise of "bumping" privileges, there is ample evidence in the 1950 negotiations that the transfer situation remained chaotic despite repeated pleas by management for some sensible limit to the practice of "job-hopping."[8]

7. Dubin, while recognizing management's dissatisfaction with seniority arrangements, suggests that the union, at least up to 1947, sought to "harmonize" its objectives with those of management. Thus, he notes that abuse of the system was curbed by certain protective devices such as foreman-steward cooperation in the matter of job qualifications, a union-imposed limitation on the frequency of "bumping," and coordination of all intraplant moves through a central transfer pool. (*Patterns of Union-Management Relations,* pp. 168–73.) However, these protective devices, introduced or accepted by the union, served the union's own interests and were not in fact motivated by a desire to ease the burden on management. The system of group piecework, e.g., required that the union impose some restriction on transfer rights in terms of worker qualifications and that "qualifying" periods be made relatively short, for "unqualified" workers were a drain on group earnings and hence a source of group dissatisfaction. Similarly, the limitation on "bumping" rights was a necessary protection for those members of the local union who found themselves constantly threatened with displacement by more senior workers.

8. *Minutes* (Sept. 6, 1950), p. 45.

This brief account of some of the issues raised at the bargaining table indicates that Studebaker management was well aware of the inefficiencies in its South Bend plant throughout the postwar period. The negotiations also show that, while local union officials were not always unsympathetic, they felt that Studebaker's cost problems were exaggerated and were largely of the company's own making. Thus they pointed, on the one hand, to the company's profitability and financial condition and hinted, on the other hand, that much of the difficulty lay in inferior plant and equipment, excessive supervisory costs, and perhaps a somewhat less than competent standards department. Under the circumstances, it is not surprising that they felt indisposed toward granting the company any significant concessions.

The full extent of Studebaker's "labor problem" was not realized, however, until after the Korean War when the company found itself on the verge of bankruptcy. The company's difficulties at this time were not confined, of course, to the labor front—a point that management itself tended to overlook in its search for a scapegoat. Nevertheless, there is convincing evidence that excesses in labor practices alone were a formidable barrier to effective competition, quite capable of imperiling the company's economic well-being. The events and developments of this critical period when the company's labor practices were first exposed to public view are documented below.

The year 1953 proved to be a difficult one for Studebaker. No sooner had it introduced its 1953 model than it encountered a series of production difficulties which prevented it from realizing its production goal during the first few months. On top of this, during the second quarter of the model year, a ten-week strike at the Borg-Warner Corporation cut off Studebaker's supply of regular transmissions, forcing the company to curtail its output of lower-priced cars and concentrate on the production of higher-priced models with automatic transmissions. Since these models moved less rapidly, the result was a buildup of dealers' stocks and some congestion of distribution channels. Finally, however, production difficulties were overcome and the

Borg-Warner strike settled, and Studebaker was able to resume two-shift operations. Unfortunately, market conditions deteriorated at the same time: used-car prices slumped and new-car sales were retarded as a result of credit tightening and the decline in farm incomes. The company faced the predicament that in the prevailing car market dealers' stocks of slower-moving models were high and interfered with new dealer buying at a time when new 1954 models were soon to go into production. To meet this situation, the company decided to curtail output, allowing dealers to draw down their inventories. Thus, in mid-September, 6,200 employees were laid off, and Studebaker launched a full-blown sales campaign to prepare the way for the 1954 model.[9]

The year 1954, however, showed only further deterioration in the company's position and, pending the merger with Packard, management appealed to the union for relief in the spring of 1954. In negotiations with the union the company explained that sales had declined by more than two thirds in the course of a year, owing primarily to the higher prices the company was forced to demand for its products. The company had recently been selling its cars below cost and this had produced an upsurge in sales, June deliveries exceeding those of the previous month by 68 per cent. But this practice could not be continued for long; costs had to be reduced as a condition of survival. Management pointed out that executive salaries had already been substantially reduced, overhead expenses trimmed, and lower prices secured from suppliers. Further economies were anticipated, moreover, from the proposed merger with Packard. But successful competition with the Big Three depended on securing a labor agreement which made Studebaker's labor costs reasonably competitive.[10]

For these negotiations, management had prepared its case

9. These events are described by Herbert O. Brayer, "Why Studebaker Laid Off 6,200 Production Workers," in *American Business* (Oct. 1953), pp. 16–17, 39.

10. Advertisement by Studebaker Corporation, *South Bend Tribune*, Aug. 8, 1954.

well. It came to the bargaining table armed with a wealth of comparative data gathered in an intensive interfirm study of wages and working conditions in the industry. The principal factors accounting for Studebaker's excessive labor costs were found to be the following:[11]

1) Hourly earnings at Studebaker for all hourly-rated employees averaged $2.39, or 18 per cent higher than the $2.03 paid by its major competitors. This difference in wage levels was confirmed in an analysis of occupational wage rates covering major operations at the Studebaker-South Bend plant and plants of the Big Three producers. Typical rate differentials for a few key occupations, selected from the 47 occupations for which comparative rate data were supplied, are listed in Table 21. Pointing to this great disparity in wage levels, Studebaker management proposed that its incentive system, designed to yield earnings 15 per cent above base rates that were approximately on a par with Detroit hourly rates, be eliminated and that an hourly rate system, based on the company's own rate schedule, be established. The relationship between the proposed rate structure and the rate structures of the Big Three is also indicated in Table 21. It appears to yield slightly higher earnings for most unskilled and semiskilled workers but somewhat lower earnings for skilled craftsmen.

2) Work standards at Studebaker were substantially below those prevailing in the rest of the industry. The extent of the deficiency was not documented, however, except for the statement that work standards in some departments were as much as 20 per cent below the levels maintained in competitors' plants.[12] The company's recommendations, flowing from its

11. This discussion is based on materials drawn from Studebaker's advertisement in the *South Bend Tribune*, Aug. 8, 1954, and from a comprehensive analysis by the company of industrial relations practices in the various firms in the industry.

12. There is reason to believe that even this estimate was unduly optimistic. It is reported that Packard officials, following the merger, undertook an analysis of Studebaker's costs and came up with the surprising conclusion that

TABLE 21. Intercompany Wage Rate Differentials in the Automobile Industry, 1954

Occupation	Chrysler	Ford	General Motors	Studebaker	
				Present rate	Proposed rate
Janitor, sweeper	$1.75	$1.745–1.845	$1.75	$2.075	$1.905
Conveyor loader	1.83	1.955	1.85	2.33	2.005
Stock handler	1.93	1.905	1.85	2.14	1.955
Assembler, major	1.98	2.005	2.00	2.44	2.055
Punch press operator, large	1.98	2.055	2.00	2.58	2.055
Drill press, multiple	2.03	2.005	2.00	2.59[a]	2.055
Lathe, regular	2.03	2.045	1.90	2.59[a]	2.055
Grinder, regular	2.03	2.095	1.95	2.63[a]	2.055
				2.59[b]	2.35[b]
Electrician	2.23–2.43	2.195–2.445	2.25–2.41	2.48[c]	2.25[c]
				2.79[b]	2.53[b]
Toolmaker	2.48–2.68	2.445–2.645	2.26–2.46	2.68[c]	2.43[c]

a. Average of individual piecework earning rates.
b. 1st class.
c. 2nd class.

Sources. Rates for Chrysler, Ford, and General Motors and proposed rates for Studebaker were compiled by the Studebaker Corporation. Chrysler rates were taken from the Chrysler "Master Agreement Schedule," Ford rates from the wage schedules of the Dearborn and Lincoln plants, and General Motors rates from the wage schedules of several Chevrolet plants in Michigan (Flint Assembly, Grand Rapids Stamping, Flint Fisher Body, and Saginaw Iron Foundry). All rates reflect cost-of-living allowances and annual-improvement-factor increases, including the 5 cents to be added to Studebaker rates on Sept. 1, 1954. Present rates for Studebaker were taken from the South Bend Tribune, Aug. 8, 1954.

study of production standards in the industry, stressed the following shortcomings at its South Bend plant. (a) There is no contractual recognition of the company's right to establish and enforce standards. (b) The company is restricted to the use of time studies in establishing standards, although experience shows that it is impossible to make time studies with the introduction of new models since complete time study would require an enormous standards department. Other means of setting standards should be permitted and have been insisted upon by other companies. (c) There should be no restrictive provisions in the contract relating to change in standards such as the present Studebaker agreement contains. (d) There should be no union participation in setting standards. (e) The company's right to discipline for failure to meet standards should not be confined to situations where the employee has previously demonstrated that he could meet the standard.

3) Plant-wide "bumping" and transfer privileges at Studebaker were excessive and resulted in waste and inefficiencies not experienced in the plants of other major producers. It was estimated that for the first four months of 1954 alone such "job-hopping" had resulted in "wasteful costs" totaling $789,000. In order to eliminate the chaotic conditions prevailing at the South Bend plant, the study committee recommended adoption of the Studebaker-Chicago provision on transfers and promotions, pointing out that "the Chicago Agreement was negotiated with a complete realization and deep appreciation of the many unsatisfactory results being obtained in South Bend." The committee's explanation of the merits of the Chicago Agreement suggests some of the ambiguities and inadequacies of the South Bend Agreement provisions: the failure to distinguish between different types of job openings and hence between different methods of filling job openings; the absence of any clear defini-

---

labor costs at South Bend, largely because of poor work standards, were almost double the industry's average. This matter is discussed more fully below.

tion of "qualifications" and "ability," especially with respect to promotions; and the requirement that all openings be cleared through the "transfer pool"—the source of multiple "bumps" and qualifying periods.

4) Paid-time-not-worked totaled 40 to 43 minutes daily per employee at Studebaker compared with the common industry practice of 24 minutes. This daily loss of 16 to 19 minutes per worker meant a cost disadvantage equivalent in effect to an hourly wage differential of more than 8 cents. The sources of the company's disadvantage in this area as of mid-1953 are summarized below.

(a) Rest periods and relief time. The Studebaker agreement provided a 5-minute rest period at the midpoint of each half day during which the lines were shut down. Other companies made no provision for rest periods as such: rest was possible only during breakdown or personal relief periods, but lines were never stopped for this purpose.

For off-line employees, relief time in other companies was provided for by an allowance in the production standard of 24 minutes (or 5 per cent) per 8-hour day, such personal relief to be taken as needed. The Studebaker agreement, on the other hand, provided for 25.3 minutes (including the 10 minutes in rest periods). For conveyor-operated departments, the practice elsewhere in the industry was to provide relief men in ratios averaging 1:22 at General Motors down to 1:12 at Hudson. At Studebaker, the agreement provided for 28.2 minutes of relief per 8-hour day (including the 10 minutes in rest periods), and the ratio in practice was 1:28.[13]

Thus Studebaker was the only concern with a provision for rest periods that shut down the lines. In addition, it was

13. It was noted that in the case of spraymen at the South Bend plant, the ratio, *contrary to the contract,* was 1:3. The next lowest ratio for spraymen in the industry was 1:7.

the only company that permitted the operation of canteens, cafeterias, and canteen wagons during work hours. Since these facilities operated during rest periods, the result was an extension of such periods.

(b) Cleanup periods. Studebaker was the only company providing for cleanup time in its national agreement. At General Motors' Buick plants it was left to the discretion of the foreman to allow time on an extremely dirty job; at Ford's Dearborn assembly plant (by supplemental agreement) spraymen and metal finishers were allowed washup time, but outside the 8-hour shift; at Chrysler's machine shop foremen could, at their discretion, allow washup time if the men were up to schedule; and at Hudson the practice was to allow a 5-minute period for cleanup on company time at the end of each half-shift. The most liberal provisions were found at Studebaker where the agreement provided a 5-minute period prior to lunch and a 10-minute period at the end of the shift, all on company time. During these periods, moreover, employees were permitted to leave the plant.

(c) Preparation periods. No provision was made for preparation time in the General Motors, Chrysler, or Hudson national agreements, nor was it the practice to grant time for such purposes in the plants of these companies. The Ford agreement allowed preparatory time at the Dearborn assembly plant, but for specified occupations only, with the allowance taken *prior to the start of the line.* The Studebaker-South Bend agreement, on the other hand, allowed the first three minutes of the shift to line employees for the preparation of tools and equipment. Apart from the more liberal allowance, the Studebaker practice was obviously inferior to Ford's; for where only some of the jobs required preparatory time, the provision of an allowance prior to the start of the line permitted the line itself to run a full 480 minutes per 8-hour shift. By con-

trast, the Studebaker provision encouraged the practice whereby off-line and "indirect" employees took advantage of the three-minute line delay, commencing work only when the line itself started.

In the light of these findings, the management committee undertaking the analysis advised that the relatively costly paid-time-not-worked provisions of the Studebaker agreement be eliminated and the agreement brought into line with the less liberal practices prevailing elsewhere in the industry.

5) Premium-pay provisions at Studebaker were more costly than those of its competitors. The company paid time and a half for Saturday and double time for Sunday as such, regardless of previous time off for any reason during the week. In the plants of rival firms, on the other hand, the employee was required to make up for any time lost for personal reasons during the preceding five days before he was eligible for Saturday and Sunday premiums. Furthermore, the Studebaker agreement provided for triple time for any holiday worked against double time in other firms, and for a night-shift premium of 10 per cent compared with the industry standard of 5 per cent for the second shift and 7.5 per cent for the third shift. The company sought naturally to have this source of disadvantage removed along with the others.

Insofar as these comparisons between Studebaker and competing firms in the industry are valid—and, it is well to note, all additional evidence suggests an even greater disparity—they reflect a highly significant difference in labor costs as of mid-1954. As a rough and certainly conservative estimate, the company was paying its workers 20 to 25 per cent more per hour and at least 33 per cent more per unit of output than were its chief competitors.[14] It is understandable, therefore, why man-

14. In the absence of comparative cost data, only the roughest sort of calculations are possible. The most that can be said with assurance is that Studebaker's hourly labor costs were at least 20 per cent above those of its principal competitors. Since the average level of work standards, based on company

agement felt that substantial concessions in labor practices were a necessary condition of survival.

After exhaustive negotiations, conducted over a period of three months, the union negotiating committee finally accepted the fact that Studebaker was operating under a severe handicap and consented to recommend certain contract modifications to the local membership. The company's situation was critical and the union leadership could no longer ignore the facts. The corporation had reported a loss of more than $19 million for the first half of 1954. Over the year the work force had been cut from 23,000 to 10,000,[15] and those workers fortunate enough still to have jobs had been averaging only $35 a week.[16] Moreover, management itself had taken the lead in its drive to economize: executive personnel had been reduced by 12 per cent, and senior executives had agreed to cuts of 20 to 30 per cent on salaries above $20,000.[17] The company had apparently held nothing back from the union. As Mr. Horvath, the local union president and a key figure in negotiations, later remarked: "They opened their books to us, something no other corporation in the country has ever done, and we saw they needed our cooperation. We wanted to do everything we could for the company and, at the same time, give our members the best possible arrangement."[18]

---

estimates, were about 10 to 20 per cent below the Detroit level, unit labor costs (even without allowance for other inefficiencies in the utilization of the work force) were therefore 33 to 50 per cent above the level in other firms.

In connection with these estimates, it is worth noting that, *after substantial wage reductions and contract improvements at Studebaker in late 1954,* officials of the merged company investigating the South Bend operation reported that unit labor costs were almost 100 per cent above the industry average. This is almost certainly an exaggeration, but it does lend support to the claim that our own estimates are highly conservative.

15. *South Bend Tribune,* Aug. 4, 1954.

16. Ibid., Aug. 6, 1954. Mr. Horvath, president of Local 5, reported that most departments had been operating "only four days a week, every other week, since the first of the year."

17. *Detroit News,* Aug. 6, 1954; *South Bend Tribune,* Aug. 6, 1954.

18. *South Bend Tribune,* Aug. 9, 1954.

According to the company, the modifications which the union negotiating committee agreed to submit to the membership would still leave Studebaker at a considerable cost disadvantage. In its meetings with management, the union had insisted upon the following conditions: (1) continuation of the 40 to 43 minutes of personal time; (2) adoption of only minor modifications in "bumping" and transfer procedures; (3) establishment of shift premiums of 6 and 8 per cent (compared with the industry pattern of 5 and 7.5 per cent); (4) payment of time and a half and double time, respectively, for Saturday and Sunday work for employees on seven-day continuous operations (compared with straight time in the rest of the industry); and (5) an increase in vacation pay from 5 to 7.5 per cent of gross earnings for employees with 15 years or more of service. Management, however, agreed to include these concessions in its proposal on the assurance of union officials that "Studebaker employees by enthusiastic teamwork would overcome this handicap."[19]

So sweetened, the company's proposal was endorsed by UAW regional and international officers and by the local's executive and negotiating committees for submission to a membership vote on August 5. Describing the terms of the proposed agreement, Raymond H. Berndt, director of the UAW's Studebaker Department and a former president of the Studebaker local, had this to say: "While these revisions grant the Company a measure of financial relief, they have been limited to those provisions where Studebaker workers enjoyed superiority over the rest of the industry. If the membership approves these changes, the contract as revised will remain equal to or superior to those with Studebaker's competitors. The improvements in the contract from the Union's standpoint are, of course, substantial."[20]

19. Studebaker advertisement in *South Bend Tribune*, Aug. 8, 1954.

20. UAW-CIO press release, Aug. 2, 1954. Concessions to the company were listed as (1) replacement of the incentive system by a system of hourly wage rates "at least equal, and in some cases superior to those in the 'Big

Despite union efforts to sell the new agreement to the membership on the grounds that the concessions granted the company were essential to survival and the stabilization of employment and take-home pay, and despite assurances that the revised contract would continue to yield more liberal benefits than Big Three contracts, the proposal was rejected by a 3 to 2 margin.[21] To some observers, the vote was "not so much a rejection of the proposed wage cut as a vote against the company's insistence that the whole agreement be considered as a 'package deal.' "[22] It was suggested that the wage reduction (approximately 18 per cent) might have been accepted had it been presented separately. Certainly, most of the speakers at the local meeting had voiced opposition to the proposed changes and, led by a former local president, they had concentrated most of their criticism on the nonwage contract revisions, including reduced shift differentials, lower holiday pay, and tighter disciplinary clauses. In any event, the general sentiment of the membership was clearly against acceptance. While there were no major disturbances, it is reported that officers of the local union were greeted with catcalls and boos as the meeting progressed.

The company, confronted with this rejection, immediately sent the union a 60-day notice of its intention to terminate the contract. Concurrently, it appealed for prompt reconsideration by the union membership, emphasizing that unless relief were

---

Three' "; (2) reduction in night-shift premium pay from a flat 10 per cent to 8 per cent for the midnight shift and 6 per cent for the afternoon shift; and (3) reduction in premium pay for holidays worked from triple time to double time. In addition, production standards clauses were to be brought into line with those of the Big Three. As a partial offset to these concessions, revisions cited as favorable to the union were (1) a full union shop; (2) improved vacation pay for those with more than 15 years' seniority; and (3) payment by the company of group insurance premiums for workers during model changeover layoffs for a period of 6 weeks instead of 4 weeks. Clearly, these gains were of more significance from a psychological than from a cost-benefit standpoint.

21. *Wall Street Journal,* Aug. 13, 1954.
22. *South Bend Tribune,* Aug. 6, 1954.

forthcoming in the form of the rejected agreement, operations would be shut down at the end of the 60-day period. "All we ask in order that Studebaker may operate successfully," said management, "is that our employees give the company eight hours of conscientious work for eight hours' pay at rates competitive with those of the rest of the industry."[23]

Studebaker's notice of intention to terminate the contract stunned and astonished rank-and-file members of the union. True, they had been warned of this at the August 5 meeting by their local president, but they had laughed it off as an empty threat. With the realization, however, that management had no intention of backing down but was determined to close operations in the absence of suitable contract revisions, a movement was launched in favor of reconsidering the company's offer. On August 10, the *South Bend Tribune* reported that petitions from the workers had caused the local union executive board to call a special meeting for August 12 at which the membership would be given an opportunity to reconsider its decision. Management had remained firm in its position that the proposed changes be voted on as a package rather than individually; and for a time it appeared that this would lessen the chances of acceptance. It was pointed out that nearly 2,000 Studebaker workers, such as maintenance men and plant guards, had not been affected by short work schedules and consequently might oppose any wage cut. Moreover, it was anticipated that William Ogden, the former local union president who had led the opposition at the earlier meeting, would again fight any change in work standards. These fears proved to be unfounded, however; at the special meeting, the membership overwhelmingly ratified the new agreement by a vote of almost 9 to 1 (5,371 "for" and 626 "against").[24]

The 1954 settlement yielded substantial cost savings, but it did not result in competitive labor costs for the company.

23. *South Bend Tribune*, Aug. 7, 1954.
24. *South Bend Tribune*, Aug. 12, 13, 1954.

Work standards were still below the levels in rival plants, and while the contract revisions provided a basis for improving standards, the more difficult task of putting these improvements into effect remained to be accomplished. Indeed, the magnitude of the standards problem was perhaps not fully appreciated until after the merger when James J. Nance, formerly president of the Packard Motor Car Company and now president of the new Studebaker-Packard Corporation, dispatched his chief financial officer, Walter Grant, to South Bend to examine the cost situation of the Studebaker Division. Grant's analysis yielded disturbing results: he estimated the break-even point to be about 282,000 cars compared with Studebaker's own pre-merger estimate of 165,000. He felt the explanation for this discrepancy lay in Studebaker's erroneous estimates of work standards and consequent serious understatement of unit labor costs which, he concluded, were almost double the industry average. Granting the possibility that these cost estimates exaggerated the situation, the fact remains that standards were most unsatisfactory, and Nance was authorized by his board of directors to return costs to competitive levels.[25]

The year 1955 witnessed a sharp reversal in the character of of union-management relations at South Bend. Early in the year the company attempted to introduce a series of revisions in work rules and job standards which brought immediate protests from the workers. Slowdowns and unauthorized stoppages occurred in a number of departments. At the same time, a strike vote by the union membership authorized a plantwide walkout by the overwhelming margin of 9 to 1. Added to their dissatisfaction over wages and working conditions, the workers sensed a rising "unfriendliness" in labor-management relations as control passed into the hands of the new company's Detroit officers, mainly executives of the old Packard Motor Car Company. Nance's campaign to raise production standards by approxi-

25. William B. Harris, "The Break-Down of Studebaker-Packard," *Fortune* (Oct. 1956), p. 224.

mately 25 per cent and his complaint in a letter to employees that the Studebaker Division was still losing money on each car produced served only to confirm these fears. To the workers it signaled the start of a new cost-saving drive on the part of the company, the prospect of layoffs, and harsher discipline.[26] Despite rank-and-file readiness to close the plant, however, the local union officers appeared willing to settle the dispute in return for certain commitments and assurances regarding changes in job standards, and by mid-February a settlement had been reached and the strike authorization canceled.

The truce was an uneasy one, however, and relations continued to deteriorate. Resentment flared high again when, in March, the company invoked its right under the 1954 agreement and instituted changes designed to tighten work standards. The incumbent union administration, under Horvath, accused the company of "bad faith" and charged violation of the contract. The opposition within the union, led again by William Ogden, was content simply to blame the Horvath group for making such revisions possible. Nor was the opposition group alone in its opinion, for in the July 1955 elections rank-and-file members expressed their resentment against both the company and the union administration by voting in a new slate of officers pledged to a program of militancy and noncooperation. With bargaining on a new contract about to begin, and with the new Detroit management determined to handle its negotiations on a firm, businesslike basis, the prospects for peaceful settlement were scarcely bright. In early July the company had announced the indefinite layoff of 1,700 hourly-rated employees (approximately 17 per cent of the work force) as a result of newly installed work standards;[27] and, in addition, it made clear in negotiations its intention to purge the contract of all provisions fostering inefficiency, including the plant-wide seniority system. These demands, as must have been anticipated, deadlocked

26. *Business Week* (Jan. 29, 1955), pp. 126, 128.
27. *Detroit Free Press,* July 7, 1955.

negotiations throughout the summer months. The local union bargainers, elected to fight any further concessions to management and acutely aware of the fate of the former administration, were naturally reluctant to give any ground. Even the International Union, which was sympathetic to the company's needs and objectives, stayed clear of the matter in the early stages. When, on expiration of the contract, however, the rank and file rejected their committee's recommendation of a day-to-day extension and closed down the plant, the International Union ordered the strikers back to work and announced its intention to participate in negotiations starting September 13.[28] Bargaining was therefore resumed, but it was not until January 12 that a new agreement was reached.

This had been a critical period for the Studebaker Division in its labor relations. It had engaged in hard, intensive negotiations throughout the greater part of a year in which there were no fewer than 85 wildcat stoppages and a complete plant shutdown for 36 days.[29] Despite these troubles, however, the company's action must be accounted a success, for while the new pact granted workers the 1955 industry pattern (valued at 21 cents per hour), it also yielded significant benefits to management—so much so, in fact, that the agreement was ratified by only the very slim margin of 2,456 to 2,139.[30] Among the more important concessions gained by the company were (1) replacement of the plant-wide seniority system by a system based on job classification with tighter transfer and "qualification" procedures; (2) improvement of work standards provisions with union recognition of the principle that "the Company is entitled to a fair day's work for a fair day's pay"; (3) reduction of rest, relief and cleanup time from 40 to 43 minutes to 24 minutes per day; and (4) reduction in the ratio of stewards to employees from 1:50 to 1:75 with a 15-hour limit on time

28. *Detroit News,* Sept. 3, 1955; *Detroit Free Press,* Sept. 8, 1955.
29. Harris, "Breakdown of Studebaker-Packard," p. 224.
30. *Business Week* (Jan. 21, 1958), p. 58.

allowed (Monday through Friday) on company pay for the purpose of adjusting grievances and meeting with management.[31]

These improvements in labor standards at Studebaker-Packard represented a significant gain in the struggle to reduce costs to a competitive level, but they did not mean an end to the company's difficulties. For the year 1955 the corporation had reported a net loss of $29 million; and for the three succeeding years its losses were respectively $43, $11.1, and $13.9 million. Indeed, it was not until the last quarter of 1958, when management's new small-car program was beginning to pay off, that the company realized a net quarterly profit ($3.7 million), its first since the final quarter of 1953. The company had therefore a 5-year record of losses when the 1955 contract expired on September 1, 1958, and the union demanded pay increases in line with the Big Three settlements. Although prospects for 1959 were considerably brighter, the company claimed that it could not, in view of its current loss position, incur additional wage costs unless and until the new-model Larks had proved a success in the market. It offered, therefore, to tie 1959 wage increases to sales. The union rejected this offer and, in late November, Studebaker-Packard's 6,200 employees walked out of the plant.[32] The strike was a short one, however; by early December a compromise settlement had been reached which preserved the formal structure of the pattern but at the same time afforded the company a measure of temporary relief. This settlement incorporated the basic features of the pattern set at Ford on September 13, but it modified their application to Studebaker-Packard in a number of respects. In the first place, it suspended the company's (5-cents-per-hour-per-worker) contribution to the SUB trust fund until such time as

31. *Agreement between Studebaker-Packard Corporation and the UAW-AFL-CIO* (Jan. 12, 1956). See also *Business Week* (Jan. 21, 1956), p. 58; and *Wall Street Journal,* Jan. 9, 1956.
32. *Business Week* (Nov. 29, 1958), p. 110.

car sales had reached certain target figures. The company would begin to pay 2.5 cents per hour into the fund when unit sales had reached 60,000 and the full 5 cents only upon the attainment of 90,000. Improvements in premium pay for shift work were similarly geared to car sales on a two-step basis. Second, the annual improvement factor of 2.5 per cent (6-cent minimum) and the 8-cent special increase for skilled workers were made effective December 1 rather than retroactively to the date of contract expiration as in the Big Three settlements. Finally, action on pensions was deferred until the contract reopening date of September 1, 1959.[33]

As it happened, the company had a successful year in 1959 and by April, car sales had passed the 90,000 mark so that SUB contributions and shift differentials were brought back into line with industry levels. The new two-year agreement signed by the company on September 5 of that year continued the wage escalation provisions of Big Three contracts and included some gains in pensions and other fringe items.[34] The negotiations of 1961 indicate, however, that the terms of the Studebaker labor contract remained above Detroit standards. Indeed, in an effort to reduce the differential in labor costs the company took a six-week strike early in 1962. As a spokesman for Studebaker stated at the time: "Our labor agreement has been a matter of amazement to our contemporaries in the industry and the envy of other unions. With the least percentage of the market, we have the most liberal working practices."[35]

Willys Motors, Inc.

The experience of Studebaker-Packard during the postwar period was repeated, though perhaps in less dramatic form, in the plants of the other independent companies. Indeed, the first

33. *Monthly Labor Review* (Jan. 1959), p. 63; UAW *Solidarity* (Dec. 8, 1958).

34. *Monthly Labor Review* (Nov. 1959), p. 1258.

35. *New York Times,* Jan. 9, 1962.

determined move by management to rid itself of pattern-plus contract terms occurred in early 1954 at Willys Motors, Inc., a subsidiary of the Kaiser Motors Corporation. Kaiser had entered the automobile manufacturing field in the lush years immediately after World War II. The venture was not a success, however, and by December 1, 1951, Kaiser's accumulated net losses amounted to over $46 million. To make matters worse, in May 1952 the Air Force canceled Kaiser's C-119 aircraft contract because of exorbitant production costs and failure to meet output targets.[36] With only further losses in prospect from automotive operations and faced with possible liquidation, Henry J. Kaiser, Sr., cast around for means to revitalize the corporation and recoup part of its losses. His solution was to propose purchase of Willys-Overland Motors, Inc., a company with a fair profit record, but without the financial resources for improvement and expansion of its operations. Unlike Kaiser Motors, Willys-Overland had a good distribution network of experienced dealers, though it was handicapped by the lack of a fast-selling passenger car. Acquisition of Willys-Overland offered Kaiser Motors an opportunity therefore to exploit its

36. William B. Harris, "Autopsy at Willow Run," *Fortune* (Aug. 1953), pp. 76, 78. According to Harris, Kaiser's initial estimated cost in January 1951 for the production of C-119's was approximately $688,000 per aircraft. Thirteen months later this figure had risen to about $1,100,000. The Air Force apparently gave serious consideration to canceling the contract at this time, but delayed the decision partly because of the costly tools involved and partly because Kaiser's management seemed to be well on the way to overcoming its production problems. But then, as Harris relates it, "the situation began to go to pieces. Under the UAW-CIO rules giving automotive workers seniority, the 'bumping' of workers on the aircraft line reached epidemic proportions. The weekly turnover at the critical mating jigs, where tail, surfaces, fuselage and nose are brought together for final assembly, averaged 20 per cent, or the equivalent of a new green crew every five weeks. By May the Air Force despaired of the output's exceeding eight or nine a month, compared to a target of twelve. Only then did Secretary Talbot crack down."

While these comments do not place responsibility for loss of contract solely on the nature of the union-management relationship, they do suggest that negotiated rules seriously hampered efficient production and at least contributed to Kaiser's ultimate failure to meet commitments.

loss carryovers and to promote its cars through a superior dealer organization. Accordingly, upon ratification of his proposal, Kaiser raised the necessary funds and in early 1953 purchased the Willys-Overland facilities.[37]

The new Kaiser-Willys operation soon ran into difficulty. The return of a buyers' market in the summer of 1953, coupled with the slowdown of production lines necessitated by the integration of Kaiser and Willys operations, cut severely into sales so that by the end of the year losses were mounting rapidly. Moreover, on March 31, 1954, the government canceled all orders for Jeeps—one of the mainstays of the Willys operation; and while a new government order was later issued for 500 Jeeps per month, this fell far short of the previous year's average monthly output of 3,125. The company found that its 1954 models were selling at a substantial loss per unit. Thus, by the spring of the year, Kaiser-Willys' position was comparable to that of Studebaker—and for somewhat similar reasons.

Convinced that costs, and particularly labor costs, had to be reduced, Henry J. Kaiser, Sr., invited Richard Gosser, UAW-CIO vice-president, to meet with Kaiser-Willys officials to discuss the wage-productivity situation in the company's plants. At this meeting, Kaiser evidently convinced Gosser that labor costs were seriously out of line and that drastic action was necessary if the company was to stay in business. Certainly Gosser did not dispute the evidence that Kaiser-Willys was paying an average piecework rate of $2.31 compared with average earnings of approximately $2.00 at Big Three plants nor that production standards were 20 to 25 per cent below competitors' levels.[38] He was also fully aware, of course, of the precipitous decline in employment from 14,000 to 7,000 (the low had

37. *Business Week* (March 28, 1953), p. 32.

38. These figures were confirmed by Emil Mazey, secretary-treasurer of the UAW-CIO, in an address before delegates from all General Motors' locals. *Proceedings of the National GM Conference, UAW-CIO* (April 29–30, 1954), p. 117.

been 4,000) and of the critical position of many older, long-seniority workers on the company's payroll. These facts, along with Gosser's high regard for Henry Kaiser, no doubt prompted the union leader to offer his assistance. In any event, Gosser later came up with a proposal for reducing the company's cost disadvantage which, at his urging, was supported almost unanimously by the members of Local 12.[39]

In this agreement, the incentive system at Kaiser-Willys was abolished and an hourly-rate system established with rates "as high or higher than those for comparable jobs in other automobile plants."[40] At the same time, provision was made for a bonus plan through which workers would share in the gains from increased efficiency. Improvements in efficiency were to be brought about by engineering changes and union-management cooperation; and the cost savings so realized were to be pooled and distributed twice yearly—50 per cent to workers, 30 per cent to the company, and 20 per cent to an engineering fund for product improvement.[41] It was also agreed that wage rates would be studied and revised where necessary.

It is not possible to state precisely how much relief was afforded the company by this settlement. Newspaper and magazine reports announced that production workers in Toledo had accepted a pay cut of 5 to 10 per cent; and Kaiser and Gosser jointly claimed that the agreement would effect savings of approximately 10 per cent in labor costs.[42] Clearly, the ultimate

39. *Business Week* (April 24, 1954), p. 146.
40. UAW-CIO press release, April 15, 1954.
41. *Detroit Free Press,* April 25, 1954. The plan envisaged a reduction of 5 per cent in the production work force, the displaced workers to be absorbed by an expansion of body work in the Toledo plant. In addition, a five-man committee, consisting of representatives of the company and the union, a production engineer, a time-study expert, and an impartial chairman, was to be set up for the purpose of reviewing work standards. According to one estimate, 4 out of 5 production jobs were timed too loosely—giving some indication of the task confronting the committee: *Business Week* (April 24, 1954), p. 146.
42. *Detroit Free Press,* April 15, 1954.

reduction in costs depended on the company's ability to tighten efficiency and, in the early stages at least, the company's efforts were remarkably successful. Only one week after the signing of the agreement, Gosser himself reported that the plant was producing 5 per cent more cars with 74 fewer workers.[43] By the year's end, 750 jobs in all had been eliminated and $300,-000 in bonus money distributed.[44]

The steps taken at Kaiser-Willys drew immediate sharp protests from a number of other UAW locals, including Karl Stellato's Ford Local 600 covering the huge River Rouge operations. In a strongly worded telegram to Reuther, Stellato denounced the Toledo "giveaway program." This brought the sharp retort from Gosser that "until Stellato knows what we are attempting at Willys, he should have the intelligence and decency to refrain from making wild statements."[45] Other locals, afraid that the agreement signaled the start of a pay-cut trend, began circulating petitions demanding the ouster of the Toledo leader. To add to the confusion, most of the UAW high command was taken by surprise—so much so, in fact, that Reuther reportedly reacted to the storm of criticism leveled against the settlement by calling Gosser to Detroit for an immediate explanation. In his own defense, however, Gosser claimed that he had earlier apprised UAW board members of his intentions at Kaiser-Willys and that Reuther had raised no objections, "probably because he never thought a group of workers would buy the idea."[46]

Now that the Kaiser-Willys agreement was a fait accompli, the International Union, recognizing the delicacy of its position in the matter, rallied behind Gosser and sought to calm the fears of its constituent locals. A series of statements was issued playing down the "wage cut" aspect of the settlement and pointing

43. *Business Week* (April 24, 1954), p. 144.
44. *Fortune* (Jan. 1955), p. 53.
45. *Detroit News,* April 18, 1954.
46. *Business Week* (April 24, 1954).

up the favored position of Kaiser-Willys workers. The stand adopted by the union was typified in the statement which Gosser himself issued on the day after the settlement:

> The proposed new agreement between the UAW-CIO and the Kaiser and Willys Corporation has been widely misinterpreted. I am convinced that the corporation's stepping up to its responsibilities by making the necessary engineering changes to properly increase efficiency in this plant and the elimination of the outmoded incentive system that has existed in this plant will in the long run not result in a wage reduction.
>
> I am sure that if these points are carried out with sincerity on the part of both management and labor the result will be a wage increase through the bonus plan. What we are doing is eliminating an outmoded incentive pay system and instituting in its stead an hourly rate system, plus a bonus payable every six months. The UAW is traditionally opposed to the piece-work system and one of our goals is its complete elimination in our industries. This is one more step in that direction.
>
> My associates and I have been meeting with company officials over a period of months to try to work out some method of putting this plant on a more nearly equal competitive basis in the industry. This could not be done with the obsolete incentive system that has been in effect.
>
> A part of the agreement is that the company will match the institution of the hourly rate system and bonus plan with engineering changes that will also add to the company's efficiency. The extent to which the company under these arrangements can approach 100% efficiency will determine the amount of bonus the workers will receive. It is impossible to say at this point just how much that will be, but it is completely inaccurate to say that our new agreement means a wage cut for the workers.

I repeat that it could and, I believe, will result in an increase in pay.[47]

Two weeks later, Secretary-Treasurer Emil Mazey, addressing himself to the same issue at the national conference of the union's General Motors Council, had this to say:

> In most incentive pay systems, when the workers make day wages above the day rate in auto plants, they make it as a result of their sweat and extra effort. Well the Union at Willys has been so strong and so militant and so effective, while the management has been exceptionally weak, that they were able to work out an incentive pay system that enabled them to make $2.31 an hour by turning out less production than is turned out in the day rate plants that we have under contract.[48]

Mazey gave the impression that the changes at Kaiser-Willys were of little consequence. He noted that the new minimum rate of $2.20 was considerably higher than the hourly rates of other manufacturers, and he assured the conference delegates that while the change from incentive to day rates normally entailed reduced earnings, this was not so at Kaiser-Willys because of the prospective bonus plan.[49]

The unfavorable publicity accorded this cooperative effort does not seem to have interfered in any significant way with implementation of the plan to reduce the company's labor costs. Nevertheless, the year 1954 was a highly unprofitable one. The consolidated net loss of Kaiser Motors and its Willys operation amounted to over $35 million; and the company was reported to be losing $200 on every car produced. In view of this experience, it is not surprising that Kaiser-Willys decided to quit the passenger car business in the following year and confine its

47. UAW-CIO press release, April 15, 1954.
48. *Proceedings of the National GM Conference, UAW-CIO* (April 29–30, 1954), p. 117.
49. Ibid., pp. 120–21.

automotive activities entirely to the production of commercial vehicles. The last Willys passenger car rolled off the production line in May and the last Kaiser in June.[50]

Although Kaiser-Willys withdrew from automobile production in mid-1955, it is worth noting that in the 1955 negotiations, settled late in the year, the company was allowed to deviate from the three-year pattern set with the Big Three producers. The agreement, affecting 4,500 workers, included an SUB plan, but company contributions to the trust fund were delayed one year and were limited to 3 cents per hour per worker compared with 5 cents elsewhere. The pact granted skilled workers the special increase of 8 cents an hour, but it did not include the general "annual-improvement-factor" increase of 2.5 per cent (6-cent minimum). Instead, the company was to begin contributing, as of October 1956, 5 cents an hour to a fund for wage adjustments, with an additional 5 cents to be paid in, beginning October 1957. This fund was not to be applied to an across-the-board increase but was to be allocated to individual jobs with rates below those of comparable jobs in Big Three plants. When queried about this below-pattern settlement, one union official simply commented that it would have been unreasonable to press for a general wage increase in view of the company's profit position.[51]

The cooperation received from the union in 1954 was thus continued into the 1955–58 period; and the concessions granted, along with Kaiser's decision to move out of automobile production, enabled the company to reverse the trend of earlier years and report a profit for 1956.

American Motors Corporation

Problems similar to those existing at Studebaker-Packard and Kaiser-Willys also came to the fore at the American Motors Corporation in the mid-1950s. This corporation had

50. *Business Week* (Dec. 15, 1956), p. 111.
51. *Monthly Labor Review* (Jan. 1956), pp. 79–80.

been formed on May 1, 1954, from the merger of the Nash-Kelvinator Corporation and the Hudson Motor Car Company. As with the other independents, mounting competitive pressure during 1953 had taken its toll of these two companies, and merger appeared to offer the best (if not the only) chance of survival in the altered circumstances. Certainly it promised the possibility of substantial cost savings, especially if bodies, frames, and engines for the cars of the two companies could be standardized, permitting use of the same dies and, hence, longer and more economical production runs. Further benefits could be expected, of course, from the integration of dealer organizations and perhaps from combined purchasing power.

In this alliance, Hudson was clearly the weaker partner. It had an illustrious name; but its plant was obsolete, its debts substantial, and its profit record unenviable. It had lost over $10 million in 1953, and the outlook for 1954 was even bleaker. By contrast, Nash-Kelvinator had realized a profit of over $14 million in fiscal 1953 (ending September 30), operated a thriving appliance division, and had considerable working capital at its disposal. It too, however, had felt the pinch in the last quarter of 1953 when its after-tax earnings had fallen to less than $1 million compared with $5.5 million in the same quarter of the previous year.[52]

After the merger, George W. Mason, formerly president of Nash-Kelvinator, assumed the presidency of the new corporation and immediately began the task of consolidating and streamlining operations. One of his first moves was to announce the transfer of Hudson's manufacturing operations from its Detroit facilities to the more modern Nash plants in Wisconsin. Another major move, taken later in the year, was to launch a determined drive to overcome the disadvantages suffered by American Motors in regard to labor costs. This campaign may be viewed, however, as an extension of earlier efforts under-

52. *Business Week* (Jan. 26, 1954), p. 28; (Nov. 27, 1954), p. 59.

taken at Nash-Kelvinator to correct the serious labor situation existing at the company's Kelvinator plant in Detroit. It will suit our purpose therefore to recount briefly the events of this earlier experience.[53]

In 1953, the Detroit Kelvinator plant employed over 2,000 workers and produced compressors for refrigerating and air-conditioning equipment. Unlike the company's other plants, it was organized by the Mechanics Educational Society of America (MESA).[54] During World War II, when labor was scarce and management overindulgent, this plant acquired the reputation of being a "loafers' paradise" wherein "it was common practice for workers to get haircuts, cook food, and shoot dice during working hours." These practices were continued into the postwar years until, in 1953, the burden proved altogether intolerable and a reorganized management decided it was time to call a halt. The job of remedying the situation fell to George W. Romney, then executive vice-president of Nash-Kelvinator. That it proved a difficult task is not surprising: the slack tempo and loose work habits of a decade are not easily reversed, as management was soon to find out. Indeed, it took more than a year of striving and three relatively long strikes (lasting 36, 34, and 65 days) to root out the worst of the maladies. Yet the company's efforts apparently paid off. It won union acceptance of a ban on the preparation of food during working hours and of a reduction in the time taken off by stewards to service worker grievances. It also established its right to transfer certain production operations to its appliance plant in Grand Rapids (because of the low level of productivity in Detroit) and won a pledge from the union that production would be

53. The following summary is based on an article appearing in *Fortune* (Jan. 1955), p. 53.

54. As of early 1955, the UAW had contracts covering 18,000 workers in American Motors' Wisconsin auto plants and 3,000 workers in the Grand Rapids, Michigan, appliance plant. MESA's contract at the Detroit appliance plant covered only 1,200 workers by this time. (*Detroit News*, March 24, 1955.)

stepped up in the Detroit plant.[55] In short, the company's determined stand earned it a new respect and a more cooperative attitude on the part of the union.

These troubles at Detroit Kelvinator involved the MESA rather than the UAW and concerned the company's appliance rather than its automotive operations. However, the labor situation in the Wisconsin auto plants under contract with the UAW also required correction and, indeed, the first tentative move in this direction coincided with the final strike at the Detroit appliance plant. In August 1954, American Motors, taking advantage of a reopening clause on nonwage matters, submitted a request for certain contract revisions to UAW Local 72 at its Nash Kenosha auto works. George W. Mason summarized the company's position: "We hope to keep wage rates high. However, this will depend on contractual changes and improved productivity. Actually, the real competitive differential is not only in what men are paid but what they produce for their pay."[56] Except for the fact the company made no plea for a wage reduction, the adjustments requested were similar to those that had been sought by Studebaker only a few weeks earlier. The union reported that the company had asked for the elimination of 22 articles in the agreement; but the emphasis was clearly on four items—idle time, plant-wide seniority, grievance procedure, and the setting of production standards. With respect to idle time, the company pointed out that workers in its plants were allowed 20 minutes a day for snacks, washup time, etc., whereas no such allowances were made in plants of the Big Three. At the Nash plant in Kenosha, for example, workers were granted a 10-minute coffee break in both morning and afternoon. The company claimed that this should at least be reduced to 5 minutes off. On the second item, plant-wide seniority, the company argued that the system led

55. *Fortune* reports that the union had "agreed to time studies to rejigger job standards, to a no-strike clause, and to the right of the company to rearrange production schedules."

56. *Detroit Free Press,* Aug. 17, 1954.

to wasteful and expensive bumping practices. Workers threatened with layoff could bump into jobs with which they were unfamiliar as long as they had the necessary seniority. Such a system fostered inefficiency and involved high training costs for the company. Management therefore sought some limitation on the exercise of seniority rights, presumably through the sort of system established at other companies wherein seniority was by occupational or departmental group. With respect to the other two items, grievance procedure and work standards, no public statements were issued detailing their shortcomings. The company simply contended that its grievance procedure was more time consuming and hence more expensive than the type employed by the Big Three and that it was unduly restricted in the determination of work standards.[57]

On the eve of negotiations, Mike Maxin, the local union president, promised that the union would give serious and sympathetic consideration to the company's proposed changes. "We realize the independents have a problem. I can't say just what the union will agree to at this time. But if the firm shows us contract provisions that are costing it more than other auto makers have to pay we will probably make concessions."[58] Despite such assurances, the company's efforts met with only partial success. Management, to be sure, secured an important new work standards clause and union cooperation in putting it into effect. However, in the following year, the company was again pressing for the other revisions included in its 1954 proposal.

On Mason's death in late 1954, Romney succeeded as president of the corporation. In subsequent bargaining with the union, he and Edward L. Cushman, a former arbitrator and university professor who had been brought in earlier to head up American Motors' labor relations, were the spokesmen and chief negotiators for the company.

In the spring of 1955, Cushman, taking the offensive, urged

57. *Wall Street Journal,* Sept. 15, 1954.
58. *Detroit Free Press,* Aug. 17, 1954.

an end to "pattern" settlements and asserted that the corporation intended "to arrive at agreements based upon the economic facts of 1955 as specifically related to American Motors."[59] With a maximum of publicity, he invited an advisory committee of distinguished economists to meet on the problem of a guaranteed annual wage for the company. All but one of the committee members had previously served on the UAW's advisory committee in 1953—a committee of which Cushman himself had been a member. Cushman also argued in a well-publicized speech that it was the duty of the UAW to bargain on the basis of each company's particular economic situation. In effect, he invited Reuther and other UAW officials to examine the company's books.

Meanwhile Romney, too, missed no opportunity to present the company's case to the public. On June 10, 1955, he appeared in Washington before the Senate Subcommittee on Antitrust and Monopoly to explain the difficulties confronting the independent producers. According to his testimony, the large companies in the auto industry enjoyed a number of competitive advantages: lower unit tooling costs for model changeovers because of volume operations; economies through the consolidation of administrative, research, and engineering expenses; and the achievement of public acceptance by the sheer impact of product volume and domination of the mass media of communication. To these advantages Romney added the labor contract, arguing that this had been "an important competitive factor, benefiting the Big Three producers." In his view, the fault here lay in "pattern bargaining" which, in the postwar years, had meant more costly settlements for the smaller companies and hence had been "an important factor in the recent trend toward mergers and liquidations of industrial enterprises." Romney criticized the union for its unwillingness to take account of the particular economic situation confronting the smaller manufacturers, though he did admit that earlier

59. *Detroit Free Press,* April 2, 1955.

negotiations had occurred while the firms in question were making profits. He promised the legislators, however, that American Motors would now insist on the elimination of cost disadvantages in its labor contracts.[60]

The company's main objective then in the 1955 negotiations was to purge its agreement of "pattern-plus" elements. In line with this desire, it not only rejected the union's original demands (estimated at 48 cents an hour) but also the Ford-General Motors settlement (estimated at 20 cents an hour). On the positive side, management cited the following evidence in support of its contention that the American Motors contract provided more liberal and costly benefits than did Big Three contracts:

1) Wage rates at American Motors plants exceeded those in Big Three plants in classifications employing the majority of workers. Assemblers, for example, received 8 to 10 cents more an hour than in the plants of competitors.

2) American Motors, because it provided time off for wash-up and snacks, received only 7 hours and 16 minutes of work for each full day's pay compared with 7 hours and 36 minutes at General Motors, Ford, and Chrysler.

3) American Motors' local agreements placed seniority on a plant-wide basis whereas major competitors handled seniority on a classification basis. The result was excessive bumping and the placement of unqualified workers on available jobs in American Motors' plants.[61]

Management asked that these "plus" items be removed and the company placed on a par with General Motors.

The widespread publicity given the company's position

60. *Statement by George W. Romney, President of the American Motors Corporation,* before the Subcommittee on Antitrust and Monopoly of the United States Senate Committee on the Judiciary (June 10, 1955), pp. 8–9.

61. *Kenosha Evening News,* July 14, 1955. Cushman also cited an example of how the corporation had been forced to lead the pattern. One of the gains hailed by the UAW at Ford in 1955 was the inclusion of vesting rights in the pension system after 10 years of service for employees aged 40 and over. Yet, as Cushman pointed out, the American Motors contract had contained this provision with no age restriction since 1953.

angered union negotiators. Leonard Woodcock, UAW vice-president and director of the American Motors Department, accused Cushman of an "out and out double-cross" in violating a mutual agreement requiring 24 hours' notice of any public statements to be issued concerning negotiations. On the following day, he berated the company's negotiating team for behaving like "a bunch of rank amateurs" and announced that strike votes had been set for August 1.[62] Nor did he allow the company's wage claims to go undisputed. Granting that the wage rates for low-skilled production workers were high, Woodcock argued nevertheless that this was offset by the fact that skilled rates in the company's plants were 15 to 20 cents below Detroit levels. Cushman persisted in his claim, however, that wage rates were indeed higher in the majority of important classifications.[63]

In an effort to break the developing stalemate, Romney wrote Reuther on July 28 re-emphasizing the cost disadvantages of the company's agreements, and offering to accept the General Motors contract—lock, stock, and barrel, as it were. He explained the company's offer as follows:

Our basic objective in principle is the elimination of contractual inequalities between ourselves and our largest competitors. To make sure that we have done all we can to make our basic position perfectly clear, let me add this: American Motors is willing to agree to all that General Motors has agreed to. We are willing to equal General Motors wage rates, fringe benefits, and non-economic contractual agreements . . .

Admittedly, application to our contracts of the principle I have stated as our objective could be complex and difficult. You, or some of your associates, or American Motors members, may question its necessity or disagree

62. *Detroit News,* July 15, 1955.
63. *Wall Street Journal,* July 15, 1955.

on the factual degree of the contractual inequality that has existed. These are additional reasons for requesting your immediate consideration of the problem at hand.

Romney proposed that the panel of economists selected by the union to advise on the guaranteed annual wage and also employed later in a consultative capacity by the company be called upon for advice in reaching "an amicable agreement on principle and on the facts." Specifically, he asked that the advice of the panel (or any three members thereof) be sought with respect to these two issues: the factual differences existing between the General Motors and American Motors contractual agreements with the UAW prior to the 1955 settlement; and the soundness of applying the 1955 General Motors settlement to present contracts of American Motors.

This offer was rejected by the union, and negotiations continued into early August with the company maintaining its opposition to a pattern settlement without some accompanying relief in the aforementioned areas. On August 10, only two days before the strike deadline, American Motors was reported to have made another offer, this time along the lines of the Ford settlement. It was qualified, however, by the request for a reduction in idle time from 44 minutes to 24 minutes, a one-year delay in pension and insurance plan improvements, and a reduction in the annual-improvement-factor increase during the first year to 3 cents.[64] The union's response was to insist on the pattern. Meanwhile, the pressure of a shutdown was removed when agreement was reached to extend the deadline to September 1. This change in union strategy was dictated by the fact that the company's plants would be closed for a few weeks in any case for inventory-taking and vacations. Even with this extension of the deadline, bargaining continued right down to the wire; and it was only after a shutdown lasting eight hours that settlement was finally announced.

64. *Wall Street Journal,* Aug. 11, 1955; *Detroit Free Press,* Aug. 10, 1955.

While the American Motors agreement contained no significant departures from the principles of the 1955 auto pattern, its estimated cost for the first year was only 14 cents compared with 19.1 to 23.5 cents for the Big Three. This lower figure resulted from the postponement of SUB contributions until September 15, 1956 (a union proposal), the deferment of certain insurance cost increases, and the absence of any provision for the adjustment of wage inequities.[65] These modifications appear modest in the light of company claims, and certainly they were less than the company had hoped for. Nevertheless Cushman regarded the settlement as one of "genuine and fundamental importance"—the first time in the history of collective bargaining in the industry that some important modifications had been made in the application of the pattern.[66] The union's view of the agreement was explained in a statement issued by Woodcock, the chief union negotiator, which said in part:

> The UAW-CIO and the American Motors Corporation have reached agreement on a new master contract which follows the Big Three pattern. We were able to work out some answers to the peculiar problems facing both the Union and the Corporation. We were able to obtain pensions for some three thousand inactive, displaced Hudson workers, many of them unable to get jobs because of their age and who would have no other security for their old age outside of Social Security payments. . . .
>
> The union proposed the one-year deferment in the GAW plan because of our strong desire to make available the necessary funds for the vested pensions for laid-off workers, in itself an historic gain. Likewise we recognize the problems AMC has had in the past; problems which

65. UAW-CIO press release, Sept. 2, 1955.

66. "You Must Bargain for Yourself!" an address by Edward L. Cushman, vice-president, industrial relations, American Motors Corporation, before the Mid-West Personnel Conference, American Management Association, Chicago, Feb. 15, 1956.

we hope the Company will be able to lick once its 1956 Ramblers come off the assembly line.

The phasing of the GAW plan will mean savings for AMC this year. . . .[67]

While the company was pleased with the results of the 1955 negotiations, it clearly viewed the union's concessions as no more than a down payment. They fell far short of the goal of competitive labor costs, and Romney was wont to remind the union of this fact. In the fiscal year ending September 30, 1955, the company had lost $6.9 million (after tax credits of $9.7 million); and in fiscal 1956, with tax credits exhausted, the company's losses (after deduction of a nonrecurring profit of $10.6 million on the sale of stock holdings) reached $19.7 million. Every effort was being made to cut costs, improve product quality, and expand sales volume. It was only natural therefore that management continued to press at every opportunity for further improvements in its contracts with the union.

Early in 1956, American Motors requested certain changes in its working agreement at the Kenosha assembly plant "to eliminate provisions that hamper the production of quality products at competitive costs."[68] The major modification sought by the company related to layoff procedures: the right of management to prohibit the exercise of bumping privileges in layoffs lasting two days or less. To allow otherwise, management contended, was impractical and contrary to prevailing practices in the industry.[69] In negotiations, management was able to convince the union's executive board of the need for such a

67. UAW-CIO press release, Sept. 2, 1955.

68. "The Future is Here," transcript of extemporaneous talk by George Romney at the third annual employee product review at Milwaukee Arena, Sept. 14, 1957, reprinted in U.S. Senate, "Administered Prices," *Hearings before the Subcommittee on Antitrust and Monopoly of the Committee on the Judiciary*, 85th Congress, 2d Session, p. 3815.

69. According to George E. Gullen, Cushman's assistant, the use of the seniority rule in these cases "would just put our labor costs out of sight." (*New York Times*, Jan. 26, 1957.)

restriction on bumping rights, but on each of the two occasions when the proposal was placed before the membership, it was voted down. With the company pressing the issue, bargaining finally reached an impasse, and on January 22 Kenosha's 5,000 production workers walked off the job in protest over accumulated layoff grievances, shutting down production of all American Motors' cars. The union leadership, following the expression of membership sentiment in the earlier votes, now argued that any attempt to restrict bumping rights was a violation of the contract. Furthermore, it found the company guilty of attempting to revise the agreement by way of the grievance procedure. Management's persistence bore fruit, however, for in the settlement of the week-old strike on January 29, the company was given the right "to furlough workers for 2 days or less without following seniority rules rigidly."[70] Moreover, by demonstrating its willingness to fight, the company had also laid the groundwork for improved future relations with the union.

Romney continued to avail himself of every opportunity to publicize and promote his campaign for a competitive labor contract. When, on May 1, 1957, Reuther invited the automobile manufacturers to join with the union in a study of problems relating to reduction of the work week, Romney responded (in a letter of May 3) with the suggestion that the study focus on "total labor costs, including the possible implications of a shorter workweek" and reminded Reuther of labor conditions at the company's plants:

> As you know, prior to the 1955 negotiations, American Motors had "pattern-plus" agreements with the UAW providing for wage rates, "fringe" benefits, and provisions for seniority, relief, and paid time off the job, which were more liberal and costly than the union required of the Big Three. We did depart by mutual agreement from the 1955 automobile pattern by delaying SUB for 15½ months,

70. *Monthly Labor Review* (March 1957), p. 366.

COMPETITIVE RELATIONS: THE INDEPENDENTS

postponing certain increased insurance contributions for a year and by providing no so-called wage inequity fund. However, despite the detailed presentation of economic facts and long hours of persuasion, the union insisted on agreements which kept American Motors in a "pattern-plus" position. The "power of persuasion" had to yield to the "persuasion of power," to use your descriptive expressions.

In his testimony before the Senate Subcommittee on Antitrust and Monopoly in early 1958, Romney elaborated on his theme that the union had forced smaller companies to exceed the pattern, seriously undermining their competitive position and contributing to concentration in the industry. Referring to the dangerous accumulation of union power, he had this to say:

> An unfortunate by-product of this development has been to aggravate seriously the competitive problems of smaller companies. True, labor leaders still pay lip service to preserving competition among employers. A week ago Tuesday, before this committee, Mr. Reuther stated: "Actually we have given a great deal of time and careful thought trying to figure out what we can do to try to check the growing concentration of economic power and control in the hands of the Big Three. We think it would be a sad thing for America and a bad thing for our union if the small companies get pushed out, and we are trying to help those." However, at his annual convention where he [Reuther] had his proposal approved, in responding to some of our employees . . . I am reliably informed he took the position that the question of whether a company like ours should continue or not was dependent upon a majority vote, and if the union program was one that was against the interests of the smaller company, why, the majority had to rule. . . .
> Through their power advantage, the union has suc-

ceeded in making smaller vehicle companies as well as many automotive parts and tool-and-die manufacturers meet the GM pattern on a plus basis. . . .[71]

While management concentrated much of its attention during this period on its automotive agreements, it by no means neglected the situation in its Kelvinator appliance plants. In 1957 the Kelvinator Division, along with the rest of the appliance industry, suffered a sharp reduction in unit sales. As Romney told the company's employees in September 1957, "Kelvinator has not made money this year. One of the necessities of 1958 is to put Kelvinator back in the black."[72] This reversal naturally focused attention on the cost situation and efficiency of Kelvinator operations vis-à-vis its major competitors in the appliance industry. It was clear that a primary requirement in restoring health to the appliance division was the reduction of Kelvinator's substantial labor-cost disadvantage. Romney explained this disadvantage in the following terms: "The insistence by the UAW on applying the automotive pattern of wages, benefits and practices to our main Kelvinator appliance plant at Grand Rapids has put the rates there substantially out of line with our competitors who deal with international unions other than the UAW. Our rates at those plants are out of line as much as 50 cents an hour as compared to our major competitors, General Electric and Westinghouse and companies of that type."[73] This then became a major issue in the 1958 negotiations, with the company reportedly prepared to close its appliance plants unless costs were reduced.[74]

The details of these negotiations which, unlike earlier ones,

71. U.S. Senate, "Administered Prices," *Hearings,* pp. 2907–09.

72. Ibid., p. 3817.

73. Ibid., p. 2909. General Motors also met the automotive pattern in its Frigidaire Division but, as Cushman pointed out to the writer, Frigidaire operations are located in Dayton where General Motors probably pays lower rates than in Detroit.

74. *Monthly Labor Review* (Sept. 1958), p. iii.

were conducted entirely without fanfare, were not disclosed. On August 22, however, the company announced that it had reached an agreement with the UAW in June covering its 1,200 employees at the Grand Rapids appliance plant. The major features of this agreement were a freeze on wages for two years, tighter work standards, and a reduction in paid relief time. It was also learned at this time that the company intended to consolidate its appliance business at Grand Rapids, closing down its compressor operations in Detroit and its laundry equipment production in Peoria, Illinois. Indeed, it was reported that the contract could be canceled by the UAW if the company failed to make the proposed transfers within six months.[75]

When news of the agreement was released, it was rumored that the parties had made a deal, the UAW exchanging concessions in return for expanded employment opportunities at the Grand Rapids plant. The settlement was bitterly denounced by officers of the MESA local representing workers at the Detroit plant. It was termed "a sellout by the UAW and a doublecross by the company."[76] These accusations were denied by the UAW. In a press release on August 26, the union explained that consolidation of appliance operations had been entirely a management decision and that the concessions granted the company had been prompted solely by the knowledge that the Kelvinator Division could not survive unless employment terms were reduced to the levels prevailing in the appliance industry.

The expansion program at the Grand Rapids facilities began almost immediately after the agreement was signed. With the lower labor costs and the economies derived from consolidation, the outlook for the appliance division improved markedly, and by October 1959 employment had risen to about 3,000.[77]

Meanwhile the automotive division, which was now operating profitably, was forced in late 1958 to meet the pattern of

75. *Monthly Labor Review* (Oct. 1958), p. 1160.
76. Ibid.
77. *Report of Reuther to the 17th Convention* (Oct. 9–16, 1959), p. 32-D.

improvements already established in the settlements at Ford and General Motors. Despite the recession, this division had made spectacular progress, largely by capitalizing on the expanding market for smaller cars. From less than 2 per cent of the car market in 1956 and 1957, American Motors had raised its share to over 4 per cent in 1958 and was to reach almost 7 per cent in 1959 and 1960. These successes were naturally reflected in the firm's profit record—$26 million in 1958, $60.3 million in 1959, and $48.2 million in 1960. Clearly, American Motors had survived its crisis though, as we noted in the previous chapter, concessions on work rules in 1961 were evidence that the terms of the company's contract had remained more liberal than those of its larger competitors.

CHAPTER 7

Competitive Relations: Determinants of the Pattern

The preceding account of the experience of the independent auto producers during the postwar period raises a number of interesting issues, the most important of which center upon the finding that until recently the smaller, less profitable companies have operated under more liberal contracts than their larger and more prosperous competitors. Since these developments are hardly consistent with the avowed objectives of union wage policy and run counter, moreover, to the general tendency for compensation levels to vary directly with the size and profitability of firms,[1] they merit further attention. In this chapter we shall seek therefore to identify the forces responsible for these adverse developments in the plants of the Independents

1. As Reynolds has stated recently, "There is considerable evidence that profitable companies . . . tend to share their prosperity with employees, even in the absence of union pressure. If a union is present it will reinforce management's good intentions and may press for even larger increases than would occur otherwise." Lloyd G. Reynolds, "Wage Behavior and Inflation: an International View," in Charles A. Myers, ed., *Wages, Prices, Profits and Productivity* (American Assembly, Columbia Univ., 1959), p. 122.

and to explain more generally the behavior of interfirm cost differentials during the period in question. Before we examine these issues, however, it is well to recognize explicitly what the present study implies for the analysis of cost behavior under collective bargaining. The implications are for the most part obvious, but they bear repeating if for no other reason than that they have been unduly slighted in empirical analyses.

First, with reference to the problem of wage measurement raised in chapter 1, it is evident that studies of the impact of collective bargaining upon competitive relations cannot safely ignore the multidimensional nature of the wage bargain and concentrate solely on wage rates or earnings as the appropriate data for cost comparisons. It is always possible, of course, that employment conditions other than wage rates will be found to be related in some systematic way to known firm characteristics, including the wage level. If such relationships exist, however, they are likely to be more subtle and varied than is normally assumed. Certainly none of the customary assumptions appears to fit the present case: there is no simple, consistent relationship over time between wage rates and other employment conditions in this small group of competing firms and, clearly, any comparison of wage rates (or indeed of wage rates and fringe benefits combined) would yield an incomplete and distorted picture of interfirm differences in labor costs.

Second, it is apparent that comparisons based on the formal provisions of the labor agreement do not always provide a true measure of the extent of cost differentials among plants and firms in an industry. The agreement terms may suggest, of course, the major differences, but it is also important to consider how these terms are applied in practice. Identical contract provisions permit wide variations in day-to-day administration in different plants, and these variations may produce widely differing results. As one leading authority has aptly stated: "The local understandings that are devised to give 'meaning' to the clauses are an important aspect of collective bargaining. . . .

An adequate comprehension of the wages and conditions of employment at various companies cannot be achieved . . . by a simple comparison of formal labor-agreement terms. How a particular term of a labor agreement works out depends on the policies and practices followed in its effectuation. . . . The labor agreement greatly influences but does not inexorably determine the conditions of employment."[2] That this position is valid is adequately supported in the present study: one searches in vain through the formal contracts for many of those marked differences which are known in fact to exist between firms. The agreement indeed is an imperfect guide to actual plant practice.

We may return now to the issue posed at the beginning of this chapter, namely, the factors underlying the development of pattern-plus situations in the plants of the Independents. It should not be necessary to point out that questions of this sort cannot be answered with any high degree of precision. Speculation and personal judgment enter inevitably into one's interpretation, and the best we can hope for is that careful examination of the available evidence will yield useful insights into the nature of the forces at work.

In diagnosing the condition of the independents, one is tempted to lay the blame for their difficulties at the feet of the UAW, for it is certainly true that this strong, militant union has succeeded in wresting from these smaller companies employment conditions superior to those established with their wealthier and more powerful competitors. But this is more a description of what has happened than an explanation. Collective bargaining is after all a process of *joint* determination, and the labor contract is the result of *agreement* between the parties. Consequently, in explaining the condition of the Independents, it is necessary to inquire into the reasons why the union was more successful in securing acceptance of its demands in these companies than elsewhere.

2. George W. Taylor, "Wage Determination Processes," in Taylor and Pierson, eds., *New Concepts in Wage Determination*, pp. 100–01.

One reason frequently advanced to explain these developments is the greater vulnerability of the smaller firm to union pressure. It is claimed that whereas a prolonged strike is serious enough for the large, adequately financed corporation—in terms of inconvenience, reduced earnings and a possible deterioration of market position—for the smaller company with limited resources it can spell bankruptcy and disaster. This was apparently what Dubin had in mind when, in his 1947 study, he referred briefly to Studebaker's "vulnerability" and to the fact that, in contrast to General Motors, "the company could ill afford to have taken a do-or-die stand in an actual situation just as a matter of eternal principle."[3] It is also, as one might expect, the view most often expressed by management itself. Thus in 1958, in response to a question raised by Senator Wiley regarding the reasons for American Motors' "pattern-plus" condition, Mr. Romney had this to say:

> Oh, a combination of things, Senator. It is a long story and a long process. But in essence it gets down to the lesser ability of the smaller company to resist the demands of the large union that has greatly excessive power in relationship to smaller companies.
>
> Now the facts are in the automobile industry that because General Motors did have more economic power and strength to use as collective bargaining developed and this union grew, they were able to resist union encroachments in areas that affected costs better than other companies, and the result is that one of General Motors' major advantages in recent years has been to maintain the efficiency of its operations on a higher level than other companies.[4]

This explanation, claiming in effect that the smaller companies were never in a position to take a strike and consequently had to seek the best agreement obtainable by peaceful means, has

3. Harbison and Dubin, *Patterns of Union-Management Relations,* p. 113.
4. U.S. Senate, "Administered Prices," *Hearings* (1958), p. 2911.

also found favor with Studebaker officials. In addition, it appears to have been accepted by most experienced "outside" observers and has even been endorsed by leading UAW officials.[5] It is therefore the popular view both within and without the industry, and as such it merits serious consideration in the analysis of competitive relations. We shall argue below, however, that this popular view, plausible and persuasive as it is, is deficient as an explanation of cost developments in the industry. Indeed, we shall attempt to demonstrate by reference to the experience of all five firms that variations in the efficiency with which respective managements handled the labor-relations function (the negotiation and administration of labor agreements) have been an important source—and perhaps *the* most important source—of differences in labor costs.

Labor-Relations Performance: The Big Three

General Motors Corporation is universally recognized as one of the nation's most efficiently run enterprises. In the automobile industry, it is the acknowledged pacesetter, the standard or bench mark against which other companies measure the quality of their performance. GM's efficiency and profitability have long been the envy and objective of its competitors; consequently, its policies and practices are continuously scrutinized by rivals seeking to improve the results of their operations. Its leadership in the field of industrial management has long been common knowledge; its policy of "decentralized operations and responsibilities with coordinated control," formulated and introduced in the 1920s, is the model for efficient operation of large-scale industrial enterprise. In the area of labor relations —our present concern—there is similar evidence of leadership. GM is undoubtedly the industry's most successful labor-relations practitioner. In this section we shall summarize the

5. See, e.g., *Proceedings of the National GM Conference, UAW-CIO* (April 29-30, 1954), p. 121; *Summary of Proceedings of the National GM Conference, UAW* (May 24-25, 1956), p. 6.

available evidence on relative labor-relations performance within the Big Three and seek to develop the reasons for differences in the level of success attained.

A fundamental requirement for effective labor relations is of course a competent management. There is no doubt that General Motors has been very fortunate in this respect. In his perceptive analysis of the 1950 GM-UAW agreement, Harbison, for example, refers to the corporation's management as "unusually efficient, farsighted and intelligent."[6] Similarly, Edward L. Cushman, vice-president in charge of industrial relations at American Motors, singles out C. E. Wilson, the chief architect of GM's labor relations in the war and postwar period, as "the automobile industry's ablest industrial relations director."[7] Even the union itself, frequently frustrated by GM bargainers, grudgingly admits respect for GM's efficiency and for the "old pro" approach of its management to labor relations and collective bargaining. These expressions of respect, acknowledging superior performance, are reflected in the company's own assessment of its capabilities in this area. Its able and efficient industrial-relations staff has pride in its accomplishments and confidence in its ability to handle relations with the union in an effective and business-like manner consistent with the preservation and improvement of the company's economic well-being. Nor is this pride and confidence unwarranted, for all available evidence points to the fact that in the labor-relations sphere GM has outperformed its rivals (and, indeed, most of American industry) in maintaining the efficiency and profitability of its operations.

Since cost and productivity data for firms in the auto industry are not available, it is not possible to compare labor costs directly. What evidence does exist suggests, however, that GM has operated with significantly lower labor costs than either of its two principal competitors. In recent years GM has enjoyed

6. Frederick H. Harbison, "The General Motors-United Auto Workers Agreement of 1950," *Journal of Political Economy, 58* (Oct. 1950), 407.
7. Cushman, "You Must Bargain for Yourself!"

a slight advantage from the standpoint of direct hourly wage costs due mainly to its persistent refusal to eliminate geographic differentials. More important, however, have been the advantages derived from the company's ability to maintain a relatively faster work pace and to avoid many of the so-called "hidden costs" flowing from restrictive union rules. Since the wage-structure aspects of competitive relations have been dealt with in an earlier chapter, attention here will be limited to the non-wage elements.

The extent of GM's advantage over Ford and Chrysler with respect to work standards and the "hidden costs" of contract provisions cannot be measured with any precision, but such an advantage is generally acknowledged. In 1950, for example, Harbison, commenting on the efficiency with which GM handled its labor relations, had this to say:

> GM has been able to maintain production standards at a satisfactory level. In this respect it appears to have a significant advantage over its competitors. In most companies in the basic industries, production standards were set rather loosely during the war. In returning to normal production after the end of hostilities, unions have tended to fight every attempt of management to tighten standards, as an unwarranted speedup. In GM, however, management never let the standards get loose during the war, and it has been consistently "tough" in maintaining and improving standards since that time. The union has been aware that the corporation stands ready to fight with all its resources any attempt to weaken its unilateral authority in this area and thus has been cautious in authorizing strikes over issues of this kind.[8]

Similarly, in a recent article dealing expressly with the "effort bargain," Kilbridge made the following estimate of interfirm productivity differentials in the industry:

8. Harbison, "GM-UAW Agreement of 1950," pp. 401–02.

It is common knowledge that Chrysler for years had a slower work pace than either Ford or General Motors. . . . An industrial engineer familiar with the Detroit automotive industry states that the Chrysler work pace was until recently about 30 per cent slower than that of General Motors and that the Ford work pace was about midway between the two. Chrysler's historically low task-level reflected the cumulative results of poor management controls, especially during the second World War, and a tradition of laxity that could not be easily overcome. The situation clearly shows that sizable intra-industry task-level differences can exist between companies in the same city organized by the same union.[9]

These judgments, it may be noted, are further confirmed in Belfer's study concerning the hidden costs in labor agreements. In Belfer's view, GM had not only been able to maintain its production standards at a "satisfactory level" but had also been successful in minimizing "many of the hidden costs lurking in the labor agreement"[10]—a finding, incidentally, supported by Harbison's study.

The clearest evidence of GM's superior labor-relations performance is provided, however, in the experience of the mid-1950s. Unlike its competitors, GM found no occasion to compare its contractual relations with the union unfavorably with those of other companies. On the contrary, it reported itself well satisfied with the provisions of its labor agreements and with its experience in operating under them. In both the 1950 and 1955 negotiations, the corporation argued that basic contract clauses had demonstrated their soundness and had fulfilled the expectations of the parties to a "significant and important extent." In its presentation to the UAW in 1955, GM sought

9. Maurice D. Kilbridge, "The Effort Bargain in Industrial Society," *Journal of Business, 33* (Jan. 1960), 13.

10. Nathan Belfer, "Hidden Costs in the Labor Agreement," *Current Economic Comment, 17* (Feb. 1955), 46.

to convince the union that the five-year agreement signed in 1950 had been mutually beneficial. It pointed to the soundness of the grievance procedure through which employee problems had been "handled effectively."[11] It drew attention to the outstanding record of contract observance during the period—a record demonstrating not only the high degree of responsibility exercised by the parties but also the fundamental adequacy of contractual procedures for settling day-to-day differences.[12] It

11. For the 18-month period ending Dec. 31, 1949, GM reported the handling of 52,146 grievances, or an average of one written grievance per year for each eight employees. These grievances were disposed of as follows:

First step (foreman-committeeman)	25,091	(48.1%)
Second step (management-shop committee)	19,070	(36.6%)
Third step (appeal committee)	6,262	(12.0%)
Fourth step (umpire)	197	(0.4%)
Unsettled (at various steps)	1,526	(2.9%)

To the company, this record, wherein almost half of all written grievances were settled at the first step and only 0.4 per cent were not resolved by the parties themselves, constituted a "rather dramatic example of . . . workability."

Under the five-year agreement still further progress in grievance handling could be reported. The disposition of grievances arising between May 29, 1950 and December 31, 1954 was as follows:

	First step	Second step	Third step	Fourth step
1950	56.4%	33.0%	10.3%	0.3%
1951	56.6	33.1	10.2	0.1
1952	58.5	31.8	9.5	0.2
1953	59.9	30.5	9.5	0.1
1954	60.95	31.12	7.88	0.05
1950–54	59.1	31.6	9.2	0.1

The corporation drew attention to the rising proportion of first-step settlements and the decline in umpire decisions as further evidence of the high and improving quality of performance under the representational sections of the agreement.

12. Time lost due to stoppages in violation of the contract had averaged only 34 minutes per employee per year over the period and was down to 3 minutes in 1954. This record was indeed "exceptional" though, to the company, the 157 local violations occurring during the period indicated that some local union officers had not yet fully accepted their responsibility.

stressed "the realistic solution of supplementary problems" through 23 national supplementary interpretations and understandings and more than 1,500 special and local agreements. Finally, it pointed to the steady improvement in employee earnings and job opportunities and in union membership and dues' revenue.

As a result of general satisfaction with its agreements and their operation, GM's proposed changes in 1955 were, in the words of its management, "refinements which experience indicated would be mutually beneficial" rather than attacks on basic contract principles and procedures. The company therefore sought such revisions as greater flexibility in the apprentice-journeyman ratio to better meet the changing needs of business, a more practical application of the provisions for equalization of overtime in order to eliminate claims for duplicate payment, and a more reasonable and realistic approach to the number of committeemen required for representation purposes when only small numbers of employees were working overtime. In line with its continuing objective of making union leadership "responsible" and labor relations "predictable and business-like," the corporation also brought to the union's attention the need for curbing scurrilous attacks on management in local union newspapers and the too-frequent use of strike votes and threats of strike over real or fictitious "strikeable issues" in order to compel local negotiations over nonstrikeable issues.

While GM endorsed the high quality of its labor-relations experience during this period, the same was not true of its principal competitors, Ford and Chrysler. With the return to a competitive market in the early 1950s, these two companies (particularly Chrysler) felt the pressure of cost disadvantages and went to considerable lengths to improve their operating efficiency. In the process they drew sharp and unfavorable contrasts between their own experience in labor relations and that of the industry's leading firm. In the case of Chrysler, efforts were directed primarily at restoring plant efficiency, especially through tighter production standards and the more effective utilization of manpower. At Ford, on the other hand, the main shortcomings (relative to GM) lay in more restrictive and burdensome contract provisions and in the poor over-all quality of union-management relations. We shall consider the nature of the problems confronting each company in turn.

As with the Independents, so too at Chrysler, the shrinkage of the auto market in 1953–54 and intensification of the competitive struggle between GM and Ford brought a sharp reversal of fortunes. Chrysler's share of the market in 1954 fell to 13 per cent from the 1953 level of almost 20 per cent, and net earnings amounted to only $19 million compared with $75 million in the previous year. During this period, it became apparent that the Chrysler organization was in need of drastic overhaul if it was to meet the challenge of renewed competition. Under new leadership in the person of L. L. Colbert, the fundamental character of Chrysler's deficiencies was brought to light: its highly centralized, "production-minded" management simply could not cope with the operating problems of a large-scale enterprise as effectively as the "decentralized" managements of GM and Ford.

In the early 1950s, Colbert undertook the task of reorganizing Chrysler's management structure. The tight system of personal control developed under Walter Chrysler and his hand-picked successor, K. T. Keller, had taken its toll. It had deprived the various operating divisions of effective control devices and of the incentives necessary to instill "efficiency-mindedness" into all levels of management. To Colbert there was only one solution—decentralization (or, as he preferred to call it, "intensification through divisionalization") along the lines developed by GM in the 1920s and introduced by the new Ford management in the years immediately after World War II.

Under the old system of management, divisional heads at Chrysler were unable to estimate the profitability of their own operations. The divisions were without controllers and had little precise knowledge of their costs of production. In particular, they had no control over transfer prices (i.e. the prices charged for company-produced parts and components). The essentially primitive nature of financial data and of cost analysis and control systems quite naturally fostered inefficiency and a lack of cost awareness throughout the organization. In addition, production scheduling was practiced at a most rudimentary level. Division managers, acting independently and on the basis of less than adequate information, set their own schedules. With monotonous regularity, these schedules proved to be overly optimistic in the early stages of new model production, requiring large cutbacks and layoffs at the turn of the year. As more than one official of the company admitted to the writer, there were, prior to the mid-1950s, less effective reaction to cost pressures at Chrysler than at GM or Ford, a lack of effective coordination between the various departments of the corporation, and inadequate regard for the costs involved in widely fluctuating output and employment.

The uncertainty and insecurity bred by excessive fluctuations naturally had an impact on worker morale and the quality of labor relations. They were not, however, the sole source of Chrysler's poor labor-relations experience. Since the beginning, the company had been plagued with an almost continuous succession of labor disputes,[13] some of which generated exceptional bitterness between the parties. To some observers, a contributing factor to strife was the generally inferior quality of Chrysler's work force—itself partly the result of excessive fluctuations. According to this view, the marginal worker was a less stable employee, "more prone to participate in wildcat strikes and other expressions of hostility."[14] But whatever merit

13. The company reported, for example, a total of 1,359 strikes during the period 1937–49: *Facts in Brief about Current Negotiations between Chrysler Corporation and the UAW-CIO* (Feb. 1950), p. 90.

14. *Automotive News* (March 4, 1957), p. 7.

there may be to such an explanation (which, incidentally, still traces the problem back to poor management), part of Chrysler's troubles must surely be related to the uninspired nature of its labor-relations policies. Up to the early 1950s, Chrysler's chief officers concerned themselves almost exclusively with production, leaving labor relations largely in the hands of a New York law firm. Whether owing to this unique arrangement or for other reasons, Chrysler's approach to labor relations was generally regarded as heavy-handed, if not inept. As *Fortune* reported the situation in 1950, "During a stormy thirteen-year bargaining history, Chrysler and the union have somehow managed to retain a deep ignorance of each other's operations and a spectacular suspicion of each other's motives."[15]

To the UAW, Chrysler during these years epitomized the "arrogant, union-busting" company; and certainly the company did little to allay the union's fears. On the contrary, it appeared to entertain a distinct preference for pronouncements and actions designed to harden antagonisms. On several occasions during the late 1940s, the union referred to a statement by Chrysler's chief economist, John W. Scoville, as typifying the company's postwar attitude toward collective bargaining:

> While I condemn collective bargaining as an assault on liberty, as an evil thing which is against the public interest, as something which will increase poverty, I realize that collective bargaining is only one chick in the whole brood of vultures that seek to pick the meat from the bones of honest men. . . . It is probable that public sentiment will change in regard to collective bargaining as industrial turmoil increases, more and more people will see the evils generated by collective bargaining and we should look ahead to the time when all Federal labor laws will be repealed.[16]

15. "Chrysler's Hundred Days," *Fortune* (June 1950), p. 72.
16. Talk by John W. Scoville before the Kiwanis Club of Detroit, Aug. 14,

The UAW's deep distrust of Chrysler's motives was, if anything, intensified by the company's behavior in the early 1950s. Most settlements in the 1950 pension negotiations were reached amicably, but at Chrysler, agreement came only after a costly and bitter strike lasting 103 days. Contrary to general industry practice, the corporation rejected the customary request by Michigan Blue Cross that it promise to deduct back premiums from worker pay checks after the strike so that insurance coverage could be continued for workers during the strike. "This would not have cost Chrysler a penny, but the company refused, and the union, with a rousing publicity blast against the heartless corporation, stepped in and paid the premiums out of its strike fund."[17] What really irked the UAW leadership, however, was the conviction that management was out to weaken the union by divorcing Reuther from his rank-and-file support. During the strike the company instituted a series of employee bulletins insinuating that the UAW leadership was interested not so much in benefits for the worker as in gaining control over the pension "kitty," accumulating a huge fund out of strike assessments, building up its political machine, and strengthening its bargaining position with other companies where negotiations were pending. This sort of behavior, whatever the motivation or provocation, meant that while Chrysler eventually yielded the same benefits to the union as GM, it managed in the process to embitter relations with union leaders and much of the rank and file.

The new Chrysler management under Colbert recognized the shortcomings of this approach. It also realized that if the company were to stage a comeback by restoring competitive labor standards in its plants, its task would be greatly simplified if it

1944, quoted in UAW-CIO press release, Nov. 16, 1945, in "Fluid Drives and Brass Knuckles: Chrysler Labor Policies—Obsolete as Hand Cranks," by Norman Matthews, Director, UAW-CIO Chrysler Dept., 1947, p. 14, and elsewhere.

17. "Chrysler's Hundred Days," p. 71.

could ensure the union's cooperation. Accordingly, Colbert sought, through Reuther, to establish a new era of friendly relations with the union. It was difficult to convince the union, however, that the old management leadership, so deeply distrusted, was now without influence. Consequently, these early overtures did little to calm relations. Disputes and "wildcats" continued, and the grievance machinery was threatened with breakdown as grievances piled up which the parties were either unwilling or unable to settle short of the umpire. Colbert next carried his appeal to the August 23 conference of the UAW's Chrysler Council. At this meeting, he outlined the company's 1955 plans and entered a plea for an end to tense relations and a beginning to friendly cooperation. This effort does not appear to have met with much success either, for the same conference passed a resolution blasting the corporation's policies and claiming that Chrysler had "begun making the mistake of blaming its plight on workers" and was attempting "to weaken the very structure and heart of the union in each Chrysler plant" by cracking down on stewards and workers alike. "They [the company] have boldly indicated their intentions in preparation for the 1955 models scheduled to begin production in October, that they intend to reduce costs on production lines and to disregard previous production agreements, thereby preparing to embark on a program of squeezing more out of the workers' hides for each hour the worker puts in the shop." The resolution concluded that any attempt to produce 1955 cars with 1935 labor standards would be met head on by the UAW and its local unions.[18]

Pending completion of its plans for revamping management, Chrysler instituted an efficiency drive with the introduction of its 1955 models in which it sought to reduce the gap between its own and its competitors' labor costs. Commenting on the drive, the UAW Chrysler Department reported in early 1955 that the corporation had adopted "a passive attitude and com-

18. *United Auto Worker* (Sept. 1954).

plete disregard toward problems concerned with the bargaining procedure . . . Through arbitrary action, the Corporation attempted to reduce or eliminate recognized relief periods, hourly break or fatigue periods and wash-up time, as well as to revise production standards thus imposing speed-up methods."[19] It further reported that there were nearly four times the normal number of grievances pending before the Chrysler Appeal Board and that several Chrysler locals were already seeking authorization to strike.[20]

Despite union opposition, Chrysler continued its efforts to eliminate waste and raise productivity to levels competitive with GM and Ford. The drive continued through 1955, reaching a climax in late 1956 when the company introduced its "new look" in management—the result of studies originated in 1954. The fundamental nature of the changes instituted—and, incidentally, the extent of past defects—were described by Frank W. Misch, vice-president, finance:

> The six-month period beginning in July 1956 was perhaps the most important turning point in the history of this company since 1928. . . . In the same six months when we were bringing out and introducing these 1957 cars, we were also making a series of fundamental changes in the organization of the company. . . . By the early Fifties, the tight structure that had served the company so well in its early years under the personal direction of Walter Chrysler clearly showed need of basic revision. In January 1954, our president, L. L. Colbert, established a separate department to concentrate exclusively on the organization of the company. . . .
>
> What we were aiming at was a management structure that would combine the advantages of strong and well-informed decision-making at the center with the advan-

19. *Report of Reuther to the 15th Convention* (March 27–April 1, 1955), p. 10-D.

20. Ibid., p. 11-D.

tages of decentralized authority, responsibility, incentive and initiative in all of the company's operating divisions. We felt the need for greater decentralization—and at the same time we had to set up a better flow of organized information from the decentralized units back to central management. We wanted the power and the creativeness that comes from semi-autonomous profit centers charged with the responsibility for showing proper return on investment—and at the same time we wanted the full benefit of the coordinated use of the resources of a large-scale industrial organization.

We were always conscious that the end objective was consistent profit margins competitive with those of the other major automobile companies. We knew that to accomplish this we needed a quite different system of cost controls from those that had served the tighter organization effectively for many years. And we needed also better techniques of forward planning to coordinate, with close efficiency and accurate timing, the development of new products, the building of new facilities, the research and development of markets, and many other related activities affecting the earning potential of the company.

Promptly after we set up our organization department we began a series of actions to develop a better flow of cost information in all parts of the company and to generate informed cost perspective in the operating divisions. Appointment of comptrollers in the divisions and the establishment of divisional purchasing staffs brought excellent results. Divisional managers began to understand much better their own operating costs; and they began to exact more from their suppliers, both inside and outside the company, in the search for lower prices of components.[21]

21. Remarks by F. W. Misch, vice-president, finance, Chrysler Corporation, at a luncheon meeting of the New York Society of Security Analysts (March 7, 1957), pp. 4–6.

This all-out effort to control costs carried naturally into the labor area. On the matter of production standards, Chrysler admitted that under the old system it had been seriously out of line with its major competitors. Mr. Misch revealed the company's deficiencies in this respect and the steps that had been taken to improve the situation:

> In September we took another major step in the direction of making our company more competitive on costs and improving its over-all operating efficiency. For two years our industrial engineers had been measuring our manufacturing operations with a view to raising our plant productivity, which was not in line with that of our major competitors. With the start of production of our completely new 1957 cars, most of the assembly-line operations would be basically changed. This changeover period was the only appropriate time to realign the assembly-line tasks. For many months preceding the start of production of the 1957 cars the analysis of work methods and standards was carried down to individual operations. The leadership of the UAW-CIO had been informed of our plans, with a full background of what was at stake. So, finally, new work standards went into effect in all of the company's assembly operations as well as in many other sectors. We have begun to make real progress towards bringing our costs into competitive relationship with the other big motor companies. We have not, however, reached a point that we can accept as even a temporary goal, and we face great and sustained effort to accomplish what the business ultimately has to have, specifically in labor efficiency. These new standards had a secondary purpose as well. They were a key element in permitting us to put into effect a broadly revised system of financial control.[22]

22. Ibid., pp. 7–8.

The introduction of new work standards on the 1957 models had immediate repercussions in the plants. A number of locals charged "speedup" and registered their protests by taking strike votes. In their accusations against the company, local officers cited a letter circulated by Colbert to all employees:

> We have developed new work standards. These standards are comparable to those of the same jobs at Ford and General Motors and they are fair in themselves. Meeting these new work standards means only that each of us will do on his own job as much work as the employee doing the same job at Ford and General Motors. It takes that much effort to give us the job security and progress we are all shooting for.[23]

In the months that followed, UAW officers, apparently convinced that the company was in need of some relief on work standards, did their best to settle peaceably the rash of disputes arising in Chrysler plants. Misch's speech, however, and the interpretations placed upon it by Detroit newspapers, especially the *Detroit Times* and the *Detroit News* of March 7, 1957, forced the International Union and the UAW Chrysler Department to disavow publicly any role in the Chrysler efficiency program. Both newspapers focused their reports on the need for drastic changes in worker efficiency,[24] on the impact of the

---

23. *Detroit Times,* March 7, 1957.

24. With respect to the inefficiencies in Chrysler operations, the *Times* simply commented that "somewhere, Chrysler had made concessions to the union that had skyrocketed costs beyond those of its competitors." The *News* was more specific: "Chrysler's efficiency headaches were a carryover from the 1930s, when the corporation built up its hourly staff. Under a centralized operation there was little consideration for production scheduling. The way to build more cars was to get more workers . . . Serious effort to correct what was generally regarded as a bad production operation did not develop until Colbert took the full reins of the company in 1953."

These reports also brought to light the fact that many of the industrial engineers hired by Chrysler to revamp work standards had formerly been in the

new system of work standards upon employment,[25] and on the role of the UAW in the introduction of the new system. The *Detroit Times* characterized the Chrysler experience as "a story of labor-management cooperation without parallel in the history of relations between the UAW and the major auto manufacturers." It disclosed some of the details of meetings held between Colbert and UAW officials to discuss the company's financial difficulties. These officials had refused to make any commitment on the company's plan to revise standards; nevertheless, according to the *Times* report, they did promise to approach the matter with an open mind and subsequently worked to avert stoppages in the numerous "standards" disputes resulting from the company's program.

Whether Misch's comments on the UAW went beyond the simple statement cited in the prepared text of his remarks (see p. 324), and whether news reports based on these comments distorted the role of union leadership in the promotion of such a program are matters about which one can only speculate. The suggestion, however, that UAW officials had in any way cooperated in major "speedup" moves was bound to evoke an immediate and violent reaction. On the same day, Reuther and the director of the Chrysler Department issued a joint statement emphatically denying any "deal":

> The inaccurate and irresponsible statements of a Chrysler vice-president who has never had anything to do with

---

employ of GM and Ford. Indeed, some of them had actually taken part in similar programs conducted at GM in the late 1930s and at Ford in 1947–48.

25. According to the *News*, the sweeping changes in work standards, affecting the vast majority of production operations at Chrysler facilities, had eliminated 20,000 jobs. The *Times* confirmed this figure and added two specific examples of job loss: "At one plant they found it more profitable to eliminate an entire operation and farm it out to one of their competitors. At another they closed down a job and gave it to an outside independent contractor. Elimination of these two operations meant a loss of jobs for upward of 2,500." It is not clear to what extent the 20,000 figure represented actual savings in manpower due to more efficient utilization of labor as distinguished from job loss through transfer of operations.

collective bargaining, have unfortunately created a completely false picture of the situation in the Chrysler Corporation and the relationship between the corporation and the UAW. This is another example of the ineptness of the Chrysler Corporation in handling its labor relations, and it comes at a time when there are more strikes pending over production standards in Chrysler Corporation plants than in the rest of the UAW combined.[26]

The statement outlined the traditional policy of the UAW on production standards: the decision as to what constitutes a "fair day's work" is a matter for collective bargaining at the plant level by the people directly involved and cannot be dictated by efficiency experts, corporation officials, or union representatives. The membership was advised that the Chrysler Corporation had been given no assurances contrary to this policy in meetings with UAW officials, and responsibility for what had occurred was placed squarely on the company. The loss of jobs at Chrysler was attributed, not to a "sell-out" on work standards, but to greater organizational efficiency, better production scheduling, improved technology, and the modernization of production facilities. In the union's view it was company inertia, the failure to do such things in the past, that accounted for much of Chrysler's troubles.[27]

The upshot of Misch's unfortunate but almost certainly innocent comment, described by the union as a "near-incredible" blunder, was to place further strain on relations already embittered by the company's efficiency drive. A number of locals immediately sought strike authorization and several sent anti-administration delegates to the UAW convention.[28] Compromise settlements were reached in most of the disputes without resort to strike action, but many of these were clearly holding

26. UAW press release, March 7, 1957.
27. *Detroit Free Press,* March 8, 1957.
28. *Business Week* (April 13, 1957), pp. 158, 160.

operations agreed to only because of extraordinary union pressures. The settlement between the DeSoto Division and Local 227, for example, modified the rates of production initially set by the company, but included at the same time the following stipulation:

> It is fully understood and agreed . . . that one of the conditions and considerations for settling the work standards disputes enclosed herein, was that such settlements were only for the balance of the present model year (1957), unless changed by technological advances, engineering changes, change of method, tools, equipment or material.
>
> Also, the mutually agreed settlements do not alter Management's position that the Work Standards are accurate and proper even though waived for the balance of the present model year, nor do such settlements limit or foreclose Management's exclusive right to continue to seek a fair day's work for a fair day's pay from all employees on operations other than those agreed upon in this Settlement Agreement.[29]

In this and other ways, the company made clear that the drive to improve efficiency through tighter work standards might be delayed but was not to be discontinued. The UAW, meantime, gave evidence of an equally strong determination to resist management's efforts. Thus, during the UAW convention, the presidents of 33 Chrysler locals agreed to order a ban on overtime in the company's plants pending the settlement of numerous disputes over work standards. Norman Matthews, director of the UAW Chrysler Department, conceded that this refusal to work overtime was a direct violation of the contract; but this did not affect his support of the order. Indeed, he threatened

29. March 21, 1957.

that if the Chrysler Corporation did not yield to this form of pressure, the union was prepared to strike one of its key plants, thus shutting down the entire Chrysler operation.[30]

The history of Chrysler's labor relations throughout the next two or three years was one of recurring crises as the company maintained its pressure to bring labor efficiency up to the level of its major competitors and as the union stubbornly resisted this pressure. On December 2, 1958, for example, the union issued another of its periodic blasts against Chrysler policies:

> The Chrysler Corporation's inept and unreasonable pressure for increased production above and beyond the capacity of its obsolescent technology is responsible for the Dodge Main strike which began this morning. . . .
>
> The Union has offered to accept Ford Motor Company production standards on the jobs in dispute at Dodge Main if Chrysler will provide comparable advanced production facilities, tools and methods to those the Ford Motor Company provides. . . .
>
> It is economically unsound and morally wrong for any corporation to require its employes to compensate by unreasonable and abnormal physical exertion the corporation's lack of modern and competitive production facilities, and managerial incompetence.[31]

Despite continuing trouble of this sort, however, Chrysler has clearly improved its competitive position with respect to labor costs and is now operating at levels of efficiency well above those attained under the old management, though still no doubt below the levels prevailing at GM and possibly Ford.

While rumor has it that Ford production standards, though superior to Chrysler's in the postwar decade, were also below

---

30. *Detroit Free Press*, April 9, 1957.
31. UAW press release, Dec. 2, 1958.

those of General Motors, Ford management has made no special reference to competitive problems in this area.[32] Instead, it has tended to focus attention on the inferior nature of certain aspects of its agreement with the union and on its relatively unsatisfactory experience in union-management relations. The principal sources of competitive disadvantage in labor relations at Ford were of course aired in early postwar bargaining sessions with the union. However, since they were first thoroughly documented in the 1955 negotiations, when the company entered an exhaustive plea for the establishment of contract terms and a working relationship with the union comparable to those enjoyed by GM, it will serve our purpose to concentrate mainly on the evidence presented in these negotiations. Unless otherwise noted, the discussion which follows is based, therefore, on proposals submitted to the UAW in the spring of 1955.

Ford's first complaint concerned the costliness of its union representation system. The company charged that contract

32. Ford management's apparent satisfaction—or, at least, lack of obvious concern—with production standards in recent years may reflect the success of earlier reforms. At one time Ford had suffered (perhaps more acutely) from all the problems that were to plague Chrysler in the post-Korean period. At the end of the war, when Henry Ford II assumed control, the company was in sorry condition. "Modern corporate management was practically unknown. . . . The responsible management group was too small and too overburdened. It had little current, precise knowledge of the company's finances. Its duties and responsibilities were hopelessly tangled among its members": *Business Week* (June 13, 1953), p. 94. In the years immediately after the war, however, the company undertook a massive reorganization and modernization program. Under the leadership of Henry Ford II and Ernest R. Breech, former president of the Bendix Aviation Corporation and an ex-GM vice-president, Ford operations were decentralized along the lines developed at GM and the various divisional and staff positions manned by first-rate executives, many of them hired away from GM and other corporations. Along with other changes, such as the establishment of individual profit centers, the institution of an elaborate system of cost controls, and the initiation of a comprehensive employee-relations program, had gone a thorough modernization of production facilities and operations, including work standards. Indeed, so complete and far reaching were the changes that today's officials insist on dating the present Ford Motor Company from the year 1946. Through these earlier revisions Ford had successfully met many of the operating problems that were to

sections providing for full-time, company-paid committeemen were unique in the industry and resulted in a "substantial competitive disadvantage." It emphasized the shortcomings of its own system compared with that of GM, noting particularly the controls against abuse and inconvenience expressly set forth in the latter's contract. To dramatize the "considerable cost advantage" enjoyed by its chief competitor, Ford estimated that, whereas the cost of providing representation under its own system in 1954 had amounted to $23.55 per employee, the cost under the GM formula would have been only $2.35.[33] This meant that Ford was paying fully ten times as much for representation as GM—a cost differential equivalent to one cent per hour per employee.[34]

The provision for full-time committeemen was the principal weakness in the Ford representation system, but it was not the only deficiency. At Ford, the contract gave sole authority to the chairman of the union bargaining unit to determine the

confront Chrysler during the intensified competition of the early 1950s, and consequently had less need to be concerned with the effects of laxity and poor management controls.

33. If Ford had operated under the terms of the GM contract, the ceiling on representation costs would have been $6.50 per employee. At GM, however, representatives are paid for time actually used rather than time allotted; and since they used only 36 per cent of their allotted time in 1954, the actual cost at Ford on an equivalent basis would have been roughly $2.35.

34. The UAW, far from disputing Ford's claim, cited the Ford data on comparative costs in its negotiations with GM as justification for its demand for a more liberal representation system. Furthermore, when the various UAW subcouncils at Ford submitted resolutions in 1955 demanding increased representation, Ken Bannon, director of the UAW National Ford Department, advised delegates: "The shoe is pinching our feet on this one, because if Ford Motor Company is prepared on one particular article or section of this contract, it is this one." Bannon pointed to local abuses of full-time representation-committeemen who spent 3 to 4 days a week out of the shop, visited poolrooms and bars during working hours and, in one local, took two-hour lunch periods. Sharply criticizing such abuses, he noted that the company was well aware of them and that, under the circumstances, it would be unfair to ask the union negotiating committee to demand additional representation: *Proceedings, Annual Conference of the National Ford Council, UAW-CIO* (Jan 12–14, 1955), p. 43.

composition of committeemen's districts within that unit, while at other companies the appropriate districts were set by mutual agreement. Union control of this function had led to a situation where some committeemen had access to all parts of the plant since the workers they represented were scattered and dispersed rather than grouped according to geographic area. It was the company's contention that "such gerrymandering was not required to provide adequate representation." A second problem related to the composition of the bargaining units themselves, and especially to the need for occasional changes in these units to conform with basic changes in the structure of the company. In this connection, management pointed out that the union had consistently opposed company participation in the establishment or revision of the representation system and had tended to switch units back and forth in a more or less arbitrary fashion. It was the company's position that bargaining units should be based on rational principles of geographic location, functional relationship, and administrative convenience.[35]

A second source of competitive disadvantage at Ford during the mid-1950s was the operation of its grievance procedure. To demonstrate the relative ineffectiveness (and costliness) of grievance handling in its plants, Ford compared its experience with that of GM in a "typical" year—the year 1953. Table 22 presents the relevant grievance records of the two companies

35. Still another difficulty confronting the company in this area was the section of the agreement authorizing the chairman of the bargaining unit to appoint alternates to serve as representatives in the absence of the regular committeemen. The company cited a case to show how this right had been abused. On June 17, 1954, the company had disciplined 24 employees, including several committeemen, for their participation in an unauthorized stoppage. According to management, the chairman of the bargaining unit retaliated by designating as alternate committeemen three of the five crane operators in the plant. Since the two remaining crane operators were unable to handle the plant's loading work, the result was considerable confusion and loss of production, including sporadic shutdowns in related assembly operations. To curb such abuses, the company proposed that the provision be modified to require management's consent in the appointment of alternates.

for that year. This comparison showed that while GM experienced as many first-stage grievances per capita as Ford, a much higher proportion of grievances at GM was resolved by the parties themselves. Thus, fewer than 10 per cent of GM's grievances were appealed to the third stage compared with over 40 per cent at Ford, and only 1.6 per cent were appealed to the umpire as against 13.7 per cent at Ford. On a per capita basis, 30 times as many umpire decisions were required at Ford as

TABLE 22. Comparison of Grievance Records at General Motors
and Ford, 1953

	General Motors	Ford
First-stage grievances	61,572	16,910
Second-stage grievances	24,690	14,128
Third-stage grievances	5,911	6,923
Grievances appealed to umpire	996	2,320
Number of umpire decisions		
Actual	62	752
Per 100,000 employees	16	520

at GM. This experience indicated serious deficiencies in the Ford grievance setup. The procedure was overloaded, particularly at the umpire level, causing much delay and confusion. With so many cases to process, adequate preparation was often impossible; and with more than 5,000 umpire opinions handed down during the decade, conflicting precedents, creating "no end of confusion in the lower stages," were an inevitable consequence. In the company's view, this record signified that inadequate attention had been given in the past to the clarification of facts and issues at the lower stages and insufficient incentive provided for the settlement or withdrawal of cases short of the umpire.

The company reviewed past efforts to overcome the grievance problem. "On several occasions [during the 1940s] the union had promised more effective screening as soon as certain internal problems [relating to factionalism and instability in Ford locals] could be worked out, and denied the necessity of providing any real incentive or penalty provisions in order to bring about improvements." These promises had not been fulfilled. There had also been a number of "bargain days" when the backlog of cases was reviewed and reduced through "superficial analysis, compromise, and a certain amount of horse-trading." This practice had provided no relief, however, for the backlog was soon re-established since "bargain days" encouraged the processing of unmeritorious grievances by raising the probability of "nuisance value" payoffs. In the 1949 agreement, an attempt was made to provide effective screening by transferring the authority to appeal grievances to the umpire from the union's regional directors to the National Ford Department. At the same time, in an effort to reduce the backlog of cases to manageable proportions, temporary umpires had been appointed to assist the permanent umpire. But these changes were of little value; there was no lessening in the volume of appeals, and the multiple umpire system threatened to become permanent. Finally, in November 1954, the parties had entered into a supplemental agreement which provided for an exchange of facts on unresolved second-stage grievances, the participation of responsible line management in the third stage, and (in the Detroit area) the transfer of responsibility for plant review board activities from the company's central industrial relations staff to the individual plant staffs. While progress had been made in some of the plants under this revised system, the company found it difficult to evaluate the over-all results since the volume of umpire grievances had remained high. "It is hard to know how much of this volume is the result of the usual upsurge of appeals which takes place at the time of union elections, how much is the result of increasing union activity as they approach the end of the five-year contract, and how much of it is the result of a speed-up in the appeal of cases to avoid the deadline of preparing fact sheets." In any event, the company concluded that the union was not meeting its responsibilities in screening out unmeritorious cases and it proposed therefore that the National Ford Department establish a committee patterned after the National General Motors Department's "highly successful Board of Review." It further proposed that each case beyond a predetermined number heard by the umpire carry an assessment of $100 on each of the parties.[36]

A third labor-relations area wherein the Ford Motor Company felt there was need for considerable improvement was that of work stoppages. In this area, Ford's experience was very much inferior to GM's as the strike statistics in Table 23 show. Ford noted that there had been altogether 408 unauthorized stoppages in its plants during the period 1950–54 (63 in 1950, 56 in 1951, 73 in 1952, 123 in 1953, and 93 in 1954) and as many as 33 in the first quarter of 1955. Comparative figures for GM were not presented, but it will be recalled (p. 315, n. 12) that GM, with approximately three times as many workers as Ford, reported only 157 local contract violations during the same period.

In an effort to curb wildcats and other unauthorized stoppages, the company had proposed during the 1949 negotiations

36. UAW officials also recognized overloading of the grievance procedure at Ford as a problem of major importance, though they argued that the company was partly responsible. In 1949, for example, the National Ford Department reported as follows: "All the umpires and assistant umpires in the country could not help us if the company continues to deny legitimate grievances. A similar difficulty faces us on the union side—if our representatives and committeemen continue to process cases that have no merit, then the grievance procedure, no matter how good it may be, will not do the job it is intended to do for the workers in the plant": *Report of Reuther to the 12th Convention* (July 10, 1949), p. 81. In succeeding reports to the biennial convention, the department continued to stress the delays caused by overloading, the need to eliminate unmeritorious grievances through proper screening, and the difficulties posed by the company's refusal to confer on lower levels of management the authority necessary to act on grievances. The 1959 report did indicate, however, that substantial progress had been made in reducing the number of umpire appeals during the 1958–59 period.

TABLE 23.   Time Lost through Work Stoppages, Ford and General Motors, 1950–1954

Year	Ford			General Motors		
	Authorized[a] hours lost per man	Unauthorized[b] hours lost per man	Total hours lost per man	Authorized hours lost per man	Unauthorized hours lost per man	Total hours lost per man
1950	0 hr 0	5 hr 43	5 hr 43	0 hr 0	0 hr 29	0 hr 29
1951	1 hr 43	1 hr 14	2 hr 57	0 hr 0	0 hr 9	0 hr 9
1952	2 hr 31	3 hr 12	5 hr 43	0 hr 0	0 hr 17	0 hr 17
1953	51 hr 3	2 hr 16	53 hr 19	0 hr 27	1 hr 8	1 hr 35
1954	5 hr 14	1 hr 39	6 hr 53	0 hr 0	0 hr 3[c]	0 hr 3
Total	60 hr 31	14 hr 4	74 hr 35	0 hr 27	2 hr 6	2 hr 33

a. *Authorized strikes* are defined as stoppages relating to production standards, rates on new jobs, and (for Ford only) health and safety which have been authorized only after exhaustion of the grievance machinery and compliance with the union's internal strike authorization procedure.

b. *Unauthorized strikes* are defined as stoppages, by or affecting five or more men and lasting at least 15 minutes, which have not been approved by the international union in accordance with the provisions of the contract.

c. This statistic was omitted from the Ford submission and is taken from GM's presentation to the UAW (see above p. 315, n. 12).

that participating employees be subject to dismissal. Reuther had rejected this proposal but at the same time had declared the objective a proper one, in keeping with union policy. According to the company's brief, he had cited the substantial progress made at GM in curbing local contract violations and had assured Ford negotiators that once the union leadership had established the necessary stability and control in Ford locals, similar progress could be anticipated. On the basis of this assurance, the company had agreed to modify its proposal. It was now the company's contention, however, that the UAW had had ample opportunity to establish responsible control over local actions, but without discernible effect. Through local contract violations, Ford was losing six times as many hours per employee as GM, and these "wasteful and unjustified" stoppages were hindering company efforts to improve productivity and competitive position—to the detriment of all concerned.[37]

While Ford's record on unauthorized stoppages was bad enough, its experience with time lost through authorized stoppages was even worse. As a result of such strikes, Ford had lost more than 100 times as many hours per employee as GM—an "intolerable situation" that the company traced directly to the "strikeable issues" provisions of its contract. These provisions were of course a feature of other auto contracts, but Ford's experience under them had been less satisfactory than that of its competitors. Ford management attributed this poorer record to the fact that, whereas the provision for permissive arbitration of such disputes had led to a reduction in authorized strikes at Chrysler and GM, it had brought no comparable relief at Ford. With few exceptions, the union had refused proposals to arbitrate "strikeable issues"; yet, as the company noted, "in all but

---

37. These unauthorized stoppages were not evenly distributed throughout the company's plants. The majority had occurred in the jurisdiction of only 7 local unions, including the large Rouge local. By contrast, there were 27 locals that had been free of unauthorized stoppages throughout the period.

one of the authorized strikes which have taken place, the Union, after the strike has occurred, has finally agreed to submit certain of the issues to arbitration in the settlements which were worked out to end these so-called authorized stoppages."

What dissatisfied and disturbed the company even more, however, were the numerous abuses of proper procedure perpetrated by the union. "Since 1949 not a single negotiation of an authorized strike notice has been restricted to the so-called strikeable issue. In almost every instance the strikeable issue has been insignificant in the negotiations which we have been forced to undertake with the union to avoid an actual walk-out or to end the walk-out which has taken place." The company cited a number of instances where the union had failed to utilize the procedure properly, had openly fabricated disputes involving production standards and health and safety conditions as a tactical move in nullifying the no-strike section of the contract, and had then compelled management to negotiate on nonstrikeable issues. Moreover, company statistics indicated a steady worsening of the situation during the period of the five-year agreement.[38]

In short, Ford's experience with authorized strikes had been "deplorable" compared with GM's. The company contended that there was need for improvement not only in union responsibility for observing the intent of the contract but also in the contract provisions themselves. Hence its conclusion that the "strikeable issues" section should be eliminated and the determination of such issues placed within the jurisdiction of the umpire.

These were apparently the major factors accounting for Ford's inferior competitive position in the 1950s. The company did cite, however, as contributory causes, certain other "harmful" practices in the areas of promotion, contracting out, and

---

38. Such a worsening is not an unreasonable expectation under a long-term contract, but GM's experience indicates that it is certainly not inevitable.

plant-wide seniority for the skilled trades. The company's difficulties in these areas are outlined briefly below.

With regard to promotions, the company's dissatisfaction was directed toward that section of the contract requiring notification to the union of promotional openings. Management drew attention to the absence of such a provision in other contracts and argued that this was the sound approach since retention by management of the right to make initial selections ensured choice of the most qualified employee and avoided unnecessary delays in the filling of job openings. The company recounted its unfortunate experience with this provision. The union had asked for some form of notification in the 1949 negotiations and had supported its demand with the argument that this would reduce the number of promotional grievances. On this basis the company had finally agreed to notify the union of such promotional openings when time permitted. Notification, however, had served only to aggravate the grievance situation, the number of first-stage promotional grievances rising from 406 in 1950, to 567 in 1953, and 498 in 1954. In addition, the provision itself had been abused. In some instances, as many as 50 names had been submitted by the union for one job opening without regard to whether the employees so designated had any desire for the promotion. In other cases, the union had refused to submit any list at all, and yet filed a grievance immediately after the selection was made. Management proposed therefore that the notification clause be eliminated since it was not serving its intended purpose and had caused a substantial loss of time in filling jobs, with consequent cost to the company.[39]

On the issue of outside contractors, the company complained

39. These were not the only difficulties confronting management in this area. It also complained of union demands that employees who were obviously unqualified be nevertheless given a trial period, of union rejection of tests designed to establish the employee's ability to meet minimum necessary job requirements, and of union insistence (in some plants) that "promotions" extend to transfers between jobs with equal pay.

that, through distortion of its policy statement concerning the contracting out of work, the union had restricted its discretion in an area in which its competitors were left unhampered. This statement had been issued in January 1949, pursuant to a union request based on rumors that the company was about to revise its policy on construction work, placing greater reliance on outside contractors. According to the company, the union had not questioned management's right to alter its policy but had been concerned only that the change be accomplished gradually in order to minimize hardship to the employees concerned. Indeed, the union had "specifically disclaimed that it was after an assurance of jurisdiction over work as such." The following excerpts from the policy statement suggest the extent of management's commitment:

> The Construction Section . . . was created to function within the limits of the greater Detroit area. . . . This Section will perform all construction work which it is feasible for the Company to do, consistent with equipment and manpower skills available, with the limitation that outside contractors may be called upon when the volume of work required exceeds the capacity of the Construction Section. . . .
>
> Where deemed advisable, contracts will be let to outside contractors under certain conditions. Such outside assistance will be engaged where peculiar skills are involved, where specialized equipment not available at Ford is required or where for other reasons economies can be realized because specialized contractors can perform the work in question. . . . We intend to continue the practice of informing Union representatives of our reasons for letting such contracts, as in the past. It should be noted, however, that management must reserve the right to make the final determination as to whether work shall be done by Ford or outside contractors. In making this determina-

tion, however, we intend always to keep the interests of Ford personnel in mind and . . . to utilize this personnel . . . wherever feasible.[40]

During negotiations later in the year, the union had sought to incorporate into the contract itself some reference to the company's policy on outside contractors. The provision finally agreed to by the parties read as follows: "It is the policy of the Company to fully utilize its seniority employees in the performance of maintenance and construction work, in accordance with its letter to the Union of January 20, 1949."[41] In explaining the intent of this agreement, management pointed out that both parties had recognized the company's unrestricted right to utilize outside contractors and that the new provision had merely confirmed the statement of unilateral policy of January 20.[42] It added, however, that the union had used the provision as an entering wedge, seeking to distort and extend the policy far beyond its original intent. Thus, union representatives had insisted that work be reserved to company employees (i.e. outside contractors excluded) even when all seniority workers were already fully employed and could not therefore handle the

40. Letter from John S. Bugas, vice-president, industrial relations, Ford Motor Company, to Walter P. Reuther, president, UAW-CIO, Jan. 20, 1949.

41. *Agreements between Ford Motor Company and the UAW-CIO* (Sept. 28, 1949), Article IV, Section 2.

42. On this point management referred to the record for clear evidence of the parties' intent. It quoted a statement by Reuther defining the union's position:

"These three qualifying factors give you plenty of protection. Let me explain their implications. Suppose you have five sheet metal workers and you needed ten, and you have to have the job done immediately, or suppose the manpower was sufficient but you didn't have the special equipment needed, or suppose . . . you had the equipment and manpower but not the guarantee on the job. In such case, you would get the work done by a contractor. Take these three factors individually or in combination and very few cases will come up that there will be any dispute on unless you deliberately farm out work. If our guys were insisting on all jobs being done inside, then you would have some reason to object."

assignment without serious delay and inconvenience to plant operations. They had also sought to extend the policy beyond the Detroit area and to gain acceptance of the principle that "the Union represents all the 'work' done in any of the negotiated classifications and . . . the Company is obligated to hire to perform such work." The company accused the union of attempting to enlist it "as an ally in an inter-union jurisdictional struggle with the AFL," and noted further that in some plants the union had even complained about the work done by service representatives under sellers' warranties. It asked therefore that the reference to contracting out be removed from the agreement on the grounds that "this Section infringes on an area of management responsibility in which our competitors are left unrestricted" and has been used by the union "as a basis for promoting confusion, unrest, dissatisfaction and baseless charges against the Company."

Finally, Ford sought relief from the costly practice of plant-wide seniority in layoffs for maintenance and construction workers at its Rouge operations. These operations embrace a number of distinct industrial activities such as steel making, metal stamping and machining, foundry work, auto assembly, and glass manufacture. During the war and early postwar years, maintenance and construction workers and other skilled employees in the Rouge complex had been under the control of a centralized department from which they were assigned to the various buildings. This centralized system of control had proved inefficient and costly, however, and with the reorganization of the company after the war, each plant at Rouge was placed on a self-sufficient basis with its own permanent skilled groups trained in the processes, equipment, and maintenance needs of that plant. This specialization led to considerable improvement in the efficiency and effectiveness of plant maintenance.

Unfortunately, from the company's standpoint, seniority arrangements for skilled groups had not been altered to conform with these changes in organization. As a result, a skilled maintenance worker laid off in one plant could still displace a less senior employee in another plant despite his unfamiliarity with the maintenance problems of that plant. The expense to the company of orienting and training such workers was of course considerable. As a rough measure of the magnitude of the problem, the company noted that there had been 1,384 "bumps" on plant-wide classifications at Rouge in the year 1954 alone and that it normally took more than three months for the transferring employee to re-establish (in the new plant) his former level of proficiency. The company asked therefore that seniority in the skilled trades be limited to individual plants at Rouge since the skilled groups were now a permanent part of the work force in each plant.

The foregoing account by no means exhausts the differences in labor-management relations at Ford and General Motors, although it does suggest the principal ways in which the labor-relations experience of the two companies has differed in the recent past. There is, however, one important facet of Ford's labor situation that we have not so far considered—namely, the competitive position of the Steel Division. Ford is the only automobile manufacturer operating an integrated steel mill, and for this reason it might be argued that the operations of that division are of little concern in a study of relative labor costs in the automobile industry. Yet, if it is true, as Ford management insists, that labor costs in the Steel Division exceed the levels prevailing generally in the steel industry and that the difference in costs is due in large part to bargaining with the UAW, then this effect is clearly relevant in the discussion of how collective bargaining affects competitive relations. The situation existing in the Ford Steel Division up through the 1950s is summarized below.

In 1949, Ford estimated that hourly labor costs in its Steel Division exceeded the average for the steel industry by 26 per cent.[43] Five years later, it claimed that this gap had been further widened to 34 per cent.[44] As management explained the development of this differential: "Steel Division labor costs have drifted from bad to worse since the UAW first organized Ford employees in 1941. Almost every new agreement that has been written concerning the Steel Division has continued and aggravated a trend that puts Ford Steel operations more and more out of line, in terms of labor costs and practices, with outside steel companies."[45] The composition of the differential in 1954 is shown in the comparison of hourly labor costs in Table 24.[46]

TABLE 24.   Comparison of Hourly Labor Costs of Ford Steel Division and the Steel Industry, 1954

	Ford Steel Division	Steel Industry
Base rate	$2.10	$1.90
Incentive	.54	.21
Overtime	.07	.03
Cost-of-living allowance	.07	.00
Night-shift premium	.08	.03
Seven-day bonus	.03	.00
Representation: union committeemen	.02	.00
	$2.91	$2.17

In its request to the union for relief in 1955, management traced the source of each component of the cost differential in detail. For our purpose it is sufficient simply to note the main

43. UAW files.

44. "Hourly Labor Cost Study: Ford Steel Division Compared with Steel Industry Averages" (Ford Motor Company, April 15, 1955). The company was of the opinion that allowance for fringe benefits would increase rather than diminish the size of the differential. On the other hand, the UAW, although not denying the existence of a differential, estimated it to be in the neighborhood of 20 per cent.

45. Ibid.

46. Ibid.

conclusions. The 20-cent difference in base rates was a direct result of the original Ford-UAW agreement of 1941. This agreement had provided (1) that the company would pay rates at least as high as those of its major competitors in each of the industries in which it operated, (2) that no Ford rates would be reduced in the process of establishing the new rate structure, and (3) that the choice of competitors for rate-making purposes woud be left to the union. For the Steel Division, the union naturally selected the rates in force at one of the highest-wage steel mills in the country at that time. Since Ford was then on an hourly-rate system, the rate structure for production classifications was based on average incentive earnings in the steel mill. The rates for maintenance and service workers, on the other hand, were set on a Rouge-wide basis at the highest levels prevailing in the auto industry, which were then above the levels for comparable occupations in steel. One effect of the initial wage bargain, therefore, was the establishment of an hourly base-rate structure in the Steel Division at least on a par with the structure of incentive earnings in the steel industry.

The 33-cent differential in average incentive premiums reflected weaknesses in the type of incentive system used in the Steel Division. The Division's incentive system had been installed in 1945 in an effort to step up labor efficiency. Over time, however, it had produced incentive earnings increasingly higher than those realized under the average steel industry system. This was due partly to more liberal coverage—especially with respect to maintenance and service occupations. But the main disadvantage of the system was found in the "per cent of base rate" method of computing incentive premiums. This method, because it permitted general wage increases to be added to base rates before the computation of incentive earnings, had the effect of "pyramiding" costs and hence was the chief source of inflated premiums in the Steel Division.

The remaining components of the cost differential arose from the union's insistence on standard Ford-UAW contract provisions which were more liberal than the provisions agreed to between the steel companies and the United Steelworkers. Shift premiums in the Steel Division, for example, averaged 13.5 and 20 cents respectively for second- and third-shift workers compared with only 6 and 9 cents in basic steel. Similarly, the 5-cent bonus negotiated for all Ford workers on continuous seven-day operations applied to 60 per cent of the Steel Division's work force but was not a feature of steel company contracts. In all, provisions of this sort, carried over directly from auto industry agreements, created a cost differential of 14 cents—or 21 cents, if the cost-of-living allowance is included.

Management denied that these cost differences were offset by higher efficiency in its steel operations. Indeed, it charged that union restrictions in such matters as the scheduling and assignment of crews had imposed on the Steel Division the "doubly crippling disadvantage" of excessive manpower at excessive pay rates.

The foregoing analysis of labor problems in Ford's auto and steel operations indicates the character and extent of the company's competitive disadvantage vis-à-vis General Motors in the mid-1950s. Since that time there appears to have been some improvement in Ford's labor-relations experience—or, at least, in management's assessment of its relative cost position in this area. It is significant, however, that while more recent negotiations have introduced some changes of benefit to the company, they have brought no *substantial* relief in many of the disputed areas. Certainly this is true of the company's steel operations, for in late 1961 management again complained to the union that hourly costs in its Steel Division were 73 cents above the level in basic steel.[47]

In this section, we have reviewed certain aspects of the labor-relations experience of the Big Three producers. The review is admittedly deficient in a number of respects, but principally in

47. *Wall Street Journal,* Oct. 9, 1961.

the absence of data that would permit direct interfirm comparisons of unit labor costs. Such data are simply not available, and we are forced to rely therefore on the sort of evidence summarized above which provides at best only a rough measure of the labor-cost differentials developed under collective bargaining. This evidence does serve, nevertheless, to indicate the ranking of the three firms by performance level; and, in conjunction with the findings of other studies and our own observations, it lends support to the following conclusions regarding the forces at work in shaping competitive relations.

The difficulties faced by Chrysler and Ford in the area of labor costs were found to result from a combination of somewhat higher average levels of employee compensation, inferior work standards, more restrictive contract provisions, and generally less satisfactory day-to-day relations with local union officers and members. Such labor-cost differences cannot be attributed simply to inability or unwillingness on the part of these two companies to withstand union pressures—and, if necessary, to accept actual stoppages. While it is true that both Ford and Chrysler have on occasion lacked the strength and financial resources of GM, neither has hesitated to put up stubborn resistance to union demands judged unreasonable or has given any indication that problems of short-run survival were so acute as to preclude a proper consideration for longer-term (competitive) interests. Evidently the source of their troubles must lie elsewhere, and the conclusion seems unavoidable that it rests essentially in the skill and efficiency with which the respective managements have handled their relations with the union.

As was noted above, the greater success of GM's labor policies has been attested to by union officials and outside observers as well as by its principal competitors. It remains now to consider some of the reasons behind this superior level of performance.

When unionism entered the auto industry in the 1930s,

GM management—characteristically alert and farsighted—was quick to recognize the need for developing a clearly defined, long-range philosophy toward labor relations and collective bargaining, a set of objectives and policies that would offer firm guidance not only in the negotiation of agreements but also in their everyday administration.[48] This philosophy, evolved in the early years of collective bargaining and pursued diligently throughout the postwar period, has produced highly gratifying results from management's point of view. As early as 1947, Harbison was able to report that "the General Motors top executives have seemed convinced that the establishment of and adherence to its policy have been more important than the settlement of specific issues and specific problems which arose in the course of collective bargaining. The corporation has striven to avoid compromise on policies and resort to expediency, even if such a course of action involved expenditure of resources."[49] If anything, this early conviction has been strengthened with the passage of years. The current GM view is expressed in a recent statement by a seasoned member of the company's industrial-relations staff:

> A policy of expediency simply will not work to produce continuing good labor relations. Union officials have said to us that they have the greatest difficulty in dealing with managements which vacillate in their position on basic issues. Conversely, they get along best with managements which follow a reasonably predictable course of action, based upon reasonable policies.[50]

We would add that there is nothing in the history of collective bargaining in the industry to contradict this point of view.

48. See Harbison, "GM-UAW Agreement of 1950," p. 400; and Belfer, "Hidden Costs in the Labor Agreement," p. 46.

49. Harbison and Dubin, *Patterns of Union-Management Relations,* p. 49.

50. George B. Morris, Jr., "Good Administration of a Labor Agreement," Addresses on Industrial Relations, Bulletin no. 27 (Bureau of Industrial Relations, Univ. of Michigan, 1959 ser.), p. 3.

The main elements of the GM approach to labor relations are well known, resembling, as they do, those of industry generally. Harbison and Belfer have summarized GM's objectives under the following headings: to protect and improve the economic well-being of the company; to preserve management's freedom in the exercise of its functions; to achieve stable, predictable and "business-like" relations with the union; and to develop collective bargaining as a means of strengthening the free enterprise system.[51] In a sense, the last three objectives are supplementary to the principal goal—namely, the survival and growth of the corporation in its present institutional form. The success of the GM approach does not lie, however, in management's ability simply to formulate such goals (which, after all, are subscribed to by the vast majority of the nation's corporations), but rather in its ability to prescribe appropriate implementing policies and to have these policies applied firmly and consistently over time throughout the entire organization.[52] As Harbison noted in 1947: "Other large companies have developed definite labor relations policies, but few have been as successful as General Motors in getting them accepted and enforced by their organizations."[53]

The central purpose of GM management in all of its dealings with the union has been to preserve the necessary flexibility and freedom to operate its plants efficiently. Thus it has insisted

51. Harbison, "GM-UAW Agreement of 1950," pp. 400–02; and Belfer, pp. 44–45.

52. The UAW has frequently accused GM of excessive centralization of decision making in labor relations. GM's response, apart from reversing the accusation, has been to emphasize that uniformity in administration is less the result of centralized decision making per se as of the firm and consistent application of clear and definite policies by all levels of management. "We don't do one thing one day and something else the next day" is a favorite GM expression—and one which, incidentally, reveals in capsule form the company's view as to one of the major weaknesses in the labor-relations practices of some, if not all, of its competitors. The quotation is from the *Transcript of the GM-UAW Negotiations* (March 16, 1948), p. 83.

53. Harbison and Dubin, p. 46.

upon full retention of its right to maintain discipline and authority over all workers in its plants and has not hesitated to exercise this right up and down the line in all cases of wrongdoing. It has been especially resolute in dealing with employees guilty of violating the "no-strike" provisions of the contract through their participation in wildcat strikes and other forms of unauthorized stoppage. Management is convinced—and the record suggests, rightly so—that this is the key to responsible union behavior. As one of its spokesmen explained recently:

> General Motors' record for discharging the leaders of unauthorized work stoppages and disciplining the participants is well-known among union ranks and among arbitrators. Our consistent adherence to this policy puts the union leaders in a position where they can bring about responsible leadership within their ranks. They, too, have an important role to play in "What Constitutes Good Administration of a Labor Agreement."[54]

Similarly, GM has been adamant in its refusal to yield concessions to the union in the area of job control when these threatened to interfere with its freedom to assign and direct the work force. Like most companies, GM has accepted the rule of seniority in layoffs and rehiring; but in successive negotiations it has flatly rejected union demands on such matters as the posting of job openings, job transfers and assignments by seniority, and no transfers without employee consent. To GM management, control over utilization of the work force is of vital concern since the success or failure of an enterprise rests ultimately on the quality of its personnel and the manner in which their skills and experience are utilized. Consequently, it will tolerate no restrictions which unduly limit its flexibility in the use of manpower.[55] Finally, GM has resolutely defended its unilateral

54. George B. Morris, p. 14.
55. While GM has a reputation as a tough bargainer and has been de-

authority to set production standards, to determine what constitutes a fair day's work; and it has been prepared to meet head-on any actions by the union to weaken or dilute this authority.[56]

In short, the effectiveness of GM's labor relations is a tribute to the ability and foresight of its management. Through firm policies established during the early stages of collective bargaining and applied consistently throughout its organization, the company has been able, on the one hand, to preserve a high degree of freedom in the exercise of vital management functions and, on the other, to develop with the union a relationship

---

scribed as rigid, narrow, and restrictive in its approach to labor relations, this has not meant that union demands for new concessions are subject to automatic veto or to offhand and arbitrary treatment. There are, it is true, certain principles which the company feels must not be compromised (especially those relating to management's right to manage); but within the broad framework of objectives and policies which constitute the company's guiding philosophy, GM officials are shrewd, hard-headed pragmatists in their approach to labor issues. They give serious attention and study to union proposals, listen carefully to all supporting arguments, and respond with detailed and well-documented explanations of their own position. These replies, moreover, reveal a sophisticated understanding of the problems involved, a firm grasp of the implications and consequences of alternative courses of action, and a thorough knowledge of past experience not only of its own but of others' relations with the union. This patience and ability to marshal evidence and analyze the facts relevant to each issue, together with an insistence that issues be discussed against a background of factual experience rather than "in the abstract," helps account no doubt for Reuther's early advocacy of the need for union research facilities and personnel to accumulate and analyze the facts of actual plant experience. To GM management, the test of a good labor-relations practice, of a good solution to a labor problem is, in the last analysis, its soundness and workability, defined in terms of its contribution to the efficiency and profitability of the enterprise. There has been no confusion of ends, no ambiguity of purpose. "Good labor relations are not an end in themselves," states the company spokesman. "The end management seeks, and is primarily responsible for, in a successful business, is to produce goods and services for customers at lower cost and with increasingly better quality." (Morris, p. 14.) Stripped of its public-relations overtones, this statement simply means that management's central purpose is the continued operation of a profitable and progressive concern.

56. Both Harbison (p. 400) and Belfer (p. 46) have cited another aspect of GM's labor policy which tends to distinguish it from its competitors—an

which, while it may be governed by an agreement that is "more of a truce than a pact for union-management harmony," has nevertheless produced a remarkable record of industrial peace.

By contrast, Chrysler and Ford— the former up to the mid-1950s and the latter up to the immediate postwar years—were both hampered by outmoded management systems, poorly equipped for the efficient handling of labor relations and collective bargaining as well as of other business functions. The greater recent success of these two companies (Ford since the late 1940s and Chrysler since the late 1950s) has come with the conscious adoption of the GM program and approach, though neither can yet lay claim to having fully overcome the legacy of problems inherited from an earlier management. In recent years both companies, as witness to their deficiencies in this area, have stressed their desire to place their contracts and the quality of their relations with the union on a par with GM's. Whether this can be accomplished depends on their ability (1) to regain something of the flexibility and freedom enjoyed by GM under its labor contracts, especially in the area

---

aggressive rather than defensive posture in bargaining. These writers were led to this conclusion by the outcome of negotiations in 1948 and 1950. Harbison explained the strategy as follows:

> It [GM] has carefully appraised the bargaining situation of the union, listening to union demands without committing itself. Then, as in 1948 and 1950, it comes forth with a prefabricated proposition—a "blue-plate special"—which it proceeds to sell the union with as few substitutions as possible. In sharp contrast to other large corporations in the basic industries, GM in recent years has never let itself say "No" to union demands, only to back down later in the face of union pressure.

In 1955, however, this strategy backfired when GM apparently attempted to seize the initiative and stall the UAW's drive for some form of annual wage by offering the union its "prefabricated" stock-loan-severance pay plan. The strategy—momentarily successful when Ford followed GM's lead by offering a similar "package"—failed when the UAW outmaneuvered Ford and settled on an SUB plan which GM was then compelled to accept, much against its will. The final settlement contained a number of the choice side items with which GM had hoped to tempt the union away from its annual wage demand.

of control over the utilization of manpower; (2) to develop in local union leadership a greater respect for established procedures; and (3) to avoid fatal lapses into lax agreement administration. This third point is important for, according to the union, many of Ford's postwar difficulties arose from its failure to show consistent firmness in disciplinary action cases (as was done at GM).[57] Its policy of sporadic toughness in administering discipline served only to create confusion, uncertainty, and ill-feeling among its workers—effects that are reflected in its inferior record on grievances and work stoppages.[58]

In concluding this section, it is perhaps well to note one additional circumstance which may have had an influence on the labor-relations experience of these firms in the postwar period. In a sense, GM probably benefited from certain "accidents" of union growth—specifically, from the early emergence of a relatively strong and responsible union leader in the person of Walter Reuther. Though highly sensitive to the political requirements of union office, Reuther was an early advocate of the need for a disciplined, contract-conscious membership; and spurred on no doubt by GM's resolve to develop "responsible"

57. *Minutes, GM-UAW Negotiations* (June 7, 1955), p. 487.

58. In the matter of grievances, part of the difference in performance between Ford and GM may be attributable to differing concepts of the role of the umpire. Since the inception of the system in 1940, GM has insisted that the powers of the umpire be strictly limited to interpreting and applying the provisions of the agreement. GM management is absolutely convinced that this narrow, legalistic approach, which confines collective bargaining to earlier stages in the procedure, has reduced the number of grievances carried to the umpire, fostered the establishment of firm precedents for the settlement of future disputes, and prevented the union from using the grievance procedure as a "bargaining" device. At Ford, on the other hand, the umpire's duties went beyond the judicial stage to embrace both mediation and conciliation. This broadened scope to the function of the umpire inevitably encouraged the processing of grievances to the final step of the procedure since possibilities existed for favorable settlements going beyond the terms of the contract. Ford management itself apparently felt this to be a flaw in its grievance setup when in the early 1950s it sought to have the umpire's powers more narrowly defined.

unionism, he managed, as first director of the union's GM Department, to establish a much firmer control and direction over the behavior of GM locals than was the case in other companies. Moreover, when he relinquished this office in the late 1940s, he appointed as his successor Thomas A. Johnstone, an equally (if not more) ardent advocate of "responsible" unionism. Johnstone's personal integrity and his insistence on strict observance at all times of the rules and procedures laid down in the contract soon earned him the respect and confidence of GM management. This is reflected clearly in the minutes of all negotiations conducted during his term in office. Indeed, Johnstone was, if anything, too "responsible" in his handling of the union's business, for in June 1951 he was removed from his post as GM director and offered a less sensitive assignment elsewhere. As *Business Week* reported the matter:

> The auto industry has long envied the stabilized conditions in General Motors plants. Johnstone is generally given much credit for this stabilization. Rather uncompromising in his ideas and considered a man of his word, he insisted that the contract be abided by to the last detail. That was one reason for GM's good work record.
>
> Johnstone's success in keeping GM affairs on an even keel helped lose him his job. Scattered locals were complaining. And Reuther himself is supposed to be irked at the fact that Detroit generally attributed the five-year escalator contract that led to much of that peaceable atmosphere to Johnstone—not Reuther.[59]

While vigorous company action and strong union leadership combined to assure reasonably stable relations at GM, these same influences were in some measure lacking at Ford and Chrysler. The relative instability experienced by these two companies was, as we have argued above, largely the result of labor policies less skillfully conceived and executed than

59. *Business Week* (February 23, 1952), p. 39.

GM's.[60] At the same time, however, relations at both companies suffered in some degree from the unsettling effects of intra-union dissension, bickering, and struggles for power. This was especially true at Ford. During the 1940s and early 1950s, Ford Local 600—to take the most significant example—was a leftist stronghold and the most important source of anti-Reutherism in the UAW. Down through the years, this large local, which has been slow to yield its autonomy and independence to the international, has been a focal point of power struggles for control and influence within the union. Caught uncomfortably in the middle of these squabbles, the company has been forced to suffer the consequences of more or less continuous electioneering. It is not at all surprising therefore that union behavior has fallen far short of the measure of "responsibility" attained at GM. In milder form, other locals in the Ford and Chrysler groups have occasionally posed similar problems for management—problems deriving from local insurgency and opposition to international leadership. Since there is evidence that this opposition tends to manifest itself in disruptive behavior of various sorts, it seems fair to conclude that the generally less firm control exercised by the international over local activities has contributed to less stable relations in the plants of these two companies. It should be noted, however, that this factor is undoubtedly less important today than in the past as international efforts to bring local actions under control have met with gradual but continuing success.

Labor-Relations Performance: The Independents

The preceding section attempted to show through a comparison of the labor-relations experience of the Big Three auto firms that ability to withstand union demands is not the sole determinant of successful labor-relations performance. If it were, the lag at Chrysler and Ford would go largely unexplained. Instead,

60. We include in this the virulently antiunion attitudes that predominated in earlier managements and bequeathed to later managements a legacy of unresolved problems and embittered relations.

it was found that labor-cost differences between these three firms were related primarily to differences in the skill with which the respective managements had handled their labor relations. Moreover, improvements in relative performance came about not as a result of intensified opposition and resistance to union demands, but more as a result of the conscious adoption of policies and practices which had demonstrated their soundness and superiority in the hands of the industry's most skillful labor-relations practitioner.

We do not deny, of course, that urgent need to avoid the consequences of nonagreement may force a company to yield concessions beyond those of its competitors, or that union coercion has on occasion driven out of business an enterprise seeking to resist unreasonable demands. Nor, for that matter, do we deny the strong compulsion on all producers to maintain production uninterruptedly. We do insist, however, that differences in financial strength (and profitability) are not the only source of intercompany differences in labor standards, and that, as far as auto manufacturing is concerned, they are a less fundamental cause than differences in managerial ability. The fact that management seeks to place the responsibility elsewhere is beside the point: few companies (except in the process of reorganizing management) can be expected to acknowledge their inefficiencies or to declare their policies ineffective and ill advised. The fact that management may choose, moreover, to stress short-run considerations at the expense of longer-term interests in its relations with the union does not thereby make the selection a wise or necessary one; it may simply reflect poor judgment or lack of adequate foresight. In this section we examine the underlying position and policies of the Independents with a view to assessing the validity of management's claim that its "labor problem" (excessive employment costs) was, and is, the result of overwhelming bargaining power in the hands of the union.

In the period under consideration it is by no means obvious

that the position of the Independents was so vulnerable as to compel them to limit their bargaining—even in the face of pattern-plus demands—to what was attainable by peaceful means. Between World War II and the end of the Korean War

TABLE 25. Selected Operating Statistics, Studebaker Corporation
and Nash-Kelvinator Company, 1946–1952
(in millions of dollars)

Year	After-tax income	Depreciation and amortization	Net working capital	Net income to net worth
		Studebaker Corporation		
1946	$ 0.9	$ 5.2	$29.1	2.3%
1947	9.1	7.7	35.0	19.0
1948	19.1	8.0	39.2	30.0
1949	27.6	8.0	56.5	32.3
1950	22.5	9.3	58.1	22.5
1951	12.6	9.2	64.7	12.0
1952	14.2	8.1	54.5	12.7
		Nash-Kelvinator Company		
1946	2.6	3.5	37.6	5.2
1947	18.1	3.0	59.0	28.0
1948	20.1	4.3	63.8	25.6
1949	26.2	10.1	71.8	26.6
1950	28.8	10.2	79.1	25.2
1951	16.2	11.7	85.9	13.5
1952	12.6	11.0	70.0	10.2

Source. Moody's *Industrials*.

these producers were operating highly profitable and financially sound concerns. Table 25 presents some of the relevant operating statistics for Studebaker and Nash-Kelvinator, the two leading Independents prior to the mergers producing Studebaker-Packard and American Motors. We have included the data on after-tax earnings, depreciation allowances and net working capital as rough measures of the flow of funds and level of resources available to these two companies to cushion against the drain on financial strength which could be expected to accompany any interruption to production—specifically, a walkout.[61] It is not our intention to use these figures, however, as a basis for estimating what the effects of firmer bargaining policies on company solvency might have been. Nor do we intend to use them in a vain effort to establish that the financial condition of the Independents was at all comparable to that of the Big Three. We present them only to dispel the notion that these companies were "sitting ducks," living a precarious existence, and hence powerless to resist not simply the "pattern" established by industry leaders in Detroit but also any additional concessions the union chose to demand. Given their profitability at the time, and the fact that the bulk of their facilities were located in smaller, lower-wage communities offering less attractive employment alternatives than Detroit, it seems at least reasonable to question their professed inability to offer any resistance whatever to so-called "pattern-plus" settlements. If anything, their weakness lay more in their unwillingness than in their inability to withstand union pressures.

But even if we admit that a firm approach to labor relations and collective bargaining offered greater hazards to the smaller companies, there still remains, to our mind, overwhelming evidence that the managements in question must share with the union the responsibility for labor contracts and practices that were unrealistic in the light of (long-run) competitive conditions. As one Detroit newspaper put it in the fall of 1954: "If union statesmanship came belatedly . . . , management responsibility in the full meaning of the term was slow to materialize, also."[62] The truth is that during the period of wartime emergency with its tight labor market and cost-plus contracts fol-

61. Incidentally, it may be noted that the debt positions of these companies imposed no evident heavy strictures on their actions.

62. *Detroit Free Press*, Aug. 11, 1954.

lowed by a lush sellers' market in autos up to the early 1950s, these companies remained largely unconcerned about the cost of expensive "side" items granted to the union. Protected from competitive pressures by abnormal demand conditions that assured easy profits, they were under no immediate spur to efficiency. In these circumstances, weak, complacent, and short-sighted managements virtually relinquished control of their plants in unrealistic contract provisions and shop practices.[63]

The Studebaker Corporation, in our view, provides a classic example of this sort of mismanagement. In the early postwar years, labor relations at this company received a good deal of publicity and no small amount of praise. In almost a hundred years Studebaker had suffered no serious labor trouble; and in 1946 its president, Paul Hoffman, was awarded the Henry Laurence Gantt Memorial Gold Medal by the American Management Association "for providing an inspiring, practical example of successful management-labor relations."[64] To many people, the Studebaker-UAW relationship constituted the sort of progressive model that offered hope for the coming of age of industrial relations in the mid-twentieth century. Its virtues were extolled by business leaders, labor officials and university scholars alike. To Harbison and Dubin, it represented "a practical working model of . . . 'constructive union-management relations,' " meaning the relations achieved "when a union and a company harmonize divergent goals into an effective working agreement."[65] Their enthusiasm was clearly conveyed by the conclusion that in such stable constructive relations lay "the greatest potential contribution of collective bargaining to the American economy."[66] These two scholars explained the Studebaker relationship in the following terms:

63. See, e.g., Harris, "The Breakdown of Studebaker-Packard," p. 222; *Detroit Free Press*, Aug. 11, 1954, and June 13, 1955.
64. John F. Sembower, "What's behind Studebaker's No-Strike Record," *Industrial Relations* (Oct. 1946), p. 5.
65. *Patterns of Union-Management Relations*, p. 202.
66. Ibid.

1) The type of union-management relations developed at Studebaker reflected the firm's precarious financial position at the time of unionization. With the company in receivership, the need to maintain continuous production convinced management of the desirability, and indeed necessity, of working with rather than against the union. Similarly, it encouraged the union to pursue policies tempered by a concern for the company's survival. Since the relationship so developed proved sound and mutually beneficial, neither party found reason to alter its approach even after the emergency itself had passed.

2) Both management and the union accepted the fact that Studebaker had to operate within the limits of wage-price patterns set in Detroit. Agreement on this point reduced the range of issues separating the parties, leaving for the most part only local problems to be resolved in bargaining.

3) Management, far from fighting the union, sought to promote and strengthen it, yielding to it in the process a substantial degree of control over jobs and the work force. As a result, the union enjoyed security and an assured status within both the plant and the South Bend community.

4) Studebaker's simple and relatively informal management structure encouraged top executives to participate directly in collective bargaining. The effect of this participation was to make such company officials thoroughly conversant with "the practical shop aspects of labor relations issues."

5) Both parties avoided doctrinaire positions in their approach to bargaining issues and instead concentrated on the substance of problems. This "problem-oriented" approach provided the flexibility necessary for the constructive solution of issues arising between the parties.

6) The relationship was marked by a fairly even balance of power. Consequently, "the possibility of strikes, slowdowns and lockouts has always been an important influence on . . . decisions," leading both parties to prefer "acceptable compromises to the risks inherent in industrial warfare."[67]

67. Ibid., pp. 204–09.

Studebaker's relationship with the union was marked by a surprising lack of formality. There was "no printed statement of labor policy or procedure, no codified rules of conduct, no commitments on the part of the company or its workers."[68] The cardinal maxim of management's approach to labor relations was summed up in the phrase "we can settle anything by talking it over."[69] In line with this policy, top management maintained an open door at all times to all employees;[70] and all levels of supervision were encouraged to shoulder their full responsibility for industrial relations leadership.

That such an approach to labor relations has commendable and attractive features cannot be gainsaid. However, the test of successful labor-management relations cannot be based solely on the degree of industrial harmony and friendliness that prevails in the plant.[71] How these contribute to efficient operation of the enterprise is certainly a more fundamental test of

68. Sembower, p. 6.

69. This aspect of management policy so impressed Sembower that he was prompted to write: "This business of sitting down and talking a subject over is more than a sentiment; it is an operating credo at Studebaker which alone might be sufficient explanation for the remarkable industrial relations record." Ibid., p. 34.

70. On Feb. 2, 1953, *Time* (p. 66) wrote of Studebaker's board chairman and president, Harold S. Vance, as follows:

Vance runs Studebaker's 25,000-man organization with no committees of any kind. Says he: 'Committees call for compromise and compromise is not solution. I solve the company's problems with the men directly responsible for them. If anyone is at fault, I am to blame . . .' Vance seldom writes a memo, does most of his business by phone, which he always answers himself. At Studebaker even the lowliest production worker can dial 496 on a company phone and hear a polite voice at the other end: 'Yes, sir, Mr. Vance speaking.'

71. On the question of industrial peace at Studebaker, two comments are in order. First, the relationship at Studebaker is properly characterized as a "secondary" or "follower" relationship. In view of the company's unwritten pledge to follow the Detroit wage pattern, it is natural to expect less strife at this point than in pattern-generating centers such as GM and Ford. Second, while there were no official strikes at Studebaker, there were apparently frequent minor walkouts and slowdowns by individuals and small groups. This appears indeed to have been a quite common method of seeking redress for alleged grievances.

success (in a market economy) since competitive survival is after all a prerequisite to any relationship whatever. What can be said of Studebaker in this respect?

When Studebaker's labor-relations policies are appraised from the standpoint of efficiency, certain serious shortcomings are apparent. These were already in evidence in the early postwar years; but they became impressively clear only with the return of competition in the early 1950s. It was by then obvious that union-management relations at Studebaker, whatever their former status, were anything but "constructive." What had once been described as "collaboration for mutual benefit" was now revealed to involve little more than weak, defensive, and often ineffective bargaining on the part of the company. Plainly, the open-door policy and liberality of Studebaker's management had been overdone. The easy availability of top officials may well have contributed to the prevailing harmony; but it also meant at times short-circuiting or bypassing the industrial-relations staff and plant supervision—the groups most competent to appraise issues and problems in this area and charged, moreover, with responsibility for administering the agreement at the shop level. Harbison and Dubin had noted this as a potential source of trouble in any constructive relationship.[72] In Studebaker's case, however, it was less a potentiality than a fact already observed in 1946[73] and subsequently brought to light in studies conducted in 1953–54 by Anna M. Rosenberg and associates.[74] It was found at this time that Studebaker had neither a supervisory-training program nor an employee-communications program. Moreover, while relations between management and the union were "cozy" at the top levels, management reportedly gave little heed to relations on the shop floor, neglected its foremen, and relied on the union to enforce discipline. Under the circumstances, it is not surprising that shop

72. *Patterns of Union-Management Relations,* p. 212.
73. Sembower, p. 32.
74. *Fortune* (Nov. 1954), p. 74.

practices and work habits left much to be desired. As *Fortune* noted, the Rosenberg plan to improve Studebaker's operations required, among other things, "not only selling a few individuals on a program or a strike settlement, but persuading thousands of supervisors and workers to change deep-rooted work attitudes."[75]

Two other key elements in Studebaker's so-called "constructive" relationship were the "problem-solving" approach to issues and the informality of bargaining procedures. In our view—and with the benefit of hindsight—these now appear to have signified little more than the absence of a carefully designed program to guide and direct decisions and actions in the labor-relations sphere. Management was apparently resigned to "playing it by ear," to seeking expedient solutions for the problems of the moment (often without proper regard for their cumulative effect on the future economic well-being of the company). The notion that "we can settle anything by talking it over," that strikes (and coercion in general) are unnecessary, that problems should (and could) be resolved amicably through reasonable discussion, certainly expresses a noble sentiment, but surely one of questionable validity in the current context of collective bargaining. Such an approach made sense perhaps under the conditions existing at the time of Studebaker's organization by the union, when an extended shutdown would certainly have produced serious financial strain if not actual bankruptcy. It made less sense, however, in the 1940s when the company was riding the wave of wartime and postwar prosperity, enjoying excellent profits and a reasonably secure financial position. Under these conditions, the company could well have afforded to take a longer view of the requirements for sound, healthy growth. Yet, whether because it feared to sully its reputation for harmonious labor relations, or was lulled by the temporary security of a strong sellers' market, or had simply failed to adapt to the radical change in circumstances,

75. Ibid.

the company continued to respond openhandedly to union demands throughout the postwar period. Nor is there any evidence, as Dubin claimed, that the company exacted a price for each concession.[76] Preoccupied with amicable settlements, reluctant to force any issue, resolved to "let sleeping dogs lie," management simply conceded too much and left the company ill prepared to meet the challenge of returning competition in the post-Korean period.

It is not implied here, of course, that Studebaker's difficulties in 1953–54 were solely (or indeed principally) a "labor problem," but merely that excessive liberality in negotiations and lax administration intensified the handicap under which the company already labored.[77] In the pursuit of policies that emphasized harmony at the expense of efficiency, the Studebaker agreement, unlike those of the company's larger competitors, was never "purged" of any undesirable features. Since there were no strikes during the period, the contract was never terminated; and since the prevalent management attitude was to avoid the initiation of any complicating issues, few contract clauses (once negotiated) were ever forcefully questioned. Moreover, in its efforts to avoid labor trouble and promote stability in the local union, management yielded all too readily to the union leader's professed need for something to "take back" to the membership. Under the circumstances, it was not surprising that labor costs mounted steadily above competitive levels.

The precarious labor situation created at Studebaker did not go unnoticed in the rest of the industry. As early as 1945, for example, when Reuther reported to GM's chief negotiator that

76. Harbison and Dubin, pp. 113, 116.

77. As we might expect, inefficient handling of the labor-relations function is normally accompanied by poor management performance in other areas. If management handles other business functions in an inferior manner, the chances are that similar inefficiencies will appear in its handling of labor relations. In other words, the quality of performance in labor relations is generally a reflection of the quality of over-all management.

Studebaker had already led the way with a 12 per cent wage increase at its South Bend auto plant, his point was simply brushed aside with the scornful comment: "I wouldn't want our plants run like Studebaker's plants are run."[78] Similarly, ten years later, Malcolm L. Denise, Ford's General Industrial Relations Manager, undoubtedly had Studebaker and other independents in mind when he made the following statement before a group of personnel executives:

> Details of working agreements do not make headlines. . . . They are undramatic, and hence they receive little public attention. . . . Yet we all know companies where a few changes in such areas as bumping rights, tryout periods or the enforcement of work standards would contribute more to the health, success and profitability of the enterprise than a reduction of several cents in hourly wage rates.[79]

In the previous chapter, we found evidence of the lack of an effective labor policy at Studebaker in the deterioration of the incentive pay plan, the overmanning of numerous operations, the extensive bumping exercised through plant-wide seniority in layoffs, the granting of excessive idle-time allowances, and so forth. The important point to note here, however, is that most of these difficulties were connected with the administration and not the negotiation of agreements. Indeed, we are reliably informed that the costly practices of plant-wide bumping and excessive idle time both resulted from supervisory errors in interpreting the contract. Prior to the 1937 agreement, Studebaker had followed the policy of allowing any laid-off senior worker to displace the employee with *least* seniority in the plant. It was the company's intention to continue this practice under

78. *Proceedings, GM-UAW Negotiations* (Oct. 19, 1945), p. 71.
79. "The 1955 Ford-UAW Contract," a talk delivered before the Fall Personnel Conference of the American Management Association, New York City, Sept. 26, 1955.

the collective bargaining agreement. However, at a later date and during the absence of the Industrial Relations Director, plant supervision agreed with the union that the laid-off worker could displace *any* employee with less seniority. Since this precedent could not be reversed without a struggle, plant-wide bumping thus became an established practice. Similarly, the company had agreed to rest periods in its contract with the union which were less than the unofficial time then allowed in the company's body division. This provision, again, was misinterpreted by supervision and the contractual rest periods became an addition to the unofficial allowances. Such errors in administration are perhaps not difficult to explain in a situation where supervisors are asked to shoulder full responsibility for industrial-relations leadership and yet are offered little or no training or guidance in what is required of them.[80]

Finally, we might recall, as symptomatic of postwar relations at South Bend, the workers' initial reaction to the company's desperate attempts to streamline labor costs in 1954. Despite the evidence of sharply reduced sales and employment, of large

80. In an obvious reference to poor contract administration at Studebaker, George B. Morris, Jr., of GM's Labor Relations Staff, had this to say recently:

> Contract negotiations and contract administration are extensions of each other—they complement each other. The way an employer administers his labor agreement—and the practices he permits to develop under it—not only controls whether the agreement operates the way he intended it to, but also has a strong bearing on what will go into the next contract. The bad administrative practices of today have a tendency to become the bad contract provisions of tomorrow.
>
> A few years ago one of the automobile companies ran full page ads in the newspapers explaining its viewpoint of its own predicament under its labor contract. The ad set forth the factors which had caused this company's labor costs to get out of hand. . . . Significantly, all but the first of these problems were the outgrowth of contract administration, not contract negotiations. Thus, while the high wage rates had been negotiated, these other problems—the loose work standards, the bumping, transferring and training, and the washup, personal time and rest periods—had been created by management's own attitude and the practices which management had permitted to develop. ("Good Administration of a Labor Agreement," pp. 1-2.)

financial losses, and of a wide-reaching retrenchment program cutting executive salaries and other costs, and despite acknowledgement by union leaders that labor costs (and benefits) were seriously out of line, the local membership summarily rejected the company's plea for relief. Based on the experience of prior years, the workers simply viewed as empty the company's threat to terminate the contract and anticipated that management would respond to rejection of its first offer with another proposal asking less drastic revisions, particularly in the area of work practices. Hence their reaction, first, of amusement and derision at the company's initial threat and, then, of shock and bewilderment when they learned that the company for once would not back down, but intended to stand firmly behind its proposal to "purge" the contract. The hasty reconsideration and capitulation which followed shortly thereafter support this interpretation.

We may conclude, then, that whatever the nature of union-management relations at Studebaker in the prewar years, the picture that emerges for the postwar period is certainly not one of constructive relations, of collaboration for mutual benefit. Instead, we find that Studebaker management—inspired as it may have been by high motives and a lofty purpose—was woefully ill prepared and ill equipped to meet the challenge of collective bargaining in a competitive environment. Even allowing that the company had fewer resources than some of its competitors with which to resist union pressures, it is still abundantly clear that many of its difficulties were due to poor judgment, lax administration, and the absence of effective controls.

Turning briefly to American Motors' predicament, we find that while there is less direct evidence concerning the root causes, here again management, lulled by cost-plus contracts and the postwar sellers' market, simply yielded more to the union than was wise and allowed incredible slack to develop in its use of manpower. George Romney's own observations on joining Nash-Kelvinator in 1948 confirm that the responsibility for the company's sad condition (concealed temporarily by the absence of competitive pressures) lay primarily with management. He found "appalling internal disorganization . . . at upper as well as lower levels."[81] There was little communication or coordination between individuals or the various departments of the company. "Plant labor relations directors didn't know whether there was a labor-relations policy or not"; "lax labor standards were hurting"; and "flagrant violations of normal work discipline went uncorrected in the Kelvinator plant in Plymouth Road adjoining the Nash-Kelvinator general offices."[82] The labor situation existing in this plant was almost beyond belief, as can be seen from the following description:

> There was a men's barbershop in the men's rest room, operated by company employees on company time, with company pay. Workers had taken company parts and made electric ranges and refrigerators for the rest room. One woman was cooking breakfast for five men every morning after they got to work as a small-scale restaurant business. Some women were cooking evening meals on company time in the rest rooms and taking them home so they wouldn't have to cook after they got home. One employee bagged a bear during the hunting season and roasted cuts of it in the big ovens used to bake moisture out of the compressors. Poker games and numbers bets flourished. If foremen tried to interfere, they were barred from the rest rooms by employee-appointed "lookouts." A law school student on the afternoon shift typed his briefs in an unused women's washroom.
>
> The men were literally working only half the time they

81. Tom Mahoney, *The Story of George Romney: Builder, Salesman, Crusader* (New York, Harper, 1960), p. 160.

82. Ibid., pp. 154, 162.

were paid, and had come to regard the situation as legitimate. One day a worker was hurt in a plant accident at 10 A.M. The rules provided that any worker who had to go home before noon because of injury should get a half day's pay. The man, however, demanded and received a full day's pay because between 7 and 10 A.M. he had already done a day's work by plant standards.[83]

As at Studebaker, so too at the Plymouth Road plant of Nash-Kelvinator, management relied principally upon the union to enforce discipline. Furthermore, the union representing the Plymouth Road production workers had also organized the foremen and plant guards. This hardly bespoke a sensible arrangement; as *Fortune* commented later, "if workers loafed, the foremen and supervisors loafed as much."[84] It is possible, of course, that labor conditions at the Plymouth Road plant, which was under contract to the MESA and not the UAW, represented a unique situation. If so, however, it was unique in degree rather than in kind. The fact remains that the selfsame management that was responsible for Nash-Kelvinator's auto operations tolerated such conditions in its appliance division and moved to correct them only under Romney's insistent prodding. Nor is there anything to suggest that management pursued a different line in its relations with the UAW. In the light of these considerations and the evidence already presented, it is difficult to deny the view—frankly endorsed by Romney himself at the time—that Nash-Kelvinator management, through lax and negligent administration up and down the line, had simply failed to meet its responsibilities and had more or less relinquished its authority over the work force in its plants.

83. Ibid., p. 162.
84. (Jan. 1955), p. 53.

CHAPTER 8

The Economic Consequences of Unionism

The foregoing chapters have dealt with the wage structure and competitive relations in the auto industry as they have developed under collective bargaining. This chapter summarizes the principal findings of the study and interprets them in the light of current ideas about the nature and economic consequences of unionism. In order to provide the perspective necessary for judging the results, however, it is well to restate at this point certain reservations as to the method of analysis employed in the study. The main points can be summarized as follows.

1) Conclusions about the actual influence of unionism depend fundamentally on the model adopted for predicting developments in the nonunion economy. Insofar as models of the nonunion labor market have been developed explicitly in studies of union impact, the choice has generally been restricted to two main types—the perfectly competitive and the imperfectly competitive. Indeed, a large part of the controversy over union wage effects has centered essentially on the relative merits of these two types of nonunion model. At a more basic level, however, it is questionable whether either of these models

(which alike assume the feasibility of a market system governed by individual as distinct from group behavior) constitutes a satisfactory alternative to the union model and hence an appropriate basis for judging actual union influence. If, as most labor historians believe, unionism is a by-product of industrialism and political democracy, performing an indispensable function in the maintenance of labor's commitment to the free enterprise economy, then any economic system that assumes the characteristic form of modern democratic capitalism must surely allow for a union movement or for some equivalent mechanism to protect and represent the interests of wage earners against the inadequacies (real or fancied) of free, competitive markets. Insofar as this view of unionism is valid, labor's response to the industrial system, expressed through collective action, is a fact of industrial life—and any model that purports to have relevance to the real world must somehow reconcile the existence of the unorganized market with labor's insistent clamor for moderation of that market's inadequacies. This is not to argue that unionism is inevitable, or that its form and effects are in any sense rigidly prescribed. It is to emphasize, however, that unionism is rooted in the system, an integral part of the configuration of free institutions that characterize Western democratic societies. Alternatives to unionism are obviously available, but it is by no means certain that they are consistent with the set of institutional arrangements which nonunion models implicitly assume.[1]

2) Even if it is granted, however, that the unorganized market provides a feasible alternative to the union market, so that wage and employment conditions are a matter of unilateral decision rather than of joint determination, there is still the

1. Incidentally, it may be argued that a more reasonable, though more limited, research objective would be to discover, not the absolute effects of unionism as such, but rather the differential effects of different kinds of unions and collective bargaining relationships. Certainly, from a policy standpoint, these are the important issues. They are also more manageable issues in that they concern existing systems.

question of constructing an appropriate decision model for management. Most of the models adopted for this purpose are derived from one or more of three sources: (1) management's behavior in preunion decades, including the depression years, when social and economic conditions were vastly different from today's; (2) management's behavior in collective bargaining, a process whose very logic, supported by the law, requires a defensive, if not actually negative, posture on the part of most managements; and (3) management's behavior as deduced from economic models of the firm which tend to focus on the wage rate as the only tool of manpower management and to portray management itself as a rather passive agent, unimaginative, unadaptive, and largely unresponsive to the varied and changing needs of workers. These sources of information and insight are of course useful, and even indispensable, in the construction of a decision model for management in the nonunion economy. They provide, however, only the raw ingredients; there is no prescription for the blend. How management, unaffected by union pressures but surely not impervious to the forces of change, would have adapted its organization, outlook, and policies to meet the challenges and opportunities posed by the swift movement of events during the last few decades remains a matter for personal conjecture. Hence, there is room for legitimate difference of opinion.

These issues are easily posed, but they are not easily resolved. We raise them for two reasons: first, because they have not received, to our mind, sufficient critical attention in the literature dealing with the effects of unionism; and, second, because they indicate possible limitations of the present analysis. We have assumed, in line with other studies, that there is no incompatibility between the system of democratic capitalism as currently constituted and the absence of labor organizations—i.e. that the same set of institutional arrangements can accommodate without undue strain either a system of organized labor markets or a system of unorganized labor markets. We have also as-

sumed that the wage practices of management, in the absence
of unionism, can be determined with reasonable accuracy from
the study of preunion behavior and of the objectives and attitudes expressed by management under collective bargaining.
We have sought, however, to retain awareness of the nature
of workers' needs in contemporary society and of the requirement that these needs be met (at least in some minimal way)
either through private decision or through governmental action.
Obviously, the interpretation of our findings as to union influence—whether they represent a measure of the actual effects
of unionism or merely of the degree to which bargained solutions have deviated from competitive (employer-determined)
solutions—must rest on the acceptability of these assumptions
to the reader.[2]

THE WAGE (OR COMPENSATION) STRUCTURE

While it would be absurd to dispute the fact that economic
forces shape the broad contours of an economy's wage structure, it is erroneous to assume that the specific pattern of wage
relationships found in an industry such as autos can be explained by reference to market forces alone. The decisions of
unions and employers are made within a fairly broad range of
discretion; their policy choices affect the method and form of
employee compensation as well as the structure of payments
among individuals, occupations, and establishments. We may
not be able to specify the precise limits of discretionary control,
but our analysis indicates that some measure of discretion exists
in wage setting so that the actual pattern of wage relationships
observed under collective bargaining is often only one of a
set of possible patterns available to the parties. To discover the
range of feasible policy alternatives and the reasons underlying
specific selections from among these alternatives are important
objectives of wage analysis.

2. This matter was explored in detail in earlier chapters. (See, especially,
chap. 1, pp. 19–27, and chap. 2, pp. 49–55.

Fringe Benefits

Perhaps the most notable development on the wage front in the last 25 years has been the rapid growth in supplementary and indirect forms of employee compensation. Under collective bargaining, unions and employers have erected a system of private benefit programs which today account for approximately one fifth of total payroll expenditures. These programs obviously influence the economy in a variety of ways, affecting, among other things, the pattern of income and expenditure flows, the functioning of labor markets, and the "welfare" role of government. While we have touched lightly on some of these influences at various points in the study, this has been incidental to our primary interest—i.e. the role of fringe benefits in the wage structure and the influence of unionism in their development.

Fringe Benefits and the Wage Structure. The important analytical question raised by the development of an elaborate system of fringe benefits is whether or not such benefits should be included in the measurement of wages and hence in wage comparisons. Although there remain a number of unresolved issues and certainly adequate grounds for differences in viewpoint, it is our judgment that the compensation structure which incorporates the value of fringe benefits into the wage measure is a more meaningful concept upon which to base the analysis of relative wage movements than is the wage-rate structure per se. In adopting this position, we do not deny of course the complications that arise in reducing fringe benefits to their cents-per-hour equivalents, nor do we imply that such equivalence should be assumed (or that wages and fringes should be combined) regardless of the purpose of the analysis.[3] Fringe benefits do differ from wages in important ways, and their inclusion in the

3. See, e.g., the approach suggested by Arthur Ross ("The External Wage Structure," in Taylor and Pierson, eds., *New Concepts in Wage Determination,* pp. 181–84) when the analysis is focused explicitly on the particular wage decisions made by unions and employers.

system of employee compensation does pose novel issues of analysis. It is important in the study of wage structure to recognize these differences and to be aware of their implications.

Employee benefit programs, whether bargained collectively or instituted unilaterally by employers, do not have the same value for all employees. This divergence in value derives from the differing circumstances, expectations, and preferences of individual workers. As a first approximation, we have valued these benefits at cost and have explored the principal ways in which they affect personal, occupational, and interplant wage relationships. It is clear, however, that fringe programs, because they represent different values to different workers, introduce a complex structure of personal inequalities into the wage system—inequalities, moreover, that almost certainly would not exist had bargaining been confined to wage rates or even to fringe programs in which participation was entirely voluntary. We know little about the actual magnitudes of these personal inequalities, but in some instances they may be quite substantial.

A second point of difference rests in the fact that wages and fringes are not perfect substitutes. As with working conditions, certain minimum standards in each of the principal components of compensation may enter into workers' job expectations; the worker's reservation price may in effect consist of a set of requirements covering certain fringe items as well as the wage rate. Thus beyond certain limits the marginal rates of substitution may tend to rise sharply and indeed it can be argued that reasonable substitution possibilities may even disappear. This is only true, however, if such minimums are socially or culturally determined and if, in addition, the employer-sponsored program is the unique source of the set of benefits in question. As long as other sources are available through which comparable benefits may be purchased by the individual, then (regardless of cultural requirements) there is *some* wage differential or wage increase that will compensate for the absence of such benefit programs in the immediate employment relationship. These considerations suggest that substitution possibilities between wages and fringes vary with the nature of the benefit as well as with the social and cultural milieu. The analytical issues encountered may be illustrated in the case of insurance and vacation plans.

It is frequently asserted that the average worker prefers an employer-sponsored insurance plan to a wage increase of equivalent cost. The reason for this preference is that the benefits provided under such a plan are otherwise not available or at least are only obtainable at considerably higher cost through the purchase of individual insurance policies. Given the nature of the alternatives, it is not difficult to explain the worker's choice. Only if he had access to similar benefits through other group plans organized outside the immediate employment relationship would the worker's estimate of the cents-per-hour (wage) value of the employer's plan (with due allowance for tax effects) approximate closely its cents-per-hour cost. Thus, insofar as employer-sponsored plans are superior to other insurance alternatives (in terms of the benefit-premium ratios), the wage value of such plans must be held to exceed their cents-per-hour cost. If these plans were made available on a voluntary basis to workers desirous of purchasing insurance protection, the equivalent wage value of the plan might be taken as the lowest price at which similar protection could be purchased outside the employment relationship. This assumes, however, that the same insurance protection is worth the "outside" price to the worker—an assumption that is surely questionable. Instead, this higher price sets a maximum on the equivalent value of the employer's plan, and the actual wage values of the plan to participating workers could be expected to range between this price and the cost of the plan. In other words, individual workers participating in the employer's plan would no doubt be prepared to trade it at different rates above its cents-per-hour cost. Of course, the fact that these plans (largely at the insistence of union leaders) are now compulsory simply increases the difficulty of imputing to them an equivalent wage value; for some workers, the compulsory plan may be worth less than its cost.

Vacation plans (and holiday programs) present a somewhat different problem. These benefits are unique in the sense that they are obtainable from only one source—the employer. In such instances, the possibilities of substitution may indeed be sharply limited, though the existence of plans granting pay in lieu of vacation indicates that, for the time being at least, insistence on periodic vacations is by no means universal. Nevertheless, the trend is probably in this direction, and to the extent that it is, vacation plans become somewhat analogous to working conditions—i.e. substitutable with wages only within (narrow) limits. This does not mean that wage comparisons between groups of workers should then exclude vacation plans. It does signify, however, that the form and composition of compensation is important apart from its size—a consideration of no small moment surely to union and management negotiators!

Unionism and Fringe Benefits. Although opinion among economists differs on the extent to which unionism has been able to affect the *level* of employee compensation, agreement is well-nigh universal that unionism has had a substantial influence upon the *form* of compensation, particularly the rapid development of fringe benefits. Indeed, it is not uncommon to find the viewpoint expressed that this extensive system of supplements to the wage rate owes its existence primarily or even entirely to union pressure. But this extreme view is surely exaggerated; for while it is true that the programs now in existence are negotiated programs and owe much of their distinctive character to union pressures, it is also true that a strong undercurrent of social and economic forces was operating in the same direction. At least our speculations cannot afford to overlook such pertinent facts as (1) the voluntary introduction into industry of many of these private benefits for production workers (and more extensively for salaried personnel) prior to union entry and to any display of official union interest; (2) the universality of the tendency among more advanced nations to divert an increasing proportion of wage-earner income to specific welfare ends; and (3) the attention given by government to the development of social policies designed to regulate the employment relationship and to protect the individual worker against a variety of contingencies. These considerations do not of course deny to unionism a significant influence, but they do suggest a broader-based sympathy and support, as well as possible alternative sources, for the same or similar benefits. In any event, our own conclusions regarding union influence on fringe developments in the auto industry are summarized below.

1) *Pension and welfare plans.* Unionism has been responsible for the development of private pension and SUB programs designed to supplement the basic governmental programs in these areas and for a more rapid expansion and liberalization of life and health insurance plans. It has not been responsible, however, for the initiation of insurance plans nor, to our mind, for the existence of basic health protection. Alternative health schemes, to be sure, would probably have proved less adequate than the negotiated plans, but health needs would certainly have been met in some way either through a system of private plans or, less likely, through government-sponsored programs.

Of course even negotiated programs may take a variety of forms. This depends on the preferences of the parties and their respective abilities to make these preferences prevail at the bargaining table. In the auto industry, if management's views had been given greater weight, the character of existing pension and welfare programs would have been altered in the following directions: pension and insurance plans would have embraced the contributory principle; pension contributions and benefits would have been linked more closely to earnings' levels, and benefit improvements would not have been extended to past service and certainly not to retired workers; and income stabilization plans would have taken the form of interest-free loans or individual savings plans.

2) *Pay for time not worked.* Contrary to the usual assumption, paid vacation and paid holiday plans in the auto industry have probably not affected annual working hours significantly but have altered mainly the timing of income payments to individuals. Since more than two thirds of the industry's workers receive pay in lieu of vacation while a substantial proportion of the remainder take their vacations in part as a substitute for layoffs, vacation plans are not unlike service-connected bonuses. Similarly, the practice of paid holidays is largely an outgrowth of the earlier preunion practice of granting unpaid holidays. It is possible, of course, that the requirement of wage payments on specified holidays has encouraged greater regularity of plant shutdowns on such days, but effective pressure in this direction is no doubt more directly related to the establishment of additional penalty rates for work on holidays.

Both paid vacations and paid holidays were adopted under collective bargaining in response to union pressure (though the actual establishment of the paid-holiday pattern at General Motors in 1947 was at the company's insistence, the UAW preferring for strategic reasons a straight cents-per-hour wage increase). It is possible, however, that similar plans—paid holidays and either paid vacations or service-connected bonuses—would have been introduced even in a nonunion system by managements concerned with stabilizing their work forces (i.e. reducing turnover and absenteeism) in a tight labor market. In the depression years, plans of this sort were unnecessary. It is well to remember, however, that the costs of turnover are substantial to a company and that many firms in predepression years adopted service plans in one form or another largely (though not exclusively) as a means of encouraging a stable, cooperative work force.

When we add to these considerations the fact that the money

expended on such plans could otherwise be used to increase wage rates, it is no longer clear just what the influence of unionism has been—except perhaps to redistribute income over time and to some extent between individuals somewhat more rapidly than would otherwise have been the case.

3) *Premium payments for time worked.* Unionism has erected a higher, more elaborate, and more rigid structure of premium payments than would have prevailed in its absence. Without unionism, a firm's operating requirements might well have compelled the payment of premiums for long or undesirable hours in an economy of high-level employment and rapidly rising living standards. However, the present need for rationing overtime indicates that overtime premiums are excessive from the standpoint of inducing the necessary supply of hours (though the fairly widespread desire to avoid second- and third-shift work suggests that shift premiums are currently below the optimal level). Moreover, given the history of the drive for shorter hours and the depression of the 1930s, it seems likely that some form of legislation embracing penalty rates as a means of regulating working hours would have been enacted. It is difficult to envision, however, the erection of a system of premium payments under the combined policies of management and government that would match the height, rigidity, and elaborateness of the system erected under collective bargaining. Unionism must therefore be accorded an influential role in the development of the present structure of premium payments, though there is every reason to suppose that this form of payment would also have been a feature (albeit a less prominent one) of any alternative nonunion wage system.

The Wage System

The distinctive features of auto plant wage systems are (1) the virtual absence of incentive methods of wage payment, (2) the use of broad occupational classifications and the relative lack of wage discrimination, (3) the absence of any commitment to job evaluation principles, and (4) the limitation of wage grievances to rates on new or changed jobs. This wage system, like any other, owes its peculiar character to a variety of influences whose separate effects are not easily distinguished, let alone measured. Nevertheless, a few summary comments suggest the direction, if not the extent, of the union's influence.

The changeover in the 1930s from incentive to hourly-rate methods of wage payment was accomplished at a time of considerable worker agitation and union pressure for the abandonment of piecework. To contend, however, that the prevalence of hourly-rate methods is therefore attributable to unionism is an oversimplification. It neglects a developing sentiment among auto managers that piecework is not necessarily superior in an industry where much of the output is machine paced, where complex scheduling requirements fix within narrow limits the number of pieces or units to be produced in a given time period, and where changes in methods, materials, processes, and assignments are more or less continuous. It also overlooks the related point that workers' needs, interests, and preferences, though certainly not adequately represented prior to the advent of unionism, cannot be disregarded with impunity even in the absence of collective bargaining. Thus, while it is tempting to assume that the changeover to hourly-rate methods, roughly contemporaneous with the rise of unionism, is a consequence of unionism, a fully satisfactory explanation must account for the speed and relative ease of the transition as well as the number of more or less voluntary abandonments. The evidence leaves room for legitimate differences of opinion, but in our view a balanced judgment supports the conclusion that unionism was a significant, but nevertheless secondary, factor in the abolition of piecework methods. It was responsible for the elimination of some incentive systems that might well have continued in operation, it speeded the abandonment of others, and it may (by virtue of its stubborn opposition to piecework) have frustrated the efforts of a few plant managers to reintroduce such systems. This last effect should be interpreted carefully, however, for the resurgence of interest in incentives during the 1940s reflected the conviction that unionism had seriously hampered plant efficiency. The union itself, therefore, was partly responsible for the change in attitude.

Broad classification titles and the relative lack of rate distinction in the wage-classification system appear to owe their origin primarily to the nature of the industry's production processes. Since the bulk of manufacturing operations are highly fractionalized, most production jobs simply do not lend themselves to meaningful differentiation. These characteristics of the wage system have been given a sharper focus, however, under collective bargaining. In the first place, the union has brought about some consolidation of job titles and job rates through pressures to eliminate wage differentials between jobs that are comparable from the standpoint of skill, effort, and working conditions. Second, it has probably encouraged management to accept and perhaps even to extend the use of broad classification titles as a protection against whipsawing. In an industry where minor changes in job content and job conditions are an almost daily occurrence, a wage-classification system that combines such titles with relatively little wage discrimination has an obvious advantage to management. Whatever its shortcomings, such a system has the virtue of stability in that it can accommodate the more or less continuous flow of minor job changes without the need for constant alteration of job titles and job rates and with less likelihood of continued bickering with the union over wage-classification grievances. The degree of flexibility enjoyed within a system of broadly defined classifications may also account, incidentally, for the lack of interest displayed by management in formal job evaluation plans. It should be noted, however, that the union is firmly opposed to this technique for rate setting and, in the one case where such a plan was proposed by management, UAW officials flatly refused to consider it.

Any wage system must of course provide procedures for

establishing rates on new or changed jobs. In the auto industry, disputes in this area are not subject to settlement by the umpire and hence are strikeable issues. The umpire may decide whether a new job has been created, whether an employee has been properly classified, and whether a job has been changed sufficiently to warrant reclassification. He may not, however, establish a classification or change a wage rate.

The exclusion of new job rate disputes from the jurisdiction of the umpire was included initially in auto agreements at the insistence of management. In the absence of specifically agreed-upon criteria for evaluating or rating jobs, management was reluctant to relinquish its control over rate setting to a third party even though this meant granting the union the right to strike during the life of the contract. In general, this provision has worked rather well for both parties and certainly it has not produced an excessive number of stoppages. Nevertheless, it has occasionally led to serious shutdowns and to accusations by management that the union had invoked the strikeable issue as a bargaining tactic to compel concessions on matters not subject to negotiation. Indeed, both Ford and Chrysler proposed extension of the umpire's authority to cover such disputes, though Ford management finally settled for a provision that confines union demands in the case of a stoppage to the specific strikeable issue.

Whatever the union's initial position on the arbitrability of new job rate disputes, it is now uncompromisingly opposed to any widening of the umpire's powers. Indeed, with the advent of automation, union efforts have been directed toward diminishing the role of arbitrators in the wage-classification area, thereby broadening the scope for bargaining. This move reflects the union's desire to break away from the traditional criteria of skill and effort underlying rate setting on nonautomated jobs and to substitute in their stead such standards as the increased responsibility implied in the larger investment and output per worker on automated jobs. Needless to say, management views the matter of rate setting in a different light. It considers the present wage system and contract provisions entirely adequate for handling the adjustments required by technological change, and it regards the union's seizure of the automation issue as little more than an opportunistic attempt to secure additional wage improvements. It is clear, however, that the union will continue to press for more favorable rates on automated jobs and probably for a simplified classification system that will facilitate the broader exercise of seniority rights.[4]

Personal Wage Differentials

The conflict between union and management wage philosophies is no more sharply revealed than in the contrasting attitudes toward personal differentials. In this area, management's wage objective has been to preserve incentives and stimulate efficiency by rewarding individual effort and ability, while the union's wage objective has been to eliminate competition between workers and put an end to opportunities for favoritism and discrimination. In this contest the union has won a decisive victory. One after another, in response to union demands, the various forms of personalized wage rates or earnings have been abolished or at least substantially modified. Merit ranges and sex differentials on production jobs have been eliminated; the gap between starting rates and job rates and the length of learning periods have been sharply reduced; full or partial automatic progression through the rate range has been established for some skilled workers; and numerous individual rate anomalies and inequities have been adjusted. In addition, the union has been an effective force in the changeover from individual piece-

4. It is to be expected, of course, that the union will in the future seek changes in the wage system beyond those mentioned here. It has already declared that "the system of employment by the hour is obsolete, uneconomic, irresponsible and unjust" and has called for acceptance of the principle of salaried status for blue-collar workers. At the same time it has gradually laid the basis for such a transition through the buildup of SUB to include short workweek benefits and severance pay.

work to hourly rates in a number of the industry's plants. All in all, this represents a considerable achievement.

There is, of course, no clear warrant for the assumption that in the absence of unionism the various forms of personal rate (and earnings) differentials contained in preunion wage structures would have been preserved intact. Nevertheless, had management's wage philosophy been given freer rein, it is reasonable to suppose that plant wage structures would have exhibited greater variety and flexibility with respect to methods of payment and would have retained some vestiges of a personalized rate system that would permit the reward of individual merit.

These conclusions apply to wage rates. When the concept of wages is broadened to take account of fringe benefits, many new kinds of personal differentials are created for which unionism has been partly responsible. The largest of these is the "seniority differential" created by the introduction of fringe programs that credit past service. Unionism did not of course originate the seniority principle or the service-connected benefit, but insofar as it has been responsible for private pension plans and more liberal vacation programs (each of which credits past service) it has been responsible for a windfall for senior workers equivalent in principle to a sizable service-connected wage bonus. Except for periodic improvements, however, the "seniority differential" is a temporary phenomenon since, for future workers, these programs are properly regarded as a form of deferred income earned in earlier years.

Occupational Wage Differentials

The occupational wage structure is not to be interpreted simply as a reflection of skill differences or of market evaluations of the relative worth of jobs. Although it is not possible to sort out the quantitative significance of each of the forces affecting occupational wage movements, nor indeed to rank these forces in order of their relative importance, our analysis indicates that unionism has exercised a substantial influence on occupational differentials in the auto industry. The major trends in occupational wage behavior are not to be explained, therefore, without reference to union wage policies and to underlying internal union developments.

A primary objective of UAW wage policy in the early years was to improve the relative incomes and living standards of low-paid workers. This early wage program was largely a reflection of the strong commitment of auto unionists to the philosophy of industrial unionism. Even without that commitment, however, it is likely that political considerations would have compelled a similar program, for few labor organizations have experienced the turbulence, strife, and instability that characterized the UAW in its formative years. In an atmosphere of vigorous democracy, intense factionalism, and shifting patterns of allegiance, policies and programs were perforce formulated with an eye to political advantage. Given the composition of the membership—the heavy concentration of workers toward the lower end of the wage scale—it is not surprising that all contending factions advocated a wage program that at best would maintain absolute wage differentials.

Even in the earliest years, however, the UAW could not afford to neglect the tensions and dissatisfactions resulting from this wage policy, particularly among the skilled trades. There is a tendency to interpret the skilled-trades problem in the UAW as a fairly recent phenomenon, but the record shows that discontent among craftsmen and the desire for a separate craft identity have their roots in the beginnings of the organization. There has never been a comfortable accommodation of craft interests within the UAW. Instead, there have been alternating periods of conflict and quiescence, of separatism and solidarity, with each crisis more acute and each solution a further capitulation to craft-oriented demands. These pressures were met initially through a series of expediencies designed to pacify the skilled trades without unduly antagonizing production workers or alarming the proponents of industrial unionism. Each move, however, has represented a further step toward separatism, toward the establishment of a distinct interest group of highly craft-conscious unionists within the industrial-union structure. This development, to be sure, has not gone unnoticed or uncriticized, but it was no doubt inevitable. Given the mounting unrest and secessionary tendencies in the trades, the growing importance of craftsmen in the industry (and union) under the new technology, and the union's desire to demonstrate to other (unorganized) groups its capacity to serve their special interests, the leadership had little choice. It could bow to the pressures of the crafts for a separate and superior status or accept the risk of a declining power base in the labor movement and nation.

The result of these internal membership pressures has been an over-all union program which represents a rather incongruous and shifting combination of industrial-union and craft-union policies with the balance tilting gradually but steadily in favor of the crafts. On the wage front, the compromise until recently has taken the form of a general policy of cents-per-hour wage adjustments designed to improve the relative wage position of the lower-paid groups, combined with a particular policy of special wage adjustments designed to placate the skilled trades. The successful implementation of these two policies has meant a substantial improvement over time in the relative wage levels of workers at both ends of the industry's wage scale. Whether wages are narrowly or broadly defined, the same trends are observed: there has been a sharp contraction of differentials among production workers and, in lesser degree, among skilled tradesmen, but a widening of differentials between these two groups. It is not our contention, of course, that these trends in occupational wages are entirely attributable to union policy. To some extent they represent the effect of underlying social and economic forces operating broadly throughout the system. Nevertheless, it is the conclusion of our analysis that unionism has contributed significantly to the reduction of differentials within the production group and has also been responsible for some slight improvement in the relative wage position of the skilled trades.

Interplant Wage Differentials

Bargained wage structures in the various auto plants exhibit much less variation than did the nonbargained structures of the preunion period. Under collective bargaining, intrafirm (or geographic) differences in plant wage levels, with the notable exception of General Motors, have been eliminated, while interfirm differences have been reduced. To be sure, some interplant differences in rates remain, but the rate ranges appearing in current occupational wage surveys are, generally speaking, quite narrow. Although we cannot predict what voluntary revisions in wage structure might have been introduced during this same period under nonunion conditions, it is evident at least that observed changes in interplant wage relationships were not forced upon firms in the industry by operating or market requirements. This consideration, and the fact that the pressure for change under bargaining so obviously stemmed from the union's demand for equal pay for equal work, is the basis of the claim that unionism has been the primary influence behind the leveling of interplant wage rates.

This conclusion is incomplete, however, without the addition of at least two qualifications. First, the union's failure to eliminate geographic differentials at General Motors probably means that this company, the largest in the industry, enjoys a slight wage advantage over its competitors. Second—and more important—if the concept of wages is broadened to include fringe benefits, particuarly of the pay-for-time-not-worked variety (such as rest and washup periods), the more liberal provisions in force at Studebaker and American Motors place these smaller firms quite clearly at the top of the interfirm wage structure. Since the production facilities of the smaller firms are located in communities where nonunion wages generally are below Detroit levels, it follows that the union has been responsible for reversing the nonunion pattern of interfirm compensation differentials or, at least, for creating differentials that otherwise would not exist.

In pressing the policy of equal pay for equal work, the UAW was pursuing the basic wage-structure objective common to all unions. In recent years, however, it is possible to detect a shift in the thinking of the leadership and the gradual emergence of a new policy that indicates some willingness to abandon the time-honored principle of the standard rate. This reorientation in outlook can be traced to the mid-1950s when the revival of intense competition in the industry threatened to engulf the smaller firms and brought about a series of mergers and one retirement which reduced the number of auto companies from nine to five. One result of the frantic search for solutions was full recognition of the extent to which the smaller companies suffered from excessively liberal labor contracts and work practices. In the postwar market such differences had occasioned little comment or discomfort; as long as all firms were earning profits, it hardly mattered that compensation levels (broadly defined) varied inversely with size and profitability. However, the post-Korean crisis and the ensuing painful adjustments compelled a reassessment of the union's wage program and gave birth to the conviction that a sounder wage policy in a highly competitive market would reverse this relationship between compensation levels and ability to pay.[5]

The first official acknowledgment of this new wage policy came in the union's profit-sharing proposal to auto manufacturers in 1958. This proposal is of course subject to more than

5. It is true, of course, that UAW spokesmen continued to deny that the union would ever subsidize inefficiency by accepting substandard wages from firms of poor profitability. Instead, as the union later indicated, it would tax efficiency by demanding superstandard wages from firms of high profitability. In other words, ability to pay would enter as a factor in wage setting above the standard but not below the standard.

one interpretation. It may be regarded as a public-relations maneuver or as a bona fide offer. In our judgment it was both. It was a bold move to clothe the usual package of bargaining demands, which the public has come to expect and increasingly resent, in a more respectable garb. The narrow, self-seeking philosophy of business unionism has always been repugnant to Reuther and his colleagues; consequently, the UAW bargaining program, however much it resembles that of less "socially motivated" unions, must be encased in social objectives. The demands may derive from the same set of compulsions (the special interests of the membership and the gains recorded or sought by other unions), yet the program must embrace a set of values implying a commitment to wider community interests. This in part explains the appeal of the profit-sharing proposal: it was an opportunity to convert an ordinary set of demands into an attack on monopoly and "administered price" inflation. But this does not preclude a genuine interest in profit sharing on the part of UAW leaders. Profit sharing offered a new approach to bargaining in a period of mounting criticism and suspicion of union motives, a chance to escape the dilemma posed for wage policy by the uneven pattern of profits among firms, and an opportunity to expand the union's sphere of influence in the affairs of the industry and perhaps even to effect a new accommodation with management. There is therefore reason to believe that UAW leaders were quite prepared to accept profit sharing in their settlements with the companies, though they can hardly have entertained high hopes that management would accede to their request.

Regardless of the interpretation one places on the profit-sharing proposal itself, however, the important point to note is that the UAW leadership for the first time openly endorsed as a sound principle of wage policy the idea of gearing wage levels at least partially to each firm's ability to pay. This in itself represents a significant departure from past wage policy and practice in the automobile industry.

COMPETITIVE RELATIONS

Our analysis of competitive relations in the industry sought to determine the character and source of labor-cost differences between firms. At an early stage of the investigation, it became apparent that the central fact to be explained was the tendency for labor costs to vary inversely with the size and profitability of firms. It was evident, moreover, that these cost variations were not attributable to differences in technical or market supply factors, but were rooted instead in the conditions of the employment relationship. The explanation most frequently encountered in the literature relates these cost differences to differences in relative bargaining power. It is argued that the smaller auto companies, because they are less strong financially and hence less able to withstand a work stoppage, have been forced by the union into granting larger concessions than their stronger competitors. Our analysis suggests, however, that this explanation is at best an oversimplification. It fails to take account of the full scope of the bargaining relationship and hence does not properly distinguish between the various sources of cost advantage (or disadvantage). It assumes a straightforward relationship between bargaining power and financial condition when in fact the relationship appears to be quite complex. It focuses excessive attention on union conduct to the relative neglect of management performance. The purpose of our concluding remarks, therefore, is to explore these matters further in the light of the study's findings.

Bargaining Power and Financial Condition

In our analysis of the factors accounting for differences in labor-relations performance, we have avoided, where possible, use of the term "bargaining power" since the concept, for present purposes, is not a very useful one. Recent studies have demonstrated that bargaining power, properly defined, embraces the totality of forces affecting the bargaining relationship and agreement—i.e. the motives, goals, and tastes of the parties, their skills in the use of persuasive and coercive techniques, and the influences originating in the economic, political, and social environment.[6] Since bargaining power is not therefore a separate, identifiable determinant of the agreement but is rather a "catchall" term for the entire range of influences, statements to the effect that differences in contract terms reflect differences in bargaining power are not very revealing. They merely define bargaining power in terms of observed results and contribute little to our understanding of the actual causes of such differences. If the forces affecting bargaining power are simply the determinants of the agreement itself, then the search for causal relationships must remain focused on these determinants.

The literature on collective bargaining contains numerous statements purporting to define the relationship between a firm's financial condition and its bargaining power—and hence the sort of contractual relations it enjoys. In our view, the majority of these statements are deficient in that they fail to

6. It was this "conglomerate" nature of the concept that led Lindblom, e.g., to conclude: "Bargaining power is best defined to include all the forces which enable a buyer or seller to set or maintain a price. All the determinants of price become the determinants of bargaining power, and the concept of bargaining power is shown to be a blunderbuss rather than a refined tool of analysis": C. E. Lindblom, " 'Bargaining Power' in Price and Wage Determination," *Quarterly Journal of Economics* (May 1948), pp. 402–03. More recently, Chamberlain has sought to define bargaining power in terms of the relative costs to the parties of agreement and disagreement on each other's terms. While this approach yields useful insights into the nature of the agreement-making process, it too stresses the all-inclusive character of the concept. As Chamberlain himself points out, the definition "takes into account the total situation—not only the striking and resistance capacities of the parties but the economic, political and social circumstances as these bear upon the cost of agreement or disagreement": Neil W. Chamberlain, *Collective Bargaining* (New York, McGraw-Hill, 1951), p. 222.

It follows from both of these studies that bargaining power cannot be defined in general but only with reference to a specific objective and a specified time period. Moreover, since the concept is a subjective one, the cost estimates or valuations that shape the attitudes of the parties and influence their behavior depend intimately on how the parties themselves perceive, interpret, and weigh the various influences impinging on the bargaining situation.

recognize explicitly that the role of financial strength and profitability in the bargaining process cannot be defined without reference to other determining forces in the bargaining situation—particularly the motives, objectives, and skills of the bargainers.[7] Even where these conditions are carefully specified, however, it is important to note that efforts to relate contract differences (or differences in labor-relations performance) to variations in financial strength and profitability are normally confined to explaining the outcome of a single bargain. Under these circumstances it is perhaps legitimate to treat financial condition as an independent variable in the bargaining process. However, where the objective—as in the present study—is to explain the interfirm pattern of labor costs as it has developed over time in a series of consecutive bargains, it is necessary to acknowledge that financial strength and the sort of contractual relations a firm enjoys are interrelated and interdependent phenomena. Indeed, without some inquiry into the origin and dynamics of the union-management relationships involved, there is no more reason to assert that financial weakness is the cause of an inferior labor contract than that loose and costly labor practices are the source of a weak financial condition.

Our own analysis does not deny that variations in financial condition had a role in determining the initial adjustment of firms to collective bargaining. At the same time, however, it lends firm support to the notion that financial strength and labor-relations performance are both reflections fundamentally of the quality of management. The direct evidence on this point

7. Whether financial weakness, for example, is a source of employer strength in bargaining depends in part on the union's concern for the firm's survival—an attitude that may turn on such considerations as the availability of other job opportunities, union wage policy, and the history and character of the union-management relationship. Conversely, whether financial strength confers a bargaining advantage on the employer is determined partly by management's willingness to stand firm and, if necessary, to undergo a strike in the face of "unreasonable" union demands. Unless such conditions are specified, the significance of financial condition and profitability as factors in the bargaining process cannot be established.

is substantial; and it is reinforced, in our view, by the finding that the firms suffering most from wasteful and expensive labor practices in their plants in the 1950s were also the ones hampered by marked inefficiencies in the performance of other business functions—inefficiencies that appeared in the form of antiquated management structures, unbalanced facilities, poor accounting and control systems, inferior marketing setups, and so forth. In short, it is our judgment that financial weakness and an inferior labor contract, while certainly interrelated, are frequently the effects of a common cause—the shortcomings of management.

Collective Bargaining and Competitive Relations

In appraising the significance of developments in competitive relations during the 1940s and early 1950s, it is well to bear in mind the unique character of the period. The distinctive features of the war and postwar decade were, on the one hand, the booming market for goods and services and, on the other, the spectacular growth of new unions in the mass-production industries.[8] For most industrial managements, dealing with strong, aggressive unions was an all but new experience and collective bargaining an untried and unfamiliar process. In the absence of established guide lines, each company was left pretty much to its own devices. This combination of circumstances—the need to develop an appropriate adjustment to a new process at a time when competitive pressures imposed at best a rather weak discipline on a firm's actions—may account in part for the marked divergence in response and performance occurring during the period. Some managements, despite the relative ease with which profits were realized, still found the incentives necessary for

8. The new unions preceded, of course, the start of World War II by a few years. But while they were already making their impact felt in the late 1930s, unions such as the UAW spent much of their energies in the prewar years on the tasks of organizing the unorganized, eliminating factional struggles for control at local and national levels, and forging stable and durable organizations.

maintaining and improving the efficiency of their operations, while others, whether through ignorance, shortsightedness, or neglect, tended to let matters slide and efficiency deteriorate as long as operations continued to yield a profit. These attitudes, themselves reflective of the skills and competence of respective managements, determined naturally the quality of over-all business performance, including the handling of labor relations. Had more normal market conditions prevailed, the effects of alternative approaches to collective bargaining would surely have become visible at an earlier stage and competitive pressures would undoubtedly have compelled remedial action in cases of unsuccessful adjustment long before conditions had deteriorated to quite the extent witnessed in the early 1950s. This being so, we can reasonably expect less variation in the future not only with respect to the quality of labor-relations performance exhibited by competing firms but perhaps too with respect to their general philosophy toward labor relations and collective bargaining. For one thing, the circumstances giving rise to the experience of the 1940s will not be duplicated; for another, that experience itself provides valuable guidance in the framing of successful policy.

Turning specifically to the automobile industry, it is clear that the key to successful labor relations was not simply the fortuitous choice of one approach over another; success lay rather in the attitudes, skills, and abilities which management brought to bear on the question of forging a suitable relationship with the union—"suitable" in the sense of meeting the challenge posed by this new organization in a manner consistent with the goals of the enterprise. Effective response to this challenge was not the result merely of some superior intuition but was rather the outcome of a careful and painstaking search, continuously engaged in, for appropriate policies and for methods to ensure the effective implementation of these policies. Of the approaches fashioned by the various companies, the most publicized were those of Studebaker and General Motors, characterized respectively as "constructive" and "restrictive." Our findings show, however, that these characterizations—connoting, as they do, the superiority of the Studebaker approach —were at best misleading. The term "constructive relations," as applied at Studebaker, was really a misnomer for weak bargaining and lax administration—for the proliferation and perpetuation of loose labor standards and costly labor practices which were simply inconsistent with the survival needs of a business organization functioning in a competitive environment. By contrast, the GM approach to labor relations, so often associated with restrictionism or containment, has so far demonstrated a consistent superiority over any other approach, either practiced or proposed, in the so-called "power centers" of American industry. Indeed, if the test of constructive labor relations is the ability to succeed in the marketplace, then GM bids fair to carry off the prize.[9]

Our analysis points to the conclusion that under collective bargaining (during the period in question) differences in labor practices were in large part attributable to differences in the

9. As stated earlier, we have judged company performance in this section on the basis of efficiency. Company A outperforms Company B in the handling of its labor relations if, other things being equal (such as technology and the conditions of labor supply), it operates with lower unit labor costs. We recognize that others may choose to emphasize different criteria in judging successful performance—e.g. the degree of worker satisfaction experienced in a company's plants—and we certainly do not underrate the significance of these other criteria or pretend to pass judgment on their relative merits. However, in a free-enterprise economy, the primary test of a firm's policies must remain their consistency with its survival requirements, and this is the matter we have chosen to explore in the present discussion. Our concern has been with competitive relations in the industry and hence with the relative cost of operations (or, more precisely, of the labor-relations systems) of competing firms. This is a pragmatic test concerned principally with what has worked best within the present framework of economic relationships rather than with what ought to work best. We leave to others such questions as the optimum balance between producer and consumer satisfactions and how such balance is best achieved and maintained.

Nevertheless, the criterion of worker satisfaction is not without interest or significance even in the present context. If, e.g., worker satisfaction can be

judgment, skill, and foresight exercised by respective managements. This conclusion challenges the notion that these differences can be traced solely to differences in financial condition,
although we cannot rule out the latter as a contributing factor.
Our previous comments have indicated how difficult it is to
evaluate the role of financial condition in the bargaining process. Nevertheless, it is our judgment that the Independents
were in a position during the 1940s to have offered much more
resistance to union pressures than they in fact did. Certainly,
financial condition does not account for the glaring weaknesses
in administrative practice which were at the root of many of
their difficulties. These weaknesses, resulting in widespread
waste and inefficiency, were clearly revealed in the agonizing
reappraisals of the post-Korean period and in the massive retrenchment and housecleaning programs undertaken (under
new or revitalized managements) in a last desperate effort to
survive. One lesson of that experience may well be that a firm
has an excellent opportunity to secure concessions from the
union when it is close to bankruptcy and the union is acutely
concerned about the preservation of job opportunities. It certainly does not follow from this, however, that resistance pos-

---

raised at no loss to efficiency (and vice versa) through a change in labor policy, we would regard such a change as desirable and the new policy superior
to the old. Where, however, these interests or objectives are in conflict (the
normal case under present conditions), the management that agrees to sacrifice efficiency, however noble its intentions, has simply accepted a competitive
disadvantage and the consequences that flow therefrom—unless, of course,
competing firms enter into similar agreements. However, this does not finish
the matter. If it were established that the degree of dissatisfaction among
employees were positively correlated with efficiency in labor relations and
that dissatisfactions would have adverse effects on future efficiency in proportion to their present intensity, we would have reason to modify our conclusions on relative performance. Unfortunately, we have no way of measuring
with any accuracy what the situation is in this respect or of foretelling what
the future holds, but we are not persuaded that these possibilities are anything
other than remote. Apart from the questionable utility to workers of at least
some forms of managerial inefficiency in labor relations, we have uncovered

sibilities were absent in earlier years. Such possibilities did in fact exist, but management simply failed to exploit them, either because it was unaware of the full seriousness of its predicament (lulled by current profits) or because it chose to avoid the challenge—preferring, as it were, the dubious advantages of industrial peace to the sterner requirements of sound and satisfactory labor relations. It is surely significant testimony on this score that these same managements also failed to respond vigorously to shortcomings in business areas remote from labor relations, that they at no point really tested the union's strength or intentions (when certainly their financial resources would have permitted interruptions of at least limited duration), and that they paid less than adequate attention to such vital matters as the education and training of supervisory personnel in their rights and responsibilities in the administration of collective agreements.

Up to this point we have offered an explanation of observed differences in labor-relations performance under collective bargaining, but not of the influence of collective bargaining and

---

no evidence to suggest that the levels of satisfaction (or dissatisfaction) existing in the plants of auto companies were related in any precise or systematic way to the effectiveness of their labor policies in controlling costs. The one exception is possibly Studebaker which, up to 1952, was generally conceded to offer a more satisfying experience to workers than any other company. However, against the higher satisfactions enjoyed at the expense of efficiency during this period must be weighed the dissatisfactions suffered as a result of sharply reduced employment and earnings at the time of returning competition, uncertainty about the firm's future, and the need to re-establish the relationship on terms substantially below those formerly enjoyed. In fact, the experience in autos is similar in this respect to that in other industries: where there are wide differences in efficiency between rival firms, the adjustment ultimately required is much more likely to affect the firm sacrificing efficiency than the firm preserving it. Competitive forces may not be the primary determinant of agreement terms (and hence of bargaining power) in the short run, but normally they exercise a most profound influence over longer periods of time. Satisfactions enjoyed at the expense of efficiency (unless the practice is widespread) are likely to be short-lived and presumably must be balanced against the dissatisfactions which inefficiency itself breeds.

unionism itself on competitive relations. The latter is an altogether different and certainly much more complicated issue since it requires us in effect to reconstruct the probable course of competitive relations over the last two decades in the absence of collective bargaining. Nevertheless, if we accept that our task is in fact to distinguish between the results of the "natural" market and the "institutional" market, to inquire into the extent to which "institutional behavior" has produced an outcome differing from that of "individual responses," then the following conclusion concerning the impact of unionism upon competitive relations seems warranted.[10]

In the absence of unionism, basic differences in managerial skills and abilities would still tend to be reflected in the handling of functions relating to the effective organization and utilization of manpower. For the companies in question, however, cost differentials would almost certainly have been narrower in the period between World War II and the Korean War and might well have been eliminated or even reversed in the period following the Korean crisis. In this context the readiness of some managements (whether justified or not) to submit to union pressures takes on a new significance; for as long as management believed itself incapable of firm resistance and acted accordingly, its behavior must be accounted a consequence of collective bargaining. The fact that it may have erred in its judgment or in its adaptation to unionism is beside the point, for what matters now is how—and not how well—management responded to the challenge of unionism. In the absence of this challenge, our findings suggest that management would certainly have been under less pressure to abandon those rights or functions essential to efficient operations, that perceived errors or shortcomings would have been more readily rectified since

10. It is necessary to bear in mind that the discussion at this point is concerned with cost relationships rather than cost levels and that the cost differences referred to are in essence the differences in what firms pay for an efficiency unit of labor.

opposition to remedial action would have been less severe, and that worker compensation (insofar as it was a factor in differential performance) would have been related more closely to area wage levels, benefiting mainly the smaller producers located outside Detroit. In our view the Independents who yielded most to unionism would have profited most from its absence. Hence our judgment that the effect of collective bargaining during the period of the 1940s and early 1950s was to reinforce, as it were, differences in the quality of management, placing thereby an added strain on the competitive positions of less favored firms.[11]

It not only appears that cost differentials would have been narrower during the 1940s in the absence of collective bargaining, but also that the "shock effect" of the post-Korean crisis would have reduced these (narrower) differentials still further and perhaps even reversed them. The precipitous decline in sales and profits, brought about by a shrinking auto market and the fierce competitive struggle for sales leadership between GM and Ford, produced, as we have seen, mass unemployment and an overwhelming pressure on labor standards before which even the union was forced to give way. Without underestimating the difficulties of introducing such changes among unorganized workers, it is evident that this same pressure would have been at least as successful in tightening labor practices in the absence of unionism, with resulting significant economies. To what extent this would have affected interfirm cost differentials depends, of course, on how other firms would have reacted to the change in market conditions. The fact, however, that pressures to econ-

11. Our position here admits the possibility of a wage advantage in favor of the smaller, non-Detroit companies during the prosperous interwar period. However, against this must be weighed, we believe, the distinct possibility that their levels of productivity would also have been lower as a result of the less effective utilization of plant personnel. Collective bargaining may have exploited and, in a sense, exaggerated the effects of differences in managerial competency, but it did not create these differences. In other words, the lack of strong competitive restraints during the period in question would still have fostered attitudes and behavior conducive to waste and inefficiency even in the absence of collective bargaining.

omize were much heavier in the higher-cost firms at the same time that these firms had greater "labor slack" to eliminate leads us to conclude that an improvement in their relative cost position would have resulted from the crisis.

In summary, it is our judgment that the influence of unionism and collective bargaining on competitive relations has been to raise the relative costs of the Independents throughout the period since World War II. We would judge further that this impact was greater during the boom years of the 1940s and early 1950s than in subsequent years. It is always possible, of course, that recent improvements in the labor policies of lagging firms will prove no more than temporary and that a return to affluence will induce some slackening of effort. For reasons already stated, however, we very much doubt a revival of the excesses and extremes that characterized the formative years of collective bargaining in the industry. The unique features of that era, as well as more recent developments, convince us not only of the power of competitive forces to sharply limit the influence of collective bargaining on competitive relations in the long run, but also of a secular tendency for collective bargaining to exercise a less disruptive influence in this respect as both management and the union become more knowledgeable and experienced in its use.

Index

Addes, George F., 115, 152
Agreements: *1937*, 108, 365; *1939*,
145 n.; *1940*, 32–33, 94, 149;
1941, 146, 150, 232, 345; *1942*,
33, 146, 232; *1943*, 94; *1945–46*,
33, 146; *1947*, 33–34, 73, 146;
1948, 34, 59, 146; *1949*, 34–35;
1950, 35, 146, 195; *1953*, 35–36,
146, 178, 195; *1954*, 287–90;
1955, 35–38, 88 n., 92–93, 147,
180, 195; *1958*, 5–6, 195, 283–
84, 305; *1961*, 249–253
American Federation of Labor
(AFL), 161, 162, 244
American Motors Corp., 4, 216,
226 n., 236, 249, 357, 388; UAW
members employed by, 5; UAW
bargaining relationship with, 11–
14; fringe benefits, 41; profit-
sharing proposal, 248–54, 257;
labor-relations experience, 291–
307; merger *(1954)*, 292; labor-
cost disadvantages, 249 ff., 293–
97, 301, 304; labor-relations performance, 367–69. *See also* Hudson Motor Car Co. and Nash-
Kelvinator Corp.
Anderson, Harry: cited, 215 n.;
quoted, 74 n., 119–20, 148 n.

Annual improvement factor. *See*
Wages
Apprentices, 161 ff., 199–200
Arbitration, 12, 94–96, 333–35,
337–38, 353 n.
Automation, 95–97, 99–104, 159
Automobile industry: classic example of mass production, 4; output
(1959–60), 4; distribution of
workers by earnings, 84; wage
dispersion, 85; attitudes toward
incentive plans, 112–33; job classifications, 136–45
Automotive Council for War Production, 118

Bakke, E. Wight, cited, 24 n.
Bannon, Ken: cited, 99 n., 100 n.,
101 n., 102 n., 232 n.; quoted,
331 n.
Bargaining. *See* Collective bargain-
ing
Beach, Muriel, cited, 190 n., 192 n.
Belfer, Nathan: cited, 348 n., 349
n., 351 n.; quoted, 314
Bell, P. W., cited, 140 n.
Berndt, Raymond H., quoted, 277
Blue Cross-Blue Shield. *See* Health
insurance

Yale Studies in Economics